Max Planck Institute for Intellectual Property
and Competition Law

For further volumes/weitere Bände:
http://www.springer.com/series/7760

MPI Studies on Intellectual Property and Competition Law

Volume 20

Josef Drexl • Henning Grosse Ruse-Khan •
Souheir Nadde-Phlix
Editors

EU Bilateral Trade Agreements and Intellectual Property: For Better or Worse?

Springer

Editors
Josef Drexl
Henning Grosse Ruse-Khan
Souheir Nadde-Phlix
Max Planck Institute for Intellectual Property
and Competition Law
Munich
Germany

ISSN 2191-5822 ISSN 2191-5830 (electronic)
ISBN 978-3-642-39096-8 ISBN 978-3-642-39097-5 (eBook)
DOI 10.1007/978-3-642-39097-5
Springer Heidelberg New York Dordrecht London

Library of Congress Control Number: 2013954812

Printed on acid-free paper

Springer is part of Springer Science+Business Media (www.springer.com)

Preface

This book brings together 14 contributions that developed from presentations and discussions during a workshop organized by the Max Planck Institute for Intellectual Property and Competition Law (MPI) with the title: *Economic Partnership Agreements of the EU: A Step Ahead in Reforming International IP Law?* The workshop was held in Frauenchiemsee (Germany) in June 2011 and gathered leading academics, practitioners, and trade negotiators from the EU and its trading partners.

As the title suggests, the main focus of the workshop and previous research at the MPI concerned a new generation of bilateral and regional agreements pursued by the European Union (EU) which have emerged after the adoption of the European Commission's Strategy for the Enforcement of Intellectual Property Rights in Third Countries in 2004 and the launching of the Global Europe Strategy in 2006. Examples are the Economic Partnership Agreement (EPA) signed in October 2008 between the then European Community (EC) and the group of CARIFORUM countries (EU-CARIFORUM EPA) and the trade agreement the EU signed with Colombia and Peru in June 2012. At the core has been the question whether the intellectual property (IP) provisions found in this new generation of EU agreements actually live up to the development rhetoric and take into account the specific developmental needs of the EU contracting partners. This question becomes particularly acute in the framework of redefined trade relations between the EU and the group of African, Caribbean and Pacific (ACP) states which includes a large number of very poor countries in Africa.

However, the workshop presentations and discussions indicated a need to go beyond the agreements the EU is negotiating with developing countries. International agreements which include IP and set standards beyond those of the Agreement on Trade Related Aspects of Intellectual Property Rights (TRIPS) have proliferated since the early nineties. This proliferation has gained such speed in the last five years that the IP standards found in these agreements, the implications for various areas of international law, and the implementation of their IP obligations demand for a broader perspective which goes beyond critically analysing potential elements for reforming the international IP system.

This broader perspective is expressed in the four parts of the book. Part I provides an overview on IP protection and enforcement standards in various types of economic partnership- and free trade agreements. It covers not only the historical context in which they need to be understood and the main substance of the IP-related obligations to be found in these agreements, but also their systemic implications and their role in the wider context of international IP norm-making. Part II then focuses on the impact IP provisions in bilateral and regional agreements have on the multilateral IP system and on various other areas of international law. Addressed are areas where the impact appears profound—such as the law of- and the on-going negotiations in the World Trade Organization (WTO) and international human rights law.

In Part III, several contributions examine the original core research question: Do especially provisions in the new generation of EU agreements take a distinct, more development-oriented and integrated approach that contains elements for a reform of the international IP system? Some provisions especially in the EU-CARIFORUM EPA on the role of sustainable development and on the flexibility to design domestic IP systems in accordance with the level of development sound promising. Their development, promise, however needs to be judged against obligations, for example on IP enforcement, that go significantly beyond the standards of TRIPS. The last part (Part IV) finally turns to an often neglected area on IP law and policy in the context of trade agreements: the questions that surround the implementation of IP provisions in the domestic law and institutional setting of the contracting parties. Here, the contributions not only analyse problems that developing countries may incur, but they also place significant emphasis on implications and problems of implementing IP provisions in the EU.

Part I starts with a contribution by *Daniel Gervais* in which he tries to situate current issues in the development of international IP norms and how this might affect bilateral IP negotiations between the EU and its trading partners. *Pedro Roffe* then draws eight lessons from recent US and EU FTAs negotiations with TRIPS-plus obligations and highlights the impact of these FTAs on the international system and the multilateral process in general. One major lesson he underlines is the asymmetry that exists between FTAs partners in different areas and levels which frequently allows stronger countries to transplant IP rules without the built-in checks and balances to their developing trading partners. In her contribution, *Jayashree Watal* focuses on the deficiencies in TRIPS negotiations for strengthening IP protection and subsequent gains made in FTAs in the form of TRIPS-plus obligations from the perspective of both developed and developing countries. In light of the asymmetries discussed by *Pedro Roffe* and the developmental concerns about strong IP protection and enforcement, she addresses the question why developing countries seek and accept FTAs with TRIPS-plus IP chapters and what effect FTAs could have in multilateral IP negotiations on the positions of developing countries that are party to FTAs.

Part II starts with a debate on the impact of TRIPS-plus obligations in FTAs on various areas of international law. At first, *Marco Alemán* measures the influence of TRIPS-plus obligations on other international IP Law by using different tools and yardsticks—such as the general principles of international law, the WTO dispute settlement bodies' decisions and IP negotiations in international fora. *Carlos Correa* then analyses in his contribution the extent to which TRIPS-plus obligations influence WTO law, particularly through treaty interpretation adopted by panels under the dispute settlement mechanism. In their conclusions, *Correa* and *Alemán* agree that the interaction between FTAs TRIPS-plus provisions and WTO Law is significant, but the impact of the former on the latter may be rather limited. On international human rights law, *Peter Yu* gives a comprehensive picture of the problems arising from the interface between intellectual property protection and human rights, in particular impediments to greater protection of human rights caused by FTAs TRIPS-plus provision, before offering a set of normative and systemic adjustments that aim to resolve such problems. The debate of Part II ends with a contribution by *Souheir Nadde-Phlix* on IP protection in EU FTAs vis-à-vis IP negotiations in the WTO. Her analysis of FTA commitments on geographical indications (GIs), plant varieties, biodiversity and traditional knowledge (TK)—contrasted with related IP negotiations at the WTO—suggests that the EU is taking advantage of the stagnancy of the Doha round of trade negotiations: In order to improve its position in the multilateral negotiations, it appears to be using the negotiated outcomes in FTAs as a means for generating a critical mass of supporters in the WTO. This IP bilateralism is a 'disguised multilateralism'—which suggests that all WTO Members may be better off in getting back to the multilateral table before potentially conflicting bilateral or regional outcomes make future consensus in the WTO even more difficult.

Part III places a spotlight on the provisions in EU FTAs and scrutinises whether they may serve as elements for reforming the international IP system. It starts with a contribution by *Frederick Abbott* in which he argues that some 'development-friendly' provisions in these agreements (such as having sustainable development as treaty objective, enhanced protection of GIs, adherence to the Madrid system and rules on the transfer of technology) may provide certain benefits to developing countries. However, they must be judged against the costs developing countries incur by accepting standards of IP protection and enforcement that primarily serve the interests of their trading partner. He is overall sceptical whether this approach or the individual provisions can serve as models for the progressive development of international IP law. In his contribution, *Keith Maskus* adds an economic dimension to the discussion by offering a qualitative exploration of two recent EU FTAs with regard to their abilities for promoting or impeding economic development, in particular by focusing on how certain IP provisions in these agreements might affect prospects for promoting innovation and development in the developing country partner. This is followed by an analysis by *Thomas Jaeger* of the IP enforcement chapters in recent EU FTAs and EPAs which shows that these chapters mirror enforcement rules in the EU and sometimes go beyond the Anti-Counterfeiting Trade Agreement (ACTA). Only the Association Agreement with Central American countries follows a more moderate approach which to some extent adopts a level of enforcement closer to the one found in TRIPS.

Part IV starts with a contribution by *Christian Pitschas* who analyses the relationship between EPAs and the EU trade policy by addressing the three main issues that affect this relationship: the objectives of EU trade policy, the EU competences in the area of trade policy and the implementation of EPAs within the internal legal order of the EU. The analysis points to the limits of the EU's Common Commercial Policy (CCP) competence and highlights the areas where—despite the development rhetoric—the EU is asking for 'WTO-plus' commitments outside IP. In his contribution *Josef Drexl* questions the general assumption that EU FTAs with TRIPS-plus standards merely oblige the EU's trade partners to take implementation measures and change their IP laws, while no such implementation requirements or changes are needed on the EU side. A close analysis of the obligations in these agreements on criminal sanctions, genetic resources, transfer of technology, competition law and concerning the general principle of sustainable development suggests that in cases where changes are required, the EU seems to overlook the need for implementation. *Tuomas Mylly* then shows how the EU's exclusive CCP competence covering "commercial aspects of intellectual property" can be used to regulate IP law *within* the EU through EU FTAs. In analysing the constitutional functions of the EU trade treaties and their rules on IP, he notices that—compared to TRIPS which generally lacks direct effect in the EU—the IP chapters in new EU FTAs could have significant effects on the landscape of EU IP law. Finally, *Xavier Seuba* highlights that the exportation of IP standards from the EU to developing countries through FTAs raises various implementation issues. He discusses several examples where such issues play out in the areas of politics (power asymmetries), economics (direct costs and welfare implications) and law (legal challenges, possible interpretations).

Overall, the careful reader will notice a sceptical tone in most, if of all, contributions about how regional and bilateral trade (and development) agreements in general and the EU ones in particular push the international IP system and its domestic implementation in national IP laws further. In our view, this should not be understood as paternalistically teaching those who negotiate these agreements about what is in their best interest and whether the overall negotiated outcome—including trade and other benefits—represents a good 'deal'. We live now in a post-TRIPS era where international IP rules commonly emanate from agreements where those rules are simply one bargaining chip that is traded off against other, in substance unrelated rules and commitments. Maybe, however, these 'deals' should not be taken for granted as the default route of international IP norm-setting. In light of the findings of this book, maybe we should reconsider whether they really lead to 'good' international IP norms. Given the political economy of international trade negotiations, the most difficult part of course then is to envision realistic alternative ways towards a reform of the international IP system.

The editors would like to express their special thanks to all those who contributed to the success of the workshop and to the publication of this book. In addition to the authors, who demonstrated great commitment and cooperation throughout the course of the project, the editors are grateful to Allison Felmy, the English editor of the Max Planck Institute, for the excellent work she has done reviewing all the contributions. The help of Ruth Claussen and Anna Mattes was crucial in the preparation of the background material for the workshop. The assistance of Joerg Hoffmann, Steffen Morawietz and Isabella Gabriel was instrumental in finalizing the formatting of the book. Finally, a special "thanks" goes to the publisher that supported the publication of this book.

Munich, Germany
April 2013

Josef Drexl
Henning Grosse Ruse-Khan
Souheir Nadde-Phlix

Contents

List of Contributors

Frederick Abbott Edward Ball Eminent Scholar, Florida State University, College of Law, Tallahassee, FL, USA

Marco Alemán Deputy Director, Patents and Innovation Division and Head, Legislative and Policy Advice Section, World Intellectual Property Organisation, Geneva, Switzerland

Carlos Correa Director, Centre for Interdisciplinary Studies on Industrial Property and Economics Law, University of Buenos Aires, Buenos Aires, Argentina

Josef Drexl Director of the Max Planck Institute for Intellectual Property, Competition and Tax Law (Munich), Honorary Professor at the University of Munich; Chairperson of the Munich Intellectual Property Law Center (MIPLC), Munich, Germany

Daniel Gervais FedEx Research Professor of Law, Co-Director, Vanderbilt Intellectual Property Law Program, Vanderbilt Law School, Nashville, TN, USA

Thomas Jaeger Senior Research Fellow, Max-Planck Institute for Intellectual Property and Competition Law, Munich, Germany

Keith Maskus Professor and Associate, Department of Economics, University of Colorado, Boulder, CO, USA

Tuomas Mylly Professor of European Law, University of Turku, Turku, Finland

Souheir Nadde-Phlix Research Fellow, Max-Planck Institute for Intellectual Property and Competition Law, Munich, Germany

Christian Pitschas Partner, Bernzen Sonntag, Attorneys-at-Law & Tax Advisors, Geneva, Switzerland

Pedro Roffe Senior Fellow, International Centre for Trade and Sustainable Development (ICTSD), Geneva, Switzerland

Xavier Seuba Senior Lecturer in Public International Law and International Relations, University Pompeu Fabra, Barcelona, Spain

Jayashree Watal Counsellor, Intellectual Property Division, World Trade Organization, Geneva, Switzerland

Peter Yu Kern Family Chair in Intellectual Property Law, Professor of Law and Founding Director of the Intellectual Property Law Center, Drake University Law School, Des Moines, IA, USA

Part I
Intellectual Property Protection in Economic Partnership- and Free Trade Agreements

Current Issues in International Intellectual Property Norm-Making

Daniel Gervais

Contents

1 Introduction

In attempting to situate current research on, and issues concerning, the development of international intellectual property (IP) norms, and how this might impact bilateral IP norm-making within the European Union (EU), I will consider a finite, and necessarily incomplete, list of substantive issues first and then turn to procedural ones.[1]

[1] Given the short nature of this comment, I will reference in the notes articles and publications where I elaborate further on the various themes.

D. Gervais (✉)
Professor of Law, Vanderbilt Law School, Nashville, TN 37203, USA
e-mail: daniel.gervais@vanderbilt.edu

J. Drexl et al. (eds.), *EU Bilateral Trade Agreements and Intellectual Property: For Better or Worse?*, MPI Studies on Intellectual Property and Competition Law 20,
DOI 10.1007/978-3-642-39097-5_1,

2 Substantive Issues

There would be a long list of issues that matter, or should matter, to EU negotiators as they approach intellectual property negotiations. I have selected five. The most important in terms of future impacts is the promotion of domestic innovation and its role in policy-making. I will then look at geographical indications (GIs), pharmaceutical research incentives, the three-step test and the recent push to shut down Internet access for unauthorized use of copyright material online ("three strikes").

2.1 Innovation

Is there a fundamental conflict of interest on innovation when it comes to intellectual property norm-making? Domestically, there is a perceived conflict between innovators and users of innovation, although many people are both. Internationally, the picture looks somewhat different as we consider the impact of economic theories such as comparative advantages.

When Adam Smith published *The Wealth of Nations* in 1776, international commerce consisted almost exclusively of goods of course.[2] The first intellectual property statutes had emerged, but relatively few goods traded internationally were protected by intellectual property rights, which were by and large territorial. The first major international intellectual property treaties recognizing the principle of national treatment/non-discrimination were adopted more than a century later, prompted by the first international exhibitions, such as the 1889 Paris World Fair (*Exposition universelle*), which gave us the Eiffel Tower.[3] In fact, trade in ideational goods whose market value was due in significant part to intellectual property (factoring in the monopoly rent) was impeded by the fear that many inventors had that their "idea" would be "stolen", which in turn prevented them from presenting their new technologies at world expos.[4] Today, trade in intangibles (in this context,

[2] Smith (1961). One could perhaps point to money changers or other banking-related services as an exception to that rule.

[3] The major treaties referred to here are the Berne Convention 1971 and the Paris Convention 1967. The first text of the Berne Convention was adopted in 1886 and the first text of the Paris Convention in 1883. For a brief look at the history, see May 2009. The tower was inaugurated on March 31, 1889 and the Expo opened on May 6th of that year. On the history of the Eiffel Tower, the French patent on the structure awarded to Eiffel and his partners and the importance of the tower for the 1889 and 1900 Expos, see Hervé (2002), pp. 8–11.

[4] See Yu (2004), pp. 323, 343–348 (discussing the 1873 international exposition in Vienna and the origin of the Paris Convention). This is reflected in the text of the Paris Convention, Article 11 (1) of which provides that the "countries of the Union shall, in conformity with their domestic legislation, grant temporary protection to patentable inventions, utility models, industrial designs, and trademarks, in respect of goods exhibited at official or officially recognized international exhibitions held in the territory of any of them".

services and goods whose value is derived from intellectual property) represents approximately 80 % of world trade, an economy whose growth and in which competitiveness is predicated on innovation. How does this translate into policy?

If one looks at the rhetoric embedded in the Agreement on Trade Related Aspects of Intellectual Property Rights (TRIPS), one finds at least a mention of technology transfer to the developing world.[5] The TRIPS Agreement was seen as the poster child for the so-called Development Theory, according to which developing economies should import the normative, judicial and administrative infrastructure of more industrialized nations to achieve a similar level of economic development. According to that theory, copying the infrastructure should lead to increased foreign investment, availability of capital and economic growth.[6] One might naturally question those foundational assumptions.[7]

A somewhat more cynical view suggests that Western powers wanted to protect intellectual property in the developing world to secure new markets and revenues for ideational goods and services protected by patents, trademarks and copyright. Companies like Apple and many others[8] saw the developing world as a potential outsourcing target to manufacture high technology products at a lower cost. Yet outsourcing is misunderstood if seen as simple cost-cutting. In reality, it is a form of knowledge transfer. It tends to evolve to progressively more complex coding and manufacturing tasks and related innovation activities, thus leading to significant innovations in the recipient (outsourced-to) country. The outsourced technology, initially involving no or low-level local innovation, progressively becomes a form of technology transfer that serves as a stepping stone to higher innovation functions and even in some cases to the emergence of the outsource as a world-class competitor.[9]

[5] See, e.g., Article 66.2 of the TRIPS Agreement.

[6] The intellectual backdrop for this theory is the Washington Consensus, according to which the recipe for economic development is to reduce the role of government, emphasize privatization, trade and capital market liberalization and deregulation. According to this view, governments must mostly protect property rights and avoid corruption. While acknowledging that there is no guarantee of fairness in wealth distribution that comes with this worldview, Washington Consensus advocates generally believe in trickle-down economics, *i.e.*, that all or most citizens will benefit from GDP growth. Some commentators, including Joseph Stiglitz (Nobel prize winner in economics) have questioned the evidence to support this view. Stiglitz (2001), p. 27.

[7] See Gervais (2009b), pp. 2353–2377.

[8] Steve Jobs, former CEO of Apple, reportedly explained to President Obama that "those jobs aren't coming back." See Duhigg and Bradsher (2012).

[9] As UNCTAD's World Investment Report 2005 notes: "In the early stages of technological activity, enterprises need not set up formal R&D departments. As they mature, however, it becomes increasingly desirable to monitor, import and implement technologies. R&D as a distinct activity may appear as early as the second level of complexity, where multifaceted technologies are involved or if local conditions demand significant adaptation. In a developing country, such R&D is feasible once the operation is fairly large scale and the necessary technical skills are available. The role of formal R&D then grows as the firm attempts significant technological improvements to introduce new products or processes".

It is, therefore, not unrealistic to see a future where Brazilian, Chinese, Indian and other companies compete head-to-head with innovation-based Western enterprises on what has mostly been the turf of the West for the past 200 years, namely innovation itself. In certain industries, this process has begun. This innovation-displacement effect of TRIPS and TRIPS-plus agreements may be accelerated when considering that a very significant proportion of researchers in Western laboratories are nationals of developing countries (such as India).[10]

Perhaps the outsourcing approach and the risk of creating new competition is not as short-sighted as might appear at first glance. Through investment and acquisition, the same capital and companies, though geographically reconfigured (an issue for Western tax authorities, which may have to move massively to sales-based taxes to replace income-based revenue, but not for the companies involved), will likely remain dominant in many, perhaps most, industries.[11] That would explain why, both in bilateral discussions and multilaterally (to the extent that the World Trade Organization (WTO) remains a viable negotiation forum for new areas), there is such an emphasis by lobby groups representing such companies on investment liberalization in parallel to IP protection.[12]

It seems fair to ask, from a policy-making standpoint, whether the domestic interests of Western negotiators are coextensive with those of multinational corporations who dictate their objectives.[13] The EU must decide how it wants to play this game of course. If innovation is seen merely as a layer of an inescapable globalization process, the authorities should not fight a losing battle to prevent innovation in developing countries. Nor can they be expected to naively allow Brazil, Russia, India, China, and South Africa (the BRICS countries) somehow to "take innovation over", however. A middle way must be found, one which focuses on cooperation and value-creating interpenetration of corporations, universities and other innovation-leading institutions. In a world of highly fungible capital, that is the best and perhaps the only way forward.

An unresolved part of the global innovation equation is whether state (or "authoritarian") capitalism is going to be able to innovate as much as traditional liberal capitalistic societies.[14] The evidence suggests that state capitalism is very

---

[10] The Financial Times reported that in order to compensate for the shortage of first-rate talent, the "clamour for brains is driving elite employers in the UK to behave like football talent scouts in India and elsewhere." Clegg (2007).

[11] One author argues that, once the proper legal system and protection is in place—and especially what he refers to as the invisible infrastructure of "asset management"—the conditions required for the "Western" capitalist model to be moveable and innovation fully to emerge will be present. See de Soto (2003).

[12] UNCTAD maintains a database of bilateral investment treaties. The list is impressive, including 48 bilateral treaties involving the United States alone. http://www.unctadxi.org/templates/DocSearch____779.aspx.

[13] Forster (2006), pp. 29–30.

[14] See Gat (2007).

good at starting new businesses (less predatory than venture capital) and at incremental innovation, but that it has not been good at generating quantum innovation leaps. As a report on state-owned enterprises in *The Economist* noted:

> [T]he pursuit of indigenous innovation could prove to be a distraction. Foxconn, a huge Taiwanese-registered electronics group, has an unrivalled ability to mass-produce iPads and the like [...] Huawei is a master of improving on other people's technology and bringing it to market at lightning speed. China's universities mass-produce graduates in disciplines that have been forgotten in the West, such as mining and heavy engineering. China would be better off exploiting these advantages rather than trying to build the next Silicon Valley.[15]

Efforts by the World Intellectual Property Organization (WIPO) to produce economic studies of intellectual property impacts will no doubt help in developing adequate policy options in this regard, as previous efforts by the World Bank and others have done in the past.[16] Put differently, the variegated picture of IP as part of a broader landscape of innovation policies should help calibrate TRIPS implementations and national policies in countries that strive to join the club of innovators. It will also allow all of us better to comprehend the social costs of certain forms of IP and allow mitigation where necessary.

Let us remember that, not long ago, even while TRIPS was being negotiated in the late 1980s and early 1990s, innovation narratives were essentially absent beyond the lip-service paid to technology transfer. This is not altogether surprising: studies on the specific impacts of IP were hard to find in the industrialized world and virtually nonexistent for the developing world. Negotiators put the policy cart before the empirical horse. I realize that there may well be a point when it comes down to politics and sheer clout, but facts can and often do matter. The EU and other major players should fully support efforts to generate and analyse data o the impact of intellectual on innovation and economic development.

2.2 Geographical Indications

This is an issue where the EU has had some bilateral successes and is leading a reform of the Lisbon register.[17] It is high time, however, to remove the few real obstacles to a true international protection of GIs. I am concerned about the notification system proposed in the WTO context, both because the WTO has no expertise in maintaining a register and because what has been proposed is mostly a repository of notifications and no more. A revamped Lisbon system implemented in the same way as the proposed TRIPS register is likely to offer better clarity and certainty to business.[18]

[15] See The Economist (2012), pp. 21–27.

[16] See Gervais (2005), pp. 505–535.

[17] See "Summary by the Chair, Fourth Session Lisbon Working Group".

[18] See Gervais (2009c), pp. 87–104.

US opposition, fueled by concerns about Budweiser beer (now an EU property!) and Kraft (maker of many food products with European-sounding names but not originating from that part of the world) can be defused. This means solving a short list of known issues. There is a precedent for this in the EU-US Wine Pact, which grandfathered a number of wine appellations considered semi-generic, including Bordeaux and Chablis for example. Beyond preserving and/or phasing out certain indications, coexistence is possible, as the case of Pisco, "officially" made in both Chile and Peru, demonstrates.[19] What matters, at a policy level at least, is to get the normative heft of GIs recognized even if this means accepting that a number of existing indications used in the "New World" are not compatible with current EU practice.

Establishing a renovated Lisbon system is similar in many ways to the succesful expansion of the Madrid system by way of a Protocol.[20] It would seem fully justified for Lisbon.

The developing world could benefit from a multilateral GI protection (beyond trademark-level protection) system that creates legal certainty and is not limited to wines and spirits, as it is in TRIPS. It is compatible with certain forms of traditional knowledge and innovation (TK&I), for example, and the deep linkages to the land that often underpins the keepers of TK&I.[21] I readily acknowledge, however, that the commercial focus of GIs will not serve all kinds of TK&I, far from it, but it is a partial solution worth exploring for products such as tea, coffee, chocolate and a number of crafts.

2.3 *Pharmaceuticals*

What exactly are the significant actual or potential markets for EU pharmaceuticals that are negatively affected by the inadequate protection of IP, whether patents or test data? Should an answer to that rather simple question inform how one makes policy choices? The issue is well known and, at the risk of oversimplification, let me summarize it as follows. When a country (typically a least-developed country)[22] has no reasonable chance of being seen as a "market" for a relatively expensive pharmaceutical, no patent should be enforceable for use in that territory. Valid concerns about exports or re-exports from that territory should be addressed, however. The Doha (paragraph 6) system tried to balance precisely those two objectives.

[19] See Fontaine (2011), pp. 2–3.

[20] See Gervais (2010), pp. 67–126.

[21] See Gervais (2012b) in Drahos and Frankel.

[22] A list of least-developed countries is maintained by the United Nations and used by the World Trade Organization to identify countries that may avail themselves of certain flexibilities, including under TRIPS. The list is available at http://www.unohrlls.org/en/ldc/25/.

The more complicated question arises when a country starts to go up on the per capita GDP scale. At some point in that ascension, some but not all people in that country can begin to afford—by which I mean pay a reasonable price for—pharmaceuticals, thus creating unfairness in access. Some might argue that some degree of unfairness is unavoidable. Fair enough, but is there a limit to the unfairness society will tolerate when the matter is life itself? Translated as a policy question, how much flexibility should the governments have to set that limit and implement corrective measures?

This debate has emerged in many countries, not just developing ones. In the United States the shifting stance on the importation of lower-priced pharmaceuticals from Canada is an illustration.[23] Should one allow parallel imports? Compulsory licensing? Price-setting, as many EU members do? For our purposes here, the question takes on a different hue: As a matter of EU policy, should bilateral agreements prohibit any such measure, especially in the wake of the Dutch seizure-in-transit case?[24]

There are other, even more complex issues to tackle. As work in the World Health Organization (WHO) has tended to demonstrate, patents have generated innovation in the field of pharmaceuticals, but (a) they have also created a number of problems, and (b) there may be better ways forward to develop treatments, especially for orphan and tropical diseases. This in turn affects patent policy. For instance, should the EU be "exporting" very low patentability criteria via bilateral agreements on biotechnological inventions? Should a mere prediction of some kind of applicability be sufficient to meet the European Patent Convention (EPC) test? Patents on "new" pharmaceuticals are increasingly granted on pre-existing genes or reformulations of existing molecules. Utility/industrial applicability is an important factor, but so is novelty (when applied to preexisting biological materials) and inventive step when applied to mere isolation or reformulation of known substances. Much more work is required, rather urgently, in this area before suboptimal policies are set in bilateral or other instruments.

It is time for a full assessment of whether the tendency to patent ever closer to basic science is generating positive innovation outcomes before underlying policy assumptions are exported to other countries in bilateral and regional trade agreements in the form of IP rules. I would also suggest that we need more work on whether patents on pharmaceuticals should be combined with other forms of exclusivity or other incentives, especially when research is publicly funded. Why couldn't the WHO, for instance, generate a list of priority research areas and coordinate public research on those treatments to limit duplication of efforts? Other models have been proposed that involve less bureaucracy, including investment recovery and awards.[25] Evidently, global health is at stake, and we owe it to ourselves to broaden the debate beyond patents and existing research pathways.

[23] See Darrow (2011), pp. 291–297.

[24] See Kumar (2010), pp. 506–519.

[25] See eg Müller-Langer (2009).

2.4 The Three-Step Test

The three-step test, which was included in TRIPS and also increasingly in bilateral and regional agreements and even in EU directives, is used to limit exceptions, and the limitations need much more work. I am well aware of the work done by the Max-Planck Institute for Intellectual Property and Competition Law[26] and others, but we need to do more.[27]

The existence of myriad variations of the three-step "theme" is disconcerting. In TRIPS alone, the negotiators played the three notes of the test in four different ways.[28] The 2013 Marrakesh Treaty mentions four (art. 11). Two WTO dispute-settlement panels have interpreted the test but also created dissonance in interpreting the steps. While I welcome the inclusion by those panels of Berne Convention history, which has yet another instantiation of the test, the normative vectors for the application of the test are still ill-defined.[29] As intellectual property increasingly has to face other rights in the global arena, this might prove a significant impediment. I would hope the EU will continue its leadership, as the likelihood that a case involving the test might reach the Appellate Body increases day by day.

2.5 "Three Strikes"

From three steps, let us move to three strikes, if I may interject copyright in this discussion. The EU has led the charge on HADOPI (*Haute Autorité pour la diffusion des œuvres et la protection des droits sur internet*) type legislation.[30] It will not work, if "work" is defined for this purpose as increasing revenue streams for right holders, especially creators. Empirical data available as of this writing supports this conclusion. At the same time, I have no sympathy for professional pirates who profit through various web sites by the ease with which copyright material can be disseminated online. However, bans are simply not *the* solution.

Debates that pit the technology companies against professional right holders such as film and record companies are the exact opposite of the optimal way forward. Both "sides" need and want the same thing, namely to make available the highest quality content possible. Because right holders have by and large refused to engage with technology companies, and refused to admit that control

[26] See the Max Planck Institute Declaration on a balanced interpretation of the three-step test available at: http://www.ip.mpg.de/en/pub/news/declaration-threesteptest.cfm.

[27] See Senftleben (2004).

[28] See Articles 13, 26.2 and 30 of TRIPS for the test itself with variations. In addition, arguably at least the notion of "legitimate interests of the owner of the trademark" in Article 17 is related to the third step of the test.

[29] Berne Convention, Article 9(2). See also Senftleben (2004), pp. 140–151.

[30] See Geiger et al. (2011).

of the Internet is unlikely to resemble control over previous distribution technologies and channels, and widely depicted technology players as profiteers and even pirates, a number of key business models have not yet emerged. Repression to let copyright holders "take back" the Internet is still seen as a good option in some quarters, which it obviously is not, at least if by control the idea is to decide when and how each Internet user can access content and exactly what can be done with it.

As with innovation, I wish that EU authorities would rely upon available empirically verifiable hypotheses in the often counterintuitive (for brick-and-mortar thinkers) ways in which Internet commerce is done before pushing copyright norms internationally. If I can make that even more specific, I am not opposed to copyright enforcement, though I was opposed to overbroad measures as proposed in the US recently, but the EU could lead the way in demonstrating that enforcement is only part of a more complex picture.

3 Procedural Issues

The two issues I discuss here as "procedural"—recognizing that process and substance are closely intertwined—are (a) the rules concerning participation in international discussions and (b) the determination of the scope of those discussions.

3.1 Participation

The rules of participation in IP norm-making have changed. Open discussion in multilateral fora such as the WTO or WIPO is only one option, and perhaps one which appeals less and less to advocates of higher intellectual property protection and enforcement. NGOs (including those often referred to as representing "civil society"), which are allowed to participate in most WIPO meetings and can get some access to officials at the WTO, are finding more and more closed doors, for example in the recently concluded negotiation of the Anti-Counterfeiting Trade Agreement (ACTA).[31] More importantly, even *countries* can no longer assume that they will be allowed to participate in norm-making processes that will ultimately affect them. To use ACTA again, negotiation meetings were held among countries dedicated to increasing the international level of intellectual property protection and enforcement. Arguably for the first time, the ACTA plurilateral 'country-club' approach entailed a reconfiguration around like-mindedness, not geography, with a

[31] See Gervais (2012a) in Burri and Cottier.

view to designing norms that will then be exported via other instruments to countries that would likely have been more critical or defended other views had they been allowed in the negotiation room.

One must bear in mind that such a change of tactics, while superficially appealing to isolate opponents and reduce what is perceived as "white noise", is not a guarantee of success. Dealing with opposition makes new rules politically easier to accept multilaterally and, conversely, shutting out part of the stakeholders may backfire, particularly in that it may lead to the deployment of countermeasures. For example, when the United States, which has traditionally been an exporter of intellectual property and thus typically benefits from national treatment in other countries, decided to abandon that cardinal rule to respond to "urgent" concerns from the computer chip industry and used reciprocity to try to impose (now obsolete) semiconductor chip (mask) protection, it lost the right to credibly oppose reciprocity when it was introduced in the EU Database Directive.[32] Similarly, ACTA members now cannot easily oppose other versions of like-mindedness, including South-South fora on IP.

There are other unintended consequences. Isolating opposition on substantive IP issues can also produce mistakes and lead to the emergence of "bad rules".[33] In this sense, having a mixture of open forum discussion and discussion with independent experts is essential. Governmental authorities often live in a bubble mostly built by and for specific interest groups. They bring "their" issues to the table but broader substantive analysis of societal outcomes is generally ignored or ridiculed. The discussion is often about the objectives, not their implementation. When it does come to implementation, each "side" will put in text it wants, which explains why many IP-related regulations of recent vintage include long lists of rights and specific exceptions. I wish the EU, which may be less subject to capture than others, would take an enlightened approach in defining EU interests on the basis of analysis, not mere assumptions.

I am certainly not arguing that more intellectual property is bad *per se* (or good for that matter—it is a matter of balance), but we now have access to more sophisticated tools to identify areas where it is more or less likely to be good, and drop the simplistic assumption—under which many still seem to operate—that more IP will *always* tend to generate positive outcomes. Hopefully, measures proposed by the EU in bilateral and other fora will be discussed openly, if not case by case, then at least in a democratic process, to ensure that they adequately

[32] Directive 96/9/EC.

[33] A recent example in the United States was the apparent abandonment (as of this writing) of the *Stop Online Piracy Act*, a bill that had a legitimate purpose of shutting down foreign "pirate" websites, but included overbroad measures that could have punished innocent third parties or put an unfair enforcement burden on their shoulders. See Weisman (2011). While the rhetorical tactics of proponents was to portray opponents as defending pirates (ie, disagreeing with them on the legitimacy of the aim of the proposed legislation), the critiques were much more about the suggested method to achieve the aim.

reflect EU values (that is, on the legitimacy of objectives) and are open to criticism on substance to avoid incorrect implementation of objectives the legitimacy of which is not in question.

3.2 Scope

The issue of scope is both procedural and substantive, of course. I treat it here as the former because the process of negotiation itself is shifting. Since 1883 (when the Paris Convention was signed), this process has been a one-way norm elevator. Each multilateral effort to revise the Paris and Berne Conventions, and the 1994 TRIPS Agreement itself, was meant to establish a higher baseline of international norms, while cabining exceptions—and, in the case of TRIPS, adding an enforcement layer.

Discussion has now moved to treaties to impose exceptions. I am referring of course to the Marrakesh treaty for blind and print-disabled users, and the proposed library treaty under discussion at WIPO.[34] Normatively, it is difficult to oppose those efforts.[35] I am not entirely sure how productive they will be in convincing WIPO members to adopt new exceptions.[36] What matters here, however, is control over the multilateral agenda and the emergence, for the first time, of this type of proposed instrument.

I see this as a key procedural issue because it also directly affects the participatory rules discussed under 2.1 above. It may be that these "exception and limitation treaties" will prompt a displacement of what many still see as the "real discussion" (more rights and enforcement) elsewhere, thus reinforcing the cycle and generating a fractal picture of international norm-making in this area.

4 Conclusion

It is difficult to conclude anything other than that the nature of upcoming debates—battles may be a more appropriate term—in the field of intellectual property is increasingly complex, outcomes difficult to predict, and approaches to making correct policy choices and defending them internationally a lot harder. Yet try we must. Global health and the future of innovation-fuelled economic development are at stake.

[34] See WIPO document SCCR/20/9 2010.

[35] See World Blind Union (2011). See also "Comment submitted by Professor Daniel Gervais to the Copyright Office of the United States" (Gervais 2009a).

[36] From the viewpoint of EU member States and the United States, I see little if any change, however, given Article 5(3)(b) and recitals 34 and 43 of Directive 2001/29/EC and Section 121 of the US Copyright Act.

References

Berne Convention for the Protection of Literary and Artistic Works (Berne Convention) (1971) (Paris text), 1161 UNTS 3; 102 Stat 2852
Clegg A (2007) In hot pursuit of the best brains. Financial Times
Darrow J (2011) Essential medicines: why international price discrimination may increasingly be the wrong solution to a global drug problem. J Law Med Ethics 39(2):291–297
de Soto H (2003) The mystery of capital: why capitalism triumphs in the west and fails everywhere else. Basic Books, New York
Directive 2001/29/EC of the European Parliament and of the Council of 22 May 2001 on the harmonisation of certain aspects of copyright and related rights in the information society, OJ 2001 L 167, 0010–0019
Directive 96/9/EC of the European Parliament and of the Council of 11 March 1996 on the legal protection of databases, OJ 1996 L 77, 0020–0028
Duhigg C, Bradsher K (2012) Apple's jobs to Obama: "jobs aren't coming back" to U.S. The New York Times. http://www.heraldtribune.com/article/20120123/ARTICLE/301239999. Accessed 23 Jan 2012
Fontaine B (2011) Report of the European Communities Trademark Association, WIPO Worldwide Symposium on Geographical Indications, pp 2–3. http://www.ecta.org/IMG/pdf/report_on_gi_symposium_lima_peru_final.pdf. Accessed 22–24 June 2011
Forster CJ (2006) China's secret weapon: science policy and global power. The Foreign Policy Center, London
Gat A (2007) The return of authoritarian capitalists. The New York Times, http://www.nytimes.com/2007/06/14/opinion/14iht-edgat.1.6137311.html. Accessed 14 June 2007
Geiger C et al (2011) What developments for the European framework on enforcement of intellectual property rights? A comment on the evaluation report dated 22 December 2010. EIPR 33(9):543–549
Gervais D (2005) Intellectual property, trade & development: the state of play. Fordham Law Rev 74(2):505–535
Gervais D (2009) Comment submitted to the Copyright Office of the United States. http://www.copyright.gov/docs/sccr/comments/2009/comments-2/daniel-gervais-vanderbilt-university-law-school.pdf
Gervais D (2009b) Of clusters and assumptions: innovation as part of a full TRIPS implementation. Fordham Law Rev 77(5):2353–2377
Gervais D (2009c) The Lisbon agreement's misunderstood potential. WIPO J 1(1):87–104
Gervais D (2010) Reinventing Lisbon: the case for a protocol to the Lisbon agreement (geographical indications). Chicago J Int Law 11(1):67–126
Gervais D (2012a) Country clubs, empiricism, blogs and innovation: the future of international intellectual property norm-making in the wake of ACTA. In: Burri M, Cottier T (eds) Trade governance in the digital age. Cambridge University Press, Cambridge
Gervais D (2012b) Traditional innovation and the ongoing debate on the protection of geographical indications. In: Drahos P, Frankel S (eds) Intellectual property and indigenous innovation. Australia National University Press, Canberra
Hervé L (2002) The Eiffel tower. Princeton Architectural Press, New York
Kumar SP (2010) Border enforcement of intellectual property rights against in-transit generic pharmaceuticals: an analysis of character and consistency. EIPR 32(10):506–519
May C (2009) The Pre-history and establishment of the WIPO. WIPO J 1(1):16–17
Müller-Langer F (2009) Creating R&D incentives for medicines for neglected diseases. Gabler, Wiesbaden
Paris Convention for the Protection of Industrial Property (Paris Convention), 14 July (1967) (Stockholm text), 828 UNTS 305
Senftleben M (2004) Copyright, limitations and the three-step test. Kluwer, The Hague

Smith A (1961) An inquiry into the nature and causes of the wealth of nations, 2 vols. Methuen, Massachusetts

Stiglitz J (2001) Information and the change in the paradigm in economics. Prize Lecture, December 8, 2001. http://www.nobelprize.org/nobel_prizes/economics/laureates/2001/stiglitz-lecture.pdf

Summary by the Chair, Fourth Session Lisbon Working Group (2011), WIPO document LI/WG/DEV/4/6, http://www.wipo.int/lisbon/en/news/2012/news_0001.html. Accessed 16 Dec 2011

The Economist (2012) Mixed Bag, pp 13-14

Timetable for the Adoption of a WIPO Treaty for an Improved Access for Blind, Visually-Impaired and Other Reading Disabled Persons, WIPO document SCCR/20/9, 4 June 2010

United States Copyright Act, Title 17 of the United States Code

Weisman J (2011) In fight over piracy bills, new economy rises against old. The New York Times. http://www.nytimes.com/2012/01/19/technology/web-protests-piracy-bill-and-2-key-senators-change-course.html?_r=1&scp=6&sq=sopa&st=cse). Accessed 18 Jan 2011

World Blind Union (2011) European Parliament votes its support for a binding “books without borders” treaty. http://www.worldblindunion.org. Accessed 13 May 2011

Yu PK (2004) Currents and crosscurrents in the international intellectual property regime. Loyola Los Angeles Law Rev 38(1):323–443

Intellectual Property Chapters in Free Trade Agreements: Their Significance and Systemic Implications

Pedro Roffe

Contents

1 Introduction

This paper provides an analysis of free trade agreements (FTAs)[1] in the realm of intellectual property rights (IPRs): it examines their content and purpose with a focus on their geographic scope. We begin with an overview and with general

---

Pedro Roffe, former staff member of the United Nations Conference on Trade and Development (UNCTAD), has been an engaged observer of international economic negotiations particularly on intellectual property and transfer of technology related questions. He has done extensive work on free trade agreements. Roffe is currently Senior Associate of the International Centre for Trade and Sustainable Development (ICTSD), Geneva.

[1] For the sake of convenience, we use FTAs as the generic term to refer to all trade agreements of a bilateral or regional character whose general purpose is to liberalise trade among the partners and that include chapters covering, generally and in a comprehensive manner, intellectual property

P. Roffe (✉)
Senior Fellow, International Centre for Trade and Sustainable Development (ICTSD), Geneva, Switzerland
e-mail: proffe@ictsd.ch

J. Drexl et al. (eds.), *EU Bilateral Trade Agreements and Intellectual Property: For Better or Worse?*, MPI Studies on Intellectual Property and Competition Law 20,
DOI 10.1007/978-3-642-39097-5_2, © Springer-Verlag Berlin Heidelberg 2014

observations on the meaning and consequences of such FTAs and lessons that can be drawn from recent trends. Subsequently, we consider the relationship between the Agreement on Trade-Related Aspects of Intellectual Property Rights (TRIPS) and the FTAs, studying the implementation modalities and how they expand the protection and enforcement of IPRs. Finally, the paper delves into the important impact of these agreements on the multilateral system by placing emphasis on their contribution to the universalisation of international IP regimes and to the potential creation of new alliances or coalitions around these issues.

2 An Overview

2.1 Main Actors and Prevalent Models

FTAs incorporating intellectual property (IP) chapters are not a generalised phenomenon, but they are a significant one, as they mark a trend towards upward expansion of norms and of their potential impact on the evolving international IP architecture.[2] Our analysis centres on FTAs concluded mainly by the United States of America (USA), the European Union (EU) and the European Free Trade Association (EFTA) with a number of partners, particularly in developing countries.

The USA and EFTA focus on deals with countries that seek preferential trade agreements with these important trading blocs. The case of the EU is more varied, covering such different types of arrangements as association agreements, FTAs proper, economic partnership agreements (EPAs) and agreements related to the integration process of newly acceding EU members (e.g. the Western Balkan countries). The latter category of agreements denotes a far-reaching integration approach between the parties and does not follow the general and more limited purpose of FTAs proper. Thus this category is not fully reflected in our analysis.[3] At the same time, while cognisant of the differences in the intensity of the partnerships sought in these agreements, particularly in the case of the EU, the author is of the view that in the area of IP, particularly when they involve developing country partners, FTAs seek similar objectives and the generalisations made in this paper apply to all of them.

provisions. They adopt in practice different denominations, namely: preferential trade agreements in the WTO parlance; free trade or trade promotion agreements in the practice of the USA and EFTA; and FTAs and association, cooperation and economic partnership agreements in the practice of the EU.

[2] See Hilty and Jaeger (2010).

[3] See Santa Cruz (2007).

The geographical scope of these agreements includes FTAs signed not only with the above three major trading blocs but also agreements negotiated by Japan, the Republic of Korea and Taiwan. China, for example, has recently concluded negotiations incorporating IP provisions with a number of countries.[4] One preliminary conclusion on this geographical reach is that over fifty developing economies have entered into negotiations on IP, in the context of FTAs, that go beyond the standards of protection multilaterally agreed upon in the context of the TRIPS Agreement. However, this trend does not include, yet, least-developed countries (LDCs)[5] nor major emerging economies (e.g. India,[6] Indonesia, Mercosur countries, Thailand). We need to bear in mind that ongoing processes are underway with some of these countries, such as Mercosur and India, who are currently negotiating FTAs with the EU that according to the ambitious objectives of the latter trading bloc would include comprehensive IP chapters. The list of middle and high-income countries that have concluded FTAs includes a large number of economies in Latin America and the Caribbean, the Mediterranean and Middle East, Africa and Europe.

Policy makers and scholars have paid particular attention to the US model, which is characterised by a long-established comprehensive strategy in the field of IP. The country became active in advancing TRIPS-plus arrangements even before the conclusion of the World Trade Organization (WTO) Agreement. In this respect, the North American Free Trade Agreement (NAFTA) represents the first major agreement, modelled on TRIPS but going beyond it in a number of areas—such as regulated products and enforcement issues. For its part, the USA-Jordan FTA of 2000 expands on NAFTA and has been used as a prototype for subsequent negotiations carried out by the USA.[7]

The US model epitomises the legislative mandate given by Congress to the United States Trade Representative (USTR) as illustrated by the expired Trade Promotion Authority Act of 2002 that, among other things, aims at

---

[4] See Yu (2011).

[5] A possible exception is Haiti in the EU-CARIFORUM Agreement, but in this case the country benefits from a number of transitional arrangements. See Economic Partnership Agreement between the CARIFORUM States, of the one part, and the European Community and its Member States, of the other part, OJ EC L 289/I/3 of 30 October 2008.

[6] It should be noted that India has signed FTAs with IP chapters that do not include the intensity of commitments found in the FTAs under analysis. For example in 2011, it signed an EPA with Japan that includes general IP principles reiterating commitments to be found in the TRIPS Agreement.

[7] Full texts of the agreements signed by the USA as of today are reproduced in the dedicated USTR website. An important source of information on this topic in the case of the countries of the Americas is the Organization of American States' (OAS) Foreign Trade Information System (SICE).

> ensuring that the provisions of any multilateral or bilateral trade agreement governing IPRs that is entered into by the USA reflect a standard of protection similar to that found in US law.[8]

The strict US model that has evolved since NAFTA has been relaxed with respect to health-related questions, as illustrated by the most recent agreements concluded by the USA with Peru, Colombia and Panama. The flexibilities embodied in these latter FTAs are limited to these three countries and do not extend to earlier FTAs signed with the USA. The health-related flexibilities incorporated in these recent agreements were the outcome of a bipartisan consensus obtained in the US Congress in 2007 allowing former President Bush to conclude outstanding trade agreements in the light of the expiration of the 2002 Trade Promotion Act.[9] It was perceived at that time that the softening of the provisions on health-related questions represented a turn in US policies that constituted a trend for future agreements. However, in the most recent FTA in which the USA is currently engaged, in the context of the Transpacific Partnership Agreement (TPP),[10] the known IP provisions appear to be comprehensive in character and do not allude, according to some sources, to the flexibilities found for example in the FTA with Peru, even if the latter is also a party to the TPP negotiations.[11]

---

[8] The Trade Promotion Authority (Trade Act of 2002) Section 2102 provides:

> (4) . . .The principal negotiating objectives of the USA regarding trade-related intellectual property are. . . (A) to further promote adequate and effective protection of intellectual property rights, including through (i)(I) ensuring accelerated and full implementation of the Agreement on Trade-Related Aspects of Intellectual Property Rights referred to in section 101(d)(15) of the Uruguay Round Agreements Act (19 U.S.C. 3511(d)(15)), particularly with respect to meeting enforcement obligations under that agreement; and (ii) ensuring that the provisions of any multilateral or bilateral trade agreement governing intellectual property rights that is entered into by the USA reflect a standard of protection similar to that found in US law; (ii) providing strong protection for new and emerging technologies and new methods of transmitting and distributing products embodying intellectual property; (iii) preventing or eliminating discrimination with respect to matters affecting the availability, acquisition, scope, maintenance, use, and enforcement of intellectual property rights; (iv) ensuring that standards of protection and enforcement keep pace with technological developments, and in particular ensuring that rightholders have the legal and technological means to control the use of their works through the Internet and other global communication media, and to prevent the unauthorized use of their works; and (v) providing strong enforcement of intellectual property rights, including through accessible, expeditious, and effective civil, administrative, and criminal enforcement mechanisms; (B) to secure fair, equitable, and non-discriminatory market access opportunities for US persons that rely upon intellectual property protection; and (C) to respect the Declaration on the TRIPS Agreement and Public Health, adopted by the World Trade Organization at the Fourth Ministerial Conference at Doha, Qatar on November 14, 2001.

Source: http://www.tpa.gov/pl107_210.pdf.

[9] Roffe and Vivas-Eugui (2007).

[10] See, in general on TPP, Herreros (2011).

[11] With reference to IP issues in the TPP see relevant information at Infojustice, Oxfam (2011), USTR.

In the case of the EU,[12] the evolution has been incremental in terms of upward harmonisation of IP minimum standards. The earlier versions endeavoured to facilitate the implementation of TRIPS and commit partners to "the highest international standards of protection",[13] expand the international architecture—via adhesion to the World Intellectual Property Organisation (WIPO) treaties, as discussed infra—and instate special arrangements on the mutual recognition of geographical indications (GIs), particularly with respect to wines and spirits (see cases of South Africa, Mexico, Chile and EUROMED Association Agreements).[14]

Subsequent agreements tend to parallel the level of ambition of the USA: they are more comprehensive in scope; go beyond the earlier TRIPS implementation-facilitating model; include issues such as the protection of data exclusivity (e.g. Peru, Colombia, Republic of Korea)[15]; extend the protection of GIs for "agricultural and foodstuffs products, wines, spirit drinks and aromatized wines"[16]; and deal extensively with enforcement issues.[17]

The degree of ambition displayed by the USA, namely, to transplant to the trading partners its own level of protection, is found in an official EU document from 2011:

> In negotiating FTAs, the IPR clauses should as far as possible offer identical levels of IPR protection to that existing in the EU while taking into account the level of development of the countries concerned.[18]

With respect to the IP disciplines covered, recent agreements of the USA, EU and EFTA are very similar.[19] Their structure follows the TRIPS Agreement, but as noted includes extensive provisions on regulated products, enforcement and copyright in the digital environment and, in the case of the EU, a detailed treatment of GIs, following with the latter's general position in international forums.

For example, in the case of the EU, the coverage on enforcement issues is broad but more ambitious and more precise than the TRIPS model, such as regarding border measures that encompass cases—as in the US FTAs—of "import, export, or

[12] For a comprehensive listing of EU agreements and respective texts, see European Commission: EU Trade.

[13] E.g., Article 46.1, Agreement on Trade, Development and Cooperation between the European Community and its Member States, of the one part, and the Republic of South Africa, of the other part.

[14] See Santa Cruz (2007).

[15] See Herreros (2011).

[16] See EU-Peru-Colombia, Art. 207, EU-Central America, Art. 247. It is interesting to note that in the cases of both Peru and Colombia and Central America, the GIs extension applies to products listed in respective Appendixes of the FTAs. In the case of CARIFORUM, see Art. 145 (protection "regardless of the class of the product on which it is used").

[17] EU-Peru-Colombia (chapter 4, Arts 234–254), EU-Central America (Chapter 3, Arts 260–273), EU-CARIFORUM (Arts 151–163).

[18] European Commission (2011), p. 21.

[19] The trade agreements signed by EFTA since the early 1990s are available on its dedicated webpage.

transit" of infringing goods. In this context it is interesting to note that the EU agreements with the Caribbean Forum (CARIFORUM), Peru-Colombia and Central America use similar formulations to that in the footnote to Article 51 of the TRIPS Agreement, with regard to the definition of counterfeit and pirated goods. However, in the case of CARIFORUM, the measures extend to designs and GIs and to the fact that the parties may agree to collaborate "to expand the scope of this definition to cover goods infringing all intellectual property rights".[20] The EU's 2010 agreement with the Republic of Korea (Article 10.67) is more precise including in the scope of border measures, infringing goods with respect to patents, plant varieties, registered designs and GIs.[21]

More generally, the EU has introduced an interesting feature in recent agreements that makes the IP chapters easier to respect by structuring their contents in a broader context of fostering innovation and creativity, as in the case of CARIFORUM.[22] These agreements also attempt to satisfy aspirations of their trading partners with respect to transfer of technology and the respect, preservation and maintenance of knowledge related to genetic resources, traditional knowledge and folklore.[23]

2.2 *What Lessons Can be Derived from Recent Trends in FTAs?*

Taking account of recent developments and of the FTAs as a whole, the following eight lessons can be drawn from recent negotiations with expansive coverage of IP issues:

First, FTAs, through the combined effect of the national treatment (NT) and most-favoured nation (MFN) principles, constitute an important trend in IP policymaking. They cover a significant number of countries but some major emerging economies are not yet among them.

Second, as was the case with TRIPS, while industry interests in IP-sensitive sectors (software, entertainment, pharmaceutical-chemical, biotech industries) play a decisive role in shaping these IP chapters, the developing countries' approach has been passive and mainly defensive in terms of damage control.[24]

---

[20] See Article 163, footnote 2, EU-CARIFORUM.

[21] See http://ec.europa.eu/trade/creating-opportunities/bilateral-relations/countries/korea/ (3 May 2011). The Free Trade Agreement was signed in October 2010, approved by the European Parliament in February 2011 and has been provisionally applied since 1 July 2011. See http://www.ip-watch.org/weblog/2011/02/20/stronger-ip-rights-granted-in-eu-korea-fta-precedent-for-future-ftas/?utm_source=post&utm_medium=email&utm_campaign=alerts (3 May 2011).

[22] For an analysis see Spence (2009).

[23] For details on some of these issues see Abbott (2013) and Drexl (2013).

[24] See, e.g., Roffe and Genovesi (2010).

Third, the incorporation of IP in the negotiations is one of the main incentives to major trading partners to engage in FTA negotiations because of the active and influential industrial lobby that sees the bilateral track as a more productive and issue-oriented process than multilateral negotiations. In this respect, one obvious motivation for major trading partners on the IP front is precisely to achieve a level of protection and enforcement that is not possible to obtain at the multilateral level due to resistance and solidarity among like-minded developing countries.

Fourth, consequently, the agenda is crowded with demands conventionally raised by those same industrial sectors and few of the concerns traditionally raised by developing countries in multilateral forums are reflected in the FTAs. But there are variances among the models under consideration.

Fifth, implementation of FTA commitments adds new layers of complexity to those laid down by TRIPS, which in a number of cases is still work in progress. Implementation of these new standards is not a straightforward exercise,[25] as it demands important resources and institutional capabilities not common in many countries.

Sixth, the implementation of FTA commitments is subject to closely monitoring processes that might call into question the continued pertinence of the "freedom of implementation" principle of Article 1.2, TRIPS.[26] Implementation is further subject to a very strict monitoring process via the "certification" act,[27] and to regular reviews of country compliance with IP obligations (see USTR annual reviews),[28] special committees established in these agreements to follow up their implementation[29] or close scrutiny by business associations.[30]

Seventh, FTAs do have an influence in multilateral processes by shaping new coalitions in these negotiations, or by softening positions previously held by some actors.

Finally, they represent asymmetric processes resulting in the transposition of legal systems, regimes prevailing in the major trading partners.[31] This importation, however, does not fully take into account the difference of situations: There is a lack of appropriate safeguards to strike adequate balances between private and public interests and broader considerations prevailing in weaker economies. This includes factors like the inadequacy of institutions, the fact that IP scholars are still

[25] See Deere (2008).

[26] See UNCTAD-ICTSD (2005).

[27] The implementation bills passed by the US Congress condition the entry into force of the agreements in the USA upon the satisfaction expressed by the executive branch that the other party has taken the necessary measures to implement effectively the provisions of the agreement.

[28] See e.g. USTR (2011) Special 301 Report, Roffe and Genovesi (2010).

[29] See Biadgleng and Maur (2011) and Roffe and Spennemann 2013.

[30] E.g. the annual reports produced by Business Software Alliance reporting global piracy trends.

[31] On the transplantation issue see Jaeger (2013) in this volume.

in a formation phase or the lack of experienced and well-trained adjudicatory bodies as well as a professional and critical IP bar.

The subsequent sections seek to explore further these broad general observations and lessons by emphasising how and to what extent FTAs have an impact on the international system and on multilateral processes in general.

3 TRIPS Minimum Standards and FTAs' Methods of Implementation

FTAs follow the WTO single-undertaking model of embracing in one agreement a number of trade-related questions such as IP, thus making it more attractive, particularly to developing country partners, to include TRIPS-plus commitments, in some cases even despite strong reservations. In line with its main source of inspiration, a standard provision in almost all FTAs is the reaffirmation of the rights and obligations under TRIPS.[32]

As has been well elaborated in the literature,[33] the TRIPS Agreement contains more than one ambiguity, leaving space for interpretation in a number of areas as well as different modes of implementation. For example, in the case of data protection, implementing countries were given leeway—respecting the broad parameters of Article 39.3—to adopt different options. This flexibility disappears in most FTAs due to their adoption of modalities used in developed countries for the exclusive protection of such data. This is the general case of US FTAs[34] and with some variations in the instance of EFTA.[35] As far as the EU is concerned, data exclusivity was not part of the first generation of agreements, for example of those negotiated with Chile and South Africa and more recently with CARIFORUM; however, this has changed with the latest generation of FTAs. Data exclusivity is part of the provisions on health-related questions negotiated in the Peru-Colombia agreement,[36] following closely the US template already transposed to these same countries in their respective agreements with the USA.[37] But it is not the case of the EU-Central America FTA; apparently, since these countries had already introduced data exclusivity into their national regimes as a result of their previous obligations towards the USA, a situation that could also have been extended to the agreement

[32] See e.g. Article 196, EU-Colombia-Peru.

[33] See UNCTAD-ICTSD (2005).

[34] See for example US-DR-CAFTA, Article 15.10.1.

[35] For example, in the case of EFTA-Rep. of Korea, the option is left to the parties to implement data protection through exclusivity or compensation. See Article 3, Annex III.

[36] See Article 231, EU-Peru-Colombia.

[37] See e.g. Article 16.10.2, USA-Peru.

with Peru and Colombia.[38] Data protection, as reported by the media, is one of the outstanding controversial questions in the current negotiations of trade agreements between the EU and India.

As in the case of data protection, where countries, particularly developing countries, have options in the implementation of Article 39.3, TRIPS, FTAs adopt an almost unique model regarding obligations on the patentability of plants and animals under Article 27.3(b). The latter provision in the case of protection of plant varieties obliges members to provide protection either by patents or by an effective sui-generis system or by any combination thereof. All the FTAs under consideration without exception commit countries to the ratification of or compliance with the International Union for the Protection of the new Varieties of Plants (UPOV) 1991, using different models to achieve the same result of consolidating plant breeder regimes in those countries.

Finally, as already implied, in the area of enforcement, the implementation options provided by TRIPS are reduced by the detailed treatment of the same issues. For example, under TRIPS there is no obligation with respect to the distribution of resources "as between enforcement of IPRs and the enforcement of law in general" (Art. 41.5). The US FTAs, while reiterating the general TRIPS principle, are more explicit, stipulating that "the distribution of resources for the enforcement of intellectual property rights shall not excuse a Party from compliance".[39] EU FTAs reproduce, *tel quel*, the TRIPS provisions with no further elaboration.[40]

One area of concern in the case of enforcement is that, under the national regimes of the USA and the EU, enforcement measures are subject to a number of caveats and general principles of law that put limits, for example, on the recourse to injunction remedies. In the case of the USA, for instance, permanent injunctive relief is subject to a so-called four-factor test requiring the plaintiff to demonstrate: "(1) that it has suffered an irreparable injury; (2) that remedies available at law are inadequate to compensate for that injury; (3) that considering the balance of hardships between the plaintiff and defendant, a remedy in equity is warranted; and (4) that the public interest would not be disserved by a permanent injunction."[41]

On the same issue and in the context of recent EU agreements, Xavier Seuba has observed that:

> when a comparison is made between the recent EU treaties containing obligations on civil enforcement, it becomes clear that they include almost the same wording of the [Enforcement] Directive. In fact, as far as the rights granted to the titleholders, the five texts are

[38] A simpler explanation for this different treatment in the agreements negotiated almost contemporaneously was the fact that at the time of the negotiations with Peru and Colombia, the latter FTA with the USA was still pending for ratification. The final signature of the Colombia agreement with the USA took place only on 21 October 2011.

[39] Article 17.11.2, Chile-USA.

[40] See Article 234.4, EU-Peru-Colombia.

[41] US Supreme Court, 547 U.S. 388 (2006).

> almost identical. The differences are located in the provisions (or the absence therein) that deal with the limits of right holders entitlements and with the rights of their competitors and IPR protected goods users.[42]

In other words, in such delicate matters as injunction measures, which are new for a number of developing countries, the FTAs establish strict obligations that do transplant legal regimes, appropriate to their stage of development, but without at the same time providing for the checks and balances—for example, those mentioned supra—that do exist in the "transplanting" countries. The issue probably is not of the FTAs per se but of the way the domestic legislation or courts of the receiving countries would finally implement those provisions, an issue that we discuss with more detail infra.

FTAs represent, thus, a particular way of implementing the minimum standards of TRIPS by choosing, as described above, one option that, as in the case of data protection, was a long-standing aspiration of developed countries as revealed in the TRIPS negotiations.[43] However, the implications of these new obligations are immense. The combined effect of the NT and MFN principles[44] means that changes in national laws are extended to all countries. Once those reforms are implemented in the national system, it would not be possible for a country to legitimately discriminate—within the scope of the relevant TRIPS provisions—between nationals of different countries. For example, exclusive protection of undisclosed data would have *erga omnes* effects not limited to the trading partners.

With respect to the relationship between FTAs and TRIPS, it is important to note that one salient feature of TRIPS concerning the application of the minimum standard principle is the freedom "to determine the appropriate method of implementing the provisions" of the Agreement "within their own legal system and practice". (Article 1.1., TRIPS).[45] We have seen that FTAs tend in a number of cases to suggest or choose one particular way of implementing those standards, as in the case of data protection. However, this aspect is a general legal consequence of agreeing in these agreements to standards that go beyond the minimum standard prescribed in TRIPS.

In the case of FTAs, particularly those with the USA, this freedom of implementation is further affected by the interplay of other factors. One of these factors relates to the transposition of language and institutions not common to the developing trading partners. The drafting style of US FTAs is peculiar to that country's

[42] Seuba 2013.

[43] See UNCTAD-ICTSD (2005), Watal (2001).

[44] It is interesting to note that the EU FTAs reproduce these two principles (Peru-Colombia, Articles 198, 199). In the case of US FTAs there is only reference to national treatment.

[45] For considerations on the boundaries of Article 1.1, TRIPS, see Kur and Grosse Ruse-Khan (2011) and Grosse Ruse-Khan (2010).

law making, which makes it difficult for those not familiar with the system to grasp the intricacies and nature of new commitments.[46]

But more cumbersome and pervasive is the process related to the actual implementation of the new IP obligations into national law, which is subject to a process of scrutiny and vetting by the major trading partner. This, known as the "certification process", finds its legitimacy in the implementation bills passed by Congress regarding the entry into force of the respective FTAs. As a matter of fact, Peru, in translating the FTA into domestic legislation, experienced a complex period of implementation before its trading partner was satisfied that the legislation met the standards of the agreement. Interested in finalising its agreement with the USA before the assumption of its new administration in 2009, Peru had to pass different legislative acts amending previous ones that did not conform to the expectations of the USA.[47] Similar instances have been reported in other countries.[48] In other words, the original FTAs are actually "renegotiated" upwards in the implementation process. For many actors, the certification means a reconsideration of the understandings reached in the original agreement implying stricter options in the national legislative implementation process.

[46] See for example how data exclusivity is formulated in US-DR-CAFTA, Article 15.10.1:

> (a) If a Party requires, as a condition of approving the marketing of a new pharmaceutical or agricultural chemical product, the submission of undisclosed data concerning safety or efficacy, the Party shall not permit third persons, without the consent of the person who provided the information, to market a product on the basis of (1) the information, or (2) the approval granted to the person who submitted the information for at least five years for pharmaceutical products and ten years for agricultural chemical products from the date of approval in the Party. (b) If a Party permits, as a condition of approving the marketing of a new pharmaceutical or agricultural chemical product, third persons to submit evidence concerning the safety or efficacy of a product that was previously approved in another territory, such as evidence of prior marketing approval, the Party shall not permit third persons, without the consent of the person who previously obtained such approval in the other territory, to obtain authorization or to market a product on the basis of (1) evidence of prior marketing approval in the other territory, or (2) information concerning safety or efficacy that was previously submitted to obtain marketing approval in the other territory, for at least five years for pharmaceutical products and ten years for agricultural chemical products from the date approval was granted in the Party's territory to the person who received approval in the other territory. In order to receive protection under this subparagraph, a Party may require that the person providing the information in the other territory seek approval in the territory of the Party within five years after obtaining marketing approval in the other territory.

[47] For instance, Peru, which fully implemented the FTA on 28 June 2008, was obliged to amend its legislation on 14 January 2009, just days before the entry into force of the agreement. One example of the changes introduced in the subsequent legislation relates to genetic resources. The latest revision includes a provision—absent in the 2008 law—clarifying that in the case of failure to comply with requirements applicable to access to genetic resources and traditional knowledge (such as access contracts) the sanctions could entail only monetary penalties, compensation, transfer of technology or authorisation for use. (See Article 120 A, law 29316 of January 2009). It has been reported that this latter amendment was the result of the certification process. See also Roca (2009).

[48] See Biadgleng and Maur (2011), Roffe and Genovesi (2010).

In the case of the EU, apparently, there is no such parallel situation as the extreme case of "certification" experienced with US agreements. But the EU might no doubt play a role in shaping the implementation process. In the FTAs under consideration there are important provisions regarding cooperation "with a view to supporting implementation of the commitments and obligations undertaken".[49] The system is reinforced by the creation in both the Peru-Colombia and the Central America agreements of a Sub-Committee on Intellectual Property.[50] Cooperation regarding implementation is also present in the CARIFORUM Agreement.[51] One could not prejudge the outcome of these modalities of cooperation but one should be cautious not to overestimate the actual implementation of FTA commitments, taking into account, among other things, the "checks and balances" that in fact exist in the "transposing" country.

4 Contributing to Making the International IP Architecture More Universal

The influence of FTAs in the multilateral system has a number of manifestations. As was implied above, FTAs go a step further in the process of harmonisation of IP standards that was initiated successfully with the conclusion of the TRIPS Agreement. One expression of this trend is the geographical expansion of the web of international agreements administered by WIPO and UPOV to the parties of FTAs. In the case of agreements signed with the USA, EU and EFTA similar provisions set forth a strict schedule of accession, ratification, application or best-endeavours obligations concerning a number of international treaties dealing with: a) substantive obligations, such as UPOV 1991, referred to above, as well as the WIPO internet treaties of 1996, b) facilitation treaties such as the PCT and c) classification treaties such as the Nice Agreement Concerning the International Classification of Goods and Services for the Purposes of the Registration of Marks. Thus, with respect to this aspect of the FTAs, their influence is profound.

As also implied above, FTAs do represent a deepening of the upward harmonisation of IP standards accelerated by TRIPS. This takes place in FTAs in two identifiable forms that produce similar effects: first, by delineating the referred ambiguities of TRIPS and second, by, intentionally or not, aligning countries to the regulatory regimes of the more advanced partner. The latter clearly responds to the

[49] EU-Peru-Colombia (Article 256) and EU-CARIFORUM (Article 164.1). See also EU-Central America (Article 275).

[50] There are some subtleties in the scope of the Subcommittees. In the case of Peru-Colombia its broad function is "to follow up on the implementation" (Article 257). In the case of Central America, the functions are focused on GIs and transfer of technology but keeps open possibilities to address other issues. (Article 274).

[51] See Art. 164, EU-CARIFORUM.

negotiating objectives of both the USA and the EU, namely, to translate into those agreements their respective prevailing standards of protection.

Examples of the first modality relate, in general, to the cases described in the previous section, for example, the commitment regarding UPOV 1991 with respect to the protection of plant varieties, and provisions in TRIPS (Art. 27.3(b)). The enforcement provisions are also a case in point, as for example with respect to the obligation that "competent authorities may initiate border measures ex officio with respect to merchandise for importation, exportation, or in transit, without the need for a formal complaint from a private party or right holder".[52]

The other side of the coin to this question of TRIPS ambiguities is the issue of the regulatory alignment with the more advanced countries. In the previous discussion we have referred to several situations that fall under this category, one of the most paradigmatic cases probably being the data-exclusivity provisions of pharmaceutical and agro-chemical products and the comprehensive treatment of enforcement issues including those related to the digital environment.

Of similar implications are the provisions on the restoration of the duration of protection in cases of administrative delays. This has been a normal pattern in US FTAs[53] with respect to administrative delays in the granting of a patent or in the commercialisation permit of products subject to regulatory approval. This trend, not present in the first generation of EU agreements, has surfaced in most recent FTAs, such as that with Peru and Colombia, which provide for a compensation in cases of curtailment of the effective patent term resulting from the first marketing approval.[54] It is to be noted that neither the EU-Central America FTA nor the CARIFORUM agreement incorporates such a provision.[55]

As pointed out, in the case of the USA, in its FTA with Peru and also with Panama and Colombia—as a result of the bipartisan agreement of 2007—the restoration for pharmaceuticals products was made optional. As also alluded, the more flexible policy prescribed in 2007 with respect to regulated products apparently is being revisited, as illustrated by recent proposals in the context of the TPP negotiations.[56]

The comprehensiveness and detailed treatment of the enforcement chapters, including minute and detailed provisions related to the digital environment, reflect the highest standards of protection prevailing in the most advanced countries. In this particular area some of the ambiguities of TRIPS and its "may" provisions disappear.

---

[52] See USA-Peru (Article 16.11.23).

[53] See for example, Chile-USA, Articles 17.9.6 and 17.10.2(a).

[54] Article 230.4 EU-Peru-Colombia:

With respect to any pharmaceutical product that is covered by a patent, each Party may, in accordance with its domestic legislation, make available a mechanism to compensate the patent owner for unreasonable curtailment of the effective patent term resulting from the first marketing approval of that product in that Party. Such mechanism shall confer all of the exclusive rights of a patent, subject to the same limitations and exceptions applicable to the original patent.

[55] This could be explained by the already existing restoration of the term obligation in Central America due to their FTA with the USA.

[56] See Infojustice and Oxfam (2011).

4.1 Do the FTAs Facilitate the Advancement of Multilateralism and the Building of New Coalitions?

FTAs are tributaries of TRIPS and very much connected to the international IP architecture and therefore should have an impact regarding negotiating positions taken by different countries in international forums. Like-minded developing countries have regularly advanced concerns regarding the upward movement towards stricter protection and enforcement of IP. An important expression of that anxiety was the launch in 2004[57] of the WIPO Development Agenda:

> IP protection is a policy instrument the operation of which may, in actual practice, produce benefits as well as costs, which may vary in accordance with a country's level of development. Action is therefore needed to ensure, in all countries, that the costs do not outweigh the benefits of IP protection. . .. Intellectual property protection cannot be seen as an end in itself, nor can the harmonization of intellectual property laws leading to higher protection standards in all countries, irrespective of their levels of development.[58]

Developing countries as whole or specific country coalitions have pursued similar objectives of redressing this IP expansion trend, already with the 2001 WTO Declaration on TRIPS and Public Health[59] and initiatives in various forums such as on genetic resources and traditional knowledge[60] and the push to deal in concrete terms with exceptions and limitations in patents and copyright.[61] They have also on a number of occasions resisted initiatives to reopen discussions on enforcement issues in the WTO Council for TRIPS and in WIPO's Advisory Committee on Enforcement.

These views have resulted in some common stands in multilateral forums on these same related issues. The question that arises, in the context of FTAs, is to what extent these agreements interfere with these international processes and with those positions advanced by coalitions of developing countries, including those negotiating FTAs. No doubt these questions are very much related to the overall considerations those countries have in entering into new commitments in FTAs. The actual question is whether these FTAs actually changed the entrenched and well-established positions of these same countries in multilateral negotiations. In other words, do FTAs weaken the position taken by those countries in multilateral

[57] The Agenda resulted in an agreement in 2007 with the adoption of 45 recommendations to enhance the development dimensions of WIPO's activities, see WIPO (2007).

[58] See WIPO (2004).

[59] WTO (2001).

[60] See Vivas-Eugui (2012).

[61] Since the adoption of the recommendations on the Development Agenda, the WIPO Standing Committee on the Law of Patents and the Standing Committee on Copyright and Related Rights have a heavy agenda dealing with exceptions and limitations.

forums or do they contribute to new alliances with their trading partners affecting the way developing countries will operate in the future in those international forums? The answer to these questions is not clear-cut. We examine below some cases where apparent conflicts might arise.

A case in point might be non-violation complaints, a standard cause of action in the General Agreement on Tariffs and Trade (GATT) system with respect to trade of goods in cases of nullification or the impairment of benefits accruing to Members under a particular agreement. Non-violation complaints were made applicable by TRIPS (Art. 64.2 and 3) to IP disputes.[62] Due, however, to their controversial nature, non-violation complaints have been subject to a special moratorium still in force impeding WTO Members from filing complaints under these circumstances. A large constituency in the WTO—not only limited to developing countries—favours a ban on non-violation complaints in TRIPS completely or the extension of the moratorium. Countries questioning the application of non-violation complaints based their position on the fact that equating the typical circumstances applying under GATT in the case of trade in goods with IP situations is not appropriate and is rather problematic due to the public interests involved in the case of IPRs. Contrary to the existing predicament in the WTO, in almost all existing US FTAs non-violation situations fall in the case of IPRs within the broad scope of the respective dispute settlement mechanisms. This by itself seeks to align countries signing FTAs to the position of those in favour of extending at the multilateral level the application of non-violation complaints to IP disputes.[63]

With respect to genetic resources and traditional knowledge, a number of developing countries have considered these issues as relevant subject areas in the quest for a rebalancing of the IP system, putting forward initiatives to protect those assets and avoid their misuse or misappropriation by third parties primarily located in industrialised country jurisdictions. In a number of forums such as the WTO and WIPO countries continue to pursue defensive (e.g. mandatory disclosure requirements in patent applications regarding the origin or source of the genetic resources and associated traditional knowledge)[64] and affirmative measures to protect those assets in one or another form of IP (e.g., in the current negotiations

[62] See UNCTAD-ICTSD (2005), pp 668–667

[63] It is impossible to ascertain whether countries that have signed FTAs with the USA have or have not changed their positions in the context of discussions on non-violation complaints in the WTO. The existing moratorium was the result of broad deals in the context of the ongoing Doha trade negotiations launched in 2001. In the TRIPS Council the actual application of non-violation complaints has been supported by a limited number of countries.

[64] See WTO (2011).

at the WIPO Intergovernmental Committee on Intellectual Property and Genetic Resources, Traditional Knowledge and Folklore (IGC)).[65]

Colombia and Peru have been important actors in pursuing internationally some of the defensive and affirmative strategies mentioned above. Colombia, for example, was instrumental in 2001 in the establishment of the IGC process in WIPO,[66] and Peru has been an active member of the coalition of countries that pursue a mandatory disclosure requirement in patent applications. Here it is interesting to compare those positions with what has been agreed on these same matters in FTAs concluded by those countries for example with the USA. Contrary to their wishes and the clear intent of their negotiators, their FTAs do not include specific provisions to deal with the precise demands made at the multilateral level. However, and highlighted at its time as one of the successes in the negotiations, the respective FTAs concluded by Peru and Colombia include side letters reflecting the understanding of the parties, among other things, of the importance of traditional knowledge and biodiversity including their contribution to cultural, economic and social development. The understanding lays out some principles, drawing on the Convention on Biological Diversity (CBD), of obtaining informed consent from the appropriate authority prior to accessing genetic resources and of equitably sharing the benefits arising from the use of traditional knowledge and genetic resources. It also underlines the importance of promoting quality patent examination to ensure that the conditions of patentability are satisfied.[67]

These understandings, however, underline the recognition "that access to genetic resources or traditional knowledge, as well as the equitable sharing of benefits that may result from use of those resources or that knowledge, can be adequately addressed through contracts that reflect mutually agreed terms between users and providers". Peru has continuously sustained the view in multilateral forums that these matters need to be addressed by an amendment to the TRIPS Agreement in terms of mandatory disclosure of the origin and source of the genetic resources and associated traditional knowledge. Does this mean that in the case of Peru the FTA has weakened its position in multilateral forums? The bilateral agreement with the USA has not prevented Peru from continuing to pursue a multilateral solution to these issues in the context of the current Doha negotiations.[68] But does this imply that the country continues to play such an active and leading role on these matters as it used to do?

[65] See WIPO (2011).

[66] Vivas-Eugui (2012).

[67] See Biodiversity and TK understanding (attached to the text of the FTA).

[68] It is to be noted that Peru subscribes to the communication of more than 100 countries in the context of the Doha negotiations for inclusion of disclosure requirements; see WTO (2008) and the Draft Decision of April (2011), WTO (2011).

With respect to related public-health issues, FTAs do appear to be consistent, on paper, with concerns expressed by developing countries on the possible impact of IP protection and enforcement on access to medicines. FTAs do specifically refer to international proclamations such as the 2001 Doha Declaration and the subsequent paragraph-six solution. In the case of the USA this is done in the agreement itself or in side letters. The former is the approach taken in recent EU agreements.[69]

Precisely in the case of the USA, as mentioned supra, recent agreements, such as those with Colombia, Panama and Peru, do include non-mandatory provisions with respect to pharmaceutical products, particularly on matters such as the restoration period and the linkage for regulated products. In other words and contrary to earlier agreements (e.g. with CAFTA, Chile, Morocco) the FTAs with Colombia, Peru and Panama do not bind those countries to compensate for delays in the granting of patents or the commercialisation of the product, nor "to not grant marketing approval to any third party prior to the expiration of the patent term, unless by consent or acquiescence of the patent owner".[70]

Notwithstanding the apparent consistency of FTAs with the 2001 Doha Declaration on health, FTAs considered as a whole might have consequences on public health particularly in cases of unbalanced implementation of the provisions dealing with data exclusivity or possible limitations to the use of instruments such as compulsory licensing,[71] pricing issues[72] and enforcement provisions in general (e.g., border measures as raised in the dispute brought by India and Brazil against the EU).[73]

Thus, a number of questions persist: Do FTAs weaken alliances among like-minded developing countries? Do they create new coalitions with major trading partners? Do provisions on health-related questions maintain consistency with aspirations of the international community, or do they break with the broader coalition behind the 2001 Doha Declaration?

4.2 The Balance of Bargaining: Who Wins What?

If one concludes that FTAs respond fundamentally to the concerns of the stronger trading partners and amply reflect those concerns, one remaining question relates to how far these agreements reflect the preoccupations that the signatory developing countries have raised at multilateral forums on the reform or improvement of the

---

[69] See Article 197, EU-Peru-Colombia.

[70] Article 17.10.2(c), Chile-USA.

[71] This was the case in earlier FTAs signed by the USA, e.g. with Jordan.

[72] Pricing issues in the case of pharmaceutical products are included in the case of the FTA with Australia and USA-Korea. It is reported that this would also be the case in the prospective TPP.

[73] See Seuba (2010).

international system, for example as made explicit in the WIPO Development Agenda. On this question, it would be interesting to examine whether countries that have adhered to the development agenda are candidates for or have signed FTAs. Two immediate cases come to mind. As a result or not of the FTA, Peru, which was a member of the Friends of Development in the launching of the WIPO Agenda, is no longer a member of the current Development Agenda Group (DAG) established in 2010[74] assembling countries that monitor the implementation of such Agenda in WIPO. South Africa, on the contrary—a country actively in favour of the WIPO Development Agenda and an active member of DAG—signed an FTA of first generation with the EU, an agreement negotiated immediately after TRIPS was concluded and whose level of ambition is not comparable with that of recent FTAs.

In order to explore these matters further we will focus on some specific cases in which developing countries have expressed apprehensions in terms of rebalancing the expansive agenda put forward by developed countries—namely, the cases of the TRIPS-CBD relationship, issues related to the transfer of technology and the EU's aggressive position on GIs. How far do FTA negotiations mirror these concerns? Related to these questions one could also refer to concerns exposed on health-related questions and TRIPS-plus enforcement measures, discussed supra.

With respect to the relationship between IP and the CBD, the main concern in this area has been the push by a number of countries for a mandatory disclosure requirement, as discussed in the previous section. Here we need to note that in the case of the EU and also of EFTA agreements, there is a trend in recent agreements to accommodate the position of developing country partners by underlining the relationship between CBD and TRIPS and encouraging provisions in national legislation on disclosure. For example, in the FTA with Peru and Colombia, "the Parties acknowledge the usefulness of requiring the disclosure of the origin or source of genetic resources and associated traditional knowledge in patent applications, considering that this contributes to the transparency about the uses of genetic resources and associated traditional knowledge."[75] A similar provision is found in the CARIFORUM Agreement[76] but not in the Central America FTA, notwithstanding the general acknowledgement of the CBD principles in the latter agreement.[77]

In the case of CARIFORUM, a special partnership is envisaged via regular consultations and exchanges on the work in WIPO of the IGC and broadly, in the WTO, on "the relationship between the TRIPS Agreement and the Convention on

[74] The Members of the Development Agenda Group established in April 2010 are Algeria, Brazil, Cuba, Djibouti, Ecuador, Egypt, Guatemala, India, Indonesia, Iran (Islamic Republic of), Malaysia, Pakistan, Philippines, South Africa, Sri Lanka, Sudan, Uruguay and Yemen. See WIPO (2010).

[75] Article 201.7, EU-Peru-Colombia.

[76] Article 150.4, CARIFORUM.

[77] See Article 229.4, EU-Central America.

Biological Diversity, the protection of traditional knowledge and folklore".[78] This "positive comity" to advance common positions in the above forums could also be perceived as a manifestation of the building of new alliances in multilateral forums, an issue also discussed in the previous section.

As pointed out above, US FTAs do not make reference to the CBD—which the USA has not ratified—and in some cases (Peru and Colombia) favour contractual solutions to the issue of disclosing the source or origin of the genetic resources.[79]

With respect to GIs—applicable only to the EU—most of the agreements, albeit under different modalities, do tend to reflect or adhere to the aggressive international EU position on GIs, examples being the recent agreements with CARIFORUM, Peru, Colombia and Central American countries. As also noted, South Africa, as well as Chile and Mexico, signed first-generation FTAs with the EU with a wide-ranging mutual recognition of GIs but at a time when the EU did not have the broad, aggressive GI agenda manifested later in the course of the Doha round of negotiations.

---

[78] CARIFORUM, Article 164: Genetic resources, traditional knowledge and folklore

1. Subject to their domestic legislation the EC Party and the Signatory CARIFORUM States respect, preserve and maintain knowledge, innovations and practices of indigenous and local communities embodying traditional lifestyles relevant for the conservation and sustainable use of biological diversity and promote their wider application with the involvement and approval of the holders of such knowledge, innovations and practices and encourage the equitable sharing of the benefits arising from the utilisation of such knowledge, innovations and practices
2. The EC Party and the Signatory CARIFORUM States recognise the importance of taking appropriate measures, subject to national legislation, to preserve traditional knowledge and agree to continue working towards the development of internationally agreed sui generis models for the legal protection of traditional knowledge
3. The EC Party and the Signatory CARIFORUM States agree that the patent provisions of this subsection and the Convention on Biological Diversity shall be implemented in a mutually supportive way
4. The EC Party and the Signatory CARIFORUM States may require as part of the administrative requirements for a patent application concerning an invention which uses biological material as a necessary aspect of the invention, that the applicant identifies the sources of the biological material used by the applicant and described as part of the invention
5. The EC Party and the Signatory CARIFORUM States agree to regularly exchange views and information on relevant multilateral discussions:

   (a) In WIPO, on the issues dealt with in the framework of the Intergovernmental Committee on Genetic Resources, Traditional Knowledge and Folklore; and,
   (b) In the WTO, on the issues related to the relationship between the TRIPS Agreement and the Convention on Biological Diversity, the protection of traditional knowledge and folklore

6. Following the conclusion of the relevant multilateral discussions referred to in paragraph 5, the EC Party and the Signatory CARIFORUM States, at the request of the EC Party or a Signatory CARIFORUM State, agree to review this Article within the Joint CARIFORUM-EC Council in the light of the results of such multilateral discussions.

[79] There are sources that have argued that in the case, for example, of DR-CAFTA-USA, there are presumptions such as "the patent applicant was in possession of the claimed invention as of the filing date" (CAFTA, 15.9.10) that could make irrelevant mandatory patent disclosure requirements. See Infojustice and Oxfam.

In the above cases, particularly with respect to Peru, Colombia and Central America, it is noticeable that the extension of the protection of GIs relates to what, in the case of the Central American countries, are called the "protected GIs" that correspond to those listed in a particular annex of the agreement. Other GIs might be added, but in those cases the parties need "to agree on the possibility of adding additional geographical indications for wines, spirits, agricultural products and foodstuffs to be protected on the basis of the rules and procedures established". In other words, such GIs, subject to their successful examination by the competent authorities, will be added to the agreed annex of protected GIs.[80] But what is discernible in these cases is the asymmetry of demands by the parties. The EU's list includes over one hundred and fifty products compared to only one for Colombia and three GIs for Peru.[81]

Finally, with respect to aspects related to transfer of technology—a long-standing demand of developing countries in international forums[82]—the FTAs reflect some expressions of concern not in the form of firm commitments but of broad principles. The US FTAs, in general, pay discreet attention to these matters—in a similar line with TRIPS—by "emphasizing that the protection and enforcement of intellectual property rights is a fundamental principle of this chapter that helps promote technological innovation as well as the transfer and dissemination of technology to the mutual advantage of technology producers and users, and that encourages the development of social and economic well-being".[83] In recent cases, such as the FTAs with Peru and Colombia, there is an attempt to advance in this area by promoting a framework for partnerships that might build a platform for public and private party involvement in the promotion of innovation and technological development.[84]

The EU FTAs of most recent vintage show a more sympathetic approach to these questions. But in the case of Peru-Colombia[85] and Central America[86] measures to promote transfer of technology are mostly perceived in the realm of exchange of views, experience and information. In the case of CARIFORUM, the respective provisions are presented in the context of "fostering innovation and creativity"[87] and in this respect the FTA describes areas of cooperation such as in science and technology; the information society and information and communication technologies; and eco-innovation and renewable energy. More specifically on transfer of technology, the agreement resembles the other two in that it emphasises

[80] See Article 247, EU-Central America.

[81] See Annex XIII, Appendix 1, to the FTA on list of GIs.

[82] See Gehl Sampath and Roffe (2012).

[83] Preamble, Chile FTA with the USA.

[84] See Article 16.12, USA-Peru.

[85] Article 255, EU-Peru-Colombia.

[86] Article 231, EU-Central America.

[87] Article 131, EU-CARIFORUM.

exchanges of views and information on practices and policies affecting technology transfer.[88]

The FTAs under consideration replicate the provision in TRIPS on the right to take measures to prevent or control licensing practices or conditions that may adversely affect the international transfer of technology and that may constitute an abuse of IPRs by right holders. An interesting consideration found in the CARIFORUM[89] and Central America[90] agreements is that anticompetitive practices might include abuses of "obvious information asymmetries" in technology transactions. Precisely these, the technology markets, are in general characterised by such asymmetry of information, particularly in the case of unequal parties. In this respect, the FTAs offer opportunities to explore this issue further.

Lastly, a positive formal step in the EU FTAs, as reflected in those with Peru and Colombia[91] and with CARIFORUM,[92] is the extension of the provisions of Article 66.2, TRIPS, on incentives for the transfer of technology to developing country partners in general and not limited to the least-developed countries as in TRIPS. We underline here the "formal step" of this type of mechanism in the light of the experience so far and controversy around the efficacy of such measures in the particular case of the LDCs.[93]

5 Final Observations

FTAs are not an insignificant or marginal phenomenon. This chapter depicts the progressive and incremental evolution that FTAs have experienced in recent years. At the beginning, immediately after the conclusion of TRIPS, their central intent, as exemplified by those to which the EU was a party, was to uphold the implementation of the Agreement and expand the international IP architecture through adherence to a network of administrative, functional and protection agreements administered by WIPO. Today, FTAs represent a major advancement in the harmonisation of IP standards. If they are not actually a universal phenomenon, still their geographical reach is significant and their influence on framing future developments not irrelevant.

From the space to legislate and the freedom left to states to determine the appropriate method of implementation (Art. 1, TRIPS) we are moving to a more restrictive framework. In areas such as patents, particularly on issues related to regulated products (e.g. pharmaceuticals) a more precise trend appears to be emerging on matters such as restoration of the duration of rights due to

[88] Id., Article 142.

[89] Id., Article 142.2.

[90] Article 231.3, EU-Central America.

[91] Article 255.5, EU-Peru-Colombia.

[92] Article 142.3, EU-CARIFORUM.

[93] See Moon (2011).

administrative delays, data exclusivity and the linkage between the commercialisation of products and the term of expiration of the patent. One of the most significant areas of expansion has been enforcement, where optional provisions in TRIPS have become binding on the parties, particularly with respect to border measures, criminal sanctions and enforcement issues in the digital environment—an area not originally covered by TRIPS. The case of enforcement and its coverage in FTAs is notable on its influence, as the case of ACTA shows. ACTA was an attempt in many respects to build on the existing FTAs to make them plurilateral and eventually a model for future law making in this area.

This chapter examines situations showing how pervasive FTAs are, and how influential in shaping new legislation in developing countries. The implementation of these standards has not been free of difficulties, particularly caused by the intent of the strong trading partners to export their models and IP culture and to influence the choice of options to solve a particular issue. The implementation alternatives left in TRIPS—on protection of undisclosed information, for instance, or on enforcement—are being narrowed down to those prevalent in more advanced countries but without taking into account the in-built checks and balances that exist in those countries.

The chapter considers further situations in which FTAs, in the light of the new and expanded commitments, might potentially influence the sustainability of traditional alliances among developing countries as well as the positions taken on specific issues (e.g. access to health, genetic resources and traditional knowledge, non-violation complaints, enforcement). We provide examples of potential conflicts, but it is too early to definitely conclude that FTAs have already influenced negotiating positions or existing alliances. More striking and revealing is the fact that, through a carefully monitored process of implementation, fundamental changes are taking place domestically. What influence this will have at the multilateral level continues to be an open question. Certainly, things will not be same as they were before FTAs.

References

Abbott FM (2013) Trade costs and shadow benefits: EU Economic Partnership Agreements as models for progressive development of international IP law. In: Drexl J, Grosse Ruse Khan H, Nadde-Phlix S (eds) EU bilateral trade agreements and intellectual property: for better or worse? Springer, Heidelberg (this volume)

Biadgleng E, Maur JC (2011) The influence of preferential trade agreements on the implementation of intellectual property rights in developing countries: a first look. Issue Paper No. 33, UNCTAD-ICTSD Project on IPRs and Sustainable Development. http://unctad.org/en/Docs/iteipc2011d01_en.pdf

Biodiversity and TK Understanding. http://www.ustr.gov/trade-agreements/free-trade-agreements/peru-tpa/final-text

Business Software Alliance 2011 Report. http://portal.bsa.org/globalpiracy2010/downloads/study_pdf/2010_BSA_Piracy_Study-Standard.pdf

Deere C (2008) The implementation game: the TRIPS agreement and the global politics of intellectual property reform in developing countries. Oxford University Press, Cambridge

Drexl J (2013) Intellectual property and implementation of recent bilateral trade agreements in the EU. In: Drexl J, Grosse Ruse Khan H, Nadde-Phlix S (eds) EU bilateral trade agreements and intellectual property: for better or worse? Springer, Heidelberg (this volume)

EFTA. http://www.efta.int/free-trade/free-trade-agreements.aspx

European Commission (2011) Communication: a single market for intellectual property rights. Boosting creativity and innovation to provide economic growth, high quality jobs and first class products and services in Europe. COM(2011)287 final, Brussels, 24 May 2011, p 21. http://ec.europa.eu/internal_market/copyright/docs/ipr_strategy/COM_2011_287_en.pdf

European Commission (November 2011) EU trade: overview of regional trade agreements. http://trade.ec.europa.eu/doclib/docs/2006/december/tradoc_111588.pdf

Gehl Sampath P, Roffe P (2012) Unpacking the international transfer of technology debate: fifty years and beyond. Issue Paper No. 36, ICTSD. http://ictsd.org/downloads/2012/11/unpacking-the-international-technology-transfer-debate-fifty-years-and-beyond.pdf

Grosse Ruse-Khan H (2010) Sustainable development in international intellectual property law – new approaches from EU Economic Partnership Agreements? Issue Paper No. 29, ICTSD. http://ictsd.org/downloads/2011/12/sustainable-development-in-international-intellectual-property-law-e28093-new-approaches-from-eu-economic-partnership-agreements.pdf

Herreros S (2011) The Trans-Pacific Strategic Economic Partnership Agreement: A Latin American Perspective. Serie Comercio Internacional, ECLAC. http://www.eclac.org/cgi-bin/getProd.asp?xml=/publicaciones/xml/6/42966/P42966.xml&xsl=/comercio/tpl/p9f.xsl&base

Hilty RM, Jaeger TR (2010) Legal effects and policy considerations for free trade agreements: what is wrong with FTAs? Max Planck Institute for Intellectual Property, Competition and Tax Law Research Paper No. 10-02

Infojustice. http://infojustice.org/tpp-analysis-november2011

Jaeger T (2013) IP enforcement provisions in EU Economic Partnership Agreements. In: Drexl J, Grosse Ruse Khan H, Nadde-Phlix S (eds) EU bilateral trade agreements and intellectual property: for better or worse? Springer, Heidelberg (this volume)

Kur A, Grosse Ruse-Khan H (2011) Enough is enough – the notion of binding ceilings in international intellectual property protection. In: Kur A, Levin M (eds) Intellectual property rights in a fair world trade system: proposals for reform of TRIPS. Edward Elgar, Cheltenham, pp 359–407

Moon S (2011) Meaningful Technology Transfer to the LDCs: A Proposal for a Monitoring Mechanism for TRIPS Article 66.2. Policy Brief No. 9, ICTSD Programme on Innovation, Technology and Intellectual Property. http://ictsd.org/downloads/2011/05/technology-transfer-to-the-ldcs.pdf

Oxfam (2011) Oxfam analysis of US proposals for IP Pharmaceutical Pricing Provisions in Trans-Pacific Partnership Agreement Negotiations. Manuscript with the author

Roca S (2009) Demócratas, salud pública y propiedad intelectual en el APC Perú-EE UU. Puentes 10(2):5–7. http://ictsd.org/downloads/puentes/puentes10-2.pdf

Roffe P, Genovesi M (2010) Implementación y Administración de los Capítulos de Propiedad Intelectual en los Acuerdos de Libre Comercio con los Estados Unidos: La Experiencia de Cuatro Países de América Latina. Inter-American Development Bank. http://issuu.com/aid-for-trade/docs/implementaci_n_y_administraci_n_de_los_cap_tulos_d

Roffe P, Spennemann C (2013) Preferential trade agreements and intellectual property rights. In: Cimoli M, Dosi G, Maskus K, Okediji R, Reichman J (eds) Intellectual property rights: legal and economic challenges for development. Oxford University Press, Cambridge (forthcoming)

Roffe P, Vivas-Eugui D (2007) A shift in intellectual property policy in US FTAs? Bridges Rev 11(5):15. http://ictsd.org

Santa Cruz M (2007) Intellectual Property Provisions in European Union Trade Agreements: implications for developing countries. Issue Paper No. 20, ICTSD Programme on IPRs and Sustainable Development. http://www.iprsonline.org/resources/docs/Santa-Cruz%20Blue20.pdf

Seuba X (2010) Free trade of pharmaceutical products: the limits of intellectual property enforcement at the border. Issue Paper No. 27, ICTSD Programme on IPRs and Sustainable Development. http://ictsd.org/downloads/2011/12/free-trade-of-pharmaceutical-products.pdf
Seuba X (2013) Checks and Balances in the Intellectual Property Enforcement Field: Reconstructing EU Trade Agreements. In: Geiger C (ed) Constructing European Intellectual Property: achievements and new perspectives. Edward Elgar, Cheltenham
SICE, Foreign Trade Information Service. http://www.sice.oas.org/agreements_e.asp
Spence M (2009) Negotiating trade, innovation and intellectual property: lessons from the Cariforum EPA Experience from a Negotiator's Perspective. Policy Brief No. 4, UNCTAD-ICTSD Project on IPRs and Sustainable Development. http://www.iprsonline.org/ictsd/docs/New%202009/Policy%20Briefs/PB%204%20Spence%20final.pdf
Supreme Court of the United States, Ebay Inc. et al. v. Mercexchange, L.L.C. Certiorari to the United States Court of Appeals for the Federal Circuit, No. 05-130. Decided 15 May 2006
UNCTAD-ICTSD (2005) Resource book on TRIPS and development. Cambridge University Press, Cambridge
USTR (2011) Special 301 Report. http://www.ustr.gov/webfm_send/2841
USTR. http://www.ustr.gov/trade-agreements/free-trade-agreements. An important source of information on this topic in the countries of the Americas is the OAS service SICE (see above)
Vivas-Eugui D (2012) Bridging the gap on intellectual property and genetic resources in WIPO's Intergovernmental Committee (IGC). Issue Paper No. 34, ICTSD Programme on Innovation, Technology and Intellectual Property. http://ictsd.org/downloads/2012/02/bridging-the-gap-on-intellectual-property-and-genetic-resources-in-wipos-intergovernmental-committee-igc.pdf
Watal J (2001) Intellectual property rights in the WTO and developing countries. Kluwer Law International, London
WIPO (2004) Proposal by Argentina and Brazil for the establishment of a development agenda for WIPO. WIPO General Assembly, Thirty-First (15th Extraordinary) Session, Geneva, 27 September to 5 October 2004, WO/GA/31/11
WIPO (2007) The 45 adopted recommendations under the WIPO Development Agenda. http://www.wipo.int/ip-development/en/agenda/recommendations.html
WIPO (2010) Document CDIP/5/9 Rev., 26 April 2010. Submitted to the Committee on Development and Intellectual Property (CDIP), Fifth Session, Geneva, 26 to 30 April 2010
WIPO (2011) WIPO work on traditional knowledge, genetic resources and traditional cultural expressions/folklore. http://www.wipo.int/tk/en/
WTO (2001) Declaration on the TRIPS agreement and public health. WTO document WT/MIN (01)/DEC/2 of 20 November 2001
WTO (2008) Draft modalities for TRIPS-related issues in the context of the Doha negotiations; see TN/C/W/52 of 19 July 2008
WTO (2011) World Trade Organisation, document TN/C/W/59 of 19 April 2011, including Draft Decision to Enhance Mutual Supportiveness Between the TRIPS Agreement and the Convention on Biological Diversity, Communication from Brazil, China, Colombia, Ecuador, India, Indonesia, Peru, Thailand, the ACP Group and the African Group
Yu P (2011) Sinic trade agreements. UC Davis Law Rev 44(3):953–1028

Is TRIPS a Balanced Agreement from the Perspective of Recent Free Trade Agreements?

Jayashree Watal

Contents

1 Introduction

This chapter is meant to provide readers with an understanding of the perceived shortcomings of the Agreement on Trade-Related Aspects of Intellectual Property Rights (TRIPS) as seen from the perspective of two of the main *demandeurs* of stronger international intellectual property (IP) protection in the Uruguay Round of

---

Jayashree Watal works (since 2001) in the Intellectual Property Division of the World Trade Organization (address: 154, Rue de Lausanne, 1211 Geneva, Switzerland; jayashree.watal@wto.org) and represented India in TRIPS negotiations from May to December 1990 (the drafting stage). This chapter is written in the author's personal capacity and does not engage the responsibility of the WTO Secretariat or WTO members either individually or jointly. The author gratefully acknowledges helpful suggestions made by Henning Grosse Ruse-Khan, Hannu Wager and Souheir Nadde-Phlix on an earlier draft.

J. Watal (✉)
Counsellor, Intellectual Property Division, World Trade Organization,
154, Rue de Lausanne, 1211 Geneva, Switzerland
e-mail: jayashree.watal@wto.org

J. Drexl et al. (eds.), *EU Bilateral Trade Agreements and Intellectual Property: For Better or Worse?*, MPI Studies on Intellectual Property and Competition Law 20,
DOI 10.1007/978-3-642-39097-5_3,

multilateral trade negotiations, namely the European Union (EU) and the United States (US). This understanding can be obtained from the parallels drawn between what these members of the World Trade Organization (WTO) sought in the negotiations on the TRIPS Agreement and what they are seeking and obtaining now in free trade agreements (FTAs). This chapter does not include any analysis of the World Intellectual Property Organisation (WIPO) internet treaties, namely the WIPO Copyright Treaty (WCT) and the WIPO Performances and Phonograms Treaty (WPPT), nor other provisions relating to copyright and domain names, which were largely the result of post-TRIPS technological and economic developments. The reader is not expected to get a comprehensive understanding of the EU or US agreements, nor about how they differ from each other or those of others, such as those of the European Free Trade Association (EFTA) or those between developing countries.

There are some obvious points of difference between the EU and US FTAs. For example, the EU focuses more than the US on beefing up the provisions on geographical indications (GIs) and enforcement of the TRIPS Agreement. Unsurprisingly, these were also largely the priorities of the EU in the Uruguay round of negotiations. What remains puzzling is why developing countries actively seek or accept FTAs with TRIPS-plus IP chapters. It is difficult not to conclude that overall these countries gain market access and other economic or political benefits that, in their perception, is worth the time-limited cost of providing stronger IP protection than required under the TRIPS Agreement. Certainly, EU agreements seemingly offer a better package for developing countries in relative terms, if only because they do not go far beyond concessions that countries have already made elsewhere and they at least formally, if not substantively, acknowledge the legitimate IP-related concerns of these countries.

2 Background on the Gains Made by IP *Demandeurs* in the TRIPS Negotiations

The pre-TRIPS world of national IP laws in the developing countries was not exactly a vacuum; there were several countries that continued with their pre-independence colonial laws, including those on intellectual property rights (IPRs). These countries were mainly in Africa. Others, mainly in Latin America and Asia, had taken a conscious decision to replace colonial IPR laws, which were presumed to benefit their colonial masters, with those that were presumed advantageous to local industry and commerce.[1]

Even among those who favoured changes to national IP laws the focus was more on patent laws, and in some cases copyright laws, rather than those on trademarks or designs. The economic rationale behind these changes was to achieve self-reliance, or lessening of dependence on imports from the then industrialized world, a natural

[1] See Watal (2007), pp. 131–132.

objective for newly independent states. This fitted well with the prevailing economic philosophy advocated by leading development economists at the time such as Raul Prebisch and Hans Singer. Many of these legislative changes were carried out upon the advice of the United Nations Conference on Trade and Development (UNCTAD), which focused on the role of both the patent and trademark systems in perpetuating Western monopolies.[2] Largely convinced by these arguments, developing countries were keen on re-tailoring even the international IP system to suit their needs. This was the logic behind their initiative to revise the Paris Convention for the Protection of Industrial Property, particularly in relation to patents, a venture which almost succeeded, and which in the end failed in WIPO just a few years before the launch of the Uruguay Round in the General Agreement on Tariffs and Trade (GATT).[3] In contrast, there was no move to revise the Berne Convention for the Protection of Literary and Artistic Works (Berne Convention), a treaty that would appear to have been considered satisfactory to all those who were party to it. Indeed, TRIPS added only a few more provisions and even excluded one existing provision on moral rights, at the insistence of the United States, which was not yet party to the Berne Convention when the Uruguay Round was launched.[4] Not as many developing countries were party to the latest versions of these two main WIPO treaties prior to the launch of the Uruguay Round and membership of these treaties has certainly benefited not just from TRIPS but also the later FTAs.

Seen against this backdrop, the gains that industrialized countries made globally in comprehensively revising upwards international IP standards and enforcement through the finalization and implementation of the TRIPS Agreement were rapid and very significant. They obtained an agreement that incorporates additional or new standards on as many as seven types of IPRs (namely, copyright and related rights, trademarks, geographical indications (GIs), industrial designs, patents, lay-out designs of integrated circuits, and undisclosed information) which now apply to as many as 159 countries/territories (as of the time of writing this chapter in April 2013).[5] TRIPS also made applicable the swift and effective dispute settlement process of the WTO, which can eventually allow the WTO member who has prevailed in the dispute to impose trade penalties on members violating the agreement. With respect to domestic enforcement, TRIPS included fairly detailed standards for domestic enforcement of IPRs, both internally and at the border. Quite importantly, TRIPS obliged protection of several new categories of IPRs, of which at least one, undisclosed information, had never been the subject of any multilateral agreement before, and another, protection for integrated circuit designs, had no

[2] See United Nations Department of Economic and Social Affairs, International Bureau of WIPO, UNCTAD Secretariat 1975 and UNCTAD Secretariat 1979.

[3] See Watal (2001), pp. 16–17.

[4] The US acceded to the Berne Convention in March 1989. See http://www.copyright.gov/circs/circ38a.pdf.

[5] Subject to transitional period arrangements that are still applicable to least-developed country members of the WTO.

effective international treaty, while others, like plant variety protection or performers' rights, were extremely limited geographically. TRIPS also covered new subject matter under existing types of intellectual property, at least for some developing countries, such as product patents for food, pharmaceuticals, chemicals, micro-organisms or copyright protection for software. Additionally, it created new rights under existing types of intellectual property for the majority of WTO members such as rental rights for computer programmes and sound recordings (and for films under certain circumstances) under copyright and related rights; and provided for protection of GIs, including a higher level of protection for GIs for wines and spirits.[6]

Yet, clearly the *demandeurs* were not satisfied because, even as the ink was drying on the TRIPS Agreement, they went on to negotiate bilateral and regional free trade agreements that contained provisions that went beyond the TRIPS requirements.

3 Some Key Unmet Demands of IP *Demandeurs* in the TRIPS Negotiations

There are several areas where the IP *demandeurs* did not obtain results to their full satisfaction in the TRIPS negotiations as seen from the demands made in both written and oral submissions during the TRIPS negotiations.[7] Some of the main areas are enumerated briefly below.

General: Although it was not a part of the written texts submitted by either the US or EU in early 1990 in the Uruguay Round, both preferred a requirement that all members adhere to national exhaustion of IPRs, or, when that seemed not possible, to at least not permit parallel imports from jurisdictions where prices were controlled or, when that was dropped, to remain silent on this issue.[8] Instead, the current permissive provision in TRIPS Article 6 excludes exhaustion of rights from dispute settlement and requires only national treatment (NT) and most-favoured-nation treatment (MFN). In 2001, the Doha Declaration on the TRIPS Agreement and Public Health made explicit that members are free to choose their exhaustion regime, without challenge, subject only to NT and MFN.

Patents: In the contentious area of patents, the US *inter alia* did not get explicit, mandatory protection for new uses for known substances (and the claim that this is implicit in the language of Article 27.1 does not seem to be the view of all) or for plant and animal inventions or for genes and gene sequences (mainly because the EU had not yet passed its Biotechnology Directive).[9] Nor did the US obtain patent term

[6] See Watal (2001), pp. 3–4.

[7] See Watal (2001), the last section of Chapters IV to XI, and Watal (2011).

[8] See Gorlin (1999), pp. 14–16 for a history of these negotiations.

[9] See Nadde-Phlix (2013) in this volume about current work in the WTO on the review of Article 27.3(b). See also WTO document IP/C/W/369/Rev.1.

extension to compensate for regulatory delays, a demand especially important for the pharmaceutical sector and made in only "best endeavour terms" in the US submission.[10] The United States also wanted to restrict the reasons for the grant of compulsory licences to only two, namely, to remedy adjudicated violation of competition laws or to address a declared national emergency. Later, when the separate provision on government use was dropped in the TRIPS negotiations, the US added the ground of public non-commercial use. The EU did not demand any restriction of the grounds for compulsory licensing but only imposed certain conditions.[11] The US further demanded that the revocation of a patent be allowed only on grounds that the patentability requirements had not been met, and this too was not accepted.[12]

Trademarks: In the area of trademarks, the demands of the EU and the US were not very contentious. However, demands were made to require the registration as trademarks of single colours, the shape of goods or their packaging, sound marks and smell marks, but eventually TRIPS made the registration of these marks contingent on their being distinctive as well as visually perceptible, and not just capable of graphical representation, as the EU had originally demanded.[13] The US and EU wanted easier standards and enforcement for well-known marks even without the registration requirement.[14]

Geographical indications: In this area, while the EU and its supporters wanted stronger and practically automatic protection of their GIs in the territories of the WTO members, the TRIPS Agreement provided for a higher level of protection for GIs covering wines and spirits only. They also wanted the further narrowing down of exceptions.[15] In this area, the push-back in the TRIPS negotiations came from the United States, Australia, Chile and others.

Test-data protection: This was a heavily negotiated result in which the US was the major *demandeur* of market exclusivity specified by the Brussels 1990 text to be for "a reasonable period of time, generally no less than five years" for test data submitted to the authorities for obtaining marketing approval for pharmaceutical and agricultural products.[16] It is interesting to note that the original US and EU texts were rather vague in the proposed language, but their growing ambition became

[10] See document MTN.GNG.NG11/W/70, Article 25 reads as follows: "Contracting parties are encouraged to extend the term of patent protection, in appropriate cases, to compensate for delays caused by regulatory approval processes."

[11] See GATT document MTN.GNG.NG11/W/70, Article 27 and Watal, (2001), Chapter X about how the current Article 31 was negotiated. See also MTN.GNG.NG11/68, Article 26, on which TRIPS Article 31 is modelled.

[12] See GATT document MTN.GNG.NG11/W/70, Article 24.2.

[13] See GATT document MTN.GNG.NG11/68, Article 10. Smell marks and sound marks are capable of being described by chemical formulae or musical notation, respectively.

[14] See GATT document MTN.GNG.NG11/68, Article 12 (2) and MTN.GNG:NG11/70, Article 12.2, which is broader.

[15] See GATT document MTN.GNG.NG11/68, Articles 20 and 21.

[16] See GATT document MTN.TNC/W/35/Rev.1 and Gorlin (1999) on the negotiating history of this provision.

apparent as negotiations proceeded.[17] The opposition to this provision came not only from developing countries but also from Canada, Australia and New Zealand, which did not at that time have market exclusivity for test data. In the end, the US did not obtain mention in TRIPS Article 39.3 of a period of market exclusivity for test data, leaving considerable ambiguity in this provision.

Enforcement: Although the TRIPS negotiations resulted in detailed provisions on enforcement procedures, these are mostly phrased in a way that makes it obligatory to provide the "authority" to courts and other enforcement agencies to take certain actions and not actually to oblige certain enforcement actions. Indeed, this part of the TRIPS Agreement has been criticised by some as one of its weakest links. Some commentators accurately predicted the difficulty in successfully bringing disputes to the WTO for violations of the TRIPS provisions on domestic enforcement.[18] Comments made by an important US official after TRIPS came into being also showed some disappointment with the TRIPS enforcement provisions.[19] *Demandeurs* such as the US and the EU had wanted more specific remedies than those eventually agreed to in TRIPS. For example, the EU proposed wording reads: "The judicial authorities shall be authorised, upon request, and *irrespective of whether the defendant has acted with intent or negligence*, to issue an order that the infringement be refrained from or discontinued." (emphasis added). Similarly, border measures were proposed to apply to all IPRs.[20] On the imposition of preliminary injunctions, it should be noted that while TRIPS provisions on provisional measures may have been new to civil law countries (both developed and developing), these were already in use in common-law countries (for example, in the Commonwealth countries).

Dispute settlement: The *demandeurs* wanted all of GATT dispute settlement procedures to apply to TRIPS, including the application of non-violation and situation complaints.[21] In the end, opposition from both developed countries such as Canada and developing countries such as India led to the current formulation of TRIPS Article 64.3.

---

[17] See GATT document MTN:GNG.NG11/W/70, Article 33 and See MTN:GNG.NG11/W/68, Article 28(b). See also Gorlin (1999), pp. 46–50.

[18] Reichman and Lange (1998), pp. 34–39.

[19] Watal (2010) cites some of these views.

[20] See GATT document MTN.GNG.NG11/W/68, Article 7 of Part 3 on Injunctions.

[21] See GATT document MTN.GNG.NG11/W/68, Article 8 of Part 5. The US in its submission simply concurred with the EU and stated that this was a good basis to proceed. See also Gorlin (1999), p. 82 and IP/C/W/349/Rev.1.

4 Unmet Demands of Developing Countries in the TRIPS Negotiations

What is often forgotten is that while most developing countries had only defensive interests to push back against the demands for strengthened IP protection, in which they were successful for various reasons in obtaining broad exceptions and limitations in TRIPS, there were some precise proposals made by them that were largely ignored. For example, developing countries in the TRIPS Uruguay Round demanded an extension of obligations for developed country members on transfer of technology (now in Article 66.2 and applicable only to least-developed countries (LDCs)) to all developing countries.

They also wanted the exclusion of biotechnological inventions, including microorganisms, and recognition of traditional knowledge (TK) and genetic resources (GR), especially in the context of plant variety protection. These demands were not put in writing and were broached by India after the Rio Earth Summit (where countries agreed to the Convention on Biological Diversity (CBD)) towards the end of 1992, by which time the text of the TRIPS was almost set and there was no willingness to even discuss these demands.[22] These unmet demands on GR and TK found their way into the Marrakesh Decision on Trade and Environment indirectly through its reference to the relevant provisions of TRIPS, and eventually came back to the TRIPS Council through the review of TRIPS Article 27.3(b) and later on through the specific mandate in the Doha Ministerial Declaration.[23]

In addition, developing countries also wanted to include the right to control anti-competitive conditions in IP licensing agreements, which eventually got included, in a somewhat watered-down form in Article 40 of the TRIPS Agreement.

5 Demands Made and Obtained in FTAs

Roffe, Maskus, Abbott and other authors in this volume summarize the demands made in FTAs negotiated by the US, EU and EFTA. Although very similar demands are made by the three jurisdictions, each lays emphasis on different subjects.

The EU has concluded several association agreements in the Mediterranean region, as well as with Chile, and more recently with the 14 CARIFORUM states, with Colombia and Peru, as well as with Korea. Many of the earlier agreements

[22] Thus WTO document WT/CTE/W/8 in describing the negotiating history of the TRIPS provisions relevant to the CBD concludes in paragraph 77 that "[t]he question of new forms of protection adapted to the particular circumstances of such peoples/local communities was not raised during the TRIPS negotiations". India's chief negotiator in the Uruguay Round, Mr. A. V. Ganesan, continued to place priority on this issue as can be seen from a speech he made in 1999, available at http://www.eximbankindia.com/old/lec990511-1.html.

[23] See Nadde-Phlix (2013) in this volume.

provide that the parties "shall ensure adequate and effective protection of intellectual, industrial and commercial property rights, in conformity with the highest international standards, including effective means of enforcing such rights". These agreements also include a list of multilateral IP conventions to which the EU member states are already party or that already apply on a *de facto* basis. Generally, the other party agrees to accede to these conventions after a transition period that ranges up to five years. The list generally includes the Paris Convention, the Patent Cooperation Treaty (PCT), the 1991 Act of the International Convention for the Protection of New Varieties of Plants (UPOV 1991) and the Budapest Treaty on the International Recognition of the Deposit of Microorganisms for the Purposes of Patent Procedure and the WIPO internet treaties of 1996, namely, the WCT and the WPPT. Thus, it is clear that the EU agreements have had the effect of enlarging the geographical coverage of the international IP system as well as deepening its provisions, in the same way as have the US or EFTA FTAs.

In the first phase of EU agreements, due to TRIPS NT and MFN provisions, the EU was able to free-ride on the highest international standards set by the US in earlier FTAs with the same countries.[24] The significant impact of the TRIPS MFN and NT principles is clear. Indeed, that exceptions to MFN do not extend to TRIPS-plus provisions was because of the EU position in TRIPS negotiations: This was because the US-Korea agreement in the early 1980s cut out EU companies from the benefit of pharmaceutical "pipeline" protection. However, in the later phase, the EU began incorporating detailed standards of IPRs into its agreements, including on test-data exclusivity, just like the US. The only obvious difference noted with US FTAs is that the more recent EU agreements cover GIs and enforcement (especially border measures) more extensively than does TRIPS or indeed other FTAs. What is unclear is why the EU changed its strategy and began spelling out other details of what was already covered by other agreements. Perhaps the EU was keen on retaining the ability to use the FTA dispute settlement system to address perceived violations of all provisions. Or perhaps the EU wanted to differentiate its own FTAs from those of the US or EFTA as being more development-friendly—for example by highlighting sustainable development as a treaty objective in Article 3 of the EU—CARIFORUM EPA.

General: There does not seem to be a demand in EU trade agreements to adhere to national exhaustion of intellectual property rights. The US, however, usually includes a prohibition to permit parallel imports, at least for products covered by copyright or patents, as it has done, for example, in the US-Singapore FTA and the US-Morocco FTA.

Patents: Availability of patents for plant and animal inventions is invariably a mandatory provision that is included in US FTAs, with the only exception confined to what is in TRIPS Article 27.2 and 3. In EU agreements, only adherence to UPOV 1991 is commonly required. The EU, of course, gets the benefit of US FTAs due to

[24] According to Roffe (2013), the EU-Central America agreement has no data exclusivity provisions because such provisions were already incorporated into national laws following an earlier US agreement.

the TRIPS MFN clause. Another clarification in US FTAs is the addition of a TRIPS Article 27.1 type of language stating explicitly that patents must be made available to new uses or methods of using the known product.[25]

A common demand in almost all US and EFTA FTAs is patent term extension for pharmaceutical patents of up to five years to compensate for regulatory delays in approving the marketing of pharmaceutical products. The EU-Korea agreement also contains this requirement.[26] Additionally, there are patent term extensions to compensate for delays in the grant of patents by patent offices. This is the case in the US-Korea FTA, where an extension of up to four years is mandatory.[27] Yet another area particular to US FTAs is patent linkage, where no regulatory approval can be given to a product whose patent term is on-going.[28]

While US FTAs generally contain language restricting the grounds for compulsory licensing to those demanded by the US in the TRIPS negotiations, namely, to remedy adjudicated violation of competition laws or to address a declared national emergency or for public non-commercial use, for example in the US-Jordan, US-Singapore, and US-Australia FTAs.[29] The EU and EFTA agreements do not contain such provisions.[30]

Trademarks: The US and EU also demand and obtain TRIPS-plus protection of trademarks in FTAs. For example, in the US-Korea FTA, a provision states: "Neither Party may require, as a condition of registration, that signs be visually perceptible, nor may either Party deny registration of a trademark solely on the grounds that the sign of which it is composed is a sound or scent."[31] This shows that a demand made in the TRIPS negotiations has found explicit recognition in a subsequent FTA. In the EU-Korea FTA, the focus was more on GIs and there is very little in the trademarks section that goes beyond TRIPS, except for procedures to ensure transparency. On the other hand, a leaked version of the EU-India agreement[32] shows that the EU has proposed going beyond TRIPS on trademarks. An EU proposal states that it would not be a requirement, as a condition for determining whether a mark is a well-known mark, that the mark has been registered or that an application for registration of the mark has been filed in the country concerned. There is a similar, if more specific, provision in the US-Korea FTA on well-known marks.[33]

---

[25] See US-Korea FTA Article 18.8.1.

[26] See Article 10.35 of the EU-Korea FTA.

[27] See US-Korea FTA Article 18.8.6 (a).

[28] See US-Korea FTA Article 18.8.5.

[29] Language that invariably accompanies the compulsory licence provision is that "the Party shall not require the patent owner to transfer undisclosed information or technical 'know how' related to a patented invention that has been authorized for use without the consent of the patent owner".

[30] See WHO-WIPO-WTO (2012), pp. 188–189.

[31] See US-Korea FTA, Article 18.2.

[32] See http://keionline.org/node/1681.

[33] See Article 18.2, sub-paragraphs 6 and 7 of the US-Korea FTA.

Geographical indications: Clearly, the subject matter of most interest to the EU is the protection of its GIs, and in this the EU-negotiated agreements are unique. As Frederick Abbott explains in this volume,[34] the EU has obtained more in the EU-Colombia-Peru EPA than it even envisages in a multilateral context in the WTO. The EU has obtained in this and other FTAs the higher level of protection accorded under TRIPS Article 23 to only wines and spirits for agricultural and food products. However, the nature of interest in GIs is essentially asymmetric. For example, the EU has obtained this level of GI protection for 150 of its products, while Peru and Colombia have obtained this in the EU for only three of their products. In the EU-Korea FTA, EU has 60 agricultural products and more than 100 wines and spirits listed as GIs to be protected in Korea, and Korea has 63 agricultural products and one spirit listed as GIs to be protected in the EU. However, due to cultural and dietary differences, the economic impact in the respective jurisdictions is a matter of empirical verification product by product, as no generalizations are possible just based on the number of GIs protected.

Test data: The one area that shows a large degree of convergence in all FTAs and that focuses on an unmet demand of the *demandeurs* for stronger IPR protection in the TRIPS negotiations is test-data protection, where the US, EFTA and in many cases the EU have demanded and obtained a clear five or more years of market exclusivity for pharmaceutical products.[35] In the case of agricultural chemicals, the period of market exclusivity is ten years. This is so in both the US-Korea and EU-Korea agreements. Of the later generation of agreements negotiated by the EU, only the EU-CARIFORUM agreement does not contain such a requirement. There are media reports that the EU-India FTA, aimed to be finalized by summer of 2013, will also not contain such a requirement.[36]

Enforcement: In the area of enforcement, border measures go beyond TRIPS provisions, as both the US and EU cover goods infringing IPRs whether through importation, exportation or transit, whereas TRIPS disciplines are required to cover only importation, the other two being optional for WTO members. Again for border measures, several EU agreements cover IPRs other than the TRIPS-required copyright pirated and trademark counterfeited goods, notably patents, plant variety protection, industrial designs and GIs. This is the case of the EU-Korea FTA, whereas the EU-CARIFORUM agreement confines itself to designs and GIs. Jaeger in this volume describes the various TRIPS-plus enforcement provisions, noting that only the Association Agreement between the EU and Central American States confines itself largely to TRIPS standards.[37] Some provisions go beyond even what

[34] See Abbott (2013) in this volume.

[35] See Table 4.1 in Chapter IV and related analysis in WHO, WIPO, WTO (2012), pp. 186–190.

[36] See, for example the EU Government Gazette, October 2012, available at: http://governmentgazette.eu/?page_id=13, where an article by the EU Trade Commissioner on the EU-India FTA states: "to avoid negative impacts on access to affordable medicines in India or elsewhere, we are not pressing for changes in India's legislation on intellectual property rights in this area".

[37] See Jaeger (2013) in this volume.

is in the Anti-Counterfeiting Trade Agreement (ACTA). For example, in practically all recent EU agreements, parties to a dispute concerning IPR infringement committed on a commercial scale have the right to demand disclosure of all appropriate "banking, financial or commercial documents under the control of the opposing entity, subject to the protection of confidential information". Similarly, these agreements specify binding guidelines for the determination of damages that, in some cases, go beyond ACTA in that they cover compensation for moral damages also. A point to be noted is that while the US agreements have changed the wording of TRIPS Article 41.5 language found in the enforcement part to have a more restrictive effect, rather than the flexibility originally incorporated into TRIPS by developing countries, the EU agreements just reproduce TRIPS language on this point.[38]

Dispute settlement: In the area of dispute settlement, the US invariably calls for the application of non-violation rules, including to IPRs, in its FTAs. This can be seen in the US-Chile, US-Singapore, US-Australia, US-CAFTA, US-Morocco and US-Bahrain FTAs.[39] Not so the EU trade agreements, not even the EU-Korea FTA.[40]

Unmet demands of developing countries: Very little is included on the unmet demands of developing countries. Transfer of technology is mentioned, if at all, only in hortatory terms in some US FTAs, with the Peru agreement going a little further in terms of setting up common platforms for public and private entities to team up for innovation and technology development. The EU agreements generally speak more about the exchange of information and practices. However, the EU-CARIFORUM agreement speaks of encouraging, developing and facilitating cooperative research and development (R&D) activities in science and technology (S&T) between the two sides. It also encourages similar cooperative production and development activities in the creative industries, a sector in which the Caribbean countries have a significant interest. Finally, the EU-CARIFORUM EPA contains a potentially meaningful provision in Art.142.2 on action that must be taken against the abuses of IP, especially via licensing practices "which may adversely affect the international transfer of technology".[41]

---

[38] Article 41.5 of TRIPS states: "It is understood that this Part does not create any obligation to put in place a judicial system for the enforcement of intellectual property rights distinct from that for the enforcement of law in general, nor does it affect the capacity of Members to enforce their law in general. Nothing in this Part creates any obligation with respect to the distribution of resources as between enforcement of intellectual property rights and the enforcement of law in general".

[39] For example, see Article 20.4.1(c) of the US-Singapore FTA, which states that dispute settlement procedures apply wherever "a benefit the Party could reasonably have expected to accrue to it under Chapters 2 (National Treatment and Market Access for Goods), 3 (Rules of Origin), Chapter 8 (Cross Border Trade in Services), or Chapter 16 (Intellectual Property Rights) is being nullified or impaired as a result of a measure that is not inconsistent with this Agreement."

[40] See Anh (2010).

[41] For a detailed discussion, see Drexl (2013) in this volume.

EU agreements with Peru, Colombia and the CARIFORUM extend Article 66.2 type benefits to these countries, unlike TRIPS, where this provision is confined to LDC WTO member countries.[42] This goes some way toward meeting the unmet demands of developing countries in the Uruguay Round. In this regard, it must be noted that LDCs complain in the WTO that the reporting of the implementation of Article 66.2 of TRIPS is not clear, as benefits accruing to developing countries that are not LDCs are also included. The meaning of "technology transfer" itself is under discussion between LDCs and developed countries in the WTO. However, one advantage in FTAs that make non-violation applicable to IP is that this type of provision could represent an area for both violation and non-violation complaints by developing country partners. This, of course, would not be the case against the EU since EU agreements generally do not have such applicability.

In the case of the agreements concluded by Peru and Colombia with the US, the language in the agreements on TK and GR is in line with the positions taken by the US in multilateral forums such as the WTO and WIPO, rather than those taken by these developing countries. The EU, on the other hand, has joined a large number of developing countries in demanding an amendment to the TRIPS Agreement to require patent applicants to disclose their use of GR and associated TK in their patent applications. In accordance with this position, in the EU-Colombia-Peru agreement there is a provision[43] that—even though it does not go beyond the EU position in multilateral forums—provides a basis for further co-operation and action in this area for Peru and Colombia.

What continues to be puzzling is why developing countries seek and accept FTAs with TRIPS-plus IP chapters and what effect FTAs could have in multilateral IP negotiations on the positions of developing countries that are party to FTAs. Further, is there really an asymmetric bargaining strength between the developing country parties to the FTA, on the one hand, and the EU and the US, on the other? The next three sections deal with these issues.

6 The Question of IP and Development

If the strengthening of IP were to unambiguously lead to higher growth and development in developing countries, there would be no reason to complain about the strengthening of such protection through FTAs or otherwise. However, it is clear from the literature that for these regulatory regimes to contribute to development, other factors need to be in place.

Stronger IP regimes have evolved and matured once a solid scientific and technological base and creative industries were in place. It is true that economists are unable to definitively answer the question if the opposite is true, namely whether

[42] See for example Article 142.3 of the EU-CARIFORUM EPA.

[43] See Abbott (2013) in this volume.

stronger IP protection leads to the development of innovation and creativity. Why, for example, did South Korea and China do so well in terms of proportion of resident patent filing to total patents filed in their countries after patent law reforms, and why did not Mexico and Brazil?[44]

What is even more puzzling is why developing countries are seeking or accepting FTAs with TRIPS-plus IP chapters if overall they would not benefit in terms of economic development. Given the widespread availability of material and experts advising against the acceptance of TRIPS-plus standards in FTAs, one has to assume that developing countries do enter FTAs on the basis of "prior informed consent", to borrow a phrase from multilateral environmental agreements. Clearly, FTAs form part of an offensive strategy on their part to gain better market access for exports of goods and services crucial to their economies. It could also be a desire for recognition and protection of their TK or GIs, especially in the EU FTAs, but as Pedro Roffe points out in this volume,[45] and as any cursory study would show, these benefits, even where they exist, are highly asymmetrical. Therefore, it appears to be true that while developing countries take a defensive position on IPRs in negotiating FTAs, they finally agree to such asymmetrical provisions in return for what in their judgement is real market access and other tangible economic or political benefits. It is true that usually IP rights are time-limited and so this may not be seen as being so damaging to domestic interests. However, it is also true that concessions made on MFN tariffs could erode over time, not least because other FTAs are signed to enlarge the list of the beneficiaries of preferential market access. Further, changes in IP laws are permanent or at least difficult to change once incorporated—on an MFN basis, as this is the TRIPS requirement—into national laws.

A significant point is that the overall benefits of an FTA package compared to costs fundamentally changed with the adoption of the TRIPS Agreement. While before the adoption of TRIPS the US used the Special 301 process as a "stick" to pressure trading partners to strengthen IP protection (or face the threat of trade retaliation), the post-TRIPS strategy has used the "carrot" of enhanced market access for products of interest to developing countries and other benefits to attract them to adopt higher IP standards. Curiously, major emerging countries are rarely party to FTAs that have IP chapters that go beyond TRIPS commitments,[46] although there are some on-going negotiations. It is not clear whether this is because major emerging economies have better bargaining power as the other side is equally keen on market access that these markets bring to the table, or because they have technical and negotiating skills to appreciate the lop-sidedness of such FTAs, or for some other reason.

---

[44] See, for example, Maskus (2012), Chapter 1 and Maskus (2013) in this volume.

[45] See Roffe (2013) in this volume.

[46] For example, the Japan-India FTA did not contain a chapter on IP and MERCOSUR countries are yet to conclude FTA negotiations with any of the major *demandeurs*.

7 FTAs' Impact on IP Negotiations in Multilateral Forums

Another unanswered question is whether one of the aims of FTAs is the dilution of like-minded solidarity in multilateral forums and whether this has occurred as a result of FTA commitments. A number of examples can be cited in this context: non-violation complaints now applicable to IPRs in most US FTAs; the narrowing of language for the protection of GR and TK or public health. However, so far there does not seem to be much evidence of the dilution of like-minded countries' solidarity in multilateral forums. For example, in the WTO, Peru is a party to a proposal for a draft Article 29*bis* TRIPS, submitted in April 2011[47] by the core group that favours a TRIPS obligation on the disclosure of origin for GRs and associated TK in patent applications—despite the language in the US-Peru FTA. There may be no contradiction here as perhaps Peru, in joining with a large number of other developing countries, can obtain something more in multilateral negotiations than it could in bilateral FTA negotiations. However, numbers alone do not really matter in winning negotiating battles at the WTO. What really matters is to stick firmly to credibly developed positions. For example, during the Uruguay round of negotiations, India was alone among developing countries in proposing the combining of the provisions on government use and compulsory licensing into one provision, thus eliminating the restrictions on grounds for compulsory licences, and this position is now reflected in Article 31 TRIPS.[48] Nevertheless, countries can change their positions following bilateral FTAs, as can be seen in the context of the vastly changed positions of Korea and Singapore from the days of the TRIPS negotiations to recent debates in the TRIPS Council—but whether these changes are due to improved economic conditions and therefore differing national interests or due to the "club" effect of FTAs is a moot point.

8 The Asymmetry Issue

With respect to the asymmetry the FTAs represent and the motivation for entering into FTAs, it is noted that developing and developed countries are matched in their eagerness to conclude FTAs. The motivations of each side may be quite different, especially in the case of smaller developing countries: perhaps these countries are keen to gain market access, and perhaps the US, EU and EFTA see this as an opportunity to change the rules of the trade game, including through strengthened IP protection, a feat difficult to achieve in multilateral forums. In other words, could both have equally mercantilist motivations? In this regard, there may be little difference between the US and the EU, even though the latter may be more adept at packaging the FTA with the addition of words such as "sustainable development" or with technical assistance packages for developing countries. However, it must be

[47] See Trade Negotiations Committee (2011).

[48] See Chapter X of Watal (2001) and Watal (2011).

noted that the more positive language in EU agreements, as against US FTAs, with respect to the disclosure requirement for inventions based on genetic resources and/or associated TK is clearly due to the difference in negotiating positions and strategies between the US and the EU in the WTO, where in the context of the Doha round of trade negotiations the EU has joined the coalition of developing countries on the issue relating to TRIPS and the CBD—in exchange for support on GIs.

Developed country negotiators state that they are often struck by the negotiating expertise and strategies employed by their counterparts—this was heard from the representative of the European Commission at the workshop on "Economic Partnership Agreements of the EU: a Step Ahead in Reforming International IP Law?" organized by the Max Planck Institute for Intellectual Property and Competition Law in June 2011 (MPI workshop).[49] Moreover, developing country negotiators should, in principle, be better informed about the pros and cons of the negotiated subject matter (such as GIs), given the vast amount of material on the Internet, and the network of civil society groups and academics willing to provide free expertise on IPRs to developing countries. However, in practice, real expertise could be ignored and sometimes the most concerned parts of the domestic administration (such as affected ministries) may not be involved in the FTA negotiations.

It is also possible that the EU negotiators too did not get all they asked for—for example, in the EU-CARIFORUM EPA, parties have only agreed to collaborate further in the expansion of border measures to encompass all IPRs, and there is no reference to test-data protection.[50] Further, knowledge, bargaining power and asymmetries are different issues, as pointed out by Frederick Abbott[51] in this volume. While there is knowledge and expertise, there may well be asymmetries in bargaining power. Sometimes the use of pressure (such as the threat to withdraw the benefits of the Generalised System of Preferences) could bring trading partners to the negotiation table. In other cases, there may be little expertise and sparse resources to obtain such knowledge or expertise. Each negotiation is clearly different depending on the differing circumstances and the interests of the negotiating parties. In the end, the outcome of each FTA should be judged on a case-by-case basis.

Could asymmetries be corrected later through creative implementation, using all available FTA/TRIPS flexibilities (e.g. Articles 7 and 8 TRIPS, Article 3 of the EU-CARIFORUM EPA (sustainable development objective) and its Article 224 providing for a general exception)? Marco Alemán introduced an idea at the MPI workshop to the effect that in order to establish a reciprocal balance of FTA commitments it should be possible to roll back from IP commitments once the market-access preferences are eroded (due to similar or greater commitments made by the trading partner to another country in another FTA). Paradoxically, this may be possible where the concept of non-violation complaints applies in the dispute settlement proceedings of the FTA as arguably legitimate expectations (to benefit from

[49] For more information about this workshop see Nadde-Phlix (2012).

[50] See footnote 2(c) of Article 63 of the EU-CARIFORUM EPA.

[51] See Abbott (2013).

enhanced market access via FTA-based trade preferences, for example) are subsequently affected by another measure (such as new trade preferences granted to other countries) that, taken at its face-value, does not violate the provisions of the FTA.

9 Concluding Remarks

In conclusion, the IP chapters of EU and US FTAs do throw light on what the *demandeurs* for stronger IP protection did not obtain in the TRIPS negotiations. Both the US and EU do seem to have obtained in their FTAs some of their unmet demands left over from the TRIPS negotiations in the Uruguay Round. It is unclear whether this will result in gains for these *demandeurs* either to increase IP protection or to moderate demands for lowering such protection in multilateral negotiating forums. The EU agreements go some way to formally acknowledge the legitimacy of long-standing demands of developing countries, including in the Uruguay Round and beyond. The subjects covered include traditional knowledge and genetic resources and transfer of technology. Perhaps such language, although symbolic, could help legitimize these demands by developing countries in other forums. In the case of enforcement of IPRs, in some cases the EU does not call for the distribution of resources for the enforcement of IPRs to a greater extent than is required for the enforcement of law in general. Also, the earlier EU agreements do not go much beyond concessions that countries have already made elsewhere. This chapter shows that, notwithstanding the severe criticism of TRIPS by civil society groups, it appears more balanced when seen from the perspective of some of the more recent bilateral and regional FTAs.

References

Abbott FM (2013) Trade costs and shadow benefits: EU economic partnership agreements as models for progressive development of international IP law. In: Drexl J, Grosse Ruse Khan H, Nadde-Phlix S (eds) EU bilateral trade agreements and intellectual property: for better or worse? Springer, Heidelberg (this volume)

Anh D (2010) Legal and institutional issues for Korea-EU FTA: new model for post-NAFTA FTAs? Sciences Po Policy Brief. http://gem.sciences-po.fr/content/publications/pdf/AHN_KOREU%20FTA%20201010.pdf

Gorlin JJ (1999) An analysis of the pharmaceutical-related provisions of the WTO TRIPS (Intellectual Property) agreement. Intellectual Property Institute, London

Jaeger T (2013) IP enforcement in EPAs as compared to standard enforcement. In: Drexl J, Grosse Ruse Khan H, Nadde-Phlix S (eds) EU bilateral trade agreements and intellectual property: for better or worse? Springer, Heidelberg (this volume)

Maskus KE (2012) Private rights and public problems: the global economics of intellectual property in the 21st century. Peterson Institute of International Economics, Washington

Maskus KE (2013) Assessing the development promise of IP provisions in European Union Partnership Agreements. In: Drexl J, Grosse Ruse Khan H, Nadde-Phlix S (eds) EU bilateral trade agreements and intellectual property: for better or worse? Springer, Heidelberg (this volume)

Nadde-Phlix S (2012) Economic partnership agreements of the EU: a step ahead in reforming international IP law? – Workshop of the Max Planck Institute for Intellectual Property and Competition Law, June 2011. IIC Int Rev Intellect Prop Compet Law 43(8):951–958

Nadde-Phlix S (2013) IP protection in EU economic partnership- and free trade agreements vis-à-vis IP negotiations in the WTO. In: Drexl J, Grosse Ruse Khan H, Nadde-Phlix S (eds) EU bilateral trade agreements and intellectual property: for better or worse? Springer, Heidelberg (this volume)

Reichman J, Lange D (1998) Bargaining around the TRIPS agreement: the case for ongoing public–private initiatives to facilitate worldwide intellectual property transactions. Duke J Comp Int Law 9(11):11–68

Roffe P (2013) The intellectual property chapters in free trade agreements: their significance and systemic implications. In: Drexl J, Grosse Ruse Khan H, Nadde-Phlix S (eds) EU bilateral trade agreements and intellectual property: for better or worse? Springer, Heidelberg (this volume)

UNCTAD Secretariat (1979) The role of trade marks in developing countries

Trade Negotiations Committee (2011) Draft decision to enhance mutual supportiveness between the trips agreement and the convention on biological diversity (TN/C/W/59)

United Nations Department of Economic and Social Affairs, International Bureau of WIPO, United Nations Conference on Trade and Development (UNCTAD) Secretariat (1975) Report on the Role Of Patent System in the Transfer of Technology to Developing Countries

Watal J (2001) Intellectual property rights in the WTO and developing countries. Kluwer Law International, London

Watal J (2007) Developing countries and the protection of intellectual property rights: current issues in the WTO. In: Bermann G, Mavroidis P (eds) WTO law and developing countries. Columbia studies in WTO law and policy. Cambridge University Press, Cambridge

Watal J (2010) The US-China dispute - a comment on the interpretation of TRIPS enforcement provisions. J World Intellect Prop 13(5):605–619

Watal J (2011) From Punta Del Este to Doha and beyond: lessons from the TRIPS negotiating processes. WIPO J 3(1):24–35

WHO, WIPO, WTO (2012) Promoting access to medical technologies and innovation: intersections between public health, intellectual property and trade

Part II
Going Beyond Trips: Impact on International Law and Policy

Impact of TRIPS-Plus Obligations in Economic Partnership- and Free Trade Agreements on International IP Law

Marco M. Aleman

Contents

1 Introduction

1.1 Delimiting the Concept of TRIPS-Plus

According to the minimum standard nature of the Agreement on Trade Related Aspects of Intellectual Property Rights (TRIPS), those that wish to become members of the World Trade Organization (WTO) must transpose into their national legal framework

The views expressed are those of the author and do not represent the international organization or its members states.

M.M. Aleman (✉)
Deputy Director, Patent Law Division and Head, Legislative and Policy Advice Section, World Intellectual Organisation (WIPO), Chemin des Colombettes 34, 1202 Geneva, Switzerland
e-mail: Marco.Aleman@wipo.int

J. Drexl et al. (eds.), *EU Bilateral Trade Agreements and Intellectual Property: For Better or Worse?*, MPI Studies on Intellectual Property and Competition Law 20,
DOI 10.1007/978-3-642-39097-5_4, © Springer-Verlag Berlin Heidelberg 2014

provisions that contain the minimum standards of protection of intellectual property (IP) rights.

The legislative implementation of the TRIPS Agreement varies from one region to the next and within one region, from one country to another. Developed countries were also in need of some adjustments as a consequence of the entry into force of TRIPS, e.g., the United States of America (US) amended its patent law to provide for a minimum term of 20 years of protection beginning from the filing date; the local working requirement was taken out of several patent laws, e.g., in the United Kingdom; and the European Patent Convention (EPC)[1] was updated in the year 2000 to ensure, inter alia, TRIPS compliance.[2] However, the level of adjustment needed in the developing world was higher and the response to commitments for implementation was not enthusiastic, a reaction to some extent justified by the perception of some Members that TRIPS' higher standards of protection would yield a net negative in terms of welfare cost.[3] Nevertheless, implementation of the TRIPS Agreement in a significant number of developing and least-developed countries (LDCs) started before the Agreement entered into force. For the TRIPS Agreement's 2000 dateline (in favour of developing countries) 28 developing country Members completed in advance their implementation process,[4] and 22 developing country Members showed outstanding legislative reforms.

TRIPS minimum standards cover the most diverse issues of patent law, e.g., requirements for patentability (Article 27.1), allowed exclusions from patentability (Article 27.2 and 3), rights conferred (Article 28), exceptions to the exclusive rights conferred by patents (Article 30), requirements in the processing and granting of compulsory licenses (Article 31), the term of protection (Article 33), and reinforced process patent protection (Article 34).

On the other hand, the TRIPS Agreement provides that Members "may, but shall not be obliged to" implement in their law more extensive protection. More extensive protection is the outcome of norms that go beyond TRIPS standards. In general, those norms are identified as TRIPS-plus. When the Agreement expressly establishes a minimum standard, for instance, a 20-year patent term, and a country decides to adopt a higher standard, e.g., allowing a patent extension under certain circumstances (such as delay in the granting process by the patent office or curtailment of the effective exclusivity period due to delays by the health authority

---

[1] No reference is made in this article to the relationship between specific provisions of the EPC and TRIPS.

[2] The definition of invention was amended to cover all fields of technology; the exclusion from patentability on the grounds of "*ordre public* and morality" was reworded in order to cover circumstances where the exploitation, but no longer the "publication" of the invention infringes these principles; methods of medical treatment continue to be excluded from patenting, but the ground was changed from the absence of industrial applicability to just the effective use of the possibility provided in TRIPS to exclude such inventions.

[3] Gervais (2009), p. 349.

[4] Some developing countries had TRIPS-compatible legislation in place well in advance of the 2000 deadline, among them Chile, Mexico and South Korea.

in granting marketing approval), the patent law goes "beyond" the standard required by the TRIPS Agreement. In the same vein, a country can renounce its right to use a given flexibility enshrined in the TRIPS Agreement, for example, excluding from patenting plant varieties instead of plants as allowed under TRIPS, whereas the latter option—plants—is a wider exclusion.

However, regarding a number of issues which are not covered by the TRIPS Agreement, e.g., utility models and traditional knowledge, it is not clear whether a national law that includes provisions dealing with one of those matters goes "beyond" the TRIPS Agreement or whether they are just not TRIPS-related. Issues not covered by TRIPS for which protection is granted by a given country are not widely considered TRIPS-plus; instead, other expressions appear in the literature such as TRIPS Extra.

The TRIPS Agreement makes it clear that any type of more extensive protection needs to be in harmony with the Agreement provisions. There are so far no examples of provisions aiming to provide for more extensive protection that have been considered by a WTO panel to be contrary to TRIPS, although the need for further analysis of this matter has already been highlighted by some delegations within the TRIPS Council Meeting.[5]

Bearing in mind that TRIPS-plus norms have the proviso of not contravening the Agreement provisions, those norms can only be drafted using the flexibility that allows Members to increase the level of protection. Therefore TRIPS-plus/extra provisions are norms that—while compatible with TRIPS—are sound or reasonable from the policy perspective of a given country which considers benefiting from this increased level of protection.

Needless to say, developing countries and LDCs whose policy choice is to fulfil the TRIPS Agreement's minimum standards will give special attention to the identification of those flexibilities towards the minimum commitments, while developed countries and some developing countries will be ready to explore more extensive protection as the consequence of particular public policies, namely promotion of innovation, foreign direct investment or trade, as well as industrial policies.[6]

Current literature refers to flexibilities such as those choices for multilateral treaty implementation that take the approach of "minimum standards protection" as the "ceiling" of commitments, while using the term TRIPS-plus to refer to commitments that go beyond that minimum standard. This is the way both concepts will be developed in this article. Nevertheless, the borderline between provisions that contain flexibility or TRIPS-plus commitment is not clearly cut, as an example will illustrate: The "best mode" requirement as provided for in Article 29 of the

[5] During the TRIPS Council meeting of 8 and 9 June 2010 delegates from India and China highlighted the importance of Article 1.1 of TRIPS for the identification of "ceilings" in more extensive protection commitments.

[6] The existence of TRIPS-plus provisions in PTAs is not the only reason for developing countries to provide more extensive protection. There are developing countries and countries in transition that have adopted a higher level of protection than that requested in the TRIPS Agreement as the consequence of a unilateral choice.

TRIPS Agreement is a "may" clause.[7] Moreover, it has been identified as an important flexibility for developing countries.[8] However, some US free trade agreements (FTAs) contain a best-mode obligation that eliminates the flexibility provided in the TRIPS Agreement as to whether to adopt this requirement or not, so it could be seen as a FTA-s TRIPS-plus provision as well.

1.2 Preferential Trade Agreements (PTAs)

Preferential trade agreements—be they free trade agreements (FTAs) or customs unions (CUs)—are a way to promote liberalization. In order to pursue liberalization, countries act simultaneously at three levels: bilateral, regional and multilateral, producing a special synergy among the different processes.[9]

PTAs are in principle regional, covering areas like the European Union (EU), the Common Market of the South (MERCOSUR), North America (NAFTA), the Common Market of the Caribbean (CARICOM), the Association of Southeast Asian Nations (ASEAN), and the Common Market for Eastern and Southern Africa (COMESA),[10] while FTAs are increasingly cross-regional.[11] To avoid confusion, the expression preferential trade agreements will be used in this article in relation to European Union economic partnership agreements (EPAs)/FTAs and Interim Agreements, because it is most descriptive of the integration systems that are currently in place.[12]

Legal analyses of the creation of PTAs focus on GATT Article XXIV, GATS Article V and the Enabling Clause[13] as the instruments that permit the creation of

[7] This provision permits Members to request the best mode in the following way: "Members ... may require the applicant to indicate the best mode for carrying out the invention known to the inventor".

[8] See Commission on Intellectual Property Rights (2002), p. 117 and Article 123(3) of the WIPO Model Law for Developing Countries on Inventions (1979).

[9] Rayasam (2006), para 22; see Sect. 3.2.2 below.

[10] Zissimos (2006).

[11] Under the WTO regional agreement information system, the world is divided by regions as follows: North America, Central America, South America, Caribbean, Europe, West Asia, Middle Asia, East Asia, Africa, Commonwealth of Independent States and Oceania.

[12] World Trade Report 2011: According to the report, one half of the PTAs currently in force are not strictly "regional", due to the inclusion of countries from different geographical areas. p. 58.

[13] Adopted under GATT 1979, this provision enables developed Members to give differential and more favourable treatment to developing countries.

CUs[14] and FTAs.[15] These provisions allow Members to adopt measures otherwise WTO-inconsistent, based on the ground of first promoting regional integration and ultimately global free trade.[16] This is known as the "regional integration exception"; however, the "race" initiated by the US and the EU[17] and followed by other developed and developing countries, particularly since the early 1990s, has produced such a proliferation of PTAs[18] that what was conceived as an exception threatens to become the rule.[19] Notwithstanding the regional exception, the wording of Article XXIV clarifies that their purpose is to facilitate trade among the constituent's territories and not to "raise barriers to the trade of other Members".

CUs and FTAs are reviewed to determine their consistency with WTO rules, so countries involved in these agreements must notify the Council for Trade in Goods/ Council for Trade in Services of their "intention", and are then examined by the Committee on Regional Trade Agreements (CRTA), which produces a report[20] for the consideration of the respective Council, which in turn produces a recommendation to the Members concerning consistency.[21] Between 1996 and 2001 no report

---

[14] A CU is defined in Article XXIV:8(a) of GATT 1994 as follows: "the substitution of a single customs territory for two or more customs territories so that i) duties and other restrictive regulations of commerce ... are eliminated with respect to substantially all the trade between the constituent territories ... or at least in respect to substantially all the trade in products originating in such territories, and ii) ...substantially the same duties and other regulations of commerce are applied by each of the Members of the union to the trade of territories not included in the union".

[15] A free trade area is defined by Article XXIV: 8(b) of GATT 1994 as follows: "a group of two or more customs territories in which the duties and other restrictive regulations of commerce ... are eliminated in substantially all the trade between the constituent territories in products originating in such territories".

[16] Members recognized the desirability of increasing freedom of trade by the development, through voluntary agreements, of closer integration between the economies of the countries *parties* to such agreements.

[17] Former French Foreign Trade Minister Christine Lagarde not just supported the new EU strategy, but added that this shift was an imperative due the fact that the US was "aggressively pursuing bilateral and regional deals, so France and Europe must join in, or risk being left behind", quoted in Bhala (2007), text above fn. 15.

[18] World Trade Report 2011: According to the report, there are almost 300 PTAs in force, p. 60.

[19] The average number of PTA participants by WTO Member in 2010 is 12.

[20] The examination of the GATS consistency has been a difficult task, because it includes economic, legal and political considerations (see Panel Report in Turkey—*Textiles*, para 9.52). In fact, experience has shown that the consensus needed to produce a report is very difficult to reach.

[21] This practice has been the subject of criticism, because this analysis of compatibility is based upon a hierarchy of norms that is not shared by all; see for example Pauwelyn, who considers that this claimed supremacy of the WTO rules over the regional trade agreements is wrong, and argues that practice shows that WTO consistency of those regional trade agreements is almost never tested, so in the author's view regional trade agreements are here to stay, whether or not they comply with WTO rules.

was adopted by the CRTA; however, after a new transparency mechanism was adopted in 2006 on a provisional basis,[22] the task has been changed from "examination" to "consideration". Thus the WTO Secretariat, based on the information provided, such as tariff concessions, MFN duties, rules of origin and import statistics, prepares a factual presentation that helps Members in their considerations.

1.3 Stepping or Stumbling Blocks[23]

The WTO recognizes the advantage of economic integration and trade liberalization among groups of Members, whose common interest facilitates deals that are less likely to happen at the global level; thus, the positive impact of increased regional trade is hoped to boost trade at the global level.

As far as the EU is concerned, in 2006 a shift in trade policy strategy was announced by the Trade Commissioner, Peter Mandelson, to "integrate trade policy into the European Union's competitiveness and economic reform agenda", which among other features includes a new generation of bilateral FTAs.[24] As expressly stated, these new FTAs are addressed to "key partners" for the purpose of building "on WTO rules by tackling issues which are not ready for multilateral discussions and by preparing the ground for the next level of multilateral liberalization".

However, some voices are being raised to draw attention to the possible negative effects of these PTAs on multilateral trade liberalization.[25]

---

[22] WTO Members are currently reviewing the transparency mechanism with the intention to adopt it as final. WTO Members are also engaged in negotiation within the Doha Round to clarify and improve the disciplines in regional trade agreements.

[23] World Trade Report 2011, p. 197. However, the WTO report expressly states that "building-block/stumbling-block imagery does not adequately characterize the relationship between PTAs and the multilateral trading system", and prefers other reasons for the new wave of deep integration agreements, namely, the requirements of international production networks.

[24] See http://www.eu-un.europa.eu/articles/en/article_6311_en.htm and European Commission 2006, p. 10. The assessment of the concrete impact of this new generation of FTAs on specific IP categories is not part of this article.

[25] See WTO Report of the Consultative Board 2004, para 85. Also see Asian Development Outlook 2006. Some authors shared this view, i.e., de Jonquières (2006): "abandonment of multilateral liberalisation in favour of bilateralism and regionalism could, in the longer term, erode the rules and disciplines underpinning the WTO".

2 MFN Clauses in GATT, GATS and TRIPS

As discussed below, the "regional integration exception" in GATT and GATS allows, in countries that are part of CUs or FTAs, certain WTO-inconsistent measures under certain conditions.[26] Thus, all the benefits granted to Members involved in these regional agreements remain at the regional level.

On IP matters, the pre-TRIPS situation was the same as described above, due to the fact that bilateral investment agreements and IP bilateral agreements did not stipulate MFN treatment.[27] The situation has changed since the entry into force of the TRIPS Agreement, due to the introduction of the MFN clause and, particularly, because exceptions provided for in Articles 4 and 5 do not include "regional integration" itself.

The MFN clause negotiation was not an easy process; several delegations expressed doubts about the positive contribution of this principle in the IP field.[28] The EU delegation expressed interest in creating exclusions from the MFN Customs Unions and Free Trade Areas,[29] but its proposal did not receive support from other delegations. The US delegation proposed a text in which MFN treatment should not be applied in the case of "any advantage, favour, privilege or immunity which exceeds the requirements of this agreement and which is provided for in an international agreement to which the contracting party belongs". This proposal is reflected in the Brussels Draft,[30] which is, with some minor changes, very similar to the final text of Article 4 of the TRIPS Agreement, with the exception of "which exceeds", which has been left out of the final text. Thus, according to the US proposal, TRIPS-plus provisions included in regional trade agreements (CUs or FTAs) were excepted from the MFN principle.[31]

The exceptions to the MFN clause for IP matters, as finally negotiated in the TRIPS Agreement, refer to "international agreements related to the protection of

---

[26] As the Appellate Body stated in Turkey—*Textiles* (WT/DS34/AB/R, para 58), there are two conditions to justify the WTO-inconsistent measure: "First, the party claiming the benefit of this defence must demonstrate that the measure at issue is introduced upon the formation of a customs union that fully meets the requirements of sub-paragraphs 8(a) and 5(a) of Article XXIV. And, second, that party must demonstrate that the formation of that customs union would be prevented if it were not allowed to introduce the measure at issue".

[27] WIPO-administered treaties, either pre or post TRIPS Agreement, do not contain MFN clauses.

[28] See MTN.GNG/NG11/27, 14 November 1990, para 4.

[29] See MTN.GNG/NG11/W/68, 29 March 1990, Article 4 of the draft Agreement on Trade-Related Aspects of Intellectual Property Rights submitted for circulation by the European Communities.

[30] (c) deriving from international agreements related to the protection of intellectual property which entered into force prior to the entry into force of this agreement, provided that such agreements are notified to the committee established under Part VII below and do not constitute an arbitrary or unjustifiable discrimination against nationals of other parties.

[31] See MTN.GNG/NG11/W/70, 11 May 1990, Draft Agreement on Trade-Related Aspects of Intellectual Property Rights submitted by the US.

intellectual property which entered into force prior to the entry into force of the TRIPS Agreement". Thus, any FTA provision on IP matters that enters into force after the TRIPS Agreement and that consists of an "advantage, favour, privilege or immunity" shall be "immediately and unconditionally" accorded to the nationals of all other Members.

3 Regionalizing in GATT/GATS and Multilateralizing in TRIPS

As far as the TRIPS Agreement MFN clause is concerned, it is clear that TRIPS-plus provisions in PTAs are global in nature. Thus no distinction is made between a TRIPS obligation and a TRIPS-plus obligation. As stated by Pauwelyn, "regionalism in IP is automatically multilateralized".[32] However, this does not mean that a widely accepted standard would be automatically accepted in the rounds of WTO multilateral negotiations (see below).

Therefore, the different way WTO rules deal with the advantages given to Members of CUs or FTAs as far as trade issues and IPR issues are concerned might call for a revision of one of the two. It seems *a priori* that "the regionalization" of trade and services preferences is subject to more criticism than the "multilateralization" of PTAs' IP benefits.

3.1 Interaction Between WTO Law and TRIPS-Plus Provisions

TRIPS-plus provisions can be categorized, according to their content, in four groups of rules. The first group consists of provisions that aim to clarify, interpret or narrow down a TRIPS flexibility, as well as provisions that go beyond the minimum standard protection of TRIPS; the second consists of provisions that develop new matters not covered by the TRIPS Agreement; the third includes provisions that repeat the text of TRIPS articles; and the fourth, provisions that contain an obligation to "apply" or "accede" to other treaties or to respect international commitments in force. In the relationship between each of these groups of rules and the TRIPS Agreement, although some elements are shared, many others are very diverse, as will be described by means of examples.

[32] Pauwelyn (2007), p. 18.

3.1.1 Provisions That Interpret or Modify TRIPS Flexibilities

A good starting point concerns provisions that add clarity to a treaty text, either because the text is vague or because it needs further interpretation. A treaty provision may be vague in order to accommodate the express will of negotiators to leave open policy space or because negotiators were not able to agree on a more precise text. Thus, some Members may retain an interest in looking for other forums to add clarity or to interpret in a particular way the multilateral provision.

One example consists of PTA provisions on the regulatory review exception.[33] Parties to these regional agreements, which are also bound by WTO rules, intend to shed some light on the compatibility of this exception with Article 30 of the TRIPS Agreement, which as we know opted for a list of conditions that an exception has to fulfil to be considered TRIPS-compatible, instead of listing what those exceptions are.

The regulatory review, or Bolar-type exception, has been included in the national laws of a significant number of countries,[34] either as a consequence of unilateral choice or after the entry into force of bilateral free trade agreements. The Bolar-type exception contained in the Canadian Patent Law (Article 55.2(1)) has been studied by a WTO panel,[35] which found that this norm was in line with the TRIPS Agreement, and in particular with Article 30. In the panel's view, this exception is "limited",[36] "do[es] not unreasonably conflict with the normal

[33] In most countries, various entities can authorize the commercialization of certain regulated products. Since this process of marketing authorization takes place in parallel with and independently of the process of protection for the invention of those products, it is possible that certain tensions arise due to the delay in granting the authorization. Two major tensions may be mentioned. On the one hand, the right holder may suffer a net loss in the effective period of patent protection, since the 20-year period of protection starts from the patent application date. But on the other hand, competitors and consumers may be deprived of the possibility of early entry into the market of non-patented products as soon as the patent expires, because competitors need to wait until the marketing authorization is granted for each one of their products, producing a *de facto* extended period of marketing exclusivity. Therefore, from the competitors' and users' perspectives, there is an interest in this administrative process for marketing authorization beginning within the period of patent protection, despite the fact that production and commercialization must wait until the patent expires. This is exactly what the regulatory review exception is about.

[34] The laws of Australia, Brazil, China, Costa Rica, The Dominican Republic, Egypt, India, Jordan, Kenya, Malaysia, New Zealand, Nigeria, Thailand, Tunisia and Zimbabwe. The EU has decided to adopt at a regional level Directive 2001/82/EC for veterinary medicinal products and Directive 2001/83/EC for medicinal products for human use, as respectively amended by Directives 2004/27/EC and 2004/28/EC.

[35] See WT/DS114/R.

[36] because of the narrow scope of its curtailment of Article 28.1 rights. As long as the exception is confined to conduct needed to comply with the requirements of the regulatory approval process, the extent of the acts unauthorized by the right holder that are permitted by it will be small and narrowly bound. Even though regulatory approval processes may require substantial amounts of test production to demonstrate reliable manufacturing, the patent owner's rights themselves are not impaired any further by the size of such production runs, as long as they are solely for regulatory purposes and no commercial use is made of resulting final products.

exploitation of patents"[37] and do[es] not "prejudice the legitimate interest of the patentee".[38]

Therefore, a PTA provision on the regulatory review exception would be considered a TRIPS-plus provision, whose aim is to add clarity regarding the compatibility of this specific exception with Article 30 of TRIPS, where this exception is not expressly stated.

Nevertheless, it is still an exception to patent rights. The use of the regulatory review exception as a mechanism to increase competition has been frequently highlighted by experts and policymakers. The Report of the CIPR[39] recommended that policymakers in developing countries introduce this exception in their patent laws. Therefore, either not all TRIPS-plus provisions provide more extensive protection or not all PTA provisions are TRIPS-plus.

Now, it would be convenient to continue with provisions that narrow down TRIPS flexibility. This is the most common ground for a TRIPS-plus provision, e.g., commitments to provide patent protection for plants or animals; to choose a given level of exhaustion or to accept some limitations on this; to limit the acceptable grounds for compulsory licenses; to provide patent protection for second medical indications; and to limit the acceptable grounds for revocation, among others.

Thus, any commitment in a bilateral agreement restricting the freedom of choice that a Member enjoys concerning a TRIPS-provided flexibility would be considered TRIPS-plus. Therefore, if two countries, via a bilateral agreement, agree to a national exhaustion regime, it is a TRIPS-plus provision, as well as if the agreement is on international exhaustion.[40] Along the same lines, it is a TRIPS-plus provision

[37] The Panel considered that Canada was on firmer ground, however, in arguing that the additional period of de facto market exclusivity created by using patent rights to preclude submissions for regulatory authorization should not be considered 'normal'. The additional period of market exclusivity in this situation is not a natural or normal consequence of enforcing patent rights. It is an unintended consequence of the conjunction of the patent laws with product regulatory laws, where the combination of patent rights with the time demands of the regulatory process gives a greater than normal period of market exclusivity to the enforcement of certain patent rights.

[38] On balance, the Panel concluded that the interest claimed on behalf of patent owners whose effective period of market exclusivity had been reduced by delays in marketing approval was neither so compelling nor so widely recognized that it could be regarded as a 'legitimate interest' within the meaning of Article 30 of the TRIPS Agreement. Notwithstanding the number of governments that had responded positively to that claimed interest by granting compensatory patent term extensions, the issue itself was of relatively recent standing, and the community of governments was obviously still divided over the merits of such claims.

[39] Commission on Intellectual Property Rights (2002), p. 59.

[40] In a document prepared by WIPO (CDIP/5/4) figures show the following distribution by region of the exhaustion level chosen by several countries: Africa (national 12, regional 16 and international 2); Latin America (national 9, regional 0 and international 14); Asia and Oceania (national 13, regional 0 and international 8); Europe (national 5, regional 31 and international 1). Thus

that allows the patentability of second medical uses, because it is a limitation on the freedom Members enjoy to define the novelty requirement, where under TRIPS Members are free to adopt their own definition. However, in the same vein, a provision in a bilateral agreement that excludes second medical indications from patent protection would also be a TRIPS-plus provision.

Therefore, what characterizes a TRIPS-plus provision is not exclusively the fact that it aims for more extensive protection, because a commitment to use the TRIPS flexibility to provide minimum levels of protection is also TRIPS-plus. Moreover, what is really important to consider in terms of a given provision being TRIPS-plus is that a particular flexibility that exists in the TRIPS Agreement is carved out through the bilateral agreement.

Finally, we can make some comments on provisions that provide for more extensive protection. What characterizes these types of TRIPS-plus provisions is the fact that they go beyond the level of protection expressly stated in the TRIPS Agreement. There are several examples of this kind of provision, e.g., patent term extension, data exclusivity instead of data protection, criminal sanctions for patent infringements or border measures on patent matters, among others.

In order to analyse the interaction of these previously mentioned PTA provisions (that clarify or narrow down a flexibility or go beyond it) and the TRIPS Agreement, some light may be shed by some international law concepts. The first and most common relationship is that both treaties relate to each other in a coherent manner. In this connection, treaty norms should be interpreted in such a way that no conflict arises.

When the same countries accede to different treaties, the normal interaction between the treaties consists in one supplementing the other or at least confirming the rights and obligations contained in the other: this coherence of international law is known as "systemic integration".[41] The Vienna Convention on the Law of Treaties (VCLT), under Article 31(3)(c), provides for a treaty interpretation in which the person interpreting takes into account, together with the context, "any relevant rules of international law applicable to the relations between the parties".

A second relationship consists of the possibility of rules that "conflict", in which case the fulfilment of commitments in a given treaty implies the violation of the other one. A contradiction or conflict only exists when two treaties cannot be interpreted in a coherent manner, bearing in mind the objective and purpose of both treaties as a whole. It may happen that two or more parties to a multilateral treaty have decided to amend that treaty between them. As a matter of fact, Article 41 of the VCLT envisages the possible amendment by "certain of the parties" of a multilateral treaty, either because the treaty provides for this amendment (Article 41.1(a)) or because the amendment in question is not prohibited by the treaty if other requirements are fulfilled, namely, it does not affect the enjoyment of

international exhaustion counts for almost 61 per cent in Latin America, about 6.6 per cent in Africa and just 2.7 per cent in Europe. National exhaustion counts for almost 40 per cent in Africa and Latin America while just 13 per cent in Europe.

[41] Pauwelyn (2007), p. 9.

other parties' rights and does not affect the object and purpose of the other treaty (Article 41.1(b)).

To solve conflicts, the treaty may provide some guidance by setting a hierarchy of norms; thus, in case of conflict one treaty shall prevail over[42] or be subject to another. In many cases, in order to protect the multilateral system, PTAs explicitly provide that the bilateral agreement does not prejudice rights and obligations under other multilateral treaties, for instance, the TRIPS Agreement.[43] Moreover, in some cases a treaty could be more precise in its reference to a prevailing part or norm of another, e.g., when PTAs make reference to general flexibilities[44] or to flexibilities in a specific field, such as those that aim to promote access to medicines.[45]

However, contradiction between different policy objectives of a TRIPS-plus provision and a rule within the TRIPS Agreement may occur in the form of e.g. a provision on data exclusivity instead of data protection or a patent term extension instead of the 20-year term; the choice for restrictions on parallel importation instead of regional or international exhaustion, which may enter into conflict with the reference that a given PTA could make to flexibilities available in TRIPS, or in other international instruments, such as the Doha Declaration, in the promotion of access to medicines. In this connection, referring to rules of international law and treaty interpretation, the PTA may prevail, either because it is *lex specialis* or because it is *lex posterior*.

This insecurity notwithstanding, it is not appropriate to conclude that this general reference to flexibilities available in such multilateral instruments as the TRIPS Agreement or the Doha Declaration is useless. This reference may prove to be very useful for the interpretation of vague provisions contained in the PTA itself. However, it seems less useful in opposing the implementation of new commitments agreed upon in the PTA, on the grounds of the existence of a given flexibility available within the multilateral instrument.[46]

---

[42] NAFTA Article 103.2 states that it prevails over GATT unless otherwise provided.

[43] See Article 196(1) and (2) of the EU-Colombia/Peru FTA, which, on the one hand, stipulates that the parties reaffirm the rights and obligations under the TRIPS Agreement and WIPO-administered treaties, and on the other hand, expressly states that provisions on IP are intended to complement or specify the rights and obligations under those previously mentioned in multilateral treaties and that "no provision of this title will contradict or be detrimental to the provisions of such multilateral agreements".

[44] See Article 197(1) of the EU-Colombia/Peru FTA: "each party may, in formulating or amending its laws and regulations, make use of the exceptions and flexibilities permitted by the multilateral intellectual property agreements".

[45] See Article 139(2) of EC-Cariforum Agreement, which states "nothing in this Agreement shall be constructed as to impair the capacity of the parties ... to promote access to medicines". In the same vein, Article 197(2) and (3) of the EU-Colombia/Peru FTA make reference to the necessary consistency of the interpretation of the FTA's IP chapter with the Doha Declaration, as well as to the WTO General Council Decision of 30 August, 2003 on the implementation of Paragraph 6 and its protocol for amending TRIPS.

[46] Grosse Ruse-Khan (2011), p. 30.

3.1.2 Provisions That Develop New Aspects Not Covered by the TRIPS Agreement

Two important matters not covered by the TRIPS Agreement that have been developed by PTAs are utility models and traditional knowledge. Both have been indicated by scholars as examples of TRIPS flexibility,[47] precisely because Members enjoy total freedom to draft the system of protection that they consider appropriate, if any. However, the view has also been expressed that matters not included within the TRIPS Agreement should not be considered flexibilities.[48]

Concerning utility models,[49] the policy space that countries enjoy in the implementation of this type of protection is quite broad, because even though it is mentioned in Articles 1, 4, 5 and 11 of the Paris Convention as an industrial property category, there is no substantive provision on it within that treaty or the TRIPS Agreement.[50] Moreover, other multilateral treaties, such as the International Patent Classification (IPC)[51] and the Patent Cooperation Treaty (PCT),[52] refer to utility models without providing any substantive minimum standard of protection for them.

Therefore, since there are no substantive provisions on utility models in WIPO-administered treaties, there is no reference to utility models in the TRIPS Agreement and the usefulness of the system is not shared by all countries alike, the conclusion concerning developed and developing countries' decisions on their national implementation derives exclusively from national policy choices. For those who do not share the opinion that utility models are a complementary tool to promote local innovation, the flexibility they enjoy consists of simply not adopting a utility model system at all.

---

[47] Deere (2008), p. 75.

[48] Delegation of Uruguay at the Fifth Session of the CDIP (26-30 April 2010) concerning document CDIP/5/4.

[49] Utility model legislation exists in a significant number of countries: of 120 countries studied in a WIPO document (CDIP/5/4Rev), there is utility model protection in 43 countries in Africa, 22 in Latin America, 19 in Asia and Oceania, and 25 in Europe. Needless to say, important differences exist between those legal norms.

[50] Article 2, subsection 2, of the TRIPS Agreement contains a reference to the Paris Convention establishing that "nothing in Parts I to IV of this Agreement shall derogate from existing obligations that Members may have to each other under the Paris Convention". The fact that this treaty does not establish any minimum standard of protection for utility models leaves WTO Members free to formulate regimes for this category of IPR.

[51] The IPC covers not only patents for invention, but also inventors' certificates, utility models and utility certificates.

[52] In the framework of the PCT, references to an application for the protection of an invention are construed as covering applications for patents for inventions, inventors' certificates, utility models, patent certificates of addition and utility certificates of addition.

Concerning subject matter of protection, countries' legislation may provide the same exclusions as in their patent laws[53] or add to the general exclusions of patent laws others that are derived from the application of a "tridimensional requirement"[54] or from some particular exclusion that applies exclusively to utility models.[55]

In this context, Article 148 of the EU-Cariforum EPA provides protection for processes and only allows for exclusion from patentability, based on *ordre public* and morality, of diagnostic, therapeutic and surgical methods and plants and animals. This provision limits the freedom those countries had under multilateral commitments to exclude other subject matter from utility model protection, namely, chemical products and processes.

Turning our analysis to genetic resources and associated traditional knowledge, it is appropriate to focus on one single aspect, namely, the transparency requirement of the disclosure of the source or origin of the biological material.[56]

The review process of Article 27.3(b) of the TRIPS Agreement has covered the issue of disclosure of the origin of genetic resources within the broader subject of the relationship between the TRIPS Agreement and the Convention on Biological Diversity (CBD)[57] and, in particular, within the objectives of that Convention of realizing a system of prior informed consent and benefit sharing in relation to the

---

[53] In the case of the Philippines, it is provided in Rule 2001 of the Patent Act that "the following shall be excluded from protection as utility models: (a) discoveries, scientific theories and mathematical methods; (b) schemes, rules and methods of performing mental acts, playing games or doing business, and programs for computers; (c) methods for treatment of the human or animal body by surgery or therapy and diagnostic methods practiced on the human or animal body. This provision shall not apply to products and compositions for use in any of these methods; (d) plant varieties or animal breeds or essentially biological processes for the production of plants or animals. This provision shall not apply to microorganisms and non-biological and microbiological processes; (e) aesthetic creations; and (f) anything which is contrary to public order or morality."

[54] For example, the Russian Federation Patent Act, in relation to inventions patentable as a utility model, states: "A technical solution relating to a device shall be protected as a utility model" (Section 1351, subsection 1). The Polish law states: "Any new and useful solution of a technical nature affecting shape, construction or durable assembly of an object shall constitute a utility model". In the Mexican Utility Model Law, protection is available for "[o]bjects, utensils, appliances or tools which, as a result of a modification in their arrangement, configuration, structure or form, offer a different function with respect to their component parts or advantages with respect to their usefulness".

[55] For instance, processes or chemical substances are excluded in the laws of a significant number of countries. Despite the fact that concern has been expressed that this back door could be used to protect non-patentable inventions, particularly in sensitive sectors such as pharmaceuticals, it is clear that many solutions are available within the utility model system itself, for example, a definition could be adopted including the requirement of embodiment, but an exclusion from patentability for those products could also be provided.

[56] A significant number of countries in all regions provide for the disclosure of the origin or source of the biological material, but particularly in Latin America followed by Europe.

[57] The Doha Declaration of November 2001 instructed the TRIPS Council to analyse the relationship between TRIPS and CBD in the framework of its review of Article 27.3(b).

access to and exploitation of biological resources.[58] In that regard, some Members have expressed their concern about the fact that patents might be granted for inventions that use biological material without respecting the provisions of the CBD.

On that topic, WTO Members have tabled different proposals. Switzerland, which had advocated a revision of the legal framework under WIPO-administered treaties (PCT and PLT)[59] proposed that the inclusion of the disclosure-of-origin issue, in the multilateral system, be explored through the revision of Rule 51*bis*1(a) (i) to (v) of the PCT, entitled "Certain National Requirements Allowed Under Article 27". A group of countries[60] proposed that a new provision (Article 29*bis*) be inserted in the TRIPS Agreement requiring patent applicants to indicate the "country providing such resources" as well as "the source in the country providing the genetic resources"; and the EU and its Member States expressed willingness to discuss the introduction of a multilateral system for disclosure within the TRIPS Council, which is not to be an obstacle for the granting and validity of patents.[61]

Another approach is taken for those that consider that national legislation on access and benefit sharing and on contracts in this field are more appropriate instruments than the patent system itself, this is known as the "national based approach". US lead the position of those that considers that the introduction of a new patent disclosure requirement "are not an appropriate solution to meet the concerns raised", while on their view the burden the inventor and IP offices assume and the uncertainties that new requirement brings, might undermine the role of the patent system in encouraging innovation, technological progress and economic development.[62]

Although some differences may be acknowledged between Article 150.4 of the EU-Cariforum EPA and Article 201.7 and 8 of the EU-Colombia/Peru FTA, they share the acceptance that disclosure of the "sources" (Cariforum), or "origin or source" (Colombia/Peru), of the biological material is a requisite of the patent application. In the case of the EU-Cariforum EPA it is qualified as an administrative requirement. The EU-Colombia/Peru FTA also provides that in their national laws the parties will regulate the "effects of any such requirement".

The relationship of this group of PTA rules (matters not covered by TRIPS) to the TRIPS Agreement is also complex from the international law perspective.

Regarding the relationship between TRIPS-plus provisions in this group and the TRIPS Agreement, the first question that arises is whether there is any possibility of

---

[58] For an in-depth analysis see IP/C/W/368/Rev.1.

[59] The Swiss proposal was first submitted for consideration at the fourth session of the Working Group on PCT Reform held in May 2003. The proposal is described as an enabling clause because it allows Member States to implement the requirement, if they so wish.

[60] Namely, Brazil, China, Colombia, Ecuador, India, Indonesia, Peru, Thailand, the ACP Group and the African Group (TN/C/W/59).

[61] Therefore the requirement should not act "*de facto o de jure*" as an additional formal or substantial patentability criterion and sanctions should fall outside patent law.

[62] See IP/C/W/469, and in the same vein IP/C/W/434, IP/C/W/443, IP/C/W/449 and IP/C/W/459.

contradiction. Taking utility models as an example, it seems a priori unlikely that contradiction exists, because no provision of the TRIPS Agreement makes reference to this matter. Therefore, the regional agreement supplements the multilateral one in a matter not covered by the latter. Accordingly, provisions on utility models in PTAs do not amount to inter-se modifications of TRIPS which would be subject to the tests of Art.41 VCLT.

Regarding the indication of the source of the biological material, as an element of the disclosure requirement, although a significant amount of legislation has been passed in very diverse regions, i.e., in Europe at the EU level[63] and at the national level by some European countries,[64] as well as in Latin America,[65] Africa[66] and Asia,[67] certain views still draw attention to its possible conflicts with Article 29 of the TRIPS Agreement.

In case of conflict between a multilateral treaty and a regional one on issues not expressly covered by the multilateral treaty, for instance, a provision on the disclosure of the origin of genetic material—not expressly covered by the TRIPS Agreement—an FTA panel may well consider that the regional treaty provision will prevail in view of the *lex specialis* principle; however, whether the same approach would be taken by a WTO panel is a matter still to be seen.

3.1.3 Provisions That Repeat the Text of TRIPS Provisions

Treaties are, in general, equal from the international law perspective. Therefore the fact that a given treaty is multilateral, as is the case with the TRIPS Agreement and WIPO-administered treaties, does not imply that such treaties are in a better position than bilateral treaties. However, if one of the treaties in question has adopted a hierarchy, a treaty may thus be subject to or prevail over the other.

Therefore, when a PTA accepts the superiority of a multilateral treaty, as is the case with the EU-Colombia/Peru FTA, what is the purpose of repeating a provision that already exists in the multilateral treaty? One example is the provision that reiterates the freedom of parties to choose the appropriate level of exhaustion of IP rights, in Article 200 of the EU-Colombia/Peru FTA, which is identical to the corresponding provision in the TRIPS Agreement.

As was mentioned before, if a hierarchy has not been established, the PTAs will often prevail due to the fact that they contain more specific provisions (*lex specialis*)

---

[63] See Article 13 of the Biotechnology Directive (Directive 98/44/EC of 6 July 1998).

[64] See Article 15(6) of the Patent Law of Belgium (consolidated version of 1 January 2010), Article 3(4) of the consolidated Patent Law of Denmark (order of 29 January 2009), and Article 49a of the Patent Law of Switzerland (last amended 1 July 2009).

[65] See the Patent Law of the Andean Community, Brazil and Costa Rica, among others.

[66] See the Patent Law of Egypt, Ethiopia, Burundi and South Africa, among others.

[67] See the Patent Law of China, India and Pakistan, among others.

and/or in the case of post-TRIPS FTAs (the majority with some exceptions, namely, NAFTA), because the FTAs are later in time (*lex posterior*).

From the international law perspective, this is not a case of "systemic integration" or "conflicting rules", because the FTA text adds nothing to what is already agreed upon at the multilateral level. However, the way those matters are addressed within the multilateral or regional dispute settlement mechanisms should be a matter for consideration.

In this respect, Article 200 of the EU-Colombia/Peru FTA, on exhaustion, does not contain an express exclusion of this matter from dispute settlement. Thus, it could be a valid subject for a regional complaint, while at the multilateral level there is no competency on the part of a WTO panel to decide on this issue, because claims are excluded from the DSU (Article 6 of the TRIPS Agreement).

3.1.4 Provisions to "Apply" or "Accede" to WIPO-Administered Treaties or to Respect International Commitments in Force

The long-established practice of EU PTAs was to require the parties to ensure adequate and effective protection of IP rights "in conformity with the highest international standards".[68] Nevertheless, some questions have arisen about what the exact meaning of "highest international standards" is, e.g., whether bilateral and regional treaties were part of those standards; whether in the case of the existence of two multilateral agreements with different standards one will be considered the "highest"; and whether future multilateral treaties negotiated after the regional agreement should also have to be considered.

In the new generation of PTAs, an exhaustive list of multilateral treaties indicates the "highest international standard", which is contained mainly in treaties not mentioned in the TRIPS Agreement or adopted after TRIPS.[69] There are three types of commitment[70]: the accession to a treaty within a certain deadline, the endeavour to accede to a treaty and compliance with a treaty.[71]

As for EU PTAs, commitments on the accession to IP multilateral treaties or endeavours to accede play a prominent role; thus these agreements include a list of treaties according to each category of IP matter.[72]

---

[68] See, for example, Article 30 of the EU-Lebanon Interim Agreement (2002).

[69] In the field of patents, commitments are related to the following treaties: the Patent Cooperation Treaty (Washington, 1970), the Patent Law Treaty (Geneva, 2000) and the Budapest Treaty (1977).

[70] In previous bilateral agreements the recognition of the importance of a number of multilateral treaties was also used.

[71] See Article 147 of the EU-Cariforum Agreement.

[72] The EU-Cariforum EPA, in some categories of IP, includes a list of international agreements to which the parties are committed to apply, to accede or to endeavour to accede, e.g., on copyright Article 143 A, on trademarks Article 144 E and on patents Article 147A(1), (2) and (3).

There is a difference between, on the one hand, incorporating a treaty by reference, as TRIPS does in Article 2, e.g., with the Paris, Berne, and Rome conventions and also the Washington Treaty and, on the other, committing to join a given treaty. The obligation in the first case is to apply the standard of that treaty, while in the second case, it consists of joining the treaty or the endeavour to join it. However, the commitment to "apply" a treaty, as incorporated by the EU in its PTAs, is equivalent to the obligation that derives from the incorporation by reference. Therefore, the EU acquires an undertaking equivalent to that assumed by Members in the framework of TRIPS regarding those conventions and treaties incorporated by reference. In this sense, the effect of the commitment to "apply" a treaty would be equivalent to a TRIPS modification that consists of the incorporation by reference of that treaty (because of the MFN principle).

The commitment to accede or endeavour to accede has no direct link with the future respect of the treaty commitments. A given country may thus be expected to accede to a treaty, but latter it may decide to fulfil or not to fulfil the commitment. Therefore, the content of a possible dispute within a regional body would be whether the country met the deadline for joining or its endeavour to accede, but fulfilment of the multilateral treaty commitments seems to remain beyond the competence of those regional bodies.[73]

In North–south PTAs, developed countries commit themselves primarily to comply with treaties to which they are already party, and developing countries to accede or to endeavour to do so.[74] A smooth transition to stronger IP protection is therefore taking place,[75] because the IP treaty that is included in the list of commitments in the FTA becomes part of the obligations under the TRIPS Agreement as a consequence of the MFN principle.[76] Those treaties are considered TRIPS-plus, because they were adopted after TRIPS, and their impact on the

[73] Thus, a claim by the EU before Cariforum/Colombia/Peru relating to violations of a multilateral treaty would be solved according to the respective treaty's rules, e.g., Article 28 of the Paris Convention and Article 59 of the PCT.

[74] However in some cases developed countries commit to accede to treaties they are not yet parties, For instance, through certain FTAs the United States of America has committed to make reasonable efforts to accede to the Patent Law Treaty (PLT), i.e., the US Korea and the US Australia (US still not a party, they just signed the treaty in 2000), as well as to make reasonable efforts to accede to the Hague Agreement Concerning the International Registration of Industrial Designs (1999), i.e., the US Korea, US Australia and US Singapor (US still not yet a party); and to make reasonable efforts to joint the Singapore Treaty on the Law of Trademarks, i.e., the US Singapore was signed in 2007 before US joined that treaty in 2008.

[75] As an example, the Singapore Treaty on the Law of Trademarks was adopted on 28 March 2006 and is reflected in the US-Korea FTA (2007).

[76] Ironically, even soft law, which by way of its incorporation in an FTA, may bind not only parties to the FTA to each other, but also such parties with other WTO members (MFN). Needless to say, it does not affect those other Members that are not part of the FTA.

international law is the same as that of any other TRIPS-plus provisions; in fact, for some authors, in this way the "TRIPS Agreement is amended, even though the amendment is not applicable to all WTO Members".[77]

3.2 *Impact of TRIPS-Plus Provisions on International Law*

Bearing in mind the different relationships previously described, the impact of TRIPS-plus provisions on international law can be assessed in two areas: first, in the dispute settlement arena and second, in terms of international negotiations underway.

3.2.1 WTO Dispute Settlement Understanding (DSU)

The DSU is designed as a mechanism to ensure the "security and predictability" of the world trade system; to this end, panels and the Appellate Body (AB) are entrusted with the task of clarifying existing provisions of the WTO rules, such as the TRIPS Agreement. However, there are limits to its function: "[the Dispute Settlement Body] DSB cannot add to or diminish the rights and obligations provided in the covered treaties"; therefore, no amendment of the covered agreements is expected to be achieved through panel decisions.

There are two points that deserve special attention. One is the way WTO panels consider TRIPS-plus rules when interpreting the multilateral norms, and also whether decisions taken by a regional panel should be taken into consideration by WTO panels. Second, attention should be given to exclusion clauses that are incorporated in PTAs.

WTO Panels' Competence Regarding TRIPS-Plus Provisions' Compatibility

Complaints related to TRIPS-plus provisions lie within the competence of the regional dispute settlement mechanism. Nevertheless, it has been argued that bilateral agreements can be used by some Members to support a given interpretation of a WTO rule, e.g., the Industry Functional Advisory Committee (IFAC) states in a report to the US Government that FTAs "have provided the vehicle ... for significant clarifications of TRIPS obligations in the FTAs' partners"[78] and Bhala, in relation to non-WTO awards on disputes over bilateral agreements, states that these

[77] He (2010), p. 272.

[78] Morin (2009), p. 186.

awards "may prove useful as guidance, even path-breaking in legal theory or rationale, for WTO panels and the Appellate Body".[79]

WTO panels have not yet relied on bilateral treaty provisions in the analysis of the TRIPS Agreement provisions. Several reasons have been given, e.g., the fact a bilateral agreement has entered into force before the TRIPS Agreement,[80] or the fact that PTAs are not considered a "relevant rule of international law applicable in the relation between the parties" in the sense of the VCLT.[81]

Another reason that has been expressed to justify the non-recourse of WTO panels to regional treaty provisions is that those provisions are not considered "a subsequent practice which establishes the agreement of the parties with its interpretation".[82] In this connection, some scholars[83] consider that provisions contained in bilateral trade agreements could eventually create new customary international law. However, in the view of other authors,[84] this would be very difficult owing to the stringent requirements imposed on the behaviour of states to be considered customary law, on the one hand, because it must reflect the general practice of states and, on the other, because states must believe that there is a legal obligation to conduct themselves in such a manner.[85]

Therefore, while regional panels are frequently open in their analysis to considering WTO case law[86] and WTO rules, the opposite is not true. Moreover, in its Report in the Argentina Poultry dispute the Panel considered that it was not bound by "rulings of non-WTO dispute settlement bodies".[87]

---

[79] Bhala (2007), p. 84.

[80] See WT/DS170/R, para 3.2. Canada, the defendant, argued that according to a NAFTA provision, the term of 20 years from filing and 17 from granting are equivalent and so in conformity with the TRIPS provision. However, the panel did not consider the NAFTA provision as a useful tool for interpretation to determine whether Canada complied with the TRIPS Agreement.

[81] See WT/DS/291, 292 and 293. The panel held that the obligation to take into account exogenous rules of international law when interpreting a WTO rule applies only to those rules that are binding on all WTO members and not to those that are binding just among disputants, as in the case of FTAs.

[82] See WT/DS114/R. The panel held that the legal situation in various countries, including the US, is not a tool for interpretation, despite Article 31 of the VCLT. The panel added that the requirement of "subsequent practice" would be difficult to satisfy, because it implies a "tacit agreement between all parties".

[83] Yu (2004), p. 397.

[84] Morin (2009), p. 188.

[85] Morin, *idem*, quoting Kindred and Saunders (2006), p. 148, argues that, since FTA signatory states accepted the TRIPS-plus provision to cover trade interests and not to cover any recent customary norm, FTAs are unlikely to serve as a basis for interpretation of new customary international norms.

[86] See NAFTA decisions in cases such as *High Fructose Corn Syrup* and *Softwood Lumber*, cited in Henckels (2008).

[87] See WT/DS241/R, para 7.41.

Exclusion Clauses in PTAs

The WTO dispute settlement system is the exclusive forum for the resolution of disputes regarding the violation of agreements covered by the DSU,[88] including the TRIPS Agreement. However, the potential for overlapping jurisdiction arises when one issue is covered by WTO as well as PTA rules.

Jurisdiction on these overlapping IP provisions may be within the competence of regional and multilateral bodies alike. As far as PTAs are concerned, normally they give parties the freedom to choose the forum where a claim should be brought, coupled with a prohibition to bring the same matter before a second forum when a process has already been launched.[89] In case no provision on exclusion clauses exists, recourse to international law doctrines may be of help, namely, the criteria of *res judicata*'[90] *lis alibi pendens*[91] or *forum non conveniens*.[92]

There are slight differences in the choice-of-forum clauses included in recent EU bilateral agreements, for instance, while in the EU-Cariforum EPA it is stated that regional arbitration bodies "shall not adjudicate disputes ... on rights and obligations under the Agreement establishing the WTO". In the EU-Colombia/Peru FTA it is stated that "disputes related to the same measure arising from this Agreement and by virtue of the WTO Agreement, may be settled under this title or under the DSU at the discretion of the complaining party".

All in all, in overlapping IP matters covered by the TRIPS Agreement and the PTA, the forum generally chosen by parties seems to be the WTO dispute settlement system,[93] but regional dispute settlement bodies are also competent to hear disputes related to TRIPS-plus provisions. Nevertheless, a matter for further consideration is what the appropriate forum is for claims about the compatibility of conflicting provisions.

3.2.2 Impact on Current and Future Multilateral Negotiation

Bilateral trade agreements[94] preceded the establishment of the IP multilateral legal system, namely, the Paris Convention (1883), so they are far from being a new

[88] See WT/DS320/AB/R, para 371.

[89] See Article 319 of the EU-Colombia/Peru FTA and Article 222 of the EU-Cariforum EPA.

[90] If something is already decided by a given body this closes off the option for further consideration by other bodies.

[91] If a dispute is still unresolved in one forum it cannot be brought before another forum.

[92] One adjudicative body considers that another tribunal is better placed to exercise jurisdiction.

[93] Up to 2010, 82 out of 443 disputes were between parties that were partners in PTAs.

[94] For instance the Cobden-Chavalier Treaty between Britain and France in 1860, which brought significant tariff reductions and an MFN clause.

phenomenon. However, mainly bilateral agreements that preceded TRIPS negotiations in the early 1990s and those after TRIPS are having a more direct impact in shaping the multilateral IP system.

As far as the EU is concerned, the EU Trade Commissioner stated that the objective of FTAs is: "to build on WTO rules by tackling issues which are not ready for multilateral discussions and for preparing the ground for the next level of multilateral liberalization". In the same vein, Susan Schwab, US Trade Representative during the George W. Bush administration said: "my experience is that bilateral, regional and multilateral treaties are in fact mutually reinforcing.... Here in these bilateral negotiations, you develop a precedent that could at some point be translated in a multilateral setting".[95]

The underlying strategy, called "competitive liberalization",[96] consists in building on bilateral agreements to advance at the same time in regional and multilateral negotiations with the intention to promote more international free trade.

Therefore, it seems clear that PTAs make a considerable contribution to multilateral negotiations.[97] Having said that, reality sends a different signal on the impact of PTAs' TRIPS-plus provisions on current multilateral negotiations. A brief review of the international agenda process may be illustrative, e.g., issues that are under consideration in the Doha Round are not necessarily those that play a more prominent role in PTAs, and parties to signatory PTA agreements, although active in promoting new bilateral agreements with peer countries,[98] are not aligned in the multilateral discussions (e.g., the WIPO Standing Committee on the Law of Patents). Some authors argue, referring to the specific issue of patents, but extendable to other categories, that "the assertion that bilateral trade deals have a huge impact on international patent law making, both by proponents and by critics, is unsubstantiated".[99]

[95] Quoted in Rayasam (2006), para 22.

[96] Zoellick (2004), p. 57.

[97] See World Trade Report 2011, which indicates that waves of regionalism have "tended to coincide with—or be immediately followed by—significant advances in GATT negotiations", p. 52.

[98] Nevertheless, a significant number of FTAs signed by developed and developing countries other than the United States of America and EU members limit IP provisions to the TRIPS commitments and do not reproduce the text of the agreements signed with the US or the EU, e.g., Australia's FTA with Singapore and Thailand or Singapore's FTA with New Zealand, Jordan and Japan.

[99] Morin (2009), p.177.

4 Conclusion: Broad Interaction but Limited Impact

The idea that PTA provisions are exclusively geared towards more extensive protection of IP rights, although valid in a significant number of cases, is not always correct, as the case of certain PTA provisions concerning matters such as the best mode requirement and the regulatory review exception shows.

TRIPS-plus provisions are immediately and unconditionally multilateralized through the MFN clause of TRIPS, which does not include the regional exception that exists for concessions concerning trade in goods and services. The implementation of TRIPS-plus provisions takes place through their inclusion in national patent laws, which harmonize IP standards of protection at a higher level than that negotiated in the TRIPS Agreement.

Despite the fact that PTAs' conflicting clauses usually place the TRIPS Agreement further up in the hierarchy, which means it will prevail in case of contradiction, general international law rules, in particular the VCLT, would give preference to TRIPS-plus provisions that interpret a multilateral norm, narrow down a flexibility or provide an increased level of protection, either because the PTAs are signed later (*lex posterior*) or because they contain special rules on the subject (*lex specialis*). Moreover, in case of conflict between a specific TRIPS-plus provision contained in a PTA and another provision of the same PTA that refers to flexibilities included in the TRIPS Agreement or in any other international instrument, such as the Doha Declaration, it seems that the former will prevail. In other words, there is no way to oppose the implementation of a given TRIPS-plus specific commitment, e.g., a patent term extension, on the grounds that it runs counter to the flexibility provided in TRIPS or Doha concerning access to medicines, except when the TRIPS-plus provision does not pass the test of Art.41 VCLT,[100] in which a case TRIPS Agreement prevails.

The consideration that WTO panels will give to PTA provisions and to regional panel decisions in their interpretation of WTO rules, for instance the TRIPS Agreement, is a matter that deserves further policy attention.

Previous experience shows the positive impact of waves of regionalism on multilateral trade negotiations. Whether the TRIPS-plus provisions of PTAs will impact current multilateral negotiations within the WTO is a matter to be seen upon

[100] VCLT. Article 41. Agreements to modify multilateral treaties between certain of the parties only.

1. Two or more of the parties to a multilateral treaty may conclude an agreement to modify the treaty as between themselves alone if: (a) the possibility of such a modification is provided for by the treaty; or (b) the modification in question is not prohibited by the treaty and: (i) does not affect the enjoyment by the other parties of their rights under the treaty or the performance of their obligations; (ii) does not relate to a provision, derogation from which is incompatible with the effective execution of the object and purpose of the treaty as a whole.
2. Unless in a case falling under paragraph 1 (a) the treaty otherwise provides, the parties in question shall notify the other parties of their intention to conclude the agreement and of the modification to the treaty for which it provides.

completion of the Doha Round. Likewise, the impact of PTAs' TRIPS-plus provisions in the current international norm-setting work done by WIPO is something that should become discernible in the near future.[101]

References

Asian Development Bank (2006) Asian Development Outlook: Routes for Asia's Trade. http://www.adb.org/sites/default/files/ADO/2006/ado2006-part3.pdf

Bhala R (2007) Competitive liberalization, competitive imperialism, and intellectual property. Liverpool Law Rev 28:77–105

Commission on Intellectual Property Rights (2002) Report: Integrating Intellectual Property Rights and Development Policy. London. http://www.iprcommission.org/home.html

de Jonquières G (2006) Global trade: outlook for agreements nears a moment of truth. Financial Times, 24 January 2006

Deere C (2008) The implementation game. The TRIPS agreement and the global politics of intellectual property reform in developing countries. Oxford University Press, Cambridge

European Commission (2006) Global Europe: competing in the world. Trade Policy Review, 4 October 2006, Brussels. http://trade.ec.europa.eu/doclib/docs/2006/october/tradoc_130376.pdf

Gervais D (2009) (Re)implementing the TRIPS agreement on trade-related aspects of intellectual property to foster innovation. J World Intellect Prop 12(5):348–370

Grosse Ruse-Khan H (2011) The international law relation between TRIPS and subsequent TRIPS-plus free trade agreements: towards safeguarding TRIPS flexibilities? J Intellect Prop Law 18(2):327–365

He H (2010) The development of the free trade agreements and international protection of intellectual property rights in the WTO era – new bilateralism and its future. IIC 41(3):253–283

Henckels C (2008) Overcoming jurisdictional isolation at the WTO-FTA nexus: a potential approach for the WTO. Eur J Int Law 19(3):571–599

Kindred H, Saunders P (2006) International law: chiefly as interpreted and applied in Canada. Edmond Montgomery, Toronto

Morin JF (2009) Multilateralizing TRIPS-plus agreements. J World Intellect Prop 12(3):175–197

Negotiating Group on Trade Related Aspects of Intellectual Property Rights Including Trade in Counterfeit Goods. (a) MTN.GNG/NG11/27, Meeting of 14 November 1990, Note of the Secretariat. http://ipmall.info/hosted_resources/lipa/trips/27.pdf. (b) MTN.GNG/NG11/W/68, Draft Agreement on Trade-Related Aspects of Intellectual Property Rights, Communication from the European Commission, 29 March 1990. http://www.tripsagreement.net/documents/GATTdocs/Draft_Agreement_on_Trade_Related_Aspects_of_IP_Rights_E_E.pdf. (c) MTN.GNG/NG11/W/70, Draft Agreement on Trade-Related Aspects of Intellectual Property Rights, Communication from the United States, 11 May 1990

Pauwelyn J (2007) Legal avenues to multilateralizing regionalism: beyond Article XXIV. HEI, September 10-12, 2007, Geneva

Rayasam R (2006) Free-Trade Evangelist. US News & World Report, 21 August 2006 (Q&A: 649 Susan Schwab, US Trade Representative during the George W. Bush administration)

[101] Work in progress developing at a different pace, depending on the subjects, namely, the Standing Committee on Copyright and Related Rights (SCCR), Standing Committee on the Law of Patents (SCP), Standing Committee on Trademarks, Industrial Designs and Geographical Indications (SCT) and Intergovernmental Committee on Intellectual Property and Genetic Resources, Traditional Knowledge and Folklore.

World Intellectual Property Organization (WIPO), Committee on Development and Intellectual Property (CDIP). (a) CDIP/5/4, "Patent related flexibilities in the multilateral legal framework and their legislative implementation at the national and regional levels", 1 March 2010, Geneva. http://www.wipo.int/edocs/mdocs/mdocs/en/cdip_5/cdip_5_4-main1.pdf. (b) CDIP/5/4 REV., "Patent related flexibilities in the multilateral legal framework and their legislative implementation at the national and regional levels", 18 August 2010, Geneva. http://www.wipo.int/meetings/en/doc_details.jsp?doc_id=153559

World Trade Organization (WTO). (a) WT/DS34/AB/R, Report of the Appellate Body of 22 October 1999 and WT/DS34/R, Report of the Panel of 31 May 1999, Turkey – Restrictions on Imports of Textile and Clothing Products. http://www.wto.org/english/tratop_e/dispu_e/34abr_e.pdf and http://www.wto.org/english/tratop_e/dispu_e/1229d.pdf. (b) WT/DS114/R, Report of the Panel, Canada – Patent protection of pharmaceutical products, Complaint by the European Communities and their Member States, 17 March 2000. http://www.wto.org/english/tratop_e/dispu_e/7428d.pdf. (c) WT/DS170/R, Report of the Panel, Canada –Term of Patent Protection, Complaint by the United States. 5 May 2000. http://www.wto.org/english/tratop_e/dispu_e/cases_e/ds170_e.htm. (d) WT/DS241/R, Report of the Panel, Argentina – Definitive anti-dumping duties on poultry from Brazil, 22 April 2003. http://www.wto.org/english/tratop_e/dispu_e/241r_a_e.pdf. (e) WT/DS/291, 292 and 293, Report of the panel, European Communities - Measures Affecting the Approval and Marketing of Biotech Products, 29 September 2006, Geneva. http://www.wto.org/english/tratop_e/dispu_e/cases_e/ds291_e.htm. (f) WT/DS320/AB/R, United States – Continued suspension of obligations in the EC – Hormones dispute, AB-2008-5, report of the appellate body, 16 October 2008. http://www.wto.org/english/tratop_e/dispu_e/ab_reports_e.htm. (g) IP/C/W/368/Rev.1, Council for Trade-Related Aspects of Intellectual Property Rights, The relationship between the trips agreement and the convention on biological diversity (summary of issues raised and points made), 8 February 2006, Geneva. http://www.wto.org/english/tratop_e/trips_e/ipcw368_e.pdf. (h) TN/C/W/59, Trade Negotiations Committee, Draft decision to enhance mutual supportiveness between the TRIPS Agreement and the Convention on Biological Diversity. Communication from Brazil, China, Colombia, Ecuador, India, Indonesia, Peru, Thailand, the ACP Group, and the African Group, 19 April 2011, Geneva. http://www.wto.org/english/tratop_e/trips_e/art27_3b_e.htm

WTO (2004) The future of the WTO: addressing institutional challenges in the new millennium. Report of the Consultative Board. WTO, Geneva

WTO (2011) The WTO and preferential trade agreements: from coexistence to coherence. World Trade Report. WTO, Geneva

Yu P (2004) Currents and crosscurrents in the international intellectual property regime. Loyola Los Angeles Law Rev 38:323–443

Zissimos B (2006) Why are trade agreements regional? Vanderbilt University, Nashville

Zoellick R (2004) US Government Accountability Office (GAO)

The Impact of the Economic Partnership Agreements on WTO Law

Carlos Correa

Contents

1 Introduction

The economic partnership agreements (EPAs) promoted by the European Union (EU) are one of its key instruments to realize its commercial interests through the liberalization of trade in goods and services and the strengthening and expansion of intellectual property rights. While EPAs would allegedly deliver a number of benefits to the EU partners,[1] their losses may outweigh the potential gains in areas of vital interest to those partners.[2]

---

[1] See, e.g., http://ec.europa.eu/trade/wider-agenda/development/economic-partnerships/.

[2] South Centre (2011).

C. Correa (✉)
Director of the Center for Interdisciplinary Studies on Industrial Property and Economics at the Law Faculty, University of Buenos Aires, Buenos Aires, Argentina
e-mail: quiess@gmail.com; ceidie@derecho.uba.ar; quies@sion.com

J. Drexl et al. (eds.), *EU Bilateral Trade Agreements and Intellectual Property: For Better or Worse?*, MPI Studies on Intellectual Property and Competition Law 20,
DOI 10.1007/978-3-642-39097-5_5, © Springer-Verlag Berlin Heidelberg 2014

In the field of intellectual property, in particular, the EU aims to support the interests of its companies in acquiring and enforcing patents, copyrights and other rights in foreign markets. This may help European companies to control foreign markets without the need for a permanent commercial presence through the export of products made in European territory.[3] EPAs rely on the minimum standards set out by the Agreement on Trade-related Aspects of Intellectual Property Rights (the TRIPS Agreement) but contain a large number of substantive and enforcement rules that go beyond the obligations established under that Agreement.[4] The increase in the levels and expansion of intellectual property protection are explicit targets of EPAs.[5] They are unlikely to contribute in any manner to support the development of EU partners and may, if full reciprocity is provided for, lead to negative economic and social effects,[6] especially in areas such as access to medicines.[7]

In some cases, the EPAs' obligations expand rights already recognized under the TRIPS Agreement ("TRIPS-plus") while in others they introduce obligations in areas not covered by the Agreement ("TRIPS-extra").[8] One example of the former is the extension of the patent term; the obligation to provide for technological protection measures (TPMs) in the area of copyright is an example of the latter. In both cases, however, new rights and obligations not existing under the TRIPS Agreement are created.

The number of countries subject to these additional TRIPS-plus obligations is substantial and may still expand if current negotiations (e.g. EU-MERCOSUR, EU-India) involve comprehensive intellectual property chapters, as actively sought by the EU. A significant number of members of the World trade Organization (WTO) will, as a result of the combined effect of US FTAs and EPAs, be obliged to grant intellectual property protection beyond what is required under the TRIPS Agreement. Despite this, proponents of such higher standards are likely to face

[3] While there is no conclusive evidence regarding a positive correlation between increased levels of intellectual property protection and inflows of foreign direct investment, several studies have shown increases in developed countries' exports, particularly to countries with strong imitative capabilities (where, in turn, technological acquisition and development is negatively affected). See, e.g., Connolly and Valderrama (2005). On the impact of stronger intellectual property rights on exports from developing countries, see Siew-Yong et al. (2011).

[4] The same applies to the FTAs signed by the USA with some developed and developing countries. The USA is currently engaged in negotiations for an Asia-Pacific trade agreement (the Trans-Pacific Partnership Agreement, or TPP) with proposals for even higher levels of protection. See, e.g., Flynn et al. (2011).

[5] For the sake of simplicity, in the analysis that follows, "EPAs" includes other free trade agreements (FTAs) entered into or under negotiation by the EU.

[6] See, e.g., Karingi et al. (2005). This study concludes that "full reciprocity will be very costly for Africa irrespective of how the issue is looked at. A focus on deepening integration with a view to enhancing intra-African trade would provide positive results", p. x.

[7] See, e.g., Shabalala (2008).

[8] For simplicity, in the remaining text only the expression "TRIPS-plus" will be used.

great obstacles if they attempt to push for a review of the TRIPS Agreement[9] along the lines of the EPAs and FTAs. Thus, the developing countries' refusal to accept a debate on enforcement measures at the Council for TRIPS and the criticism by China and India of the Anti-Counterfeiting Trade Agreement (ACTA)[10] suggest that the WTO continues to be an unfriendly forum for further expansion of intellectual property protection.

Given this unfriendly environment for TRIPS-plus reforms in the WTO, their proponents are likely to continue to seek them at the plurilateral, regional and bilateral levels (ACTA is, in fact, an outstanding example in this regard), as well as in the World Intellectual Property Organization (WIPO).[11]

While a direct influence of EPAs (and other FTAs) in terms of a possible review of the WTO multilateral rules regarding intellectual property is, thus, unlikely, the interpretation of the TRIPS standards may be affected by the adoption and implementation of TRIPS-plus standards in EPAs.

This chapter examines, first, the possibility of an expansive interpretation of TRIPS obligations under the dispute settlement mechanisms of EPAs; second, it discusses the extent to which a WTO panel may enforce TRIPS-plus obligations contained in EPAs. For this purpose, the case of test data protection is analyzed as an example of the possible implications of TRIPS-plus obligations for the interpretation of the TRIPS Agreement.

2 TRIPS Under EPAs' Dispute Settlement Mechanisms

EPAs not only include TRIPS-plus provisions. They also oblige the parties to comply with the obligations provided for by the TRIPS Agreement. Article 139.1 of the EU-CARIFORUM EPA, for instance, establishes that "[t]he EC Party and the

[9] In accordance with Article 71 of the Agreement, "[t]he Council [for TRIPS] may also undertake reviews in the light of any relevant new developments which might warrant modification or amendment of this Agreement". However, any amendment of the Agreement needs approval by two thirds of the WTO members. The only amendment proposed so far (incorporation of a new Article 31*bis* based on the WTO Decision of 30 August 2003 relating to compulsory licenses for the export of medicines) has been open to approval since December 2005.

[10] At the session of the Council for TRIPS of August 2010, for instance, China and India, supported by a number of other developing countries, expressed their concerns about enforcement provisions in bilateral, regional and plurilateral agreements, specifically in the draft ACTA, that went beyond the standards of the TRIPS Agreement.

[11] Norm-setting activities in WIPO have been practically frozen for the last fifteen years as a result of the reluctance of developing countries to embark on negotiations that could lead to higher standards of protection without a proper assessment of their possible development impact. The Singapore Treaty on the Law of Trademarks (so far ratified by 25 countries) is the only international treaty adopted within WIPO in that period. The WIPO General Assembly in 2011 called for a Diplomatic Conference on the Protection of Audiovisual Performances which eventually adopted a new treaty on the matter.

Signatory CARIFORUM States shall ensure an adequate and effective implementation of the international treaties dealing with intellectual property to which they are parties and of the Agreement on Trade-related Aspects of Intellectual Property". Article 139.4 clarifies that in addition and without prejudice to their existing and future international obligations, the EC Party and the Signatory CARIFORUM States "shall give effect to the provisions of this Section [Section 2, Chapter 2]".

The CARIFORUM text makes it clear, hence, that the parties must comply, on the one hand, with the TRIPS Agreement and, on the other, with the additional obligations established in the EPA. As a result, a country party to an EPA may invoke, under the EPA's dispute settlement system, the violation of a particular TRIPS-plus obligation established by an EPA as well as a violation of a TRIPS obligation.

The dispute settlement provisions in all the EPAs are similar.[12] They allow for a choice of forum between the WTO and the EPA dispute settlement system, provided that the subject of the dispute is regulated under the substantive provisions of WTO agreements and the particular EPA.[13] This opens the door for "forum shopping": the complaining party will probably choose the forum most likely to provide a judgment favorable to its own position. One important issue is, therefore, the extent to which the interpretations of TRIPS provisions that may be given by EPA arbitration panels may substantially differ from those of a WTO panel or Appellate Body, and whether such interpretations may subsequently influence WTO jurisprudence.[14] Rulings in the context of free trade agreements have influenced WTO jurisprudence in some cases. For instance, in *Brazil—Tyres* the WTO panel referred to a MERCOSUR ruling in support of its finding that Brazil's exemption for MERCOSUR imports was not "arbitrary" within the meaning of Article XX of the General Agreement on Tariffs and Trade (GATT) of 1994.[15]

Notwithstanding the fact that the interpretive rules of the Vienna Convention on the Law of Treaties (VCLT) may be applied under the EPAs and the WTO dispute settlement systems,[16] the concept of "subsequent practice"[17] and an "evolutionary interpretation" of TRIPS provisions may increase the chances of interpretations beyond what would otherwise be admissible under the WTO dispute settlement

[12] Except for the provisions in the EPAs with Eastern and Southern Africa (ESA) and the East African Community (EAC), which indicate that the dispute settlement provisions will be further negotiated.

[13] Once a party has instituted a dispute settlement proceeding under one of those systems, it can institute a proceeding on the same measure under the other system after the first proceeding has ended.

[14] A different issue, not addressed here, is the extent to which the TRIPS preamble and provisions may have a "mitigating effect" on interpretations given under EPA dispute settlement mechanisms to TRIPS-plus provisions. See, e.g., Xiong (2011).

[15] *Brazil—Measures Affecting Imports of Retreaded Tyres* (DS332) available at http://www.wto.org/english/tratop_e/dispu_e/cases_e/ds332_e.htm.

[16] See, e.g., Part III, Article 18 of the EU-CARIFORUM EPA.

[17] Article 31.3(b) VCLT.

mechanism.[18] In addition, the procedures are different[19] and the EPA dispute settlement systems lack a clear development orientation.

While the EC is bound to exercise due restraint in asking for compensation or adopting remedies in cases of violation of EPA provisions, and should take account of the developing country party,[20] "EPA DS [dispute settlement] mechanisms are a modified version of the WTO DS. The important point is that most of the modifications are reflections of the proposals that the EU put forth for the reform of the WTO DSU [Dispute Settlement Understanding]".[21]

In connection with the EU-ACP agreements,[22] for instance, it has been noted that "analysis of the EPAs DS [dispute settlement] provisions indicates that the deal reached in ACP-EU negotiations has serious shortcomings in terms of its developmental credentials. It seems to be difficult to give a pass mark to the EPA DS mechanisms with respect to their performance on development friendliness".[23]

Moreover, differences in the legal context of EPAs and the TRIPS Agreement may be critical for the interpretation of a TRIPS provision under an EPA dispute settlement system. EPAs (and other FTAs) have as a clear objective the expansion and strengthening of intellectual property rights, thereby providing an inherently biased context for interpretation of substantive and enforcement obligations. The EPA provisions that may be used to elaborate on the contextual framework for their interpretation are not the same as in the TRIPS Agreement.

The EU-CARIFORUM EPA, for instance, refers to Article 8 of the TRIPS Agreement and to the need to ensure a balance between the interests of right-holders and users. It states that

> The EC Party and the Signatory CARIFORUM States agree that the principles set out in Article 8 of the TRIPS Agreement apply to this Section. The Parties also agree that an adequate and effective enforcement of intellectual property rights should take account of the development needs of the CARIFORUM States, provide a balance of rights and obligations between right-holders and users and allow the EC Party and the Signatory CARIFORUM States to protect public health and nutrition. Nothing in this Agreement shall be construed as to impair the capacity of the Parties and the Signatory CARIFORUM States to promote access to medicines.[24]

[18] Some WTO rulings have relied on an "evolutionary interpretation" (see Marceau 2001), but WTO members are not allowed to expand existing obligations.

[19] See, e.g., Karli M (2008). Thus, the dispute settlement mechanisms under EPAs do not offer the possibility of a review of the legal arguments as currently done by the Appellate Body in WTO.

[20] Id., p. 26.

[21] Id., p. 5.

[22] African, Caribbean and Pacific countries that are signatories of the Lomé Convention (1975) and the Cotonou Agreement (2000).

[23] Karli M (2008), p. 33.

[24] Title IV, Chapter II, Section 2, Article 1.2.

However, among the "Principles" of the intellectual property chapter of the cited EPA there is no reference to Article 7 of the TRIPS Agreement,[25] which specifically puts the protection and enforcement of intellectual property in the context of social and economic welfare[26] and is of key relevance for balancing the rights and obligations under the Agreement. Importantly, although Article 7 refers to the contribution that intellectual property *should* make, it is included in the text of the Agreement and not in the preamble and should, hence, "be given greater weight than the treaty's preambular provisions".[27] In *Canada-Patent Protection of Pharmaceutical Products*, a WTO panel stated that the "goals and the limitations stated in Articles 7 and 8.1 must obviously be borne in mind . . . as well as those of other provisions of the TRIPS Agreement which indicate its object and purposes".[28]

The Doha Declaration on the TRIPS Agreement and Public Health (hereinafter "the Doha Declaration")[29] also provides significant elements for the interpretation

[25] Instead, the objectives set forth in the "Innovation and Intellectual Property" chapter are about innovation, competitiveness and protection of intellectual property rights (as an objective in itself), without social or welfare considerations:

Article 132. Objectives. The objectives of this Chapter are to:

(a) promote the process of innovation, including eco-innovation, of enterprises located in the Parties;
(b) foster competitiveness of enterprises and in particular micro-, small and medium-sized enterprises of the Parties;
(c) facilitate the production and commercialisation of innovative and creative products between the Parties;
(d) achieve an adequate and effective level of protection and enforcement of intellectual property rights;
(e) contribute to the promotion of technological innovation and to the transfer and dissemination of technology and know-how;
(f) encourage, develop and facilitate cooperative research and development activities in science and technology between the Parties, as well as to develop lasting relations between the Parties' scientific communities;
(g) encourage, develop and facilitate cooperative production and development activities in the creative industries between the Parties, as well as to develop lasting relationships between the Parties' creative communities;
(h) promote and strengthen regional cooperative activities involving the outermost regions of the European Community, so as to allow these regions and the CARIFORUM States to mutually benefit from their proximity and neighbourhood situation by developing an innovative and competitive regional area.

[26] Article 7: "The protection and enforcement of intellectual property rights should contribute to the promotion of technological innovation and to the transfer and dissemination of technology, to the mutual advantage of producers and users of technological knowledge and in a manner conducive to social and economic welfare, and to a balance of rights and obligations".

[27] Yu (2009), p. 1004.

[28] Paragraph 7.26.

[29] See WT/MIN(01)/DEC/2, http://www.wto.org/english/thewto_e/minist_e/min01_e/mindecl_trips_e.htm.

of TRIPS provisions, particularly those directly or indirectly related to public health. Paragraph 5(a) of the Declaration spells out one of the "flexibilities" in the TRIPS Agreement: "In applying the customary rules of interpretation of public international law, each provision of the TRIPS Agreement shall be read in the light of the object and purpose of the Agreement as expressed, in particular, in its objectives and principles".

References recognizing the importance of the Doha Declaration may be found in the chapters on intellectual property in many EPAs and in other FTAs.[30] However, with the exception of the EU-CARIFORUM EPA,[31] such chapters contain substantive TRIPS-plus provisions that may affect access to drugs. In addition, those references may play a role in interpreting other provisions of the agreements when they are ambiguous, but would not help to mitigate clearly worded TRIPS-plus obligations. In the case of the EU-Colombia-Peru FTA, a reference to the importance of the Doha Declaration is complemented by a provision stating that "in interpreting and implementing the rights and obligations under this Title, the Parties shall ensure consistency with this Declaration".[32]

In summary, while EPAs are not likely to trigger changes in WTO rules concerning intellectual property rights, they may affect the way in which the TRIPS rights and obligations are interpreted under the EPAs' dispute settlement mechanisms. There is a risk of expansive interpretations of the TRIPS obligations that overlook public interests and welfare considerations.[33] Although this risk exists, it is uncertain whether such interpretations may influence, in turn, the way in which disputes are resolved in the WTO, since panels and the Appellate Body are

[30] See, e.g., Article 147(b) of the EU-CARIFORUM EPA; Article 197.2 of the EPA with Peru and Colombia. The US-Chile FTA preamble refers to the "principles" of the Doha Declaration. The preamble of the Anti-Counterfeiting Trade Agreement (ACTA) also contains a reference to the Doha Declaration.

[31] However, Article 163 of the EU-CARIFORUM EPA is TRIPS-plus in requiring signatories to adopt procedures "to enable a right holder who has valid grounds for suspecting that the importation, exportation, re-exportation, entry or exit of the customs territory, placement under a suspensive procedure or placement under a customs free zone or a customs free warehouse of goods infringing an intellectual property right may take place, to lodge an application in writing with competent authorities, administrative or judicial, for the suspension by the customs authorities of the release into free circulation or the retention of such goods." This provision exceeds the enforcement obligations of Article 51 of the TRIPS Agreement, which only requires that WTO members adopt procedures to enable a right holder to act in relation to the *importation* of *counterfeit trademark or pirated copyright*. This provision may unduly block trade in legitimate products, including products in transit, particularly as it may be applied to the alleged infringement of patents that would be extremely difficult for custom authorities to establish on a reasonable basis. See, e.g., Seuba (2010).

[32] Article 197.2. This rule may be useful in some circumstances, for instance, to interpret some exceptions in the agreement, such as the one relating to data exclusivity (Article 231.4). For a general analysis on this issue, see Grosse Ruse-Khan (2011), p. 1.

[33] For instance, an arbitration panel may find admissible the EU's interpretation—discussed below—that Article 39.3 of the TRIPS Agreement imposes an obligation to grant exclusive rights on test data, even in the absence of specific wording to that effect in the EPA.

bound to consider both Articles 7 and 8 of the TRIPS Agreement and, specifically in the case of public health-related matters, the elements provided by the Doha Declaration.

3 Limits to a "More Extensive Protection"

Article 1.1 of the TRIPS Agreement stipulates: "Members shall give effect to the provisions of this Agreement. Members may, but shall not be obliged to, implement in their law more extensive protection than is required by this Agreement, provided that such protection does not contravene the provisions of this Agreement".

This provision means that the imposed obligations constitute the "floor" or base for intellectual property protection, that is, they are *minimum* standards. While developing countries were able to clarify that WTO members "shall not be obliged to . . . implement in their law more extensive protection", this provision opened the door for an aggressive action by the TRIPS proponent countries to later expand such protection through bilateral or regional agreements.

The incorporation of TRIPS-plus standards in EPAs and other FTAs is based on the presumption that TRIPS-plus standards, whatever their content and impact, will not violate the TRIPS Agreement. However, this presumption is not absolute, as indicated by the final proviso of the quoted Article 1.1: "provided that such protection does not contravene the provisions of this Agreement".

The interpretation of this proviso has attracted little attention so far; most commentators seemed to have assumed that, given that the TRIPS Agreement only established a floor, increased levels of protection will, as a matter of principle, never contravene the Agreement's provisions or that the effects of the proviso are limited.[34] But this is not necessarily the case.[35]

Conflicts between more extensive protection and the provisions of the TRIPS Agreement may arise in two circumstances: such protection may be unilaterally created by national laws, or be based on obligations contained in other international treaties, such as an EPA, entered into by two or more WTO members. In the former case, any other WTO member may question the consistency of the higher national legal standards with the TRIPS Agreement. In the latter, challenges may equally be brought by any member, but controversies may also arise between the parties to an EPA. If this were the case, a WTO panel and/or the Appellate Body may need to evaluate the TRIPS consistency of a TRIPS-plus standard contained in another treaty binding the same parties.[36]

The customary principles of treaty interpretation, in particular the principle of an "effective interpretation" (*effet utile*), require the interpreter to give a specific

[34] See, e.g., Frankel (2009).

[35] See, e.g., Grosse Ruse-Khan and Kur (2008).

[36] This hypothesis is considered in the next section.

meaning to the proviso in Article 1.1. This principle has been referred to by the WTO Appellate Body on several occasions.[37] In *Canada-Dairy*, for instance, it was stated that

> the task of the treaty interpreter is to ascertain and give effect to a legally operative meaning for the terms of the treaty. The applicable fundamental principle of *effet utile* is that a treaty interpreter is not free to adopt a meaning that would reduce parts of a treaty to redundancy or inutility.[38]

Similarly, in *Argentina-Footwear (EC)*, the Appellate Body held:

> Yet a treaty interpreter must read all applicable provisions of a treaty in a way that gives meaning to *all* of them, harmoniously. And, an appropriate reading of this "inseparable package of rights and disciplines" must, accordingly, be one that gives meaning to *all* the relevant provisions of these two equally binding agreements.[39]

"To contravene" means to be in "conflict with (a right, principle, etc.), especially to its detriment".[40] According to international law principles, a conflict between provisions in two international treaties, such as an EPA and the TRIPS Agreement, may arise when three conditions are present: a) the WTO members are also parties to the EPA; b) the EPA and the TRIPS Agreement covers the same subject matter; and c) the provisions at stake impose obligations that cannot be reconciled.

Two provisions would be deemed to refer to the same subject matter when their *object* is the same, for instance, protection of test data, border measures or preliminary injunctions. The extent to which the content of the respective provisions are in conflict may be narrowly or broadly interpreted.

Article 30 of the VCLT has been interpreted as incorporating a legal presumption against conflicts, which supports a narrow understanding of "conflict" as situations where different treaties provide for mutually exclusive obligations, that is, obligations that cannot be complied with simultaneously.[41] Under this interpretation,

> States are presumed to enforce their treaty obligations in good faith. The good faith principle also implies that States are presumed to have negotiated all their treaties in good faith, that is, taking into account all their other international law obligations (general principles, custom and treaty obligations). In this sense, States' obligations are cumulative and, thus, should be read together. In this context, the WTO agreement, as with any other treaty, should be interpreted taking into account other relevant and applicable rules between the same parties, with a view to avoiding conflicts with other relevant rules of international law applicable to the relations between the same countries.[42]

---

[37] See, e.g., Van Damme (2009).

[38] See WT/DS103/AB/R, WT/DS113/AB/R, WT/DS103/AB/R/Corr.1, WT/DS113/AB/R/Corr.1, para 133.

[39] See WT/DS121/AB/R, para 81.

[40] http://oxforddictionaries.com/definition/contravene?q=contravene.

[41] See, e.g., Jenks (1953), quoted by Marceau (2001), p. 1084.

[42] Marceau (2001), p. 1089.

Box 1: Eroding TRIPS Flexibilities in the EU-Colombia-Peru FTA

- **Copyright**
  - Technological measures and rights management information
  - Recognition of *droit de suite*
- **Trademarks**
  - Protection of sounds as trademarks
  - Obligation to introduce opposition proceedings and provide public electronic applications and registration databases
- **Geographical indications (GIs)**
  - Expanded level of protection for GIs not related to wines and spirits
- **Industrial designs**
  - Increased rights conferred by registration
- **Test data**
  - Exclusivity of 5 years for pharmaceuticals and 10 years for agricultural chemical products
- **Enforcement**
  - Several provisions inspired by the EC Directive on the Enforcement of IPRs (2004/48) and the European Customs Regulation (1383/2003).
  - Liability of online service providers inspired by the EC Directive on E-commerce (2000/31).

Source: based on a comparative table prepared by Souheir Nadde-Phlix, research fellow, Max Planck Institute for Intellectual Property and Competition Law.

Narrowly construed, the concept of "conflict" would not apply to situations where the provision of one of the treaties is stricter but not incompatible with that of another treaty, such as when it provides discretion or flexibility for a party to opt for an implementation of the obligation on a particular subject matter that is less restrictive than that imposed by the other treaty. Thus, EPAs provide for obligations beyond those imposed by the TRIPS Agreement that erode many of its "flexibilities".[43] As an illustration, Box 1 describes a number of TRIPS-plus

[43] There is extensive literature on the "flexibilities" accorded by the TRIPS Agreement, particularly (but not only) in relation to public health. See, e.g., Velasquez G, Correa C, Seuba X (2012).

obligations found in the EU Colombia-Peru FTA that eliminates TRIPS flexibilities in different fields.

However, under a narrow interpretation, a conflict could only be found when an EPA contravenes "a *mandatory* TRIPS provision instead of an *optional* one".[44] This means that EPAs' obligations on intellectual property that deprive parties of the possibility of adopting alternative, less stringent levels of protection would not "contravene" any TRIPS provision.

Although a narrow interpretation of "conflict" seems a logical outcome of the need to apply international treaties in a mutually supportive and coherent form,[45] a broader understanding is possible, especially in cases where the provision of one of the treaties may undermine or defeat the purpose of the other treaty. Thus, the panel in *European Communities—Regime for the Importation, Sale and Distribution of Bananas (EC—Bananas III)* adopted a broad concept of conflict between treaties' provisions. It stated:

> As a preliminary issue, it is necessary to define the notion of "conflict" laid down in the General Interpretative Note. In light of the wording, the context, the object and the purpose of this Note, we consider that it is designed to deal with (i) clashes between obligations contained in GATT 1994 and obligations contained in agreements listed in Annex 1A, where those obligations are mutually exclusive in the sense that a Member cannot comply with both obligations at the same time, and (ii) the situation where a rule in one agreement prohibits what a rule in another agreement explicitly permits.[46]

In a footnote to this paragraph the panel further elaborated on this concept:

> For instance, Article XI:1 of GATT 1994 prohibits the imposition of quantitative restrictions, while Article XI:2 of GATT 1994 contains a rather limited catalogue of exceptions. Article 2 of the Agreement on Textiles and Clothing ("ATC") authorizes the imposition of quantitative restrictions in the textiles and clothing sector, subject to conditions specified in Article 2:1-21 of the ATC. In other words, Article XI:1 of GATT 1994 prohibits what Article 2 of the ATC permits in equally explicit terms. It is true that Members could theoretically comply with Article XI:1 of GATT, as well as with Article 2 of the ATC, simply by refraining from invoking the right to impose quantitative restrictions in the textiles sector because Article 2 of the ATC authorizes rather than mandates the imposition of quantitative restrictions. However, such an interpretation would render whole Articles or sections of Agreements covered by the WTO meaningless and run counter to the object and purpose of many agreements listed in Annex 1A which were negotiated with the intent to create rights and obligations which in parts differ substantially from those of the GATT 1994. Therefore, in the case described above, we consider that the General Interpretative

[44] Grosse Ruse-Khan (2011), p. 24. Emphasis in the original.

[45] See, in particular, Article 31(c) of the VCLT, which requires the interpreter to take into account "any relevant rules of international law applicable in the relations between the parties".

[46] WT/DS27/R/USA, Report of the Panel, para 7.159. The cited "General Interpretative Note" states that: "In the event of a conflict between a provision of the GATT 1994 and a provision of another Agreement in Annex 1A ..., the provision of the other Agreement shall prevail to the extent of the conflict."

> Note stipulates that an obligation or authorization embodied in the ATC or any other of the agreements listed in Annex 1A prevails over the conflicting obligation provided for by GATT 1994.[47]

A conflict between a TRIPS Agreement provision and a TRIPS-plus provision may exist when, as noted by the panel, "a rule in one agreement prohibits what a rule in another agreement explicitly permits". This may be the case, as exemplified below, where an EPA requires "data exclusivity" that prohibits a member from doing what otherwise the TRIPS Agreement allows (registration of a pharmaceutical or agrochemical product relying on test data developed by third parties).

While the "general rule of interpretation" contained in the VCLT indicates that "any subsequent agreement between the parties regarding the interpretation of the treaty or the application of its provisions" is to be taken into account, together with the context,[48] the concepts of "interpretation" and "application" need to be cautiously considered in order not to add to the obligations assumed by the parties. The Appellate Body has held in this regard that

> We further observe that, in its commentary on the Draft Articles on the Law of Treaties, the International Law Commission (the "ILC") describes a subsequent agreement within the meaning of Article 31(3)(a) of the *Vienna Convention* "as a further *authentic element of interpretation* to be taken into account together with the context". In our view, by referring to "authentic interpretation", the ILC reads Article 31(3)(a) as referring to agreements bearing specifically upon the interpretation of a treaty. In the WTO context, multilateral interpretations adopted pursuant to Article IX:2 of the *WTO Agreement* are most akin to subsequent agreements within the meaning of Article 31(3)(a) of the Vienna Convention....
>
> In our view, the term "application" in Article 31(3)(a) relates to the situation where an agreement specifies how existing rules or obligations in force are to be "applied"; *the term does not connote the creation of new or the extension of existing obligations....*[49]

In accordance with this view, despite the wording in EPAs suggesting that they "specify" TRIPS obligations (see next section), they include provisions that create new obligations or extend the existing ones. If this is the case, the existence of a conflict may be established and there would be no obligation under the WTO dispute settlement to apply such provisions. In light of Articles 3.2 and 19.2 of the DSU, the WTO agreements should "prevail over any other norms to the extent of any inconsistency".[50]

---

[47] Id., fn. 401.

[48] Article 31.2(a).

[49] EC—Bananas III (Article 21.5—Ecuador II) / EC—Bananas III (Article 21.5—US), paras 390-391 (WT/DS27/AB/RW2/ECU, WT/DS27/AB/RW/USA, WT/DS27/AB/RW2/ECU/Corr.1, WT/DS27/AB/RW/USA/Corr.1) (emphasis added).

[50] Bartels (2001), p. 502.

4 Data Exclusivity: A Possible Conflict with TRIPS?

This section discusses a possible conflict between the provisions of the TRIPS Agreement and those of EPAs requiring "data exclusivity", that is, the grant of rights to exclude the use of or reliance on test data by a third party to obtain marketing approval of a pharmaceutical or agrochemical product.

4.1 Test Data Protection Under TRIPS

Article 39.3 of the TRIPS Agreement stipulates the following:

> Members, when requiring, as a condition of approving the marketing of pharmaceutical or of agricultural chemical products which utilize new chemical entities, the submission of undisclosed test or other data, the origination of which involves a considerable effort, shall protect such data against unfair commercial use. In addition, Members shall protect such data against disclosure, except where necessary to protect the public, or unless steps are taken to ensure that the data are protected against unfair commercial use.

The TRIPS Agreement mandates the protection of test data on the safety and efficacy of pharmaceutical and agrochemical products (when a number of requirements are met) under the discipline of *unfair competition*. Paragraph 3 of Article 39 must be read, in effect, in conjunction with paragraph 1 of the same article, which provides: "In the course of ensuring effective protection against unfair competition as provided in Article 10*bis* of the Paris Convention (1967), Members shall protect undisclosed information in accordance with paragraph 2 and data submitted to governments or governmental agencies in accordance with paragraph 3".

If Article 39.3 is interpreted in light of the VCLT, as applied by the GATT/WTO jurisprudence,[51] whatever the intention of the proponents[52] of said article was, the only obligation under this provision is to refrain from obtaining another party's undisclosed test data by means of dishonest practices (such as bribing employees or espionage). This provision does not ban the use of or the reliance on such data by a drug regulatory agency for the marketing approval of a competing product. Thus, the provision does not require the establishment of a period during which such data are subject to exclusive rights or to the payment of compensation to the originator of the data for using or relying on them. Exclusive rights amount to a drastic derogation of the general principle of free circulation of knowledge and

[51] See, for instance, *India—Patents*, where the Appellate Body held that "[b]oth panels and the Appellate Body must be guided by the rules of treaty interpretation set out in the Vienna Convention, and must not add to or diminish rights and obligations provided in the WTO Agreement" (WT/DS50/AB/R, para 46).

[52] During the negotiations, the USA submitted a text that included restrictions on the use of or reliance on test data, but this proposal lacked support and was finally dismissed. See Correa (2002).

information. They cannot be inferred from a text that, unlike other provisions of the TRIPS Agreement,[53] does not indicate in any manner an obligation to provide for a *ius excluendi*.

Interestingly, despite the fact that many countries with significant markets for pharmaceuticals (e.g. Argentina, Brazil, India, Thailand, Venezuela) do not grant "data exclusivity", the USA only once submitted a complaint under the DSU alleging violation of Article 39.3. The case was brought against Argentina. Although the Argentine government refused to change its pro-generics legislation—permissible in its view under Article 39.3 of the TRIPS Agreement—and did not adopt data exclusivity, the case was settled by mutual agreement[54] after near two years of consultations. No other similar complaint has been brought to the WTO, suggesting that developed countries are conscious that they could not prevail in a case on the matter and that bilateral or regional agreements, such as EPAs—where the asymmetry in political and economic power forces potential partners to accept TRIPS-plus obligations[55]—offer an effective alternative route.

4.2 Conflicts Rule and Test Data Protection Under EPAs

The EU FTA with Peru and Colombia stipulates in Article 196.2 ("Nature and scope of the obligations" under Title VII on intellectual property) that:

> The provisions of this Title shall *complement and specify* the rights and obligations of the Parties under the TRIPS Agreement and other multilateral agreements related to intellectual property to which the Parties are party, and therefore, no provision of this Title will contradict or be detrimental to the provisions of such multilateral agreements.[56]

The term "complement" means that new rights and obligations are added; to "specify" suggests that such rights and obligations already exist under the TRIPS Agreement and that the EPA will only *develop* them or include specifics for their implementation. As mentioned above, the EC has argued in the case of test data that the EPAs' provisions do not add to existing obligations under the TRIPS Agreement. According to the EC,

> the only way to guarantee that no "unfair commercial use" within the meaning of Article 39.3 shall be made is to provide that regulatory authorities should not rely on these data for

[53] See, e.g., Article 16 ("The owner of a registered trademark shall have the exclusive right to prevent all third parties not having the owner's consent from . . ."); Article 26 ("The owner of a protected industrial design shall have the right to prevent third parties not having the owner's consent from . . ."); Article 28.1 ("A patent shall confer on its owner the following exclusive rights: (a) where the subject matter of a patent is a product, to prevent third parties not having the owner's consent from the acts of . . .").

[54] See World Trade Organization Dispute Settlement Body, Notification of Mutually Agreed Solution According to the Conditions Set Forth in the Agreement, WT/DS171/3, WT/DS196/4, IP/D/18/Add.1, IP/D/Add.2 (20 June 2002).

[55] See, e.g., Drahos (2003).

[56] Emphasis added.

> a reasonable period of time, the determination of what is a reasonable period of time being left to the discretion of the Members. . ..
>
> In theory, any country maintaining an *effective* system to implement obligations under 39.3, even if different from non-reliance over time, would not be in breach of its TRIPS obligations, but we are not aware of many alternatives and it is clear that what the TRIPS-negotiators had in mind was data exclusivity over a certain period of time. On the other hand, as it does not set any time limit, Article 39.3 would not prevent a country from providing for data exclusivity for an unlimited period of time.[57]

Of course what (some) TRIPS negotiators "had in mind" (in the EC's view) is not a sufficient basis for an interpretation of the provision that would dramatically expand the obligation of the WTO members. The EC has attempted to explain what it deems simply a "lack of clarity" on the basis of the difficulties faced in the negotiations:

> It must be admitted that the wording of Article 39.3 does not, from a *prima facie* reading, appear to impose data exclusivity during a certain period of time. This lack of clarity is the obvious result of a difficult negotiation process where divergences of views arose between developing and industrialised countries as to the necessity of EC/US like type of data protection as well as among industrialised countries on the length of the data exclusivity period.[58]

Article 196.2 of the EU FTA with Peru and Colombia spells out the general presumption of compatibility of the treaties negotiated in good faith. However, despite the statement contained in said Article ("no provision of this Title will contradict or be detrimental to the provisions of such multilateral agreements", including the TRIPS Agreement), such contradiction or detrimental effect may exist. On the one hand, some TRIPS standards may be deemed to provide for the maximum permissible level of protection, such as in the case of the idea/expression dichotomy, the citation right found in Article 10(2) of the Berne Convention[59] and enforcement obligations subject to the general requirement of fairness and equity contained in Article 41.2 of the TRIPS Agreement. On the other hand, some EPA provisions may prevent conduct allowed by the TRIPS Agreement in a manner that amounts to a conflict of law, as interpreted above.

Test data for pharmaceutical and agricultural products is one of the areas where the EU typically requires its potential partners to provide TRIPS-plus obligations.[60] Divergences on this issue have blocked a free trade agreement with India and constitute one of the potentially most controversial issues in the EU-MERCOSUR FTA negotiations.[61] Although the EU was not able to obtain the level of protection it desired,[62] the FTA between the EU and Peru and Colombia exemplifies well the EU's ambitions on this matter. Box 2 contains the test data regime incorporated in that agreement.

---

[57] European Commission Issue Group on Access to Medicines (2001), at 19, 21.

[58] Id., at 19.

[59] Grosse Ruse-Khan and Kur (2008).

[60] Such requirements are also a key element of US FTAs. See, e.g., Roffe and Spennemann (2006).

[61] None of the MERCOSUR countries grant data exclusivity for pharmaceuticals.

[62] The EU demanded ten years of data exclusivity for test data for pharmaceuticals, but it finally agreed on five years, the same term that Colombia and Peru had previously accepted in their FTAs with the USA.

Box 2: Test Data Protection Under the EU-Peru-Colombia FTA
Article 231

1. Each Party shall protect undisclosed test or other data related to safety and efficacy of pharmaceutical products[78] and chemical agricultural products, in accordance with the Article 39 of the TRIPS Agreement and its domestic legislation. [fn 78: . . . For Peru, the protection of the undisclosed information of such products shall be granted against disclosure and the practices that are contrary to honest commercial practices, in accordance with Article 39.2 of the TRIPS Agreement, in absence of specific legislation regarding thereof.]
2. According to paragraph 1, and subject to paragraph 4, when a Party requires, as a condition of approving the marketing of pharmaceutical or of agricultural chemical products which contain new chemical entities, the submission of undisclosed test or other data related to safety and efficacy, that Party shall grant an exclusivity period normally of five years from the date of marketing approval in the territory of that Party for pharmaceutical products, and 10 years for chemical agricultural products, period during which a third party may not commercialize a product based on such data, unless he/she presents proof of the explicit consent of the holder of the protected information or his/her own test data.
3. For the purpose of this Article, a "new chemical entity" is the one which has not been previously approved in the territory of the Party for its use in a pharmaceutical or chemical agricultural product, pursuant to its domestic legislation. Accordingly, the Parties need not apply this Article with respect to pharmaceutical products that contain a chemical entity that has been previously approved in the territory of the Party.
4. The Parties may regulate:
   (a) exceptions for reasons of public interest, situations of national emergency or extreme urgency, when it is necessary to allow access to those data to third parties; and
   (b) abbreviated marketing approval procedures in its territory, relied on a marketing approval granted by another Party. In such case, the period of exclusive use of the data submitted in connection with obtaining the approval shall begin from the date of the first marketing approval relied on, when the approval is granted within six months from the filing of a complete application.
5. With regard to chemical agricultural products, the Parties may provide procedures which make it possible to remit or refer to the undisclosed information on safety and efficacy related to tests and studies that involve

(continued)

Box 2 (continued)

vertebrate animals. During the term of protection, the interested person in using such information shall compensate the holder of the protected information. The costs of such compensation shall be determined in a fair, equitable, transparent and non-discriminatory manner. The right to this compensation shall apply for as long as the protection of the undisclosed information on safety and efficacy lasts.

6. In accordance with the provisions of Article 197 paragraph 5, the protection provided in this Article does not prevent a Party to adopt measures in response to the abuse of intellectual property rights or practices which unreasonably restrain trade.

The EU's attempt to present the enhanced protection of test data (by means of data exclusivity) as a mere development or specification of Article 39.3 of the TRIPS Agreement is evident. Paragraph 1 of Article 231 stipulates: "Each Party shall protect undisclosed test or other data . . . in accordance with the Article 39 of the TRIPS Agreement and its domestic legislation". Moreover, paragraph 2 of the same article stipulates that, "[a]ccording to paragraph 1, and subject to paragraph 4, . . . that Party shall grant an exclusivity period. . . ." This wording suggests, then, that the required exclusivity is granted *in accordance with* the TRIPS Agreement.

However, such exclusivity is in conflict with the doctrine of unfair competition under which test data must be protected, as per the terms of the provisions in Articles 39.1 and 39.3. It is well established and beyond dispute that this doctrine does not confer exclusive rights, but empowers an affected party to take legal actions (provisional or permanent injunctions, claims for damages etc.) in the case of dishonest commercial practices. Introducing data exclusivity prevents a national authority from granting marketing approval to a pharmaceutical or agrochemical product by relying on test data developed by a company different from the applicant, unless authorized to do so by the data "originator". Hence, Article 231 prohibits what the TRIPS Agreement permits. On the basis of the analysis made above, this situation may be understood as a conflict between the two treaties' provisions, that is, a situation where TRIPS-plus provisions *contravene* those in the TRIPS Agreement.

It might be argued, however, that the object of Article 39.3 is protection against unfair commercial practices and that data exclusivity is one of the possible measures to obtain this protection, even more effectively than through a regime of unfair competition. Although this argument certainly carries some weight, the TRIPS provisions must be interpreted in light of Articles 7 and 8 of the Agreement, that is, through a pro-development lens.[63]

---

[63] See Yu (2009), p. 1027.

Box 3: The Doha Declaration on the TRIPS Agreement and Public Health

...

4. We agree that the TRIPS Agreement does not and should not prevent members from taking measures to protect public health. Accordingly, while reiterating our commitment to the TRIPS Agreement, we affirm that the Agreement can and should be interpreted and implemented in a manner supportive of WTO members' right to protect public health and, in particular, to promote access to medicines for all.

In this connection, we reaffirm the right of WTO members to use, to the full, the provisions in the TRIPS Agreement, which provide flexibility for this purpose.

5. Accordingly and in the light of paragraph 4 above, while maintaining our commitments in the TRIPS Agreement, we recognize that these flexibilities include:

In applying the customary rules of interpretation of public international law, each provision of the TRIPS Agreement shall be read in the light of the object and purpose of the Agreement as expressed, in particular, in its objectives and principles.

...

Significantly, paragraph 19 of the Doha Ministerial Declaration instructed the TRIPS Council to take into account in its work the objectives and principles set out in Articles 7 and 8 of the TRIPS Agreement.[64] Moreover, the Doha Declaration on the TRIPS Agreement and Public Health provides important elements for the interpretation of the TRIPS provisions as they relate (as is the case of Article 39.3) to public health. Box 3 includes some of the relevant paragraphs of the Declaration, which explicitly refers to the application of Articles 7 and 8 of the Agreement for reading "each provision" thereof.

Although the Doha Declaration is not strictly an "authoritative interpretation" under WTO law (in terms of Article IX.2 of the Marrakesh Agreement Establishing the WTO), it does provide a framework for a pro-public health interpretation of TRIPS provisions. The European Commission, for instance, stated in a report that

> in the case of disputes (e.g. in the context of WTO dispute settlement procedures) Members can avail themselves of the comfort provided by this Declaration. Panelists are likely to take account of the provisions of the TRIPS Agreement themselves as well as of this complementary Declaration, which, although it was not meant to affect Members' rights and obligations, expresses the Members' views and intentions. Hence, the Declaration is part of the context of the TRIPS Agreement, which, according to the rules of treaty interpretation, has to be taken into account when interpreting the Agreement.[65]

Clearly, protection of data under an unfair competition regime is the best option from the perspective of public health, as it forbids dishonest practices while not unduly delaying the entry of legitimate generic competition. As noted in a UNAIDS report,

---

[64] http://www.wto.org/english/thewto_e/minist_e/min01_e/mindecl_e.htm.

[65] European Commission (2001), p. 2.

> an approach to test data protection, which allows regulatory authorities to rely on the data but not provide generic companies access to it, has important public health benefits. It ensures that generic producers do not need to conduct trials on compounds that have been proven to be efficacious, thus avoiding the imposition of additional costs that may be passed on to the consumer. This approach may also be important for preventing unnecessary and unethical tests, such as repeated human trials for each version of the medicine.[66]

Interestingly, in a "Draft recommendation of the European Ombudsman in his inquiry into complaint 2560/2007/BEH against the European Medicines Agency (EMA)",[67] the Ombudsman dismissed a restrictive interpretation given by the EMA to Article 39.3 of the TRIPS Agreement—which was considered enforceable in the EU legal system—and found that

> Article 39(3) of the TRIPs agreement refers to the protection of data submitted in the framework of marketing approval "against unfair commercial use". Thus, it appeared that, leaving aside the issue of protecting the public, the response to whether access can be granted pursuant to this provision hinged on the future use of disclosed data or the availability of steps to prevent certain future use. . . .
>
> Thus, the Ombudsman considered that granting private access to the complainants, with a view to conducting the scientific study envisaged by them, could reconcile the complainants' interest in getting access with the interest in protecting data against unfair commercial use, in line with Article 39(3) of the TRIPs agreement.[68]

This opinion does not address the issue of availability of test data for the marketing approval of competing products, but does suggest a pro-public health approach in interpreting the EU obligations under Article 39.3. Although EMA's refusal to provide the data would have attained the purpose of protecting them against a possible unfair commercial use, the Ombudsman opted for an interpretation that preserved the legal capacity of the competent authority to release the information for a public health purpose.

Given the possibility of "forum shopping" and that the WTO dispute settlement mechanism "appears to 'attract' jurisdiction rapidly for all WTO-related matters",[69] the EU might hypothetically bring a complaint under this mechanism relating to the protection of test data (for instance, in connection with the extent of the exceptions "for reasons of public interest" allowed under paragraph 4 of Article 231 of the EPA

---

[66] UNAIDS (2011).

[67] The complainants were researchers working for the Nordic Cochrane Centre who applied, via the Danish Medicines Agency, to the European Medicines Agency (EMA) for access to clinical study reports and corresponding trial protocols concerning certain anti-obesity drugs to independently verify their accuracy. These reports and protocols had been submitted to EMA with a view to obtaining marketing approval. See http://www.ombudsman.europa.eu/et/cases/draftrecommendation.faces/pt/4883/html.bookmark.

[68] Id., paras 23 and 39. The Ombudsman made the preliminary finding that, "in view of the insufficiency of its reasoning, EMA's refusal to grant access amounted to an instance of maladministration" (para 41).

[69] Marceau (2001), p. 1082.

with Peru and Colombia) and argue that the data exclusivity regime contained in the FTA with Peru and Colombia just *develops* Article 39.3, and that it is not only compatible with the TRIPS Agreement but is the only way of interpreting Article 39.3 in order to prevent unfair commercial practices effectively.[70] The panel and the Appellate Body would be required, in such a case, to assess whether there is conflict between the TRIPS provision and the FTA regime, beyond the issue of the possible non-compliance by the complained party. In the absence of such assessment, the proviso of TRIPS Article 1.1 would be reduced to inutility, in violation of the already mentioned principle of effective interpretation.

As argued above, in this hypothetical situation, the panel and the Appellate Body may find such conflict if the relevant provisions are interpreted in the framework of Articles 7 and 8 of the TRIPS Agreement and of the Doha Declaration. Importantly, the WTO dispute settlement mechanism should serve "to preserve the rights and obligations of Members under the covered agreements",[71] and one right of WTO members is to adopt measures to protect public health. Even if a conflict were not found, the panel and the Appellate Body would need to recognize that the TRIPS Agreement does not impose any obligation to grant exclusive rights in respect of test data.

5 Conclusions

Given the different context in which the TRIPS and the EPA provisions are likely to be read in case of disputes, arbitral decisions taken in the framework of EPA dispute settlement mechanisms may lead to expansive interpretations of the obligations under the TRIPS Agreement. There is a potential risk that these interpretations may influence those to be made under the WTO dispute settlement mechanism. However, such risk is limited by the constraint imposed, *inter alia*, by Article 3.2 of the DSU and the adherence of the WTO bodies to the customary principles of treaty interpretation enshrined in the VCLT.

The TRIPS Agreement did not issue a blank check for the introduction of TRIPS-plus standards through other international treaties or national laws. Although the limits of what may "contravene" the TRIPS provisions are not precise, there are situations where this may be the case. Given that the TRIPS Agreement and the EPAs' chapters on intellectual property cover, in many cases, the same subject matter and that parties to an EPA may opt for the WTO forum, its

[70] It is worth noting that in *European Communities—Measures Affecting Trade in Large Civil Aircraft*, the Appellate Body admitted to consider, under Art.31 (3) c) of the VCLT, the extent of an obligation under the Agreement on Subsidies and Countervailing Measures in the light of a provision contained in a EU—US bilateral agreement. See, Appellate Body Report WT/DS316/AB/R, para.845-850, available at http://www.wto.org/english/tratop_e/dispu_e/cases_e/ds316_e.htm.

[71] Article 3.2, DSU.

panels and the Appellate Body may be faced with the need to consider the relationship between TRIPS and EPA provisions and, in particular, to evaluate a possible conflict between them. A conflict may be found when the TRIPS-plus provision prohibits a WTO member from doing what is otherwise permitted under the TRIPS Agreement, in a way that does not contribute to the social and economic welfare of the member concerned and, in particular, where such provision undermines the member's right to protect public health.

References

Bartels L (2001) Applicable law in WTO dispute settlement proceedings. J World Trade Law 35(3)

Connolly M, Valderrama D (2005) Implications of intellectual property rights for dynamic gains from trade. Am Econ Rev 95(2):318–322

Correa C (2002) Protection of data submitted for the registration of pharmaceuticals. Implementing the standards of the TRIPS agreement. South Centre/WHO, Geneva

Drahos P (2003) Expanding Intellectual Property's Empire: the Role of FTAs. ICTSD. http://ictsd.org/downloads/2008/08/drahos-fta-2003-en.pdf. Accessed 3 Jan 2012

European Commission (2001) WTO Ministerial Declaration on the TRIPS Agreement and Public Health. European Commission, Brussels, 19 November 2001

European Commission Issue Group on Access to Medicines (2001) Questions on TRIPS and data exclusivity. http://trade.ec.europa.eu/doclib/docs/2006/may/tradoc_122031.pdf. Accessed 30 Jan 2012

Flynn S, Kaminski ME, Baker BK, Koo JH (2011) Public Interest Analysis of the US TPP Proposal for an IP Chapter. Program on Information Justice and Intellectual Property http://infojustice.org/tpp-analysis-december2011. Accessed 23 Jan 2012

Frankel S (2009) Challenging TRIPS-plus agreements: the potential utility of non-violation disputes. J Int Econ Law 12(1023):1033

Grosse Ruse-Khan H (2011) The International Law Relation between TRIPS and Subsequent TRIPS-Plus Free Trade Agreements: towards safeguarding TRIPS flexibilities. J Intellect Prop Law 18(2):1. http://ssrn.com/abstract=1849204. Accessed 20 Jan 2012

Grosse Ruse-Khan H, Kur A (2008) Enough is enough - the notion of binding ceilings in international intellectual property protection (2008). Max Planck Institute for Intellectual Property, Competition & Tax Law Research Paper Series No. 09-01. http://ssrn.com/abstract=1326429 or doi:10.2139/ssrn.1326429. Accessed 3 Jan 2012

Jenks W (1953) The conflict of law-making treaties. Br Yearb Int Law:425 et seq

Karingi S, Lang R, Oulmane N, Perez R, Sadni Jallab M, Ben Hammouda H (2005) Economic and welfare impacts of the EU-Africa Economic Partnership Agreements. African Trade Policy Centre. http://vi.unctad.org/tda/papers/Partial%20Equilibrium%20Models_Ralf_David/Economic%20and%20Welfare%20impacts%20of%20EU-Africa%20EPAs%20(2005)[1].pdf. Accessed 3 Jan 2012

Karli M (2008) Assessing the development friendliness of dispute settlement mechanisms in the economic partnership agreements & an analytical and comparative guide to the dispute settlement provisions in the EU's FTAs. Occasional paper, European Studies Centre. University of Oxford, Oxford

Marceau G (2001) Conflicts of norms and conflicts of jurisdictions. The relationship between the WTO agreement and MEAs and other treaties. J World Trade 35(6):1081–1131

Roffe P, Spennemann C (2006) The impact of FTAs on public health policies and TRIPS flexibilities. Int J Intellect Prop Manage 1(1/2):75–93

Seuba X (2010) Free trade of pharmaceutical products: the limits of intellectual property enforcement at the border. ICTSD, Geneva

Shabalala D (2008) Intellectual Property in European Union Economic Partnership Agreements with the African, Caribbean and Pacific Countries: what way forward after the Cariforum EPA and the Interim EPAs? CIEL. http://www.normangirvan.info/wp-content/uploads/2008/05/shabalala-iprs-in-the-epas.pdf. Accessed 18 Jan 2012

Siew-Yong Y, Chen-Chen Y, Kee-Cheok C, Nai-Peng T (2011) Does protecting intellectual property rights matter for trade? The case of China's exports to ASEAN-5. Afr J Bus Manage 5(2):524–530. http://www.academicjournals.org/AJBM

South Centre (2011) Economic Partnership Agreements in Africa: a benefit-cost analysis. Analytical Note, November 2011. http://www.southcentre.org/index.php?option=com_content&view=article&id=1646:economic-partnership-agreements-in-africa-a-benefit-cost-analysis&Itemid=67&lang=fr. Accessed 3 Jan 2012

UNAIDS (2011) Doha+10 TRIPS flexibilities and access to antiretroviral therapy. http://www.unaids.org/en/media/unaids/contentassets/documents/unaidspublication/2011/JC2260_DOHA+10TRIPS_en.pdf. Accessed 3 Feb 2012

Van Damme I (2009) Treaty interpretation by the WTO appellate body. Oxford University Press, Oxford

Velasquez G, Correa C, Seuba X (2012) IPR, R&D, human rights and access to medicines. An annotated and selected bibliography. South Centre, Geneva

Xiong P (2011) Trips-plus provisions and the approaches to interpretation of free trade agreements and trips: do they affect public health? http://www.law.anu.edu.au/anzsil/ielig/xiong.pdf. Accessed on 15 Feb 2011

Yu P (2009) The objectives and principles of the TRIPS agreement. Houston Law Rev 46(4):1004

EU Economic Partnership Agreements and International Human Rights

Peter K. Yu

Contents

 Kern Family Chair in Intellectual Property Law and Director, Intellectual Property Law Center, Drake University Law School. An earlier version of this chapter was presented at the Max Planck Institute for Intellectual Property and Competition Law Workshop on "Economic Partnership Agreements of the EU: A Step Ahead in International IP Law?" in Frauenchiemsee, Germany. The author would like to thank Josef Drexl, Henning Grosse Ruse-Khan and Souheir Nadde-Phlix for their kind invitations and hospitality and Peter Beyer, Josef Drexl, Henning Grosse Ruse-Khan, Paul Kuruk, Tuomas Mylly, Xavier Seuba, Hanns Ullrich and the workshop participants for their valuable comments and suggestions. He is also grateful to Linzey Erickson and Lindsey Purdy for excellent research and editorial assistance. An expanded version of this chapter, with a focus beyond the EU EPAs, is available at Florida Law Review 64: 1045–1100.

P.K. Yu (✉)
Drake University Law School, Intellectual Property Law Center, 2700 University Ave, Des Moines, IA 50311, USA
e-mail: peter_yu@msn.com

J. Drexl et al. (eds.), *EU Bilateral Trade Agreements and Intellectual Property: For Better or Worse?*, MPI Studies on Intellectual Property and Competition Law 20, DOI 10.1007/978-3-642-39097-5_6, © Peter K. Yu 2014

1 Introduction

In the past decade, the European Union has been actively pushing for the establishment of bilateral, plurilateral and regional economic partnership agreements (EPAs) with its trading partners. These agreements aim to promote free trade, facilitate economic integration and stimulate local development. Of great concern in the intellectual property area are those EPA provisions that call for high standards of protection and enforcement that exceed what is required by the Agreement on Trade-Related Aspects of Intellectual Property Rights (TRIPS Agreement) of the World Trade Organization (WTO).

This chapter examines the impact of the intellectual property chapters in the EPAs on the protection of human rights. It begins by outlining the challenges inherent in any analysis of the interface between intellectual property and human rights. It reminds readers that some of the rights protected under the intellectual property chapters in the EPAs do overlap with rights recognized in existing international or regional human rights instruments. Taking seriously this overlap, the chapter discusses the compatibilities between intellectual property rights and human rights and the resulting synergies created by the EPAs.

The chapter then examines the various impediments the EPAs have posed to greater protection of human rights. In particular, it discusses the conflicts and inconsistencies within the EPAs, lost opportunities for promoting human rights and the indirect systemic tension that the agreements have generated within the human rights system. The chapter concludes with a discussion of normative and systemic adjustments that seek to alleviate the tension or conflict between the intellectual property chapters in the EPAs and the international human rights system.

2 Inherent Challenges

Until recently, policymakers, scholars and activists paid little attention to the implications of the intellectual property system for the protection of human rights. Their position changed, however, with the adoption of the TRIPS Agreement and the increasing push for TRIPS-plus standards through bilateral, plurilateral and regional trade and investment agreements. Although the growing discussion has enriched our understanding of both human rights and intellectual property laws, significant challenges remain in any discussion of the interface between human rights and intellectual property. This section explores three of these challenges.

2.1 IP Rights as Human Rights?

The first challenge concerns the human rights attributes of intellectual property rights. Traditionally, policymakers, international bureaucrats, academic commentators and civil society organizations examine the interface between intellectual property and human rights by using either the conflict approach or the coexistence approach.[1] The conflict approach views the two sets of rights as being in fundamental conflict. The coexistence approach, by contrast, considers them essentially compatible.

Although each of these approaches has benefits and drawbacks, both ignore the fact that *some* attributes of intellectual property rights are protected in international human rights instruments while other attributes do not have any human rights basis at all. Thus, instead of inquiring whether intellectual property and human rights conflict or coexist with each other, it is important to distinguish the human rights attributes of intellectual property rights from the non–human rights aspects of intellectual property protection.

For example, the protection of corporate trademarks is unlikely to be considered a human right, unless one accepts the right to property as a human right *and* equates intellectual property with personal property. Likewise, trade secrets owned by corporations do not have any human rights basis, because they are created or developed by employees. Other examples of existing intellectual property rights that lack human rights aspects are rights in works made for hire, employee inventions, and non-original, non-creative databases; neighboring rights for broadcasters and phonogram producers; exclusive rights for clinical trial data; and protections for the economic investments of institutional authors and inventors.

Article 27(2) of the Universal Declaration of Human Rights (UDHR) states explicitly that "[e]veryone has the right to the protection of the moral and material interests resulting from any scientific, literary or artistic production of which he [or she] is the author". Article 15(1)(c) of the International Covenant on Economic, Social and Cultural Rights (ICESCR) further requires state parties to "recognize the right of everyone ... [t]o benefit from the protection of the moral and material interests resulting from any scientific, literary or artistic production of which he [or she] is the author".

In view of these provisions, the tension between the intellectual property chapters in the EPAs and the existing international human rights instruments is not the simple categorical tension between intellectual property rights and human rights. Rather, tension exists between the non–human rights aspects of intellectual property protection and human rights, including the human rights attributes of intellectual property rights. Although commentators tend to emphasize the conflicts between intellectual property rights and human rights, the intellectual property chapters, in certain circumstances, can create synergy between the EPAs and international or regional human rights instruments.

---

[1] Helfer (2003), pp. 48–49; Torremans (2008), pp. 196–197.

2.2 No Consensus on Human Rights?

The second challenge concerns the type of human rights that the analysis should cover. Despite decades of efforts establishing the international human rights system, countries have yet to agree on the nature, scope and meaning of human rights obligations. While the Vienna Declaration and Programme of Action states that "[a]ll human rights are universal, indivisible and interdependent and interrelated", the document is mostly aspirational.[2] Many governments, policymakers and commentators still have yet to view all forms of human rights as having the same weight and priority. Many of them continue to prioritize civil and political rights over rights of later generations, such as economic, social and cultural rights (second-generation rights) or collective rights for minorities, indigenous peoples and traditional communities (third-generation rights).

To complicate matters, policymakers and commentators subscribe to different conceptions of human rights. While some take a highly *philosophical* approach that relies heavily on first principles and natural law, others take a more *positive* approach that focuses on compromises in existing international or regional human rights instruments. As Richard Falk observes:

> The positivists consider the content of human rights to be determined by the texts agreed upon by states and embodied in valid treaties, or determined by obligatory state practice attaining the status of binding international custom. The naturalists, on the other hand, regard the content of human rights as principally based upon immutable values that endow standards and norms with a universal validity.[3]

Some commentators also question how relatively trivial matters such as intellectual property rights can be equated with such fundamental rights as the prohibition on genocide, slavery and torture; the rights to freedom of thought, expression, association and religion; and the rights to life, food, health, basic education and work.[4] That question was, indeed, raised during the drafting of the UDHR. Alan Watt, the Australian delegate, declared that "the indisputable rights of the intellectual worker could not appear beside fundamental rights of a more general nature, such as freedom of thought, religious freedom or the right to work".[5]

Although both the philosophical and positive approaches have merits, this chapter focuses on the latter, for at least three reasons.[6] First, the drafting histories of the UDHR and the ICESCR have shown that it is difficult enough for countries to achieve a *political* consensus on the rights recognized in the instruments. Given the divergent interests, backgrounds, beliefs and cultures, countries are very unlikely to succeed in achieving an international *philosophical* consensus on these rights.

---

[2] Vienna Declaration and Programme of Action, 12 July 1993, para 5.

[3] Falk (1992), p. 44.

[4] Yu (2007d), p. 713.

[5] Morsink (1999), p. 221.

[6] On the weakness of this approach, see Yu (2007d), pp. 715–716.

As Jack Donnelly reminds us, "few issues in moral or political philosophy are more contentious or intractable than theories of human nature".[7] Thus, it makes great pragmatic sense to focus on rights that have already attained international consensus, if not universal agreement.

Second, international human rights instruments thus far have received significant attention in the international debate concerning the human rights implications of intellectual property protection. The plain language of these instruments is therefore likely to have a significant impact on the future development of the international intellectual property system. While commentators may question whether the UDHR has now achieved the status of customary international law,[8] this declaration, along with other international and regional human rights instruments, has undeniably achieved an international normative consensus.[9]

Third, based on the usual approach to drafting international agreements, the provisions in the international human rights instruments do not necessarily have a commonly agreed-upon purpose (other than a broad one, such as the promotion of human dignity and respect). As James Nickel points out, "people can agree on human rights without agreeing on the grounds of human rights".[10] Moreover, international instruments cannot escape the *realpolitik* of international negotiations no matter how much foresight the drafters had. As one commentator observes:

> [H]uman rights codifications inevitably convey a somewhat incomplete, or even biased, image of what human rights really are. All of them have been drafted and enacted under specific political and economic circumstances, and therefore reflect the mindsets and specific concerns of their drafters and the time they lived in. They are often the fruit of political compromise—a constraint to which moral truth is not exposed.[11]

According to Professor Donnelly, human rights are far from "timeless, unchanging, or absolute; any list or conception of human rights—and the idea of human rights itself—is historically specific and contingent".[12]

2.3 *Human Rights for Corporate Owners?*

The final challenge concerns the increasing willingness of the European Court of Human Rights (ECtHR) to extend human rights protection to non-individuals, such as corporate owners of intellectual property rights. As Laurence Helfer and Graeme Austin observe:

[7] Donnelly (2003), p. 16.

[8] Yu (2007c), p. 1046, fn. 16.

[9] Donnelly (2003), p. 17.

[10] Nickel (2007), p. 177.

[11] Cornides (2004), p. 137.

[12] Donnelly (2003), p. 1.

> Some in the human rights community ... fear that intellectual property owners—in particular, multinational corporations—will invoke the creators' rights and property rights provisions of international instruments to lock in maximalist intellectual property rules that will further concentrate wealth in the hands of a few at the expense of the many.[13]

In *Anheuser-Busch, Inc v. Portugal*, for example, the Grand Chamber of the ECtHR extended the coverage of Article 1 of Protocol No. 1 to the European Convention of Human Rights to both registered trademarks and trademark applications of a multinational corporation.[14] The case concerned a dispute over Portugal's cancellation of the application by a multinational brewery for the BUDWEISER trademark in an effort to protect the appellation of origin BUDĚJOVICKÝ BUDVAR owned by its longstanding Czech rival. Focusing on the right to property, the ECtHR considered the term "possessions" to include trademarks and trademark applications. Following this decision, even a faceless corporation may receive human rights–like protection for its intellectual property.

The willingness of the ECtHR to extend human rights protection to the intellectual property of corporate entities is particularly important to our analysis of the human rights implications of the EPAs. To be certain, one could make a strong argument that corporations aggregate the disparate human rights interests of individuals, such as their individual shareholders. One could also cite the many social benefits created through lawsuits brought by resourceful corporate entities on behalf of individuals whose rights have been violated. Nevertheless, given the considerable disparity in power between transnational corporations and individuals (or even governments representing some of these individuals[15]), the tension created by a system that allows *corporate* owners to demand greater *human* rights protection at the expense of individuals is inherently troubling.

As a conceptual matter, such an expansive view of human rights is also highly problematic. As Professor Donnelly declares emphatically, "[c]ollectivities of all sorts have many and varied rights. But these are not—cannot be—human rights, unless we substantially recast the concept".[16] It is one thing to give corporations standing to bring human rights claims on behalf of individuals, but quite another to allow corporate owners to claim that their "human" rights have actually been violated.[17] This chapter therefore focuses only on individuals; it does not explore the EPA's impact on the human rights–like protection afforded to corporate owners that the ECtHR has recently recognized.

Moreover, if corporate owners have rights, they should also have human rights responsibilities. The lack of such responsibilities is indeed the reason why we need to better balance the protection and enforcement of intellectual property rights against international human rights commitments. In recent years, international

---

[13] Helfer and Austin (2011), pp. 504–505.

[14] *Anheuser-Busch, Inc. v. Portugal*, 45 ECHR 36 (2007) (Grand Chamber).

[15] Hestermeyer (2007), pp. 94–95.

[16] Donnelly (2003), p. 25.

[17] Yu (2007c), pp. 1130–1131; Yu (2007d), p. 730.

human rights bodies have increasingly outlined the vast responsibilities of corporate owners in areas involving intellectual property protection and enforcement.

For example, in its authoritative interpretative comment on the right to health, the Committee on Economic, Social and Cultural Rights declares: "While only States are parties to the [ICESCR] and thus ultimately accountable for compliance with it, all members of society— . . . including . . . the private business sector—have responsibilities regarding the realization of the right to health".[18] The preamble to the Human Rights Guidelines for Pharmaceutical Companies in Relation to Access to Medicines similarly states: "Pharmaceutical companies, including innovator, generic and biotechnology companies, have human rights responsibilities in relation to access to medicines".[19] Guideline 26, in particular, stipulates that these companies "should make and respect a public commitment not to lobby for more demanding protection of intellectual property interests than [that] required by TRIPS, such as additional limitations on compulsory licensing".

3 Compatibilities and Synergies

Although commentators remain concerned about the adverse impact of intellectual property rights on the human rights system, the protection and enforcement of those rights can be consistent with a country's human rights commitments. In fact, because some attributes of intellectual property rights are protected by international or regional human rights instruments, greater protection of those attributes can promote the protection of human rights.

In the EPAs, the intellectual property chapters include provisions covering a wide variety of intellectual property rights, ranging from copyrights to patents and from geographical indications to *sui generis* database protection. Although an ongoing debate exists concerning whether international human rights instruments recognize the right to property[20] and whether intellectual property should be identified as personal property,[21] many commentators have equated the protection of intellectual property rights with the protection of human rights. Their view is indeed strongly supported by the ECtHR's interpretation of Article 1 of Protocol No. 1 to the European Convention of Human Rights. Intellectual property is also explicitly covered in the right-to-property provision in Article 17(2) of the Charter of Fundamental Rights of the European Union, which recently entered into force following the adoption of the Lisbon Treaty on the Functioning of the European Union.

---

[18] Committee on Economic, Social and Cultural Rights (2000), para 42.

[19] The Guidelines were included as an annex in Human Rights Council (2008).

[20] Yu (2007d), pp. 731–736.

[21] Raustiala (2007), p. 1032.

Even for those refusing to equate intellectual property rights with human rights, the intellectual property chapters do protect important human rights attributes of intellectual property rights. To begin with, these chapters protect the *material* interests in the creations of individual authors and inventors as recognized in international human rights instruments. While not all forms of intellectual property rights should be protected at the level of human rights, copyrights and patents clearly implicate the material interests of individual authors and inventors.

The intellectual property chapters also offer important protection to the *moral* interests in the creations of individual authors and inventors. For instance, the provisions on copyright and related rights help strengthen the protection of moral rights; they ensure proper identification and attribution of the creative work and prevent the work from being recoded or otherwise modified in a manner that would prejudice the author's honor or reputation. The provisions on copyright management information and the requirement that the EPA parties ratify the 1996 Internet Treaties of the World Intellectual Property Organization (WIPO) also serve similar purposes. In addition, the provisions on patents help ensure the recognition of individual inventors, whose contributions patent grants will acknowledge.[22]

Likewise, the provisions on geographical indications can help indigenous peoples and traditional communities obtain the much-needed protection of the moral and material interests in their creations.[23] The provisions on the protection of traditional knowledge and cultural expressions can also preserve the ways of life and economic and cultural heritage of these individuals and communities.[24] By fostering the equitable sharing of benefits, these provisions thereby promote the right to self-determination, the right to development, the right to cultural participation and development and the right to the benefits of scientific progress of these individuals and communities. As far as biodiversity, seeds, plant genetic resources and traditional agrarian practices are concerned, such protection could implicate the rights to adequate food and health.

From the human rights standpoint, the protection of traditional knowledge and cultural expressions is rather important. As stated in the Declaration on the Rights of Indigenous Peoples, which the United Nations General Assembly adopted in September 2007:

> Indigenous peoples have the right to maintain, control, protect and develop their cultural heritage, traditional knowledge and traditional cultural expressions, as well as the manifestations of their sciences, technologies and cultures, including human and genetic

---

[22] Article 4*ter* of the Paris Convention for the Protection of Industrial Property stipulates that "the inventor shall have the right to be mentioned as such in the patent".

[23] Nevertheless, the protection of geographical indications could also undermine the protection of human rights if the former creates a trade barrier by imposing unfair restrictions on the ability of local producers to rename, label, remarket or brand their products. Musungu (2009), p. 31.

[24] Helfer and Austin (2011), p. 3.

> resources, seeds, medicines, knowledge of the properties of fauna and flora, oral traditions, literatures, designs, sports and traditional games and visual and performing arts. *They also have the right to maintain, control, protect and develop their intellectual property over such cultural heritage, traditional knowledge, and traditional cultural expressions.*[25]

Although this Declaration does not cover intellectual property rights per se, the protection of indigenous heritage is likely to have serious ramifications for the protection of intellectual property rights. The Declaration's focus on the protection of "cultural heritage, traditional knowledge and traditional cultural expressions" also echoes provisions in the UDHR, the International Covenant on Civil and Political Rights, the ICESCR, and other international and regional human rights instruments.[26]

Moreover, the EPAs include in their intellectual property chapters abuse-of-rights provisions to promote competition, which complement other EPA provisions related to competition law. The chapters also include technology transfer provisions, which could promote the protection of human rights, in particular the right to the benefits of scientific progress. The scope and extent of such protection, however, will depend on how seriously signatory countries take the obligations under those provisions. For example, Articles 66.2 and 67 of the TRIPS Agreement outline the obligations of developed countries to promote technology transfer, technical cooperation and legal assistance in developing and least-developed countries. Even though the Doha Ministerial Decision of 14 November 2001 reaffirmed the mandatory nature of these obligations, developed countries thus far have failed to take them seriously.

Finally, if trademark protection in the EPAs could be extended to cover personality interests, such as those protections found under the right of publicity in the United States, the intellectual property chapters could provide important protection to individuals—especially celebrities—against the unauthorized use of their names, likenesses, images, voices or other personal attributes. Such protection may also enhance the protection against privacy intrusions, which goes hand in hand with personality rights.[27] Although the right to privacy is generally not covered within the scope of intellectual property rights, the intellectual property chapters do contain provisions to ensure proper protection of personal data and of informational privacy.

---

[25] United Nations Declaration on the Rights of Indigenous Peoples, 13 September 2007, Art. 31(1) (emphasis added).

[26] Universal Declaration of Human Rights, 10 December 1948, Art. 27(1); International Covenant on Civil and Political Rights, 16 December 1966, Art. 27; International Covenant on Economic, Social and Cultural Rights, 16 December 1966, Art. 15(1)(a); Convention (No. 169) Concerning Indigenous and Tribal Peoples in Independent Countries, 27 June 1989, Art. 15(2).

[27] Zapparoni (2004), p. 706.

4 Conflicts, Inconsistencies and Lost Opportunities

Although the intellectual property chapters in the EPAs can promote the protection of human rights, they can also frustrate such protection. Indeed, many commentators believe that the chapters would frustrate such protection more than they promote it. The human rights impediments created by the EPAs can arise in two different ways: (1) directly through the tension created by the language used in the intellectual property chapters in the EPAs and (2) indirectly through an emphasis on trade, economic partnerships and non-multilateral approaches that eventually divert time, resources, energy and attention from the further development of the international human rights system. This section discusses direct impediments, and the next section examines indirect impediments.

At the normative level, direct human rights impediments can take the form of conflicts or inconsistencies between the intellectual property chapters and international human rights instruments. They can also take the form of lost opportunities resulting from the failure of the EPAs to promote the protection of human rights, even though such protection would not create any direct conflict within the intellectual property chapters.[28] These lost opportunities are due in large part to the misguided and unproven assumption that more intellectual property rights are always better. At times, developed countries and their policymakers seek to strengthen the levels of protection and enforcement of intellectual property rights *at all costs*, without taking full account of the many spillover effects in the human rights arena.

To help us better understand the potential conflicts, inconsistencies and lost opportunities, this section focuses on three debates in areas where intellectual property rights have posed significant challenges to the protection of human rights. It does not, however, identify each individual provision in the intellectual property chapters in light of the large number of interrelated provisions involved and the wide variety of human rights implicated in the debates.

The most widely cited debate concerns the much-needed access to essential medicines in less-developed countries,[29] which is impeded by the strong protection of patents and clinical trial data as well as heightened measures that restrict parallel imports while mandating the seizure of in-transit generic drugs. This debate has caught the attention of the WTO, WIPO, the World Health Organization (WHO) and other international intergovernmental bodies.

The debate over access to essential medicines implicates both the right to life and the right to health. Article 3 of the UDHR explicitly provides: "Everyone has the right to life, liberty and security of person". Article 25(1) further recognizes that

[28] Musungu (2009), p. 35.

[29] The TRIPS Agreement distinguishes between developing and least-developed countries. This chapter uses the term "less-developed countries" to denote both developing and least-developed countries. When referring to a specific country group, the chapter may return to use of the terms "developing countries" and "least-developed countries".

every person has "the right to a standard of living adequate for the health and well-being of himself [or herself] and of his [or her] family, including food, clothing, housing and medical care and necessary social services". Echoing this provision, the preamble to the WHO Constitution declares: "The enjoyment of the highest attainable standard of health is one of the fundamental rights of every human being without distinction of race, religion, political belief, economic or social condition". While the right to life has arguably entered into customary international law, a raging debate continues over the legal status of the right to health.[30]

Regardless of the legal status of the right to health, the HIV/AIDS crises in less-developed countries have led many policymakers, commentators and activists to question the expediency and appropriateness of the existing intellectual property system. Indeed, concerns over these crises led WTO members to adopt the Doha Declaration on the TRIPS Agreement and Public Health, which "recognize[d] the gravity of the public health problems afflicting many developing and least-developed countries, especially those resulting from HIV/AIDS, tuberculosis, malaria and other epidemics".

A few years later, the member states adopted a pioneering protocol to formally amend the TRIPS Agreement by adding Article 31*bis*.[31] If ratified by two-thirds of the WTO membership, the proposed amendment will allow countries with insufficient or no manufacturing capacity to import generic versions of patented pharmaceuticals. As of this writing, more than a third of the 159 WTO member states, including the United States, India, Japan, China and members of the European Union, have ratified the proposed amendment.[32]

Interestingly, some commentators have suggested that the right to health can go in the opposite direction. For example, victims of harmful diseases can use this right to argue for the need to provide incentives for pharmaceutical manufacturers to develop drugs that treat, prevent or cure diseases. Although the intellectual property system provides the much-needed incentives for the development of new pharmaceuticals, commentators continue to disagree over whether some of these incentives can be generated outside the intellectual property system or through other funding models, such as grants, subsidies, prizes, advance market commitments, reputation gains, open-source drug discovery, patent pools, public-private partnerships or equity-based systems built upon liability rules.[33] There is also an ongoing debate concerning the optimal levels of patent protection for less-developed countries and whether existing protections have already exceeded those levels.[34] As Josh Lerner observes: "Almost all economists would agree that some intellectual property protection is better than no intellectual property protection

[30] e.g. Borges Barbosa et al. (2007), pp. 131–133; Hestermeyer (2007), pp. 76–136.

[31] Yu (2007a), pp. 872–886.

[32] World Trade Organization (2011).

[33] Pogge et al. (2010); Van Overwalle (2009); Yu (2007c), pp. 1089–1092.

[34] Maskus and Reichman (2005), pp. 36–39.

at all. But this does not mean that very strong protection is better than a more moderate level of protection".[35]

A second debate concerns access to information technology, communications infrastructure, computer software, electronic databases and digital content. Such access is impeded by the protection of copyrights, databases and technological measures. This debate implicates the rights to education and freedom of expression. Because education directly affects one's ability to fully realize oneself, the impeded access has troubled those adopting the human capabilities or human flourishing approaches to human rights.[36] The issue regarding access to knowledge further ties the debate on intellectual property and human rights to the older debate about the global digital divide[37] and to a much newer one concerning access to knowledge.[38]

Thanks to the internet and new communications technologies, the debate on access to information technology has now caught the attention of not only civil liberties groups, but also the United Nations and other international intergovernmental organizations. Held in two phases in Geneva and Tunis, the World Summit on the Information Society sought to address the concerns raised by the growing digital divide in less-developed countries and the possibility that these countries might lose out on many unprecedented opportunities generated by the information revolution.[39] This summit led to the launch of the Internet Governance Forum (IGF), which was created to promote a "multilateral, multi-stakeholder, democratic and transparent" policy dialogue on internet governance.[40] IGF meetings have since been convened in Athens, Rio de Janeiro, Hyderabad, Sharm El Sheikh, Vilnius, Nairobi and Baku.

In recent years, the adoption of the graduated response system has elicited strong criticisms in the human rights arena.[41] Of primary concern are the human rights implications of internet disconnection, the system's most draconian sanction. From the human rights standpoint, using suspension or termination of internet service as a remedy to alleged copyright infringement is highly problematic. As Frank La Rue, the Special Rapporteur on the Promotion and Protection of the Right to Freedom of Opinion and Expression, declared in his recent report:

> The Special Rapporteur considers cutting off users from Internet access, regardless of the justification provided, including on the grounds of violating intellectual property rights law, to be disproportionate and thus a violation of article 19, paragraph 3, of the International Covenant on Civil and Political Rights. . . .
>
> The Special Rapporteur [further] calls upon all States to ensure that Internet access is maintained at all times, including during times of political unrest. In particular, the Special

[35] Lerner (2010), p. 32.

[36] Helfer and Austin (2011), p. 322. On the human capabilities and human flourishing approaches to human rights, see Nussbaum (2001, 2011); Sen (1999).

[37] Yu (2002).

[38] Kapczynski (2008); Krikorian and Kapczynski (2010).

[39] Yu (2005).

[40] World Summit on the Information Society (2005), paras 72–73.

[41] Yu (2010c).

> Rapporteur urges States to repeal or amend existing intellectual copyright laws which permit users to be disconnected from Internet access, and to refrain from adopting such laws.[42]

The Special Rapporteur's concern and request are understandable. After all, repressive governments have recruited internet service providers to serve as gatekeepers to help censor digital content and restrict information flows.[43] While the graduated response system protects intellectual property rights holders, as opposed to governments, its impact on individual freedom of expression is not that different from the impact of government censorship.

Indeed, as I have pointed out elsewhere, the developed countries' increasing push for draconian measures to respond to enforcement problems in the digital environment has slowly backfired on their longstanding interests in promoting free speech, free press, human rights and civil liberties abroad.[44] From the human rights standpoint, those EPA provisions that call for internet disconnection, greater intermediary liability for internet service providers and tougher criminal penalties for unauthorized dissemination of online content have raised very serious concerns.

The final debate concerns the role of the intellectual property system in response to challenges posed by global climate change. As the debate has emerged only recently, it is unclear what rights will be implicated, what limitations and exceptions will be introduced and how and whether the overall intellectual property system will be changed. Indeed, the rights involved are more likely to be covered in the category of lost opportunities than in the category of conflicts or inconsistencies.

Nevertheless, it is worth noting that the debate will implicate such important human rights as the rights to health, adequate housing, adequate food, water and development.[45] Because of the asymmetry in resource endowment, less-developed countries with significant populations and resources in areas vulnerable to floods, hurricanes, typhoons, tsunamis, severe drought, desertification or forest decay will likely suffer more than others if the intellectual property system is not better managed to respond to climate change.

5 Systemic Tension

In addition to the above conflicts and inconsistencies, the intellectual property chapters in the EPAs have created considerable tension between the intellectual property and human rights systems. Even in areas where no direct conflicts or inconsistencies arise, the chapters could distort the work of the international human

[42] Human Rights Council (2011), paras 78–79.

[43] Yu (2010a), p. 715; Yu (2010c), p. 1402.

[44] Yu (2011a), pp. 928–929.

[45] International Council on Human Rights Policy (2010), p. 4.

rights system by creating an undue emphasis on trade, economic partnerships and non-multilateral approaches. They could also divert time, resources, energy and attention from the further development of the international human rights system.

5.1 *Intellectual Property v. Human Rights*

Compared with the intellectual property system, the human rights system has a distinctively different culture, language and forum structure as well as drastically different approaches to negotiation and conflict resolution. The position human rights advocates take often does not coincide with that taken by intellectual property rights holders and their supportive governments.[46] The latter's views are often colored by the trade-based—and, at times, trade-only—approach developed through the founding of the WTO and the adoption of the TRIPS Agreement. It is therefore no surprise that commentators have heavily criticized the WTO panels and the Appellate Body for failing to protect important human rights.[47]

Indeed, the tension between the WTO and the international human rights system has led UN human rights bodies to heavily criticize the TRIPS Agreement. For example, in Resolution 2000/7, the UN Sub-Commission on the Promotion and Protection of Human Rights (UN Sub-Commission) stated that "the implementation of the TRIPS Agreement does not adequately reflect the fundamental nature and indivisibility of all human rights".[48] Noting the "apparent conflicts between the intellectual property rights regime embodied in the TRIPS Agreement, on the one hand, and international human rights law, on the other", the Sub-Commission underscored the "social function of intellectual property" and reminded governments of "the primacy of human rights obligations over economic policies and agreements". The resolution also requested "[g]overnments and national, regional and international economic policy forums to take international human rights obligations and principles fully into account in international economic policy formulation".

Likewise, Mary Robinson, the UN High Commissioner for Human Rights, released a report highly critical of the TRIPS Agreement.[49] The report provided five observations concerning the potential challenge for developing a human rights approach to the Agreement. First, the High Commissioner noted:

---

[46] Gervais (2008), p. 22.

[47] Broude (2010); Howse (2000).

[48] Sub-Commission on Human Rights (2000).

[49] Commission on Human Rights (2001).

> [T]he overall thrust of the TRIPS Agreement is the promotion of innovation through the provision of commercial incentives. The various links with the subject matter of human rights—the promotion of public health, nutrition, environment and development—are generally expressed in terms of exceptions to the rule rather than the guiding principles themselves and are made subject to the provisions of the Agreement.

Second, "while the [TRIPS] Agreement identifies the need to balance rights with obligations, it gives no guidance on how to achieve this balance". Third, because of the required minimum standards, the TRIPS Agreement has taken away a high degree of autonomy and a considerable amount of policy space from the WTO member states. Fourth, and relatedly, "the protection contained in the TRIPS Agreement focuses on forms of protection that have developed in industrialized countries". The protection less-developed countries are required to offer therefore does not always take account of local needs, interests and conditions. Finally, under the current international intellectual property system, limited attention has been devoted to the protection of "the cultural heritage and technology of local communities and indigenous peoples".

Notwithstanding these concerns, the High Commissioner recognized the flexibilities built into the TRIPS Agreement and noted that "much still depends on how the ... Agreement is actually implemented". While these flexibilities are important and may help retain the balance in the international intellectual property system, it is important to remember that countries need expertise and resources to take advantage of these flexibilities. As UNCTAD reminded us in *The Least Developed Countries Report 2007*:

> Even with its inbuilt flexibilities, the TRIPS Agreement is highly problematic for [least-developed countries] owing to the high transaction costs involved in complex and burden-some procedural requirements for implementing and enforcing appropriate national legal provisions. [These countries] generally lack the relevant expertise and the administrative capacity to implement them.[50]

In sum, as shown in the UN Sub-Commission's and High Commissioner's analyses of the human rights impact of the TRIPS Agreement, obligations in international intellectual property agreements—including the EPAs—could create tension between the intellectual property and human rights systems. Even if tension does not exist on the surface, the obligations could create a mismatch between the adopted standards and local conditions.[51] They could also divert the scarce economic resources from other important public needs. Such diversion is particularly likely in the enforcement area.[52]

---

[50] UNCTAD (2007), p. 99.

[51] Yu (2006), pp. 42–50; Yu (2007a), pp. 889–891.

[52] Fink (2009), p. 2; Li and Correa (2009), p. 210; Musungu (2009), p. 61; Xue (2009), p. 143; Yu (2010b), pp. 2–6.

5.2 Bi/Plurilateral v. Multilateral

Although the intellectual property chapters in the EPAs have created significant tension between the intellectual property and human rights systems, the bilateral and plurilateral approaches the European Union used to establish these agreements have raised additional concerns. By going outside the multilateral system, the EPAs have undermined the existing multilateral approach to international norm-setting in both the intellectual property and human rights arenas.

As commentators have widely recognized, the development of the highly controversial Anti-Counterfeiting Trade Agreement (ACTA), the equally problematic Trans-Pacific Partnership Agreement and other TRIPS-plus non-multilateral agreements is not only an effort to strengthen the protection and enforcement of intellectual property rights, but also an indictment of the deficiencies in the TRIPS Agreement and the multilateral approach used in completing the WTO rounds of trade negotiations.[53] By changing countries' preference for multilateral approaches, the establishment of EPAs has therefore posed significant challenges to the stability of both the international trading system and the international human rights system.[54] These bilateral and plurilateral negotiations may further alienate a country's trading partners, thereby making it more difficult for the country to undertake multilateral discussions in the future.[55]

Even worse, by fragmenting the international regulatory system, the continued push for EPAs has forced countries to divert scarce time, resources, energy and attention from other international intergovernmental initiatives, including the further development of the international human rights system. In less-developed countries where resources are scarce and where personnel dedicated to the negotiation of international human rights instruments may overlap with those involved in developing international intellectual property agreements, the negotiation of EPAs will inevitably deplete resources that could otherwise be used to strengthen human rights protection.

It is important to remember that not every country has the ability to undertake discussions in a multitude of fora—in this case, in both intellectual property and human rights fora as well as in both multilateral and non-multilateral processes. Even the United States or the European Union could not devote the same amount of time, energy and attention to the multilateral process had they been asked to negotiate a large number of bilateral and plurilateral agreements alongside the ongoing multilateral negotiations.[56] With significantly more limited resources, less-developed countries most certainly would do much worse.

[53] Atik (2012), p. 145; Yu (2011c, d), pp. 511–514.

[54] Yu (2011b), p. 976.

[55] Cho (2004), p. 239; Leaffer (1991), p. 297; Yu (2011b), p. 976.

[56] Directorate General for Trade (2005), p. 5; Schott (2004), pp. 15–16.

Moreover, as Eyal Benvenisti and George Downs insightfully observe, the growing proliferation of international regulatory institutions with overlapping jurisdictions and ambiguous boundaries could help powerful countries preserve their dominance in the international arena.[57] The growing complexities could also result in what Kal Raustiala describes as "strategic inconsistencies", which help alter, undermine or put pressure on unfavorable norms in the international human rights system.[58] Such complexities could further upset the existing coalition dynamics between international actors and institutions, thereby threatening to reduce the bargaining power and influence less-developed countries have obtained through past coalition-building initiatives.[59]

6 Reconciliation and Adjustments

To reconcile the conflicts and inconsistencies, and to alleviate the tension, between the intellectual property and human rights systems, this chapter proposes two different sets of adjustments. The first set focuses on normative challenges, while the second responds to systemic challenges.

6.1 Normative Adjustments

As discussed earlier, some attributes of intellectual property rights are protected by international human rights instruments. A satisfactory resolution of the tension between the intellectual property and human rights systems therefore requires a careful delineation of the different attributes of intellectual property rights. After all, the Committee on Economic, Social and Cultural Rights stated clearly that, "[i]n contrast to human rights, intellectual property rights are generally of a temporary nature, and can be revoked, licensed or assigned to someone else".[60]

From the human rights standpoint, there are two different types of conflicts: external conflicts and internal conflicts.[61] External conflicts arise at the intersection

[57] Benvenisti and Downs (2007).

[58] Helfer (2004), p. 14; Raustiala (2007), pp. 1027–1028.

[59] Okediji (2003), p. 373; Yu (2007b), pp. 17–18.

[60] Committee on Economic, Social and Cultural Rights (2006), para 2. On this general comment, see Helfer (2007).

[61] In addition to these two sets of conflicts, which are true conflicts, it is also worth noting the possibilities for false conflicts (similar to those identified by conflict-of-law scholars). One commentator, for example, contends that market failures can precipitate false conflicts. Foster (2008), pp. 305–306.

between human rights and the non–human rights aspects of intellectual property protection. Internal conflicts, by contrast, arise at the intersection between rights protecting the human rights attributes of intellectual property and other forms of human rights. These conflicts take place within the human rights system even though they also implicate intellectual property protection.

With respect to external conflicts, countries can consider the introduction of limitations and exceptions either within the intellectual property system or without. Externally, countries can embrace the principle of human rights primacy the UN Sub-Commission outlined in Resolution 2000/7. In the event of a conflict between intellectual property rights and human rights, countries can ensure proper protection of human rights by using certain human rights to pre-empt intellectual property rights. For example, the rights to life and health can be used to safeguard against the over-protection of pharmaceutical patents or clinical trial data. To some extent, greater utilization of the human rights system may help less-developed countries uphold the flexibilities in the TRIPS Agreement.

Nevertheless, authors, inventors or their corporate owners may abuse the human rights system. Because those attributes or forms of intellectual property rights that do not have any human rights basis are likely to be deemed less important through a human rights lens, without the proper safeguards, pre-emption based on the principle of human rights primacy could significantly reduce the incentives generated by the existing intellectual property system.

Internally, countries can proactively introduce limitations and exceptions into the intellectual property system. They can also adopt safeguard provisions to ensure better protection of human rights. A recent example is Article 27 of ACTA, which, as a compromise, includes safeguard clauses in three sub-provisions to preserve "fundamental principles such as freedom of expression, fair process, and privacy".[62] Although these clauses may be a redeeming feature of this highly controversial treaty, it remains to be seen whether they can alleviate the tension between intellectual property rights and human rights. After all, ACTA member states, especially the powerful ones, could deem the safeguard provisions as merely hortatory, as they did in regard to Articles 7 and 8 of the TRIPS Agreement and to the Doha Declaration.[63] The effectiveness of these safeguard clauses could also be undermined by a member state's insistence that the human rights conflicts have been internally resolved through the flexibilities built into the intellectual property system.

A better alternative, therefore, is for countries to clearly delineate the limitations or exceptions available to individuals. Article 6(4) of the EU Information Society Directive, for instance, requires each member state to

[62] Anti-Counterfeiting Trade Agreement, 1 May 2011, Arts 27.2–27.4.

[63] Chon (2006), p. 2843; Correa (2007), p. 93; Gorlin (1999), p. 16; Yu (2009), p. 1003.

> take appropriate measures to ensure that rightholders make available to the beneficiary of [the specified] exception or limitation provided for in national law ... the means of benefiting from that exception or limitation, to the extent necessary to benefit from that exception or limitation and where that beneficiary has legal access to the protected work or subject-matter concerned.

Such a clearly delineated exception not only strikes a better balance in the intellectual property system, but also ensures the proper recognition of the human rights interests of individual users.

With respect to internal conflicts, however, the resolution of these conflicts will require more complicated approaches. In an earlier work, I outlined three different approaches that can be used to resolve these conflicts: (1) just remuneration; (2) core minimum; and (3) progressive realization.[64] For the purposes of this chapter, the most important is the just remuneration approach, which is specially designed for situations involving an unavoidable conflict between two sets of human rights. Under this approach, authors and inventors hold a right to remuneration, rather than maintaining exclusive control; meanwhile, individuals obtain a human rights–based compulsory license, as opposed to a free license.

Consider, for example, a conflict involving a newspaper's freedom of expression and the author's moral and material interests in his or her creation.[65] If the publication of a news account is of significant public interest and high political value (for example, when the author is a public figure), the human rights interest in freedom of expression will ensure the publication of the news account (that is, no injunction). Meanwhile, the author will receive proper compensation for the injury to the creative interest through the introduction of a human right–based compulsory license. Although this outcome may not please either party, it strikes a reasonable compromise from the human rights standpoint.

6.2 *Systemic Adjustments*

At the systemic level, countries can consider building the infrastructure needed to promote the protection of human rights. For example, a country can demand the inclusion of human rights impact assessments before the adoption of new EPAs or the introduction of new legislation that seeks to implement those agreements. Impact assessment has become increasingly common in not only the human rights

64 Yu (2007c), pp. 1094–1123.

65 This hypothetical draws on the famous case of *Ashdown v. Telegraph Group Ltd.*, [2002] EWCA (Civ) 1142. The case concerned the publication by the *Sunday Telegraph* of a yet-to-be-published minute written by Paddy Ashdown, the former leader of the Liberal Democrats in the United Kingdom, of his secret meeting with Prime Minister Tony Blair shortly after the 1997 general elections.

field, but also in the areas of public health and biological diversity.[66] Assessment, evaluation and impact studies also constitute one of the six clusters of recommendations WIPO adopted in October 2007 as part of its Development Agenda.[67]

In addition, countries can take advantage of the existing human rights infrastructure to monitor the impact of intellectual property rights on the protection of human rights. For example, commentators have suggested the use of monitoring mechanisms to alleviate the tension between intellectual property rights and human rights. While these monitoring mechanisms may not be as powerful as a mandatory conflict resolution mechanism, they have significant benefits. As Molly Beutz Land explains:

> Although these institutions do not have the ability to sanction or reward states based on their records of compliance other than by publishing conclusions regarding the state's compliance, the very act of a state reporting to a committee fosters greater transparency, provides human rights organizations with an opportunity to expose and challenge state actions and decisions, and forces the state to provide reasons for its conduct.[68]

7 Conclusion

Since the adoption of the Cotonou Agreement in 2000, the European Union has used the Agreement's framework to negotiate an ambitious set of bilateral, plurilateral and regional EPAs. Thus far, the high standards of intellectual property protection and enforcement incorporated into the Agreement's intellectual property chapters have raised significant tension between the intellectual property and human rights systems. While some provisions in the chapters arguably have strengthened those attributes of intellectual property rights that have human rights status, others have created considerable impediments to the protection of human rights. It is therefore imperative that countries strike a more appropriate balance between the protection and enforcement of intellectual property rights and the commitments made in international or regional human rights instruments.

[66] e.g., Convention on Biological Diversity, 5 June 1992, Art 14(1)(a); Commission on Intellectual Property Rights, Innovation and Public Health (2006), p. 10; Committee on Economic, Social and Cultural Rights (2006), para 35.

[67] World Intellectual Property Organization (2007).

[68] Beutz Land (2009), pp. 29–30.

References

Atik J (2012) ACTA and the destabilization of TRIPS. In: Lidgard HH, Atik J, Nguyen TT (eds) Sustainable technology transfer: a guide to global aid & trade development. Kluwer Law International, Alphen aan den Rijn, pp. 121–147

Benvenisti E, Downs GW (2007) The empire's new clothes: political economy and the fragmentation of international law. Stanford Law Rev 60:595–631

Beutz Land M (2009) Protecting rights online. Yale J Int Law 34:1–46

Borges Barbosa D, Chon M, Moncayo von Hase A (2007) Slouching towards development in international intellectual property. Michigan State Law Rev 2007:71–141

Broude T (2010) It's easily done: the *China—Intellectual Property Rights Enforcement* dispute and the freedom of expression. J World Intellect Prop 13:660–673

Cho S (2004) A bridge too far: the fall of the fifth WTO ministerial conference in Cancún and the future of trade constitution. J Int Econ Law 7:219–244

Chon M (2006) Intellectual property and the development divide. Cardozo Law Rev 27:2821–2912

Commission on Human Rights (2001) Report of the High Commissioner on Economic, Social and Cultural Rights: The Impact of the Agreement on Trade-Related Aspects of Intellectual Property Rights on Human Rights. E/CN.4/Sub.2/2001/13

Commission on Intellectual Property Rights, Innovation and Public Health, World Health Organization (2006) Public Health, Innovation and Intellectual Property Rights: Report of the Commission on Intellectual Property Rights, Innovation and Public Health

Committee on Economic, Social and Cultural Rights (2000) General Comment No. 14: The Right to the Highest Attainable Standard of Health (Article 12 of the International Covenant on Economic, Social and Cultural Rights). E/C.12/2000/4

Committee on Economic, Social and Cultural Rights (2006) General Comment No. 17: The Right of Everyone to Benefit from the Protection of the Moral and Material Interests Resulting from Any Scientific, Literary or Artistic Production of Which He or She Is the Author (Article 15, Paragraph 1(c), of the Covenant). E/C.12/GC/17

Cornides J (2004) Human rights and intellectual property: conflict or convergence? J World Intellect Prop 7:135–167

Correa CM (2007) Trade related aspects of intellectual property rights: a commentary on the TRIPS Agreement. Oxford University Press, Oxford

Directorate General for Trade, European Commission (2005) Strategy for the Enforcement of Intellectual Property Rights in Third Countries. OJ 2005 C 129, 3

Donnelly J (2003) Universal human rights in theory and practice, 2nd edn. Cornell University Press, Ithaca

Falk R (1992) Cultural foundations for the international protection of human rights. In: An-Naim AA (ed) Human rights in cross-cultural perspectives: a quest for consensus. University of Pennsylvania Press, Philadelphia, pp. 44–64

Fink C (2009) Enforcing intellectual property rights: an economic perspective. In: The Global Debate on the Enforcement of Intellectual Property Rights and Developing Countries. International Centre for Trade and Sustainable Development, Geneva, pp. xiii–26

Foster SE (2008) The conflict between the human right to education and copyright. In: Torremans PLC (ed) Intellectual property and human rights. Kluwer Law International, Alphen aan den Rijn, pp. 287–306

Gervais DJ (2008) Intellectual property and human rights: learning to live together. In: Torremans PLC (ed) Intellectual property and human rights. Kluwer Law International, Alphen aan den Rijn, pp. 1–23

Gorlin JJ (1999) An analysis of the pharmaceutical-related provisions of the WTO TRIPS (Intellectual Property) Agreement. Intellectual Property Institute, London

Helfer LR (2003) Human rights and intellectual property: conflict or coexistence? Minnesota Intellect Prop Rev 5:47–61

Helfer LR (2004) Regime shifting: the TRIPS Agreement and new dynamics of international intellectual property lawmaking. Yale J Int Law 29:1–83
Helfer LR (2007) Toward a human rights framework for intellectual property. UC Davis Law Rev 40:971–1020
Helfer LR, Austin GW (2011) Human rights and intellectual property: mapping the global interface. Cambridge University Press, Cambridge
Hestermeyer H (2007) Human rights and the WTO: the case of patents and access to medicines. Oxford University Press, Oxford
Howse R (2000) The Canadian generic medicines panel: a dangerous precedent in dangerous times. J World Intellect Prop 3:493–507
Human Rights Council (2008) Report of the special rapporteur on the right of everyone to the enjoyment of the highest attainable standard of physical and mental health. A/63/263
Human Rights Council (2011) Report of the special rapporteur on the promotion and protection of the right to freedom of opinion and expression. A/HRC/17/27
International Council on Human Rights Policy (2010) Technology transfer in the UNFCCC and other international legal regimes: the challenge of systemic integration. http://www.ichrp.org/files/papers/181/138_technology_transfer_UNFCCC.pdf. Accessed 24 June 2011
Kapczynski A (2008) The access to knowledge mobilization and the new politics of intellectual property. Yale Law J 117:804–885
Krikorian G, Kapczynski A (2010) Access to knowledge in the age of intellectual property. Zone Books, New York
Leaffer MA (1991) Protecting United States intellectual property abroad: toward a new multilateralism. Iowa Law Rev 76:273–308
Lerner J (2010) The patent system in a time of turmoil. WIPO J 2:28–37
Li X, Correa CM (2009) Towards a development approach on IP enforcement: conclusions and strategic recommendations. In: Li X, Correa CM (eds) Intellectual property enforcement: international perspectives. Edward Elgar, Cheltenham, pp. 207–212
Maskus KE, Reichman JH (2005) The globalization of private knowledge goods and the privatization of global public goods. In: Maskus KE, Reichman JH (eds) International public goods and transfer of technology under a globalized intellectual property regime. Cambridge University Press, Cambridge, pp. 3–45
Morsink J (1999) The universal declaration of human rights: origins, drafting, and intent. University of Pennsylvania Press, Philadelphia
Musungu SF (2009) Innovation and intellectual property in the EC-CARIFORUM EPA: lessons for other ACP regions. IQsensato, Geneva
Nickel JW (2007) Making sense of human rights, 2nd edn. Wiley-Blackwell, Oxford
Nussbaum MC (2001) Women and human development: the capabilities approach. Cambridge University Press, Cambridge
Nussbaum MC (2011) Creating capabilities: the human development approach. Belknap Press of Harvard University Press, Cambridge
Okediji RL (2003) The international relations of intellectual property: narratives of developing country participation in the global intellectual property system. Singapore J Int Comp Law 7:315–385
Pogge T, Rimmer M, Rubenstein K (eds) (2010) Incentives for global public health: patent law and access to essential medicines. Cambridge University Press, Cambridge
Raustiala K (2007) Density and conflict in international intellectual property law. UC Davis Law Rev 40:1021–1038
Schott JJ (2004) Free trade agreements: boon or bane of the world trading system? In: Schott JJ (ed) Free trade agreements: US strategies and priorities. Peterson Institute of Economics, Washington, pp. 3–19
Sen A (1999) Development as freedom. Anchor Books, New York
Sub-Commission on Human Rights (2000) Intellectual property rights and human rights. E/CN.4/Sub.2/RES/2000/7

Torremans PLC (2008) Copyright (and other intellectual property rights) as a human right. In: Torremans PLC (ed) Intellectual property and human rights. Kluwer Law International, Alphen aan den Rijn, pp. 195–215
UNCTAD (2007) The least developed countries report 2007: knowledge, technological learning and innovation for development. UNCTAD, Geneva
Van Overwalle G (ed) (2009) Gene patents and collaborative licensing models: patent pools, clearinghouses, open source models and liability regimes. Cambridge University Press, Cambridge
World Intellectual Property Organization (2007) The 45 adopted recommendations under the WIPO Development Agenda. http://www.wipo.int/ip-development/en/agenda/recommendations.html. Accessed 21 November 2009
World Summit on the Information Society (2005) Tunis agenda for the information society. WSIS-05/TUNIS/DOC/6(Rev. 1)-E
World Trade Organization (2011) Members accepting amendment of the TRIPS Agreement. http://www.wto.org/english/tratop_e/trips_e/amendment_e.htm. Accessed 11 December 2011
Xue H (2009) Enforcement for development: why not an agenda for the developing world? In: Li X, Correa CM (eds) Intellectual property enforcement: international perspectives. Edward Elgar, Cheltenham, pp. 133–156
Yu PK (2002) Bridging the digital divide: equality in the information age. Cardozo Arts Entertain Law J 20:1–52
Yu PK (2005) The trust and distrust of intellectual property rights. Revue Québécoise de Droit Int 18:107–140
Yu PK (2006) Anticircumvention and anti-anticircumvention. Denver Univ Law Rev 84:13–77
Yu PK (2007a) The international enclosure movement. Indiana Law J 82:827–907
Yu PK (2007b) International enclosure, the regime complex, and intellectual property schizophrenia. Michigan State Law Rev 2007:1–33
Yu PK (2007c) Reconceptualizing intellectual property interests in a human rights framework. U.C. Davis Law Rev 40:1039–1149
Yu PK (2007d) Ten common questions about intellectual property and human rights. Georgia State Univ Law Rev 23:709–753
Yu PK (2009) The objectives and principles of the TRIPS Agreement. Houston Law Rev 46:979–1046
Yu PK (2010a) Digital copyright reform and legal transplants in Hong Kong. Univ Louisville Law Rev 48:693–770
Yu PK (2010b) Enforcement, economics and estimates. WIPO J 2:1–19
Yu PK (2010c) The graduated response. Florida Law Rev 62:1373–1430
Yu PK (2011a) Digital copyright and confuzzling rhetoric. Vanderbilt J Entertain Technol Law 13:881–939
Yu PK (2011b) Sinic trade agreements. UC Davis Law Rev 44:953–1028
Yu PK (2011c) Six secret (and now open) fears of ACTA. SMU Law Rev 64:975–1094
Yu PK (2011d) TRIPS and its Achilles' heel. J Intellect Prop Law 18:479–531
Zapparoni R (2004) Propertising identity: understanding the United States right of publicity and its implications—some lessons for Australia. Melbourne Univ Law Rev 28:690–723

IP Protection in EU Free Trade Agreements vis-à-vis IP Negotiations in the WTO

Souheir Nadde-Phlix

Contents

1 Introduction

Ten years after the adoption of the Doha Declaration on the TRIPS Agreement and Public Health by the World Trade Organization (WTO), the Doha round and hence the multilateral trading system are almost stagnant. Despite the efforts made by the WTO Secretariat and a few developing countries to revitalize the negotiations on pending intellectual property (IP) issues or issues related to the Agreement on Trade Related Aspects of Intellectual property Rights (TRIPS), decisions at the WTO's Eighth Ministerial Conference[1] were limited to the extension of deadlines concerning TRIPS-related matters without any improvement on the negotiations

[1] The Eighth Ministerial Conference was held in Geneva from 15 to 17 December 2011. See http://www.wto.org/english/thewto_e/minist_e/min11_e/min11_e.htm.

S. Nadde-Phlix (✉)
Former Research Fellow at the Max Planck Institute for Intellectual Property and Competition Law, Munich, Germany
e-mail: souheir.nadde@googlemail.com

J. Drexl et al. (eds.), *EU Bilateral Trade Agreements and Intellectual Property: For Better or Worse?*, MPI Studies on Intellectual Property and Competition Law 20, DOI 10.1007/978-3-642-39097-5_7, © Springer-Verlag Berlin Heidelberg 2014

front. The adopted decisions deal with (1) the extension of the deadline for members to accept a TRIPS amendment on public health,[2] (2) the extension of the least-developed countries' (LDCs) transition period under Article 66.1 of the TRIPS Agreement[3] and (3) the extension until 2013 (the date of the Ninth Ministerial Conference) of the "moratorium" on bringing non-violation complaints to the WTO dispute settlement body.[4]

Surprisingly, the recession of IP negotiations at the multilateral level is faced by a proliferation of IP negotiations at the bilateral and regional levels under so-called free trade agreements (FTAs),[5] which include comprehensive IP chapters going in most cases far beyond the TRIPS level of protection (also known as TRIPS-plus protection). Accordingly, a lot of the concessions made to developing countries in the IP field under the multilateral trading system have been either distorted or lost. In particular, flexibilities provided for in the TRIPS Agreement have been paralyzed, removed or reduced.[6]

For many years, the most criticized FTAs with regard to TRIPS-plus standards were those negotiated by the United States (US), Japan and the European Free Trade Association (EFTA), respectively, the European Union (EU) being the most moderate until recently. The adoption of the Strategy for the Enforcement of Intellectual Property Rights in Third Countries by the European Commission in 2004 and the launching of the Global Europe Strategy in 2006 brought the EU to a similar level with the aforementioned countries as part of a "tough new approach on intellectual property rights".[7] The EU has thus shifted from the former FTA template of essentially seeking accession of its trade partners to multilateral IP conventions to a detailed and elaborated template similar to the one used by the US.

While the recourse to FTAs by developing countries is driven by their need to access markets with better conditions than those provided at the WTO, developed countries use FTAs as a means to achieve at the bilateral level what they have failed

---

[2] Available at http://www.wto.org/english/tratop_e/trips_e/ta_docs_e/3_wtl829_e.pdf.

[3] Available at http://www.wto.org/english/thewto_e/minist_e/min11_e/official_doc_e.htm. WTO members agreed by consensus on 11 June 2013 to extend the transition period until 1 July 2021, with a further extension possible when the time comes. See http://www.wto.org/english/news_e/news13_e/trip_11jun13_e.htm.

[4] Available at http://www.wto.org/english/thewto_e/minist_e/min11_e/official_doc_e.htm.

[5] For the purpose of this paper the term "free trade agreements" also designates economic partnership agreements (EPAs), association agreements (AAs), regional trade agreements (RTAs) and, in general, all bilateral or regional trade agreements whose purpose is to liberalize trade among the parties.

[6] It is worth noting here that the US proposals for stronger IP protection in several IP fields that were rejected during TRIPS negotiations (such as the inclusion of strong protection for data exclusivity) are now part of the new generation of FTAs, namely, those negotiated by the US, EFTA and the EU. See Mercurio (2006), p. 226.

[7] See http://ec.europa.eu/trade/creating-opportunities/trade-topics/european-competitiveness/.

to gain in WTO and other multilateral fora,[8] especially in areas related to trade, such as IP and the Singapore issues.[9] Therefore, it is not surprising that many of the issues that are still not settled in the TRIPS Council and other WTO bodies, such as geographical indications (GIs), biotechnology, biodiversity, traditional knowledge (TK) and transfer of technology, are subject to TRIPS-plus commitments in FTAs.

The question is hence whether these IP commitments set new rules that affect IP negotiations in related areas at the multilateral level. In other words, are IP provisions in new EU FTAs related to issues under negotiation at the WTO substitutes for the IP multilateral system or just a bridge to overcome the deadlock of the WTO negotiations? Is the Doha Declaration on the TRIPS Agreement and Public Health the latest IP achievement at the WTO front or will future WTO ministerial conferences witness additional achievements?

An analysis of the IP issues under negotiation in WTO and related TRIPS-plus provisions in new EU FTAs will answer some of these questions. However, for the purpose of this chapter, the focus will be limited to WTO negotiations on GIs, plant varieties, TK and biodiversity and related provisions in EU FTAs concluded with the CARIFORUM States,[10] Central America, Colombia and Peru and South Korea.

Therefore, after discussing the new IP standard in recent EU FTAs and shedding light on the misuse of TRIPS flexibilities (Part II), this chapter provides a brief analysis of IP provisions in EU FTAs on GIs, plant varieties, biodiversity and TK and related IP negotiations at the WTO, which shows that the EU limits itself to IP concessions that reflect the EU level of protection, and hence does not make concessions on issues that have not yet been regulated at the Community level. It also shows that although such FTAs obligations do not set new IP rules which directly impact on the outcome of the negotiation process at the WTO, however they create a new state of play regarding these negotiations and changes in coalitions among WTO members (Part III). The chapter then concludes with the necessity for WTO Members to get back to the multilateral table before potentially conflicting bilateral or regional outcomes make future consensus in the WTO even more difficult (Part IV).

---

[8] See Woolcock (2007) and Mercurio (2006), pp. 235–237.

[9] The Singapore issues are the four issues—trade and investment, trade and competition policy, transparency in government procurement and trade facilitation—that were introduced to the WTO agenda at the December 1996 WTO Ministerial Conference in Singapore.

[10] CARIFORUM is the Caribbean Forum of African, Caribbean and Pacific (ACP) States, which includes all members of the Caribbean Community (Antigua and Barbuda, the Bahamas, Barbados, Belize, Dominica, Grenada, Guyana, Haiti, Jamaica, Saint Lucia, Saint Vincent and the Grenadines, Saint Kitts and Nevis, Suriname and Trinidad and Tobago) and the Dominican Republic. Cuba is also a member of CARIFORUM but is not part of the ACP Group and did not participate in negotiations.

2 New EU FTAs: New IP Standards

Under the new generation of FTAs, the trend is to bring the level of IP protection into line with the domestic legislation of the respective developed-country partner. While this trend is dictated by US laws as a "US negotiating objective",[11] the EU applies it as part of its Global Europe Strategy, which provides that "[i]n negotiating FTAs, the IPR clauses should as far as possible offer identical levels of IPR protection to that existing in the EU while taking into account the level of development of the countries concerned".[12] In practice, this feature is translated in EU FTAs into IP provisions that are, to a large extent, inspired by the EU Directives without taking into consideration the level of development of the parties concerned. This means that a TRIPS-plus standard continues to be the basis for IP protection in these agreements.

The Economic Partnership Agreement (EPA)[13] between the European Community (now the EU) and the CARIFORUM group of Caribbean Countries (EU-CARIFORUM EPA) is the first example in a series of agreements that transformed drastically the traditional trade preference relationship that existed between the EU and its trade partners from developing countries. As regards IP, the EU-CARIFORUM EPA incorporates various forms of TRIPS-plus protection measures ranging from the inclusion of new areas of IP rights to the implementation of higher IP standards and the elimination of options and flexibilities available under TRIPS.[14]

The EU-CARIFORUM EPA serves as a reference point for EPA negotiations with other regional groups of African, Caribbean and Pacific (ACP) countries[15] and

---

[11] The US Trade Act of 2002, under which the US president is provided with the power to conclude trade agreements ("trade promotion authority", or the so-called "fast track"), states that "the principal negotiating objectives of the United States regarding trade-related intellectual property are (A) to further promote adequate and effective protection of intellectual property rights, including through ... (i)(II) ensuring that the provisions of any multilateral or bilateral trade agreement governing intellectual property rights that is entered into by the United States reflect a standard of protection similar to that found in United States law". See US Trade Act of 2002, Sec. 2102(b)(4), available at http://uscode.house.gov/download/pls/19C24.txt.

[12] See European Commission (2010), p. 13. See also European Commission (2011), p. 21.

[13] EPA negotiations are part of the implementation of the Cotonou Agreement, which has been the framework for the EU's relations with ACP countries since 2000 and covered aid, trade and political cooperation. After the expiry on 31 December 2007 of the Cotonou trade regime and the WTO waiver that covered it, a comprehensive agreement was signed with the Caribbean countries and a series of interim agreements were made with the African and Pacific countries as transitory measures to secure the ACP-EU trade regime awaiting the signature of comprehensive regional EPA agreements. For more information about EPAs see http://ec.europa.eu/trade/creating-opportunities/bilateral-relations/regions/africa-caribbean-pacific/.

[14] See Santa Cruz (2007), Shabalala et al. (2008) and Third World Network (2009).

[15] While none of the interim (or "stepping stone") EPAs initialed with other ACP regions and countries contains substantive provisions on IP, most of them include a "*rendez-vous* clause" in which the parties agree to negotiate a more comprehensive EPA including IP issues.

for new FTAs the EU is negotiating with other developing countries. The main difference between EPAs and other FTAs remains however the EU definition of EPAs as instruments to advance development objectives. According to the EU, EPAs aim at promoting sustainable development and growth, poverty reduction, better governance and the gradual integration of ACP countries into the world economy.[16]

Still, EPAs are agreements that extend IP protection beyond TRIPS, whereby the *acquis communautaire* (or EU *acquis*) is the standard of protection for various IP categories. This is also the case of all FTAs newly concluded or negotiated by the EU, namely: the Association Agreement (AA) between the EU and Central America (EU-CA),[17] the EU FTA with Colombia and Peru (EU-Col-Peru)[18] and the EU FTA with South Korea (EU-South Korea),[19] which differ from the EU-CARIFORUM EPA mainly by name (AA or FTA), while the content, with the exception of the development dimension that characterizes EPAs,[20] is almost identical.

---

[16] According to a representative of the Directorate General for Trade at the European Commission, the EU's trade agreements (IP chapters of FTAs/EPAs) are negotiated with the aim of helping European export businesses of all sizes to protect their IP, including geographical indications, from violations and maintain their competitiveness. They respect the EU *acquis*, fundamental rights and TRIPS flexibilities. They are negotiated—not imposed on the EU's trading partners. In addition to the above, EPAs have a role of promoting trade between the Parties, through trade development, sustainable growth and reduction of poverty. This statement was made by Dominika Svozilova, Administrator and Policy Officer at the European Commission, Directorate General for Trade, Intellectual Property and Public Procurement Unit, during the workshop on "Economic Partnership Agreements of the EU: A Step Ahead in Reforming International IP Law?" organized by the Max Planck Institute for Intellectual Property and Competition Law (MPI) and held in Frauenchiemsee from 25 to 27 June 2011. See Nadde-Phlix (2012), p. 958.

[17] The EU-CA AA was signed on 29 June 2012. Countries of the CA Region include Panama, Guatemala, Costa Rica, El Salvador, Honduras and Nicaragua. See http://trade.ec.europa.eu/doclib/press/index.cfm?id=689.

[18] The EU-Col-Peru FTA was signed on 26 June 2012. Based on the principle of regional integration, the FTA remains open for signature by Bolivia and Ecuador, the other two members of the Andean Community. See http://ec.europa.eu/trade/creating-opportunities/bilateral-relations/regions/andean/.

[19] The FTA between the EU and South Korea was initialled on 15 October 2009, signed on 6 October 2010 and entered into force in July 2011. See http://ec.europa.eu/trade/creating-opportunities/bilateral-relations/countries/korea/.

[20] Other FTAs also contain provisions on sustainable development; however, they are of a general nature compared to the provisions on sustainable development in the EU-CARIFORUM EPA, which are incorporated as an objective of the agreement that should be "applied and integrated at every level of [the parties'] economic partnership, in fulfilment of the overarching commitments set out in Articles 1, 2 and 9 of the Cotonou Agreement, and especially the general commitment to reducing and eventually eradicating poverty in a way that is consistent with the objectives of sustainable development". See Article 3(1) of the EU-CARIFORUM EPA. Here, a core question is whether such a high level of IP protection would help EPAs remain instruments to advance development objectives. For an analysis of the topic of sustainable development in international IP Law see Grosse Ruse-Khan (2010).

Like many FTAs concluded with developing countries, these new agreements provide for equal treatment for parties that are unequal in capacity and hence result in unequal outcomes.[21] IP protection in FTAs is affected most by this unfair balance. This is not only because market access prevails over every other issue in those agreements,[22] but also because the legal transplantation to developing countries of new IP rules occurs without the checks and balances necessary for any regulatory convergence.[23] Another reason lies in the nature of the TRIPS Agreement itself. By definition, the TRIPS Agreement sets a minimum standard of protection for IP rights[24] and hence opens the door for WTO Members to increase the level of protection unilaterally (at a national level) or through FTAs.[25] The increase of the level of protection is then multilateralized by virtue of the national treatment (NT)[26] and the most-favored-nation (MFN) principles.[27]

One might argue that the option for increasing TRIPS standards is limited by flexibilities enshrined in the TRIPS Agreement itself.[28] However, the problem arises when developing countries renounce their right to benefit from such flexibilities.

The main examples are found in the "may" clauses under TRIPS that are made mandatory or simply eliminated in FTAs. For instance, the option given to WTO Members in Article 1.1 to implement in their law a TRIPS-plus level of protection has been made mandatory in FTAs. Although this option is limited by a ceiling under which the extensive protection must not contravene the provisions of the

[21] See Khor (2005), p. 2.

[22] Market access is considered by developing countries as the main reward from FTAs. Developing countries attracted by market access find themselves with a level of IP protection they have to struggle at economic, social and judicial levels to implement. They also find themselves with IP concessions that are in obvious contradiction with their positions at multilateral fora.

[23] For further analysis of this issue see Roffe (2013) and Seuba (2013) in this volume.

[24] See Article 1.1 of the TRIPS Agreement, which states that "Members may, but shall not be obliged to, implement in their law more extensive protection than is required by this Agreement, provided that such protection does not contravene the provisions of this Agreement".

[25] For a discussion about "why the TRIPS Agreement allows members to give more extensive protection" see Frankel (2008), pp. 189–192.

[26] See Article 3.1 of TRIPS.

[27] Unlike other WTO agreements such as the General Agreement on Tariffs and Trade (GATT) and the General Agreement on Trade in Services (GATS), the TRIPS agreement does not exempt FTAs from the application of the MFN principle, under which "any advantage, favour, privilege or immunity granted by a Member [of the WTO] to the nationals of any other country shall be accorded immediately and unconditionally to the nationals of all other [WTO] Members". See Article 4 of TRIPS, Article XXIV of the GATT and Article V of the GATS.

[28] According to one scholar: "Flexibilities can be classified under four clusters: (a) flexibilities as regards transitional periods, (b) flexibilities as regards the method of implementation of TRIPS obligations, (c) flexibilities as regards standards of protection (upwards or downwards), and (d) flexibilities as regards enforcement. Beyond these four clusters of flexibilities, WTO members are free to protect fields of IP not covered by the TRIPS Agreement as they see fit (that is, without being obliged to comply with TRIPS provisions and principles)". See Pires de Carvalho (2010), p. 62.

TRIPS Agreement, according to scholars the effectiveness of this ceiling is questionable.[29]

Other examples of the "may" clauses that are made mandatory under FTAs are found under exceptions and limitations of protected rights, such as in Article 24 of TRIPS, which deals with exceptions to the protection of GIs and related international negotiations. According to paragraph 9 of Article 24, WTO Members are not obliged to protect GIs "which are not or cease to be protected in their country of origin, or which have fallen into disuse in that country". In other words, WTO Members may protect such GIs if they so wish. However, some members have decided not to do so, instead committing to FTA clauses that transform the optional TRIPS provision for not protecting such GIs into a mandatory one.[30]

Another form of flexibility is the option given to WTO Members under Article 27.3(b) of TRIPS to determine the appropriate system for the protection of plant varieties either by patents or by an effective *sui generis* system or by any combination thereof. This flexibility has been limited in some FTAs to one option, that is, the adoption of a *sui generis* system of protection through the adherence to the 1991 Act of the International Convention for the Protection of New Varieties of Plants (UPOV 1991).[31]

TRIPS flexibilities may constitute good assets for WTO Members to pave the ground for a more balanced IP system, provided they are preserved and used in an efficient and optimal way.[32] Yet, experience shows that reaching a balanced IP system is not the objective of FTA partners. As stated previously, while developing countries are driven by their need to access markets with better conditions than those provided under the multilateral system, the EU and other developed countries are guided by their desire to achieve in FTAs what they have failed to gain at the WTO front, especially in areas related to trade, such as IP and the Singapore issues.

Despite all consequences on the IP field, developing countries are not complaining about the proliferation of FTAs. They are major players in this FTA game, as without their consent no agreement can be reached. They do not perceive TRIPS-plus concessions as a negotiation failure.[33] What matters is to get the whole

[29] See Kur and Grosse Ruse-Khan (2008), p. 45, who indicate that "[o]n the issue of operationalising ceilings under TRIPS, one may thus conclude that while Art.1:1 2nd sentence offers a workable general ceiling rule prohibiting additional protection which contravenes TRIPS, the specific provisions on IP limitations are not drafted in a way which allow to put this general rule into (effective) operation".

[30] See Article 243 of the EU-CA AA and Article 207(b) of the EU-Col-Peru FTA.

[31] See Article 232 of the EU-Col-Peru FTA, Article 149(2) of the EU-CARIFORUM EPA and Article 15.1(2) of the FTA between the US and Central America and the Dominican Republic (CAFTA-DR FTA).

[32] See Yu (2009), p. 1046.

[33] It is worth mentioning here that IP is still a new area in developing countries, the impact of which is still to be defined in economic terms. Moreover, developing countries lack the financial and human resources necessary to assess the consequences of their FTAs' IP commitments at the economic and societal levels.

deal as one component and not one component of the whole deal. Ensuring specific economic interests in foreign markets is a legitimate target and the basis for international trade. It is easy to say that developed countries impose TRIPS-plus levels of protection on developing countries using market access as a carrot and the withdrawal of trade benefits as a stick. However, if developing countries agree to negotiate IP at the bilateral or regional levels, it is because they expect a more beneficial package at these levels than at the multilateral level.[34] As one scholar has noted, WTO Members did not commit themselves "to ensuring that regional integration compliment the Doha round of negotiations". They could have post-poned all new FTAs and Customs Unions until they completed the round. Instead, they raced each other to conclude FTA deals. Perhaps a consensus would have been reached at the multilateral level if WTO Members had not had the option of joining an FTA.[35]

The reward is definitely bigger and more profitable in bilateral negotiations than in multilateral fora. Hence, many of the unresolved IP issues at the multilateral level[36] are dealt with under new FTAs the EU is negotiating with its trade partners. For instance, concessions have been made on issues that are still under negotiation in the TRIPS Council and other WTO bodies, in particular GIs, plant varieties, TK and biodiversity, which will be discussed in the following section.

3 WTO IP Negotiations and Related IP Commitments in FTAs

The question here is whether the IP obligations in FTAs on GIs, plant varieties, TK and biodiversity set new IP rules that affect related IP negotiations in the WTO. In other words, is the EU taking advantage of the stagnancy of the Doha round in order to create a new state of play and improve its position in the multilateral negotiations, using the negotiated outcomes in FTAs as a means for generating a

[34] The EU is no longer the godfather of African countries (especially those which were former European colonies) seeking a fair distribution of wealth through preferential treatment as trading partners. The EU's charitable episode ended with the signature of the first EPA, which sets the scene for a new trend of agreements putting African countries on similar footing as the rest of the world. However, it seems that the EU-CARIFORUM EPA has served as a lesson for the other African countries that have signed interim EPAs with the EU. In addition to lobbying political support in the EU, which resulted in the extension by the EU Parliament of the deadline for signing EPAs from January 2014 to January 2016, African countries are now claiming fair negotiations and a win-win situation. For the reaction of Namibia and other ACP countries on the EU Parliament decision see http://www.bilaterals.org/spip.php?article22087.

[35] See Bhala (2007), p. 83.

[36] See Taubman et al. (2012), pp. 196–219. See also http://www.wto.org/english/tratop_e/trips_e/trips_e.htm.

critical mass of supporters in the WTO on issues of concern to the EU such as GIs, plant varieties, TK and biodiversity?

3.1 Geographical Indications

3.1.1 Overview of WTO Negotiations on GIs

The two issues on GIs debated in the TRIPS Council under the mandate given by the Doha Ministerial Declaration are (1) the creation of a multilateral register for wines and spirits[37] and (2) the extension of the higher level of protection, as provided by Article 23 of the TRIPS Agreement, beyond wines and spirits (GI extension).[38]

With regard to the multilateral register for wines and spirits, the negotiations started in 1997 and are still on-going. To date three sets of proposals have been submitted, representing the different positions of WTO Members.[39]

The EU's position is found in the proposal submitted in 2008[40] by the EU (then the European Community, or EC) and a number of countries including Colombia, Peru, India, the ACP Group and the African Group, which suggests that the registration of a GI in the Register should be considered as *prima facie* evidence that the term met the definition of "geographical indication" prescribed by TRIPS Article 22.1. The proposal suggests also that this evidence be challenged in individual WTO Members under national procedures, and it allows for assertions by domestic authorities on the genericness exception (or the existing possibility not to protect GIs that have become generic terms) laid down in Article 24.6 only if these are substantiated.

The second proposal, known as the "joint proposal",[41] submitted in 2005 by the US and other WTO Members (including South Korea and the Dominican Republic) and last revised in 2011, suggests setting up a voluntary system whereby notified GIs would be registered in a database that would be mandatory only for WTO Members choosing to participate in the system.

---

[37] The door was left open under the TRIPS Agreement for negotiating a multilateral system of notification and registration of GIs for wines (Article 23.4 of TRIPS) and for reviewing the application of GI provisions of the Agreement by the TRIPS Council (Article 24.2 of TRIPS). The Doha Ministerial Declaration extended the mandate under Article 23.4 to also cover spirits, confirming a decision taken at the 1996 Singapore Ministerial Conference, and added to it the question of the possible extension of the higher level of protection for wines and spirits as provided by Article 23 of TRIPS to cover GIs for all products. See Taubman et al. (2012), pp. 90–91 and 200–201.

[38] See http://www.wto.org/english/tratop_e/trips_e/gi_background_e.htm.

[39] See Taubman et al. (2012), pp. 202–205. See also http://www.wto.org/english/news_e/news11_e/trip_ss_13jan11_e.htm#current_proposals.

[40] See WTO document TN/C/W/52 of 19 July 2008.

[41] See WTO document TN/IP/W/10/Rev.4.

The third proposal[42] was submitted by Hong Kong, China, and consists of a compromise under which a registered GI would be preliminary *prima facie* evidence which could be challenged only in those countries choosing to participate in the system.

With regard to GI extension, the Doha Ministerial Declaration identifies the question of extending the protection of GIs provided for in TRIPS Article 23 to products other than wines and spirits as an implementation issue.[43] WTO Members are divided on this question. Advocates of the extension, led by the EU, call for the renegotiation and amendment of TRIPS in order to apply the additional protection provided in Article 23 of TRIPS to GIs to all other products, including applying *mutatis mutandis* the exceptions provided in Article 24 of the Agreement. Opponents of the GI extension, which include the US, Colombia and several other countries, claim that Article 22 of TRIPS provides an adequate level of protection for GIs and that enhancing GI protection would disrupt existing legitimate marketing practices. They further claim that there is no mandate on GI extension under the Doha Ministerial Declaration to undertake negotiations on the text of the TRIPS Agreement.[44]

3.1.2 GI Protection in EU FTAs

The EU has a rich agricultural heritage, and most of its GIs, accordingly, are agricultural products. Enhancing GI protection worldwide through multilateral and bilateral negotiations is a key objective for the EU. Therefore, GI protection is an essential component of all EU FTAs in which the EU standard is the basis for protection.[45]

For instance, the EU-CARIFORUM EPA provides that no later than 1 January 2014 the signatory CARIFORUM States must establish a system of protection of GIs[46] that is in harmony with the EU standard.[47] Among these requirements are the

[42] See WTO document TN/IP/W/8.

[43] See the Doha Ministerial Declaration paragraphs 12 (Implementation Issues) and 18 (TRIPS). Available at: http://www.wto.org/english/thewto_e/minist_e/min01_e/mindecl_e.htm#implementation.

[44] Paragraph 12 of the Doha Declaration, which deals with implementation issues, is interpreted differently by WTO Members. While the EU and other advocates of the GI extension argue that the "outstanding implementation issues" are part of the Doha "single undertaking", the US and other opponents of the extension argue that these issues can only become negotiating subjects if the Trade Negotiations Committee (TNC) decides to include them in the talks. The TNC so far has not done so. For further information about this debate see http://www.wto.org/english/tratop_e/trips_e/gi_background_e.htm. See also Taubman et al. (2012), pp. 204–205.

[45] See http://ec.europa.eu/trade/creating-opportunities/trade-topics/intellectual-property/geographical-indications/.

[46] See Article 145 A(2) of the EU-CARIFORUM EPA.

[47] See Article 145 of the EU-CARIFORUM EPA.

establishment of a registration system for GIs,[48] the limitation of the protection to those GIs "which are produced in accordance with the relevant product specifications"[49] and the expansion of the additional protection for wines and spirits to all other products protected as GIs.[50]

A strong protection of GIs, including the establishment of a register for GIs[51] and the extension of the additional protection of wines and spirits to all products,[52] is also found in the EU-CA AA.[53] By the entry into force of the AA, Central America should have established a *sui generis* system for the protection of GIs that is in harmony with the EU standard of protection.[54] The scope and coverage of the protection includes only GIs that are recognized and declared as such in their country of origin.[55]

The parties to the EU-South Korea FTA recognize GIs for agricultural products and foodstuffs and wines,[56] agree on the elements for the registration and control of GIs, including a register for GIs,[57] and expand the additional protection for wines and spirits to all other agricultural products and foodstuffs protected as GIs.[58]

A quick look at the GI provisions under the EU-Col-Peru FTA[59] shows that the parties have reached a deal regarding the different categories of GIs protected and the level of protection in their respective countries. The EU-Col-Peru FTA came at a time when a *sui generis* system of GI protection was already in place in each of the parties to the agreement. It is therefore not surprising that a requirement to establish a GI register is missing from the FTA. But it is surprising, considering the high priority given this issue by the EU, that the agreement is missing a requirement to extend the additional protection of wines and spirits to all other agricultural products and foodstuffs,[60] although neither Colombia nor Peru provide for such a higher level of protection in their national legislation.[61] However, as part of its obligation under the Lisbon Agreement for the Protection of Appellations of Origin and their International Registration (Lisbon Agreement), Peru has to provide on its

[48] See Article 145 A of the EU-CARIFORUM EPA.

[49] See Article 145 B(2) of the EU-CARIFORUM EPA.

[50] See Articles 145 B(3) and 145 C(2) to (4) of the EU-CARIFORUM EPA.

[51] See Articles 244 and 245 of the EU-CA AA.

[52] See Article 246 of the EU-CA AA.

[53] See Articles 242 to 250 of the EU-CA AA.

[54] See Article 244 of the EU-CA AA.

[55] See Article 243 of the EU-CA AA.

[56] See Articles 10.18 to 10.26 of the EU-South Korea FTA.

[57] See Article 10.18(6) of the EU-South Korea FTA.

[58] See Article 10.21 of the EU-South Korea FTA.

[59] See Articles 207 to 214 of the EU-Col-Peru FTA.

[60] See Article 210 of the EU-Col-Peru FTA.

[61] Legislation relating to the protection of GIs in Colombia and Peru is available at: http://www.wipo.int/wipolex/en/results.jsp?countries=CO&cat_id=5 (for Colombia) and http://www.wipo.int/wipolex/en/results.jsp?countries=PE&cat_id=5 (for Peru).

territory greater protection to all products that are considered appellations of origin (AOs),[62] including products of the other parties to the Lisbon Agreement.[63] Moreover, the EU-Col-Peru FTA protects GIs that are

> indications consisting of the name of a particular country, region or locality or a name which, without being that of a particular country, region or locality, refers to a particular geographical area, and which identify a product as originating therein where a given quality, reputation or other characteristic of the product is exclusively or essentially due to the geographical environment in which it is produced, with its inherent natural and human factors.[64]

This is more a definition of an AO than a GI as defined by TRIPS.[65] In other words, the protection goes only to a narrower category of GIs, that is, the AO, also known in the EU as the Protected Designation of Origin (PDO). The TRIPS definition of GIs is much wider in scope, as it refers to GIs in general (known in the EU as Protected Geographical Indications or PGIs) and does not require conditions such as natural and human factors.[66] However, the EU GIs listed in Appendix 1 of Annex XIII of the EU-Col-Peru FTA[67] are not limited to PDOs (or AOs) but also include PGIs.[68] This means that EU GIs are protected under the FTA regardless of their compatibility with the definition provided by the Agreement. Moreover, Appendix 2 of Annex XIII lists non-agricultural products that qualify as GIs. This is in contradiction with the EU system, which does not protect this category of products as GIs.[69] It seems therefore that the parties to the FTA have reached a compromise whereby the EU GIs will be treated as AOs in Colombia and Peru, while the non-agricultural products that qualify as GIs in Peru and Colombia will be protected as GIs in the EU.[70] Finally, the EU-Col-Peru FTA limits the protection of GIs to those recognized and declared as such in their country of origin.[71]

---

[62] The Lisbon Agreement requires member states to protect the AO product "against any usurpation or imitation, even if the true origin of the product is indicated or if the appellation is used in translated form or accompanied by terms such as 'kind,' 'type,' 'make,' 'imitation,' or the like" (Article 3 of the Lisbon Agreement).

[63] See Article 1 of the Lisbon Agreement. Several countries of the EU are members of the Lisbon Agreement. See http://www.wipo.int/treaties/en/ShowResults.jsp?lang=en&treaty_id=10.

[64] See Article 207 of the EU-Col-Peru FTA.

[65] All AOs are GIs but not all GIs are AOs.

[66] See Article 22.1 of the TRIPS Agreement.

[67] Available at: http://trade.ec.europa.eu/doclib/docs/2011/march/tradoc_147725.pdf.

[68] For an analysis of the GI provisions in the EU-Col-Peru FTA, see Covarrubia (2011), pp. 330–338.

[69] The protection of non-agricultural GI products is ensured at the EU level through the Community trade mark (CTM) regime, which allows for the protection of geographical names under certain conditions. For more information about the protection of non-agricultural GI products see Insight Consulting, Origin and Agridea (2009).

[70] See Covarrubia (2011), pp. 330–338. It will be interesting to analyze whether such commitments are compliant with the EU legislation on the protection of non-agricultural products.

[71] See Article 207(b) of the EU-Col-Peru FTA.

In sum, with the exception of the EU-Col-Peru FTA, extending the additional protection for wines and spirits to all other products protected as GIs and establishing a GI register in harmony with the EU standard are the two pillars of GI protection in new EU FTAs, which endorse the EU's position at the multilateral front.

Moreover, by limiting the protection of GIs to those protected in their country of origin and those that have not fallen into disuse in that country,[72] the EU is making the exception of TRIPS Article 24.9 mandatory.[73] This provision, as well as the provision limiting the protection of GIs to those "which are produced in accordance with the relevant product specifications",[74] could be interpreted as favoring the EU proposal at the WTO for a GI registration system over alternative protection systems such as trademark supplemented, in many countries, by laws and regulations on unfair competition and consumer protection.[75]

In all the above-mentioned FTAs, the list of goods on which the EU claims or wishes to claim GIs is considerably longer than the list claimed by the other parties to the agreements. It goes without saying that the EU is using FTAs in order to protect European GIs in other jurisdictions using EU standards as the basis for the protection. The question is then whether GI negotiations are still relevant in the WTO framework if the problem for the EU is almost resolved and the GI systems are well regulated in most EU trading partners. In this case, the WTO dispute settlement system may be a reason for the EU to continue to push its FTA approach to become law in the WTO.

Exporting the European GI system to EU's trade partners remains an important achievement for the EU. In addition to strengthening the EU's position at the WTO and other multilateral fora, European GIs now enjoy the EU level of protection in many of the EU trade partners. To some extent this might affect related WTO negotiations; however, in practice, the debate in the WTO will continue as long as the US opposes such protection.

3.2 *Plant Varieties*

3.2.1 Overview of WTO Negotiations on Plant Varieties

Article 27.3(b) gives WTO Members the flexibility to determine the appropriate system for the protection of plant varieties by patents, by an effective *sui generis* system or by any combination thereof. It also states that the provisions of

[72] See Article 243 of the EU-CA AA and Article 207(b) of the EU-Col-Peru FTA. Under Article 145(A)(1) of the EU-CARIFORUM EPA and Article 10.21(4) of the EU-South Korea FTA the exception of TRIPS Article 24.9 is kept optional for the parties to the FTAs.

[73] See above discussion at p. 8.

[74] Such as in Article 145 B(2) of the EU-CARIFORUM EPA.

[75] See Santa Cruz (2007), p. 6 and Vivas-Eugui and Spennemann (2006), p. 40.

subparagraph 27.3(b) should then be reviewed four years after the date of entry into force of the WTO Agreement, that is, in 1999.

Negotiations at the WTO on plant varieties were addressed in the review of Article 27.3(b), which began in 1999 as required by the TRIPS Agreement, in the form of discussions about the provisions of Article 27.3(b) itself, the links between TRIPS and the Convention on Biological Diversity (CBD) and the links between IP, TK and folklore.[76] The debate on biotechnology, TK and biodiversity is still on-going in the TRIPS Council and other international fora such as the WIPO Intergovernmental Committee on IP and Genetic Resources, Traditional Knowledge and Folklore. Proposals for dealing with these complex subjects were submitted and discussed in detail by WTO Members in the TRIPS Council. The WTO Secretariat has prepared three separate documents summarizing the discussions in the TRIPS Council relating to the relationship between TRIPS and the CBD,[77] the review of the provisions of Article 27.3(b)[78] and the protection of TK and folklore,[79] respectively.

Regarding plant varieties, the debate in the TRIPS Council focused on the elements that constitute an effective *sui generis* system, the relationship between the TRIPS provision and UPOV and the relationship with TK and farmers' rights, in particular on how to strike a balance, in the protection of plant varieties, between the interests of the community as a whole and protecting farmers' rights and traditional knowledge and ensuring the preservation of biological diversity.[80]

The EU's position on the debated questions reflects the EU's internal legislation and policy on biotechnology, biodiversity and related issues.[81] It also reflects the EU's support for implementing the TRIPS Agreement in light of the CBD objectives.[82]

[76] It is to be noted that the Doha Ministerial Declaration (paragraph 19) instructs the TRIPS Council "in pursuing its work programme including under the review of Article 27.3(b), the review of the implementation of the TRIPS Agreement under Article 71.1 and the work foreseen pursuant to paragraph 12 of this declaration, to examine, inter alia, the relationship between the TRIPS Agreement and the Convention on Biological Diversity, the protection of traditional knowledge and folklore, and other relevant new developments raised by members pursuant to Article 71.1. In undertaking this work, the TRIPS Council shall be guided by the objectives and principles set out in Articles 7 and 8 of the TRIPS Agreement and shall take fully into account the development dimension". See http://www.wto.org/english/thewto_e/minist_e/min01_e/mindecl_e.htm.

[77] See WTO document IP/C/W/368/Rev.1.

[78] See WTO document IP/C/W/369/Rev.1.

[79] See WTO document IP/C/W/370/Rev.1.

[80] See WTO document IP/C/W/369/Rev.1. See also Taubman et al. (2012), p. 206.

[81] See EC Regulation No. 2100/94 on community plant variety rights and EC Regulation No. 98/44 on the legal protection of biotechnological inventions.

[82] See WTO documents IP/C/W/383 and IP/C/W/369/Rev.1.

3.2.2 Protection of Plant Varieties in EU FTAs

The protection of plant varieties has always been on the FTA agenda of the EU. Under the old generation of FTAs the protection was indirect, through a requirement (or a best-endeavor provision) to accede to or implement the 1978 or 1991 Acts of the UPOV Convention. The new EU FTAs include a more elaborated and detailed text on the protection of plant varieties requiring a level of protection in accordance with the TRIPS Agreement and including a requirement (or a best-endeavor provision) to accede to or implement UPOV 1991.

For instance, the EU-CARIFORUM EPA requires the parties to the Agreement to protect plant varieties in accordance with the TRIPS Agreement and to consider acceding to UPOV 1991.[83] It also gives the parties "the right to provide for exceptions to exclusive rights granted to plant breeders to allow farmers to save, use and exchange protected farm-saved seed or propagating material".[84] In this respect, the EU-CARIFORUM EPA, on the one hand, leaves the parties the freedom to provide for exceptions to the so-called plant breeders' rights, and on the other hand, by requiring the parties to accede to UPOV 1991, limits farmers to saving seeds only for use on their own fields[85] and hence prevents them from exchanging or transferring the saved material to others.[86]

As is apparent, these two requirements are contradictory. Accordingly, the parties to the Agreement, in particular the CARIFORUM States, will have to choose between using the exception to the "plant breeders' rights" or acceding to the UPOV 1991,[87] given that the right granted to them with one hand (the right for the "farmers' exemption") is withdrawn with the other (the parties "shall consider acceding to the UPOV Act of 1991"). One scholar has suggested that the only way to save this "farmers' exemption" and make it effective is if CARIFORUM States

---

[83] See Article 149(2) of the EU-CARIFORUM EPA.

[84] See Article 149(1) of the EU-CARIFORUM EPA.

[85] Article 15(2) of UPOV 1991 provides for an optional exception: "Notwithstanding Article 14, each Contracting Party may, within reasonable limits and subject to the safeguarding of the legitimate interests of the breeder, restrict the breeder's right in relation to any variety in order to permit farmers to use for propagating purposes, on their own holdings, the product of the harvest which they have obtained by planting, on their own holdings, the protected variety or a variety covered by Article 14(5)(a)(i) or Article 14(5)(a)(ii)". For an analysis of the related UPOV clauses, see Pires de Carvalho (2010), pp. 308–315.

[86] According to one scholar, "even as regards protected plant varieties, there is no mechanism that may prevent small farmers from continuing their traditional practices of saving and re-sowing seeds. Small farmers are not seed traders, and therefore they are not affected by the limits imposed by Article 15(2) of the UPOV 1991. Anyway, UPOV Members may define those limits in the form of quantities of seeds saved or sizes of the pieces of land involved". See Pires de Carvalho (2010), p 313.

[87] The impact of this provision is more problematic for the Dominican Republic, which is the only member among the CARIFORUM States to have joined UPOV 1991.

decide not to join UPOV 1991 after they show that they have considered acceding to it.[88]

It is important to note that the EU and developing countries do not share the same opinion with regard to the interpretation of the provisions of UPOV 1991 regarding farmers' exemptions.[89] According to the EU the UPOV 1991 allows contracting parties to "limit rights so as to permit farmers to save seeds harvested from their own plantings for replanting in subsequent years".[90] This view is contested by developing countries, which believe that

> UPOV 1978 allows farmers to save, exchange and, to a limited degree, sell seeds of protected varieties, whereas UPOV 1991 turns these actions into privileges and exceptions, giving the government discretion as to whether to permit farmers to save seeds for use on their own holdings and making it subject to "reasonable restrictions" and the protection of the "legitimate interests" of the breeder. Further, the exception only applies to saved material that has been harvested on the same holdings and not to propagated material.[91]

The question is still debated at the TRIPS Council. Therefore, the EU is trying to make its trade partners abide by UPOV 1991 in order to strengthen its position and coalitions at the multilateral level.

With regard to the EU-CA AA, at first glance, the parties appear to have been more cautious when negotiating the protection of plant varieties, as, in addition to limiting the level of protection to that provided by TRIPS, the parties are granted the "farmers' exemption" with no requirement to adhere to or apply UPOV 1991.[92] However, Central American countries had already committed to a much higher level of protection under the FTA between the US and Central America and the Dominican Republic (CAFTA-DR FTA), which, due to the MFN treatment, is also applicable to all WTO Members, including the EU Member States. According to the above, the right of the parties to the EU-CA AA to provide exceptions to "plant breeders' rights" would be in contradiction with the commitment of Central America under the CAFTA-DR FTA[93] to adhere to UPOV 1991. This raises questions about the relation between the MFN rule in TRIPS that allows EU right holders to claim stronger protection derived from CAFTA-DR FTA and the right to introduce an exception for farmers under the AA. As later and more specific agreement, the AA may prevail in the relations between EU and CA states. Of course, this right to introduce a farmer's exception beyond UPOV 1991 would only apply

[88] See Musungu (2008).

[89] See WTO document IP/C/W/383, pp. 14–17 and WTO document IP/C/W/369/Rev.1, pp. 20–22.

[90] Idem.

[91] Idem.

[92] See Article 259(1) and (3) of the EU-CA AA.

[93] See Article 15.1(2) of the CAFTA-DR FTA.

vis-à-vis EU right holders, not those from the US or other countries in relation to which CAFTA-DR states are bound to apply UPOV 1991.

The EU-Col-Peru FTA is more straightforward regarding the protection of plant varieties. Article 232 of the FTA clearly binds its parties[94] to the promotion and protection of plant varieties based on UPOV 1991, including the optional exception to the right of the breeder as referred to in Article 15(2) of UPOV 1991.[95]

The same applies to the FTA with Korea, which requires the parties to the agreement to provide for the protection of plant varieties and to comply with UPOV 1991.[96]

It seems from the above that the EU has made up its mind about the negotiations at the TRIPS Council regarding the protection of plant varieties by "an effective *sui generis* system" that is TRIPS-compliant, similar to or in harmony with the EU standard, which is bound by UPOV 1991 to which the EU is party and that favors farmers' rights while maintaining biodiversity. It is therefore expected that any new EU FTA or EPA will follow the paths of the aforementioned FTAs and will require its contracting parties to adhere to UPOV 1991 or simply apply its provisions. The increase in the number of countries (in particular DCs) acceding to UPOV or abiding by its provisions will definitely strengthen the EU's position at the TRIPS Council in the debate relating to the protection of plant varieties, but this will not resolve the problems raised unless a consensus among all WTO Members is reached.

3.3 *TK and Biodiversity*

3.3.1 Overview of WTO Negotiations on TK and Biodiversity

The relationship between the TRIPS Agreement and the CBD was also discussed in the TRIPS Council under the review of Article 27.3(b) of TRIPS. The focus was on two main issues dealing with (1) whether there exists a conflict between the two international instruments and (2) whether there is a need for amending TRIPS to ensure that both instruments are applied in a non-conflictual and supportive way.[97] The two issues were extensively debated in the TRIPS Council along with the related proposals for resolving the problems arising from the TRIPS-CBD relationship. The discussions show that WTO Members support the CBD objectives, including those relating to prior informed consent and equitable benefit sharing; agree on the need to avoid erroneous patents, including through the use of databases to preclude the grant of patents on existing TK or genetic resources (GR); but

[94] Peru became a party to UPOV 1991 on 8 August 2011, while Colombia has been a party to the 1978 Act of UPOV since 13 September 1996.

[95] See Article 232 of the EU-Col-Peru FTA.

[96] See Article 10.39 of the EU-South Korea FTA.

[97] See WTO document IP/C/W/368/Rev.1.

disagree on how this should be implemented within the TRIPS framework. Several proposals on a disclosure requirement in patent applications to enforce prior informed consent and equitable benefit sharing (hereinafter "disclosure proposals") have been discussed; however none of them has reached consensus.[98]

One proposal would make disclosure a TRIPS obligation. Supported by the African Group, Brazil, India, Colombia, Peru, the Dominican Republic and other developing countries, this proposal suggests that TRIPS be amended to require patent applicants to disclose the country of origin of GR and TK used in the inventions, evidence that they received prior informed consent and evidence of fair and equitable benefit sharing.

A second proposal supported by Switzerland, suggests the amendment of the Regulations of the WIPO Patent Cooperation Treaty (PCT) so that countries are enabled to require patent applicants, in the case of inventions directly based on GR or TK, to disclose the source of GR and TK when they apply for patents.

A third proposal submitted by the US supports the use of national legislation and contractual arrangements based on the legislation to better achieve the CBD's objectives on access to genetic resources and benefit sharing.

A fourth disclosure proposal, located outside patent law and supported by the EU, suggests the establishment of a mandatory disclosure relating only to the origin or source of genetic materials for all patent applicants at the national, regional and international levels, with penalties for non-compliance outside the patent system.

However, in 2008 the EU position has changed substantially after the EU (then EC) supported the negotiating proposal submitted to the Trade Negotiating Committee (TNC) by a group of WTO Members (mainly developing countries and emerging economies in addition to the EU) aiming at amending the TRIPS Agreement to include a mandatory requirement of disclosure of the country providing/source of genetic resources, and/or associated TK.[99] The proposal, which calls for a "procedural decision" to negotiate three intellectual property issues in parallel (two on GIs and the disclosure proposal), was rejected by other WTO Members.[100]

Finally, in 2011, a new proposal was submitted to the TNC by a group of developing countries and emerging economies. The proposal, which consists of a "draft decision to enhance mutual supportiveness between the TRIPS Agreement and the Convention on Biological Diversity" calls for the amendment of TRIPS to introduce a mandatory disclosure mechanism bearing in mind the principles, objectives and definitions of TRIPS; the CBD; and the Nagoya Protocol on Access to Genetic Resources and the Fair and Equitable Sharing of Benefits Arising from their Utilization (Nagoya Protocol).[101]

---

[98] See Taubman et al. (2012), pp. 207–210. See also WTO document IP/C/W/368/Rev.1.

[99] See WTO document TN/C/W/52.

[100] See Watal (2013) in this volume.

[101] See WTO document TN/C/W/59.

3.3.2 Protection of TK and Biodiversity in EU FTAs

The protection of TK and biodiversity is a new component in the IP chapters of new EU FTAs. In many cases, the TK and biodiversity-related provisions reflect existing obligations under the CBD in addition to recognizing the importance of the CBD's objectives and principles.[102] A further feature of these provisions is their lack of any mandatory obligation to disclose the country providing/source of genetic resources, and/or associated TK.[103]

For instance, Article 150 of the EU-CARIFORUM EPA, which covers GR, TK and folklore, contains provisions specifying the intellectual property rights of indigenous and local communities that reflect existing obligations under the CBD, to which the EU and all CARIFORUM States are parties.[104] Other provisions address the relationship between TRIPS and the CBD by allowing the parties to the Agreement to "require as part of the administrative requirements for a patent application concerning an invention which uses biological material as a necessary aspect of the invention, that the applicant identifies the sources of the biological material used by the applicant and described as part of the invention".[105] This provision is optional, as it authorizes but does not mandate national governments to apply it. Accordingly, the CARIFORUM States can make use of its provision; however, they cannot oblige the EU to apply it.

Additional provisions deal with the importance of taking appropriate measures for the preservation and protection of TK, including a *sui generis* system developed at the multilateral level,[106] the exchange of views and information on relevant multilateral discussions (in WIPO and WTO)[107] and the review of Article 150 of the EU-CARIFORUM EPA in the light of the results of such multilateral discussions.[108]

In the case of the EU FTA with Colombia and Peru, two countries known for their richness in GR, the related provisions in the agreement are more elaborated than in other FTAs. In addition to reaffirming the objectives and main principles of the CBD[109] and recognizing the usefulness of databases for the grant of patents on TK or GR subject-matter,[110] the EU-Col-Peru FTA includes a best-endeavor clause

---

[102] See Article 150 of the EU-CARIFORUM EPA, Articles 196(4) and 201 of the EU-Colombia and Peru FTA, Article 229(4) and (5) of the EU-CA AA and Article 10.40 of the EU-South Korea FTA.

[103] For an analysis and comments on Article 150 of the EU-CARIFORUM EPA, see Vivas-Eugui and Oliva (2010), pp. 11–13. See also Drexl (2013) for an analysis of the implementation in the EU of the provisions on GR, TK and folklore in recent EU FTAs.

[104] See Articles 8(j) and 16(5) of the CBD.

[105] See Article 150(4) of the EU-CARIFORUM EPA.

[106] See Article 150(2) of the EU-CARIFORUM EPA.

[107] See Article 150(5) of the EU-CARIFORUM EPA.

[108] See Article 150(6) of the EU-CARIFORUM EPA.

[109] See Articles 196(4) and 201(1), (2), (3) (4) and (6) of the EU-Col-Peru FTA.

[110] See Article 201(11) of the EU-Col-Peru FTA.

to facilitate the exchange of information about patent applications and granted patents related to GR and associated TK so that such information can be considered when determining prior art in substantive patent examinations.[111] It also includes a provision on cooperation in the training of patent examiners in reviewing related patent applications[112] and a provision on collaboration in the application of domestic frameworks on access to GR and TK in accordance with applicable international and domestic law.[113] Moreover, the door is left open for the parties to the FTA to review the IP Chapter subject to the results and conclusions of multilateral discussions.[114]

On the relationship between TRIPS and the CBD, the EU-Col-Peru FTA acknowledges "the usefulness of requiring the disclosure of the origin or source of genetic resources and associated traditional knowledge in patent applications, considering that this contributes to the transparency about the uses of genetic resources and associated traditional knowledge".[115] It also adds that "the Parties will provide, in accordance with their domestic law, for applicable effects of any such requirement so as to support compliance with the provisions regulating access to genetic resources and associated traditional knowledge, innovations and practices".[116] Although one scholar interprets this provision as an obligation that would require the EU to amend its current Directive on Biotechnology in order to determine the effects of the lack of fulfilment,[117] another scholar suggests that Article 201 of the EU-Col-Peru FTA states principles of protection "subject to national legislation" that fail to create clear obligations of the EU to protect GR, TK and folklore.[118]

Regarding the EU-South Korea FTA, the provisions on GR and TK are similar to the ones provided in the EU-CARIFORUM EPA excluding any mention of the disclosure requirement issue.[119] As regards the EU-CA AA the protection of GR and TK is limited to reiterating the principles found in Article 15 of the CBD.[120]

In this context, it is worth mentioning that the EU, Peru, Colombia, Central America, South Korea and the CARIFORUM States[121] are members of the CBD and therefore are bound by its provisions. Many of these countries are also

[111] See Article 201(9) of the EU-Col-Peru FTA.
[112] See Article 201(10) of the EU-Col-Peru FTA.
[113] See Article 201(12) of the EU-Col-Peru FTA.
[114] See Article 201(13) of the EU-Col-Peru FTA.
[115] See Article 201(7) of the EU-Col-Peru FTA.
[116] See Article 201(8) of the EU-Col-Peru FTA.
[117] See Vivas-Eugui and Oliva (2010), pp. 13–17
[118] See Drexl (2013) in this volume.
[119] See Article 10.40 of the EU-South Korea FTA.
[120] See Article 229(4) and (5) of the EU-CA AA.
[121] Saint Lucia and Saint Vincent and the Grenadines have not yet ratified the CBD.

signatories of the Nagoya Protocol and hence will be bound by its provisions once the Protocol enters into force.[122]

It is clear from the above that the EU limits itself to IP concessions that reflect the level of protection available at the Community level.[123] Accordingly, in cases where a solution has yet to be adopted in the EU (such as on the protection of TK and biodiversity), the concessions in FTAs are left open or with no mandatory effect until a proper regulation finds its way at the Community level or until an agreement is reached at the multilateral level. In this sense, a safeguard clause has been included in most EU FTAs[124] which enables parties to the Agreements to review the provisions relating to biodiversity and TK in the light of the results and conclusions of the related multilateral discussions.[125]

In this regard, the clause on disclosure requirement in the EU-CARIFORUM EPA would be a gain for DCs and not only the CARIFORUM States (as it covers part of their 2011 proposal to the TNC) if it were made mandatory. However, it seems that the EU will maintain a neutral position on this issue until it regulates the question internally or until an agreement is concluded internationally.

In Sum, the analysis shows that IP obligations on GIs, plant varieties, TK and biodiversity in new EU FTAs do not set new IP rules which directly impact on the outcome of the negotiation process at the WTO. However they create a new state of play regarding these negotiations and changes in coalitions among WTO members.

4 Conclusion

The EU's use of the *acquis communautaire* as a model for FTAs is motivated by its desire to achieve in FTAs what it has failed to achieve in multilateral negotiations. While scholars are sounding a note of warning regarding the consequences of TRIPS-plus commitments in FTAs on developing countries, the latter are racing each other to make more FTA deals notwithstanding the level of IP protection to which this commits them, provided market access is guaranteed and trade benefits are maintained.

The analysis of IP provisions on GIs, plant varieties, TK and biodiversity in new EU FTAs and related WTO negotiations shows that these provisions strengthen the EU position at the multilateral level without affecting the black letter law of the IP multilateral system.

---

[122] See http://www.cbd.int/abs.

[123] An exception to this is available under the provisions on criminal enforcement in the EU-South Korea FTA and the EU-CA AA; cited in Drexl (2013) in this volume.

[124] The AA with Central American countries does not include such provisions.

[125] See Article 150(6) of the EU-CARIFORUM EPA, Article 201(13) of the EU-Colombia and Peru FTA and Article 10.40(3) of the EU-South Korea FTA.

It is important to note that IP bilateralism is a "disguised multilateralism"—to the extent that it has multilateral effects: The strength of FTAs comes from the TRIPS Agreement, which established a solid ground for international IP protection. While TRIPS MFN and NT principles are protecting the international IP system from fragmentation, TRIPS flexibilities and limitations are safeguarding it from abuse and manipulation. Problems arise, however, when countries waive their rights for flexibilities under TRIPS and when they commit to contradictory IP rules in FTAs with different parties.[126] This will upset the carefully negotiated balance in the multilateral framework and destabilize the international IP system. It is therefore time to turn back to the multilateral table before potentially conflicting bilateral or regional outcomes make future consensus in the WTO even more difficult.[127]

Acknowledgment The author would like to thank Henning Grosse Ruse-Khan for his valuable comments.

References

Aleman M (2013) Impact of TRIPS-plus obligations in economic partnership- and free trade agreements on international IP law. In: Drexl J, Grosse Ruse Khan H, Nadde-Phlix S (eds) EU bilateral trade agreements and intellectual property: for better or worse? Springer, Heidelberg (this volume)

Bhala R (2007) Competitive liberalization, competitive imperialism, and intellectual property. Liverpool Law Rev 28:77–105

Correa C (2013) The impact of the economic partnership agreements on WTO law. In: Drexl J, Grosse Ruse Khan H, Nadde-Phlix S (eds) EU bilateral trade agreements and intellectual property: for better or worse? Springer, Heidelberg (this volume)

Covarrubia P (2011) The EU and Colombia/Peru free trade agreement on GIs: adjusting Colombian and Peruvian national laws? J Intellect Prop Law Pract 6(5):330–338

Drexl J (2013) Intellectual property and implementation of recent bilateral trade agreements in the EU. In: Drexl J, Grosse Ruse Khan H, Nadde-Phlix S (eds) EU bilateral trade agreements and intellectual property: for better or worse? Springer, Heidelberg (this volume)

European Commission (2010) Communication: Trade, Growth and World Affairs – Trade Policy as a core component of the EU's 2020 strategy. COM(2010) 612 final. http://europa.eu/legislation_summaries/employment_and_social_policy/eu2020/em0043_en.htm

European Commission (2011) Communication: a single market for intellectual property rights. Boosting creativity and innovation to provide economic growth, high quality jobs and first class products and services in Europe. COM(2011) 287 final. http://ec.europa.eu/internal_market/copyright/docs/ipr_strategy/COM_2011_287_en.pdf

European Commission, Directorate General for Trade CARIFORUM(2008) Fact sheet CARIFORUM-EC EPA: Innovation and Intellectual Property. http://trade.ec.europa.eu/doclib/docs/2008/october/tradoc_140978.pdf

---

[126] See above examples on EU and US FTAs concluded with the Dominican Republic and Central America.

[127] See the speech of WTO Director-General Pascal Lamy at the University of International Business and Economics in Beijing on 20 September 2012. Available at: http://www.wto.org/english/news_e/sppl_e/sppl246_e.htm.

Frankel S (2008) The legitimacy and purpose of IP Chapters in FTAs. In: Buckley R, Lo VI, Boulle L (eds) Challenges to multilateral trade: The impact of bilateral, preferential and regional agreements. Wolters Kluwer, Alphen aan den Rijn, pp 185–200

Grosse Ruse-Khan H (2010) Sustainable development in international intellectual property law – New approaches from EU economic partnership agreements? Issue Paper No. 29, International Centre for Trade and Sustainable Development (ICTSD) Programme on IPRs and Sustainable Development. http://ictsd.org/downloads/2011/12/sustainable-development-in-international-intellectual-property-law-e28093-new-approaches-from-eu-economic-partnership-agreements.pdf

Hilty R, Jaeger T (2010) Legal effects and policy considerations for free trade agreements: what is wrong with FTAs? Max Planck Institute for Intellectual Property, Competition & Tax Law Research Paper No. 10-02. http://ssrn.com/abstract=1534486 or http://dx.doi.org/10.2139/ssrn.1534486

Insight Consulting, Origin and Agridea (2009) Study on the protection of geographical indications for products other than wines, spirits, agricultural products or foodstuffs. European Commission, Directorate General for Trade. http://trade.ec.europa.eu/doclib/docs/2011/may/tradoc_147926.pdf

Khor M (2005) Bilateral/regional free trade agreements: an outline of elements, nature and development implications. Third World Network (TWN). http://www.twnside.org.sg/pos.htm

Kur A, Grosse Ruse-Khan H (2008) Enough is enough – the notion of binding ceilings in international intellectual property protection. Max Planck Papers on Intellectual Property and Competition & Tax Law, Research Paper No. 09-01). http://ssrn.com/abstract=1326429

Malpani R (2012) The EU-India free trade agreement: is it the end of the world as we know it? http://blogs.oxfam.org/en/blog/12-02-09-eu-india-free-trade-agreement-it-end-world-we-know-it

Mercurio B (2006) TRIPS-plus provisions in FTAs: Recent Trends. In: Bartels L, Ortino F (eds) Regional trade agreements and the WTO legal system. Oxford University Press, Oxford, pp 215–237

Musungu SF (2008) CARIFORUM EPA and beyond: Innovation and Intellectual Property in the EC-CARIFORUM EPA - Lessons for other ACP Regions – Working Paper – Deutsche Gesellschaft für Internationale Zusammenarbeit (GIZ, former GTZ) GmbH. http://www.giz.de/Themen/en/SID-4A112C28-F85DFCC4/dokumente/gtz2008-en-epa-CARIFORUM-and-beyond-innovation-and-intellectual-property.pdf

Nadde-Phlix S (2012) Economic partnership agreements of the EU: a step ahead in reforming international IP law? – Workshop of the Max Planck Institute for Intellectual Property and Competition Law, June 2011. IIC 43(8):951–958

Pauwelyn J (2007) Legal avenues to multilateralizing regionalism: beyond Article XXIV. HEI, September 10–12 2007, Geneva

Pires de Carvalho N (2010) The TRIPS regime of patent rights, 3rd edn. Wolters Kluwer, Alphen aan den Rijn

Roffe P (2012) Intellectual Property, Preferential Trade Agreements and the Multilateral System. In: Meléndez-Ortiz R, Bellmann C, Rodriguez MM (eds) The future and the WTO: confronting the challenges. A collection of short essays. ICTSD Programme on Global Economic Policy and Institutions, Geneva, pp 58–62

Roffe P (2013) Intellectual property chapters in free trade agreements: their significance and systemic implications. In: Drexl J, Grosse Ruse Khan H, Nadde-Phlix S (eds) EU bilateral trade agreements and intellectual property: for better or worse? Springer, Heidelberg (this volume)

Santa Cruz M (2007) Intellectual Property Provisions in European Union Trade Agreements: Implications for Developing Countries. Issue Paper No. 20, ICTSD Programme on IPRs and Sustainable Development. http://www.iprsonline.org/resources/docs/Santa-Cruz%20Blue20.pdf

Seuba X (2013) Implementation issues arising from intellectual property chapters contained in trade agreements between the European Union and developing countries. In: Drexl J, Grosse Ruse Khan H, Nadde-Phlix S (eds) EU bilateral trade agreements and intellectual property: for better or worse? Springer, Heidelberg (this volume)

Shabalala D, Bernasconi N (2007) The European Approach to Intellectual Property in European Partnership Agreements with the African, Caribbean and Pacific Group of Countries. Center for International Environmental Law (CIEL). http://62.58.77.233/library/files/CIEL_EN_180407_CIEL_EU-approach-to-IP-in-EPA.pdf

Shabalala D, Orellana M, Bernasconi-Osterwalder N, Plagakis S (2008) Intellectual Property in European Union Economic Partnership Agreements with the African, Caribbean and Pacific Countries: What way Forward after the CARIFORUM EPA and the interim EPAs? Center for International Environmental Law (CIEL). http://www.ciel.org/Publications/Oxfam_TechnicalBrief_5May08.pdf

Taubman A, Wager H, Watal J (eds) (2012) A handbook on the WTO TRIPS agreement. Cambridge University Press, Cambridge

Third World Network (2009) EU EPAS: economic and social development implications: The case of the CARIFORUM-EC Economic Partnership Agreement. http://twnside.org.sg/title2/par/CARIFORUM.Feb09.doc

Vivas-Eugui D, Oliva MJ (2010) Biodiversity related intellectual property provisions in free trade agreements. Issue Paper No. 4, ICTSD Project on Genetic Resources, Natural Resources, International Trade and Sustainable Development. http://ictsd.org/downloads/2011/12/biodiversity-related-intellectual-property-provisions-in-free-trade-agreements.pdf

Vivas-Eugui D, Spennemann C (2006) The treatment of geographical indications in recent WTO discussions and in regional and bilateral agreements. ICTSD, TRALAC and CIEL, Recent Multilateral and Bilateral Trends in IP Policy Making: Lessons and Challenges for Africa. http://ictsd.org/downloads/2009/01/gis20dv2020cs20rev2020sa20dialogue-pdf.pdf

Watal J (2013) Is TRIPS a balanced agreement as seen from the perspective of bilateral/plurilateral free trade agreements? In: Drexl J, Grosse Ruse Khan H, Nadde-Phlix S (eds) EU bilateral trade agreements and intellectual property: for better or worse? Springer, Heidelberg (this volume)

Woolcock S (2007) European Union policy towards Free Trade Agreements. ECIPE Working Paper No. 03/2007. http://www.felixpena.com.ar/contenido/negociaciones/anexos/2010-09-european-union-policy-towards-free-trade-agreements.pdf

Wright L (2004) Trade promotion authority: fast track for the twenty-first century. William & Mary Bill of Rights Journal 12:979-1006. http://scholarship.law.wm.edu/wmborj/vol12/iss3/18

Yu P (2009) The objectives and principles of the TRIPS agreement. Houston Law Rev 46:797–1046

Part III
Emerging Elements for Reforming the International IP System?

Trade Costs and Shadow Benefits: EU Economic Partnership Agreements as Models for Progressive Development of International IP Law

Frederick M. Abbott

Contents

1 Background and Basic Issue

Other chapters in this volume address from a critical perspective the potential impact of European Union (EU) economic partnership agreement (EPA) provisions regulating intellectual property (IP) on economic and social development. As a general matter, developing countries accept as EPA commitments obligations to implement higher and more protective standards of intellectual protection (IP) protection. These obligations supplement the baseline standards of the World Trade Organization's (WTO) Agreement on Trade Related Aspects of Intellectual Property Rights (TRIPS), and are often referred to as "TRIPS-plus" commitments. The TRIPS Agreement is drafted at a moderate level of specificity, and WTO Members are accorded a margin of flexibility regarding the manner in which

F.M. Abbott (✉)
Edward Ball Eminent Scholar Professor of International Law, Florida State University College of Law, 425 W Jefferson St, Tallahassee, FL 32301, USA
e-mail: FAbbott@law.fsu.edu

J. Drexl et al. (eds.), *EU Bilateral Trade Agreements and Intellectual Property: For Better or Worse?*, MPI Studies on Intellectual Property and Competition Law 20,
DOI 10.1007/978-3-642-39097-5_8, © Springer-Verlag Berlin Heidelberg 2014

IP-related obligations are implemented.[1] In addition to the margin of flexibility regarding implementation, WTO Members may take advantage of express exceptions and limitations to the rights of IP right holders, such as limited exceptions to patent rights (Article 30) and compulsory or government use licensing of patents (Article 31). The IP titles (or chapters) in the EU EPAs to varying degrees operate to restrict or limit the flexibilities otherwise enjoyed by WTO Members in their implementation of TRIPS obligations.

There is a general theory of intellectual property rights suggesting that countries at different levels of economic development have different best interests in the strength of IP protection, and that these best interests change over time.[2] Countries that have limited capacity for leading-edge technological innovation may be better off with weaker IP protection that provides more leeway for copying innovation undertaken elsewhere. As the capacity of countries to innovate improves, best interests may shift from appropriation-friendly IP regimes to more protective IP regimes.[3] A commitment to implement TRIPS-plus obligations prior to achieving a threshold level of innovation capacity may, in fact, impede economic and social development. Even countries that have achieved a high level of domestic innovative capacity may suffer from overprotective IP standards in various ways. For example, a proliferation of patents without sufficient regard for identifying and rewarding genuine innovation may unduly block R&D by the scientific community.[4] In areas such as public health, a balance must be struck between interests in rewarding innovation and interests in making innovative technologies available to the public.[5]

The developing country partners in the EPAs certainly are aware that they are conceding policy flexibility in accepting the IP provisions, and that by doing so, *inter alia*, they may be limiting the ability of their domestic industries to make use of EU-generated innovation. There are, however, reasons that developing countries may elect to concede flexibilities relating to IP to the EU that must be assumed to tilt the overall balance of concessions more in their favor, such as improved access to EU markets for their exports.

This chapter addresses a somewhat limited question: Approaching the matter from the standpoint of the EPA IP provisions, do certain elements introduced to create a more development-friendly balance suggest themselves as models for future development of the international IP system? In particular, this chapter will look at four aspects that EU negotiators may view as development-friendly: (1) the incorporation of "sustainable development" as an objective; (2) obligations to

---

[1] See WTO, WT/DS50/AB/R 1997, and Art. 1.1, TRIPS Agreement.

[2] See, e.g., Maskus (2000).

[3] Abbott (2005c).

[4] See, e.g., US Federal Trade Commission (FTC) (2003), Chapter 3.

[5] See, e.g., Abbott (2011).

implement higher standards of protection for geographical indications (GIs); (3) obligations to adhere to Madrid System-related trademark agreements; and (4) references to transfer of technology.

2 Sustainable Development and IP

While most or all of the EPAs include reference to sustainable development, at least in their general objectives, this section will focus on the references to sustainable development in the EPA between the EU and Colombia and Peru (EU/CP EPA).[6] This recent EPA includes fairly detailed treatment of the relationship between biodiversity and IP that goes beyond what is found in other EPAs, presumably reflecting the long-standing interest within Colombia and Peru in this relationship. Decision 391 of the Andean Community (signed in 1996) established a Common Regime on Access to Genetic Resources.[7] Decision 486 of the Andean Community, of September 2000, establishing Common Provisions on Industrial Property,[8] integrates the Common Regime of Decision 391.

Article 4(1) of the EU/CP EPA provides that among the objectives of the agreement are: "(g) to promote international trade in a way that contributes to the objective of sustainable development, and to work in order to integrate and reflect this objective in their trade relations". The objective of sustainable development is incorporated in the preamble of the Agreement establishing the WTO (WTO Agreement). In its decision in the *Shrimp-Turtle* case the Appellate Body had recourse to that principle as it interpreted Article XX of the General Agreement on Tariffs and Trade (GATT) 1994.[9] It used that reference as an important source of

---

[6] See Trade Agreement between the European Union and Colombia and Peru, available at http://trade.ec.europa.eu/doclib/press/index.cfm?id=691.

[7] Decision 391, Common Regime on Access to Genetic Resources, available at http://www.comunidadandina.org/ingles/normativa/d391e.htm.

[8] Decision 486, Common Intellectual Property Regime, available at http://www.comunidadandina.org/ingles/normativa/d486e.htm.

[9] WTO, WT/DS58/AB/R 1998.The Appellate Body stated, at paragraphs 129–132:

> While Article XX was not modified in the Uruguay Round, the preamble attached to the WTO Agreement shows that the signatories to that Agreement were, in 1994, fully aware of the importance and legitimacy of environmental protection as a goal of national and international policy. The preamble of the WTO Agreement—which informs not only the GATT 1994, but also the other covered agreements—explicitly acknowledges "the objective of *sustainable development*":
>
> The *Parties* to this Agreement,
>
> *Recognizing* that their relations in the field of trade and economic endeavour should be conducted *with a view to raising standards of living, ensuring full employment and a large and steadily growing volume of real income and effective demand*, and *expanding the production of and trade in goods and services*, while allowing for the optimal use of the world's resources in accordance with the *objective of sustainable development*, *seeking*

interpretative guidance. It is fair to assume that parties interpreting the EU/CP EPA might similarly rely on the objective of sustainable development as an interpretative source. As a concrete example, if one of the parties adopted an IP-related exceptional measure to implement a climate change mitigation policy and was challenged concerning the "limited" or "reasonable" character of that exceptional measure, the interpreter might have recourse to the general principle to support the adoption of the exceptional measure.

The principle of sustainable development was incorporated in the Rio Declaration and related documents in 1992,[10] and thereafter in the WTO Agreement preamble. While it is useful to acknowledge it in the EU/CP EPA as well, the parties to that agreement have already accepted its general applicability in trade relations. From that standpoint, this acknowledgment is not a concession by the EU in favor of Colombia and Peru.[11]

Chapter 2 of Title VII on Intellectual Property refers to "Protection of Biodiversity and Traditional Knowledge".[12] Article 201 on Protection of Biodiversity is

---

> *both to protect and preserve the environment and to enhance the means for doing so* in a manner consistent with their respective needs and concerns at different levels of economic development ... [emphasis added].
>
> Given the recent acknowledgement by the international community of the importance of concerted bilateral or multilateral action to protect living natural resources, and recalling the explicit recognition by WTO Members of the objective of sustainable development in the preamble of the WTO Agreement, we believe it is too late in the day to suppose that Article XX(g) of the GATT 1994 may be read as referring only to the conservation of exhaustible mineral or other non-living natural resources [footnotes omitted].

[10] See Brown Weiss (1992) and Rio Declaration on Environment and Development (1992).

[11] The EU/CP EPA establishes a Subcommittee on Trade and Sustainable Development. Article 15 (1)(f), EU/CP EPA. The provisions on trade in services also incorporate a reference to sustainable development, at Article 107(1).

[12] Article 201 provides:

> *CHAPTER 2*
> *Protection of Biodiversity and Traditional Knowledge*
> Article 201
>
> 1. The Parties recognise the importance and value of biological diversity and its components and of the associated traditional knowledge, innovations and practices of indigenous and local communities. The Parties furthermore reaffirm their sovereign rights over their natural resources and recognise their rights and obligations as established by the CBD with respect to access to genetic resources, and to the fair and equitable sharing of benefits arising out of the utilization of these genetic resources.
> 2. The Parties recognise the past, present and future contribution of indigenous and local communities to the *conservation and sustainable use of biological diversity* and all of its components ...
> 3. Subject to their domestic legislation, the Parties shall, in accordance with Article 8 (j) of the CBD respect, preserve and maintain knowledge, innovations and practices of indigenous and local communities embodying traditional lifestyles relevant for the *conservation and sustainable use of biological diversity*, and promote their wider

perhaps the best exemplar of a specific use of the concept of sustainable development in relation to IP to be found in the EU/CP EPA.[13] In it, the parties go beyond

application conditioned to the prior informed consent of the holders of such knowledge, innovations and

4. In accordance with Article 15 paragraph 7 of the CBD, the Parties reaffirm their obligation to take measures with the aim of sharing in a fair and equitable way the benefits arising from the utilization of genetic resources. The Parties also recognise that mutually agreed terms may include benefit-sharing obligations in relation to intellectual property rights arising from the use of genetic resources and associated traditional knowledge.
5. Colombia and the EU will collaborate in further clarifying the issue and concept of misappropriation of genetic resources and associated traditional knowledge, innovation and practices so as to find, as appropriate and in accordance with the provisions of international and domestic law, measures to address this issue.
6. The Parties shall cooperate, subject to domestic legislation and international law, to ensure that intellectual property rights are supportive of and do not run counter to their rights and obligations under the CBD, in so far as genetic resources and associated traditional knowledge of the indigenous and local communities located in their respective territories are concerned. The Parties reaffirm their rights and obligations under Article 16 paragraph 3 of the CBD in relation to countries providing genetic resources, to take measures with the aim to provide access to and transfer of technology which makes use of such resources, upon mutually agreed terms. This provision shall apply without prejudice to the rights and obligations under Article 31 of the TRIPS Agreement.
7. The Parties acknowledge the usefulness of requiring the disclosure of the origin or source of genetic resources and associated traditional knowledge in patent applications, considering that this contributes to the transparency about the uses of genetic resources and associated traditional knowledge.
8. The Parties will provide, in accordance with their domestic law, for applicable effects of any such requirement so as to support compliance with the provisions regulating access to genetic resources and associated traditional knowledge, innovations and practices.
9. The Parties will endeavour to facilitate the exchange of information about patent applications and granted patents related to genetic resources and associated traditional knowledge, with the aim that in the substantive examination, particularly in determining prior art, such information can be considered.
10. Subject to the provisions of Chapter 6 (Cooperation) of this Title, the Parties will cooperate on mutually agreed terms in the training of patent examiners in reviewing patent applications related to genetic resources and associated traditional knowledge.
11. The Parties recognise that data bases or digital libraries which contain relevant information constitute useful tools for patentability examination of inventions related to genetic resources and associated traditional knowledge.
12. In accordance with applicable international and domestic law, the Parties agree to collaborate in the application of domestic frameworks on access to genetic resources and associated traditional knowledge, innovations and practices.
13. The Parties, previous mutual agreement, may review this Chapter subject to the results and conclusions of multilateral discussions.

[13] Title IX is titled Trade and Sustainable Development and includes in Article 272(4)–(5) language similar to that found in the Title on IP. There is a dispute settlement mechanism involving a group of experts' recommendations (Article 285) associated with the Subcommittee on Trade and Sustainable Development.

the express obligations of the patent provisions of the TRIPS Agreement by acknowledging the usefulness of requiring the disclosure of the origin or source of genetic resources in patent applications (subparagraph 7), and obligating parties to "provide, in accordance with their domestic law . . . for applicable effects of any such requirement so as to support compliance with the provisions regulating access to genetic resources and associated traditional knowledge, innovations and practices" (subparagraph 8).

The European Union has commonly taken the position in the TRIPS Council and in proposals regarding the relationship between the Convention on Biological Diversity (CBD) and the TRIPS Agreement that disclosure of origin and source of genetic resources is a useful concept,[14] and the EU Biotechnology Directive of 1998 includes a reference to this in Recital 27.[15] It is fair to say that in the EU/CP EPA, the EU accepts in principle what it has already accepted, including in EU legislation. The EU does not go beyond its domestic position, such as by committing to a particular form of remedial action to redress noncompliance. It is also fair to say that the EU does not go beyond what is found in the subsequent Nagoya Protocol on this subject.[16] In other words, each of the parties to the EU/CP EPA has reaffirmed its existing position from international and domestic forums. It may be said that this is preferable, at least in the case of Peru, to the outcome achieved in the US/Peru FTA, in which Peru acknowledged that contract-based solutions to problems of access and benefit sharing were adequate. But if the question is, has Colombia or Peru obtained a concession from the EU that might offset "hard obligations" on IP that they have accepted elsewhere in the agreement, the answer appears to be "no".

With respect to general incorporation of the objective of sustainable development in the EU/CP EPA, and the specific reference in the context of biodiversity and IP, it may be "better than not" that it is included. It is difficult, however, to construe its incorporation as a concrete concession in favor of Colombia and Peru. As a matter of the general development of international law, it is useful that parties continue to reinforce the vibrancy of the principle. But this does not justify the trade-off of a tangible interest.

---

[14] See, e.g., Abbott (2005b). See also ILA Reports.

[15] (27) Whereas if an invention is based on biological material of plant or animal origin or if it uses such material, the patent application should, where appropriate, include information on the geographical origin of such material, if known; whereas this is without prejudice to the processing of patent applications or the validity of rights arising from granted patents.

[16] See, e.g., CBD Secretariat.

3 Enhanced Protection of GIs

The European Union is a strong advocate of enhanced protection of GIs at the WTO and in bilateral and regional negotiations.[17] So far, its efforts to incorporate broader and higher protection in the TRIPS Agreement have not succeeded. A principal reason for its lack of success at the WTO is opposition by the United States. There are two reasons why the United States has objected to enhanced GI protection: (1) it is a major exporter of agricultural products and is concerned that enhanced GI protection may restrict its export markets; (2) retail grocery chains, restaurants and other food service industry groups in the United States are concerned about the potential for claims and litigation by EU producers for infringement of GIs.[18] The EU is not alone in its support of enhanced GI protection. There are a number of developing country governments that believe their countries would benefit from enhanced GI protection. Similarly, the United States is not alone in its opposition. Major agricultural exporting countries, including those in the Cairns Group, share the worries of the United States.

There are detailed proposals from the EU and other WTO Members concerning more detailed GI protection systems within the context of the WTO Doha Development Round. Since negotiations concerning a multilateral register for GIs for countries that accept it are part of the built-in TRIPS Agreement agenda, at least some aspects of enhanced GI protection are not strictly speaking dependent on the outcome of the WTO Doha Development Round, but might be considered separate TRIPS business.

The question whether enhanced protection of GIs would be favorable to economic and social development of developing countries has been debated for many years. The EU and like-minded countries argue that enhanced protection: (1) would benefit local agricultural producers by allowing them to obtain higher prices and better market penetration in export markets; and (2) would protect local consumers against poor-quality imitations. Those who are skeptical of the potential benefits observe: (1) there will be domestic costs arising from displacement of local agricultural producers who may have been using foreign-originating GIs, and potentially higher prices to consumers; (2) protection of GIs in a foreign market is costly both in terms of registration and in terms of bringing legal claims against infringers, and those advocating enhanced GI protection tend to downplay these costs; and (3) consumers tend to be able to distinguish between locally produced and foreign products, and in any case are likely to be price sensitive. It seems reasonable to suggest that the answer whether enhanced GI protection will benefit a developing country is "case specific", depending on an economic analysis of the potential economic gains and losses from the factors just described. Because of the existing imbalance in terms of GI-denominated products in favor of the EU, it seems likely that the EU would be more likely to gain in an exchange of GI

[17] See, e.g., Abbott (2008). See also ILA Reports.

[18] See Abbott (2005a), pp. 350–352.

concessions than most or all developing countries. It is, however, possible to envisage circumstances in which the EU *and* an EPA partner would gain from reciprocal concessions.

Colombia, and to a somewhat lesser extent Peru, are WTO Members that have been sympathetic to enhanced GI protection. Colombia has a strong export interest in its coffee sector and the protection of related GIs. Looking once more through the template of the EU/CP EPA, the parties have negotiated a much higher level of protection for GIs than is required by the TRIPS Agreement baseline. The relevant provisions are at Section 2, Articles 207 to 214, of Title VII. The enhanced protection provisions include a broader definition of GI, a broader subject matter scope of high-level protection requirements (extending to agriculture and food stuff products), and a limitation on the use of GIs in production. Products for which a high level of protection is mandated are set out in an Annex. That Annex XIII is heavily skewed in favor of EU-origin products (approximately 160 for the EU, 3 for Peru, 1 for Colombia). Article 210 establishes a very wide set of rights in favor of the owner of a GI registered in its country of origin, extending to products "like" the GI-protected product, and against uses that exploit the reputation of the GI. Products protected at a high level enjoy protection against "any misuse, imitation or evocation even if the true origin of the product is indicated or if the protected name is translated, transcribed, transliterated or accompanied by an expression such as 'style', 'type', 'method', 'as produced in', 'imitation', 'flavour', 'like' or similar", and further against any false or misleading indication on packaging or advertising liable to convey a false impression as to origin, or any other practice liable to mislead the consumer. GIs are superior to trademarks submitted after an application for protection of the GI in its country of origin. With this broad scope, the EU has achieved substantially more protection than it has even proposed within the framework of the WTO.

Because the EU has secured a high level of protection for over 150 GIs in Colombia and Peru, while Colombia and Peru have secured similar protection in the EU for just a few products, there does on its face appear to be a substantial imbalance between the potential gains in export markets for the different parties. EU exporters will presumably gain market share in Colombia and Peru based on higher levels of protection, which they can afford to enforce. Colombia and Peru may face displacement of local producers, and potentially higher consumer prices. Colombian and Peruvian consumers may have better assurance that the products they purchase are "genuine" imports from the EU.

Based on this exemplar, it is somewhat difficult to posit the GI-related provisions of the EPA as a model for improving economic and social development in developing countries. There may, however, be other EPA partners with a stronger base of GI-protected products for which the results of the negotiations would be more balanced. And it may be that local agricultural producers and food preparation industries will evolve around new developing country GIs.

4 Trademark Registration

Trademarks serve as identifiers distinguishing the goods and services of enterprises.[19] This form of IP permits consumers to identify particular qualities and characteristics of products they prefer, and encourages enterprises to invest in the quality and performance of their goods and services. The principal economic risk associated with trademarks is that they provide a vehicle for investment in advertisement (or goodwill) that may not be validly associated with quality, skewing purchasing decisions of consumers.

Many developing countries maintain rigid and inefficient trademark registration systems that, for example, require separate applications for each class of goods or services, require the appointment of local counsel or agent to file and prosecute applications, and/or do not accept registrations through international mechanisms such as the Madrid System (i.e., the Madrid Agreement and Madrid Protocol) operated through the World Intellectual Property Organization (WIPO).

Multinational corporations and well-capitalized local businesses have the financial resources needed to file and prosecute trademark applications in developed and developing countries. It is, however, a burden on small and medium-sized businesses in developing countries to file and prosecute trademark applications locally and, perhaps more important, to file and prosecute trademark applications in foreign countries. The Madrid System, while imperfect (e.g., once an objection has been raised locally by the trademark office or a third party, parties may require retention of local counsel or agent to further prosecute an application), nevertheless permits small and medium-sized enterprises to secure international protection of their brands with modest expenditure. The Trademark Law Treaty precludes countries from requiring separate applications for each class of goods or services, and standardizes application forms.

The EU EPAs with CARIFORUM, Columbia and Peru (among others), obligate these countries to join, or make their best effort to comply with, the Madrid System and Trademark Law Treaty. Because this system is beneficial to small and medium-sized businesses in developing countries, and encourages their participation in export markets, the requirement of adherence is an example of the type of provision that may generally benefit developing countries, leaving aside the fact that these countries should not require the encouragement of the EU to undertake such commitments.

The situations of trademarks and geographical indications share some common characteristics. Both involve protection of identifiers. Yet in the preceding section of this chapter some skepticism is expressed regarding the value of increasing protection of geographical indications from a developmental standpoint. The reason for this stems from the existing imbalance in stakeholder interests, as exemplified in the EU/CP EPA, and in the obstacles to creating new protectable GIs. The EU owns

---

[19] See discussion of international trademark registration system generally in Abbott et al. (2011), pp. 434–442.

the preponderance of existing registered GIs, and considerable investment is required to create a new GI. By way of contrast, the use of trademarks is prevalent throughout the world, and the cost of developing a new trademark is modest. It is probably more realistic for small and medium-sized enterprises in developing countries to develop new product and service brands for their local markets, and to enter export markets at least at a modest level, than it is for them to create new protectable GIs.

5 Technology Transfer

In principle, bilateral and regional trade agreements provide an excellent opportunity for promoting technology transfer among participating countries. The CARIFORUM countries pressed the European Union in negotiations during 2007 and 2008 to include significant north-south technology transfer obligations in their EPA. The result is reflected in Articles 131 to 142 of the EU/CARIFORUM EPA. A somewhat less ambitious effort is reflected in the EU/CP EPA at Article 255.

The EU/CARIFORUM EPA obligates the EU only to "facilitate and promote" the participation of CARIFORUM countries in its various framework programs and specific programs, including programs designed to facilitate competitiveness among entrepreneurs, participation in research and development programs, exchange of scientific and technical personnel and cooperation among research institutions. From discussions with CARIFORUM negotiators, this author understands that European Commission negotiators cited their lack of capacity to bind EU program budget commitments as grounds for unwillingness to include firm obligations with respect to financing of transfer of technology programs in the EPA. Whatever may be the reason, the terms of the EU/CARIFORUM EPA and the EU/CP EPA follow a familiar pattern—as also evidenced in the TRIPS Agreement—of failure of developed country governments to incorporate firm obligations regarding funding of transfer of technology programs in trade agreements. The soft commitments that are included, e.g., to promote cooperative efforts, typically have not produced meaningful results. This has been well-documented in the case of the TRIPS Agreement transfer of technology provision (Article 66.2) (drafted in favor of least-developed countries). Though it is somewhat difficult to prove the negative, there is an understanding among experts involved in this area that the result has been largely the same under the bilateral/regional agreements. The same phenomenon can be seen in the context of multilateral negotiations regarding the United Nations Framework Convention on Climate Change (UNFCCC) where, so far, there is virtually no concrete action on the subject of technology transfer.

The point here is not that it is unhelpful to include soft commitments regarding transfer of technology in EPAs, but rather to contrast this with hard commitments that would represent a tangible form of trade concession. Colombia and Peru have made significant concessions to the EU in terms of protection of pharmaceutical products, geographical indications and other IP matters. The CARIFORUM countries have perhaps made a less significant level of IP-related concessions in light of the somewhat less developed state of their IP regimes at the time the EPA was concluded. In each case, however, it would have been useful to offset the developing country IP concessions with a commitment from the EU to provide support to their innovation infrastructures through concrete measures. A soft commitment to "think about" transfer of technology in a favorable way is not a model for future negotiations in support of developing countries.

6 EPAs as a Model for Progressive Development of International IP Law

The chapters in this volume largely present a critical perspective on the terms of the IP provisions in the EPAs. Particular concerns are raised in the field of patents and data exclusivity that affect access to medicines, as well as to provisions that may affect access to climate change mitigation technologies, and other areas of social welfare concern. More generally, there is concern that the EPAs deprive developing country partners of the margins of flexibility allowed under the TRIPS Agreement to pursue development-friendly industrial policies.

This chapter addresses provisions of the EPAs that might be perceived as introducing elements more favorable to developmental interests. The inclusion of sustainable development as a general objective of the EPA may assist developing countries that have implemented IP flexibilities where a conflict over textual interpretation arises. The objective of sustainable development already is acknowledged in a range of international agreements, including the WTO Agreement, and its acknowledgment in the EPAs is a modest contribution to developmental objectives. The provisions of the EU/CP EPA that address sustainable use of biodiversity do not add to commitments already made in the context of the CBD, the recent Nagoya Protocol, or by the EU in other multilateral negotiating forums. The provisions on transfer of technology suffer from a lack of concrete commitment. Particularly in the present economic environment, where EU governmental resources are strained, it is not clear that the soft statements of sentiment will have a significant practical result. In the field of GIs, the EU as a practical matter has negotiated a significant IP benefit for its agricultural exporters. Judging by the list of GIs attached to the EU/CP EPA, the benefit to developing country party exporters is small, and must be weighed against the potential displacement of local agricultural producers by EU GI-protected products. Developing countries might well benefit from joining the Madrid System trademark registration system, but can obviously do so without a mandate from an EPA.

Developing country parties to EPAs with the EU assess the overall trade benefits and costs of the agreement, and consider political factors as well. The chapters presented in this volume strongly suggest that the IP chapters of the EPAs represent a cost. The provisions in the IP chapters that reference sustainable development, transfer of technology and other potentially development-friendly objectives or undertakings may provide some benefits at the margin, but they are not constructed in such a way as to offset concrete costs in areas such as access to pharmaceutical technologies. They appear largely to be in the nature of "window dressing", more shadow than substance. In this regard, they do not lend themselves as models for the future development of international IP law. Constructed in some other way, they might.

References

Abbott FM (2005a) Geographical indications at the Hong Kong ministerial. ICTSD session on recovering multilateralism in IP policy making: can the WTO deliver? Reprinted (2011). In: Abbott FM, Cottier T, Gurry F (eds) International intellectual property in an integrated world economy, 2nd edn. Aspen, New York

Abbott FM (2005b) Preservation and use of genetic resource assets and the international patent system. Study for the Ministry of Foreign Affairs of Norway, Hong Kong Ministerial Revision. http://papers.ssrn.com/sol3/papers.cfm?abstract_id=1924481

Abbott FM (2005c) Toward a new era of objective assessment in the field of TRIPS and variable geometry for the preservation of multilateralism. J Int Econ Law (8)1:77–100

Abbott FM (2008) Post-mortem for the Geneva mini-ministerial: where does TRIPS go from here? ICTSD Information Note No. 7. http://ictsd.org/i/publications/16949

Abbott FM (2011) Intellectual property and public health: meeting the challenge of sustainability, Global Health Programme Working Paper No. 7/2011. http://papers.ssrn.com/sol3/papers.cfm?abstract_id=1965458

Abbott FM, Cottier T, Gurry F (eds) (2011) International intellectual property in an integrated world economy, 2nd edn. Aspen, New York

Biennial reports of the Committee on International Trade Law of the International Law Association regarding developments in TRIPS. http://www.ila-hq.org/en/committees/index.cfm/cid/24

Brown Weiss E (1992) Introductory note, United Nations Conference on Environment and Development, 31 I.L.M., 814

CBD Secretariat: About the Nagoya protocol. http://www.cbd.int/abs/about/

Rio Declaration on Environment and Development (1992) Report of the United Nations Conference on Environment and Development, Rio de Janeiro, 3-14 June 1992, Annex I. http://www.un.org/documents/ga/conf151/aconf15126-1annex1.htm

International Law Association (ILA) (2000-2012) Biennial Reports of the Committee on International Trade Law regarding developments in TRIPS. http://www.ila-hq.org/en/committees/index.cfm/cid/24

Maskus K (2000) Intellectual property rights in the global economy. Petersen Institute for International Economics. Petersen Institute for International Economics, Washington

US Federal Trade Commission (FTC) (2003) To promote innovation: the proper balance of competition and patent law and policy. http://www.ftc.gov/os/2003/10/innovationrpt.pdf

World Trade Organization (WTO). (a) WT/DS50/AB/R, Report of the Appellate Body, India - Patent Protection for Pharmaceutical and Agricultural Chemical Products, 19 December 1997. http://www.wto.org/english/tratop_e/dispu_e/tripab.pdf. (b) WT/DS58/AB/R, Report of the Appellate Body, United States - Import Prohibition of Certain Shrimp and Shrimp Products, 12 October 1998. http://www.wto.org/english/tratop_e/dispu_e/58abr.pdf

Assessing the Development Promise of IP Provisions in EU Economic Partnership Agreements

Keith E. Maskus

Contents

1 Introduction

Since launching its "Global Europe Strategy" in 2006 the European Union (EU) has actively sought negotiations with developing countries to conclude free trade agreements (FTAs) and economic partnership agreements (EPAs) that have a significant focus on enhanced protection of intellectual property rights (IPRs). In pursuing its own "TRIPS-plus" agenda in these EPAs, the EU follows the lead of the United States, Japan and the European Free Trade Area. The United States in particular demands strong protection for patent owners, particularly in

K.E. Maskus (✉)
Professor of Economics, Department of Economics, University of Colorado, Boulder, CO, USA
e-mail: keith.maskus@colorado.edu

J. Drexl et al. (eds.), *EU Bilateral Trade Agreements and Intellectual Property: For Better or Worse?*, MPI Studies on Intellectual Property and Competition Law 20,
DOI 10.1007/978-3-642-39097-5_9,

pharmaceuticals and agricultural technologies, and extensive rules covering digital copyrighted materials. This strategy has attracted considerable criticism because the high standards of protection sometimes seem inconsistent with the needs and preferences of developing-country partners.[1]

Perhaps aware of this problem, EU negotiators have agreed to language in recent EPAs that recognizes the primacy of economic development goals for agreement partners, including in the context of IPRs. For example, in the EU FTA with Colombia and Peru, approved by the European Commission in 2011, Article 197 asserts the rights of parties to make use of the exceptions and flexibilities in multilateral intellectual property agreements, take steps to safeguard public health and take measures to prevent the abuse of IPRs. These provisions essentially incorporate limitations on IPRs set out by the World Trade Organization (WTO) Agreement on Trade-Related Aspects of Intellectual Property Rights (TRIPS), the Doha Declaration and related proclamations. At the same time, however, the FTA calls for extended periods of exclusivity for confidential test data, protection of digital rights management systems from circumvention, strong legal rights to geographical indications (GIs) and extensive enforcement obligations, all in excess of TRIPS requirements. Whether such provisions truly are friendly for development remains an area of intense debate among intellectual property (IP) scholars and practitioners.

In this chapter I offer a qualitative exploration of two recent EU agreements—the EU-CARIFORUM EPA and the EU-Colombia-Peru FTA—in terms of their evident abilities either to promote or to retard economic development. Inevitably, such discussion must be placed in a broader context regarding the global system of IPRs. Thus, I will focus on three basic questions. First, what provisions in these agreements seem to offer genuine promise for enhancing economic development prospects? For this purpose the next section of the chapter reviews the relevant language. Second, the EU's intense policy focus on globalizing protection of GIs appears strongly in these agreements. How likely is it that strong protection in this area will be beneficial for the partner countries and developing nations more generally? This issue is considered in Sect. 3.

Third, the EU agreements pay some attention to the need for protecting traditional knowledge, especially arising from the use of genetic resources, an area outside the scope of TRIPS. How this idea would play out in actual policy remains unclear at this point, as I discuss in Sect. 4. Concluding remarks are offered in the final section.

[1] Roffe and Spennemann (2006); Maskus (2006).

2 Development Objectives in the EU Trade Agreements

Let us begin with a review of development-related basic objectives in these two agreements.

2.1 EU-CARIFORUM EPA

This EPA is supposed to "contribut[e] to the reduction and eventual eradication of poverty" through an agreement that is consistent with sustainable development and the Millennium Development Goals (Article 1(a)). For this purpose, the Parties, "taking into account their respective levels of development and consistent with WTO obligations" will establish a "progressive, asymmetrical liberalization of trade between them and reinforce, broaden and deepen cooperation in all areas relevant to trade and investment" (Article 1(f)). Two elements are particularly relevant here. First, paying attention to respective development levels should offer flexibility to the CARIFORUM partners with respect to key IP provisions, as noted below. Second, the commitment to asymmetric trade liberalization presumably envisions larger cuts in trade barriers, and greater reforms toward stronger and more harmonized IPRs, in the Caribbean partners.

One of the agreement's central principles is to promote sustainability. Thus, Article 3.1 notes that "the objective of sustainable development is to be applied and integrated at every level of the economic partnership." Further, Article 3.2 notes that the Parties "shall fully take into account the human, cultural, economic, social, health and environmental best interests of their respective population and future generations." The implications of such language for a reformed regime of IPRs within CARIFORUM are unclear, primarily because the direct linkages between intellectual property protection and sustainable development are ambiguous and controversial. Presumably, however, this passage also supports a reasonable degree of flexibility in limiting the scope of patents, trade secrets and plant variety rights in order to promote public health, educational and environmental objectives.

Turning next to IPRs, specifically covered in Chapter 2 of the agreement, there is one interesting innovation. Specifically, the Parties "recognize that the protection and enforcement of intellectual property plays a key role in fostering creativity, innovation and competitiveness, and are determined to ensure increasing levels of protection *appropriate to their levels of development*" (Article 131.2; emphasis added). Thus, while the accord surely envisions significant enhancements in protection in the CARIFORUM nations, this provision offers considerable scope for avoiding full IP harmonization with the EU.

The IP chapter incorporates a wide range of objectives (Article 132). The foundational goal is to achieve an adequate and effective level of protection and enforcement of IPRs. Such protection is then presumed to foster competitiveness of enterprises, especially those of small and medium size, and promote innovation and the transfer and dissemination of technology and know-how. While these are standard aims of virtually all FTAs and EPAs, the EU-CARIFORUM accord goes beyond them to encourage, develop and facilitate cooperative R&D activities in science and technology (S&T) between the Parties and similarly to encourage cooperative production and development activities in the creative industries.

The attention to S&T is a novel formulation in trade agreements. To achieve it, the EPA sets out a full set of aspirations on cooperation in Article 136. Among the more interesting are calls for cooperation in establishing joint research networks, fostering researcher exchanges and proposals to participate in the Seventh Framework Programme for Research and Technological Development (FP7) and development of links between the private and public sector. Further, the agreement lists similar objectives in the areas of information and communications technologies and in eco-innovation and renewable energy. For example, it aims to promote exchange of information on standards and interoperability issues (Article 137) and encourage eco-innovation networks, including through public-private networks (Article 138).

As an economic matter, if there is real substance to these technology-transfer and knowledge-sharing objectives, then the EPA will be of considerable benefit for S&T development and industrial transformation. Many commentators have called for a more open and collaborative approach to S&T sharing but no prior trade agreement calls for it.[2] If the EC really were to open up some publicly funded grant programs to participation by Caribbean scientists, even in partnership with EU research networks, it would represent an important step toward achieving sustainable knowledge transfers that could build the scientific and educational capacities of partner countries. There is reason to question this commitment, however, due to the significant opt-out in Article 134. In particular, CARIFORUM nations may participate in "existing and future framework programmes" but only to the extent permitted by EC internal rules (and those of EC members) governing such access. It will be interesting to see if this commitment amounts to anything meaningful as the EPA is implemented.

Like TRIPS and the FTAs negotiated by the United States, the IP chapter of the EU-CARIFORUM EPA declares that policy reforms will encourage technology transfer and diffusion. To be sure, statistical evidence suggests that stronger patent laws are an important pre-condition for expanding international technology flows through FDI and licensing.[3] An important caveat, however, is that such findings seem to pertain only to reforms in larger and middle-income emerging economies. It seems optimistic to expect this positive outcome in the small and poor economies of the Caribbean region unless the offsetting trade benefits of the EPA combine with patent reforms to encourage more technology flows. It should also be noted that Article 142 of the EPA contains no specific obligations for EC countries to expand technology transfer. Rather, the language refers to increased information flows and marketing opportunities, while exhorting the CARIFORUM nations to improve their business environments for inward technology transfer. Undoubtedly,

[2] Barton and Maskus (2006).

[3] Park (2008); Branstetter et al. (2006).

the latter is an important element of economic transition, which may be facilitated by the EPA in total. Overall, however, the IP chapter offers little concrete to encourage technology flows.

It is also worth noting that Article 142.2 also stipulates that both the EC and CARIFORUM States "shall take measures, as appropriate, to prevent or control licensing practices or conditions pertaining to intellectual property rights which may adversely affect the international transfer of technology and that constitute an abuse of intellectual property rights or an abuse of obvious information asymmetries in the negotiation of licenses." It is likely that the CARIFORUM countries would find it difficult to undertake and sustain an effective competition regime to discipline such abuses, given limited resources and expertise in this area. However, Article 142 does not seem to rule out the possibility that EC competition authorities could take action against firms that engage in abusive licensing practices in CARIFORUM. Any such extraterritorial application would be controversial, but could be an affirmative route toward disciplining anticompetitive practices in the developing world.[4] It remains to be seen whether this intriguing possibility could be operationalized in the context of the EPA.

Where the EU-CARIFORUM agreement departs significantly from recent US FTAs, in a direction that most would consider favorable for sustainable development, is the absence of TRIPS-plus protection for pharmaceuticals.[5] Rather, Article 147B reaffirms the significance of the policy flexibilities noted in the Doha Declaration on TRIPS and Public Health. It further commits both Parties to implement the 2005 amendment to TRIPS permitting poor countries to import medicines produced under a compulsory license elsewhere to meet their specific needs. In short, the EPA places no restrictions beyond TRIPS on the ability of CARIFORUM partner states to issue compulsory licenses, import medicines in parallel markets or other competition-oriented limitations on patents. Indeed, Article 139.2 states that nothing in the agreement shall be interpreted to limit the capacity of member countries to promote access to medicines.

In contrast, the obligations to enforce IPRs go far beyond anything envisioned in TRIPS, which comports with the EU's strong focus (along with the United States and other developed countries) on improving global enforcement. Thus, the EU-CARIFORUM EPA calls for the sharing of private banking and financial information in infringement cases, seizure of financial assets, issuance of preliminary injunctions and calculation of damages from infringement on a markedly comprehensive definition of costs.[6] These conditions are similar to the strong protections set out in the Anti-Counterfeiting Trade Agreement (ACTA), a pact

---

[4] See also Drexl (2013) in this volume discussing Article 142(2) in detail.

[5] On these provisions, such as extended patent terms, lengthy test data protection and restrictions on generic entry, see Roffe and Spennemann (2006). It should be noted that where the United States has negotiated such rules, they would apply equally to IPRs owned by pharmaceutical companies from the EU.

[6] See also Jaeger (2013) in this volume discussing IP enforcement provisions.

agreed by major developed and emerging economies to combat trade in counterfeit goods.[7] Whether authorities in the Caribbean nations might have sufficient resources and capabilities to meet these expectations remains doubtful.

2.2 EU-Colombia-Peru FTA

This free trade agreement is quite similar to the EU-CARIFORUM EPA in its general treatment of IPRs. For example, a key general provision of Title VII (on intellectual property) recognizes the importance of maintaining balance between the rights of IP holders and the public interest, including education, culture, public health, environmental protection and so on. It also explicitly notes that Parties may make use of the limitations and flexibilities offered by TRIPS and other agreements, including especially those regarding access to medicines and measures taken to prevent the abuse of IPRs. Further, both agreements note the importance of technology transfer and encourage the development of joint research activities and networks, facilitation of scientific exchanges and the like. Neither agreement imposes positive obligations on the EU to foster technology transfer, however.

Another area of flexibility in the agreements is worth noting. Regarding trademarks, partners in both the EPA and the FTA were able to negotiate a limited fair-use exception, under which a firm may apply descriptive terms regarding the kind and quality, intended purpose, or geographic origin of goods so long as they are used in good faith and not as trademarks. This provision permits a limited continued use of descriptors in good faith without achieving authorization of the trademark owner. In copyrights, both agreements commit parties to abide by the provisions of the WIPO Copyright Treaty and the WIPO Performances and Phonograms Treaty, which call for legal restrictions against technical measures taken to defeat digital rights. However, the Peru-Colombia FTA has considerably more extensive copyright provisions, including a minimum protection term of life plus 70 years (or 70 years for works created by an entity other than a natural person), which goes beyond the TRIPS (and, therefore, the EPA) rule of 50 years. The FTA also calls for the protection of moral rights and performance and broadcast rights, none of which are mentioned in the EPA.

The EU-Colombia-Peru FTA takes greater pains to protect patent owners in pharmaceuticals than does the EPA. Specifically, the FTA permits countries to make exclusive rights available in cases where the effective patent term is curtailed due to unreasonable delays in marketing approval. It also requires that Parties grant exclusivity periods for protecting undisclosed test data submitted to government authorities in applications for marketing rights, with these periods being five years

[7] Yu (2011). It should be noted that ACTA encountered considerable opposition by legislatures in the EU, Mexico and other nations and its ultimate ratification into law is doubtful.

for pharmaceutical products and ten years for chemical agricultural products. These protection terms, which are consistent with EU procedures, are not mentioned in the CARIFORUM EPA, presumably because Caribbean countries approve such products on a simple registration basis rather than performing regulatory examinations. Still, there are no further TRIPS-plus rules in the FTA regarding patented pharmaceuticals, again underscoring the more flexible approach the EU takes to this issue in comparison with the United States.

Regarding enforcement of IPRs, the two agreements set out largely the same central provisions, including resort to preliminary injunctions against suspected infringement, suspension of the release of goods into commerce and a comprehensive definition of economic damages.[8] Interestingly, the provisions of the EU-CARIFORUM EPA on release of financial records and blockage of access to financial accounts do not appear in the FTA. On another front, the latter explicitly states that internet service providers are not to be held liable for unwittingly transmitting or storing infringing materials. However, those providers do have a "take down" obligation to remove or disable access to such materials when they become aware of them.

2.3 *Summary*

In general terms, the various objectives set out in these two agreements seem consistent with the notion that the EU's trading partners should retain a significant degree of flexibility in limiting the scope of IPRs in order to promote sustainable development. This is particularly evident in the area of public health and access to medicines, where the agreements take the TRIPS Agreement and the Doha Declaration as their foundations. Indeed, the only TRIPS-plus provision is the requirement in the EU-Colombia-Peru FTA for preserving the confidentiality of test data in pharmaceuticals and agricultural chemicals for periods consistent with EC law. Moreover, these agreements both open doors for additional access to scientific and technical exchanges, potentially raising access to EU-generated knowledge on behalf of these developing countries. It remains to be seen how effective such commitments may be for expanding actual transfers of technology.

In contrast to this pro-development orientation in IP law, the enforcement obligations set out in both agreements are considerably stronger and more prescriptive than the baselines set out in TRIPS. This approach is consistent with the emphasis that the EU and other developed economies increasingly place on the importance of expanding border enforcement, increasing civil and criminal penalties and raising defenses against internet copyright infringement.

---

[8] See again Jaeger (2013) in this volume.

3 Geographical Indications

One truly distinctive feature of recent EU EPAs and FTAs is their insistence on extensive provisions regarding the protection of GIs. Specific mention of GIs is rarely made in corresponding agreements made by the United States. This situation reflects the stark difference in approaches to protecting the place names attached to goods by reason of specific quality characteristics or production processes.[9] The United States, along with many other "new world" producers of wines, spirits and food products, argues that product quality and innovation and entrepreneurial flexibility within a geographic area can be sufficiently promoted by certification marks and collective marks. The former are available to any firm that demonstrates through a certification process that its product meets certain quality conditions, which may include geographical origin, such as "Napa Valley wine". Collective trademarks, such as "California Blue Almonds," are owned by an association of producers and may or may not refer to products from a particular origin. In contrast, core members of the European Union, such as France, Spain, Portugal and Italy, have a long tradition of preserving the use of geographical names directly for those producers located in a region who produce goods according to precise specifications. In the EU use of a GI is reserved exclusively for qualified producers in a region, making it a more restrictive mechanism than a certification or collective mark.

There is a strong trade-policy reason for this emphasis on GIs in trade agreements. Specifically as it shifts away from strict price supports the EU's agricultural policy now emphasizes the gains in rural incomes and wealth that may stem from producing premium-priced goods with the benefit of protected GIs.[10] These income benefits are larger the greater the geographical scope in which a country's GIs are registered. In consequence, the EU places a strong priority on pushing globally stronger protection for GIs in its trade policy.

3.1 GIs in the Agreements

Both the trade agreements considered here feature extensive sections on GIs. Thus, the EU-CARIFORUM EPA obligates Caribbean countries to establish a system of GI protection by January 1, 2014. The most significant requirements are as follows. First, the registration system must be reserved for "goods originating in the geographical area concerned and that are produced in accordance with the relevant product specifications" (Article 145.B.2). The clause regarding product specifications evidently commits these partners to recognize EU-registered GIs based on such technical processes, a considerably stronger standard than that

[9] Fink and Maskus (2006).

[10] Josling (2006).

envisioned in TRIPS or in the United States. It also reserves GIs for Caribbean goods that meet specified production characteristics, rather than simply for products made in a designated region. This language would seem to preclude reliance on collective marks as a system of GI protection, pushing CARIFORUM nations closer to the EU standards.

Second, the agreement calls for "higher level" protection of GIs by banning their use by goods not from a geographical origin, even if the usage would not confuse consumers about the true origins of those products (Article 145.B.3). It also precludes such use even if the place name is accompanied by terms such as kind, style, imitation, or type. These conditions apply to all classes of products, not just wines and spirits. Third, applications for trademarks that are similar to, or contain, a protected GI in the same product class must be refused registration. Further, if a GI application is made prior to a similar trademark application the latter must be denied if the former is ultimately approved. Thus, GIs are given priority over other types of marks in the protection system.[11] It is evident that such priority could raise uncertainty about the prospects for protection for other marks.

Turning to the FTA with Colombia and Peru, each partner is required to provide high-level protection for the GIs posted to Annex XIII, which lists nearly 100 established EU indications covering wines, sprits and foodstuffs along with one Colombian GI (a kind of fruit) and three Peruvian GIs (two vegetables and pisco, the famous liquor). It is noteworthy that the EU GIs include several designations that are considered generic or semi-generic in many other countries, such as Champagne, Chablis, Roquefort and sherry. The specific language makes a distinction between protection for wines and spirits and for other goods. For the former products usage of words such as style, type or imitation is precluded even if there is no likelihood of consumer confusion. For the latter goods unauthorised use of protected GIs is not permitted where it may create such confusion, even if such descriptors are added (Article 210(1)(b)). Thus, the likelihood of consumer confusion is the condition determining the legal usage of words such as style or imitation for GIs other than wines and spirits. Parties may protect other (unlisted) GIs according to their own laws and regulations, though governments may request that new indications may be accorded the higher-level treatment, subject to a review. Note also that Article 207 states that no GIs may lapse into generic use so long as they remain protected in their country of origin. Finally, trademarks that could cause confusion with a GI may not be registered or must be invalidated, but only if the trademark application is made after the corresponding GI application. Moreover, Parties need not protect a GI if doing so could mislead consumers in cases where a well-known trademark exists. Overall, while there are similarities in the two agreements, the EU-Colombia-Peru FTA offers a narrower scope of protection for GIs than does the EU-CARIFORUM EPA.

[11] Another example of this preference arises in Article 144 F, in which the fair use limitations on trademark rights are somewhat broader than those regarding GIs.

3.2 The Development Potential of GIs

Given the importance the EU places on geographical indications in its regional trade agreements it is worth asking whether such protection is likely to promote sustainable economic and rural development in developing-country partners. A number of poor countries, such as India, Thailand and Sri Lanka, see considerable promise in adopting and protecting strong GI systems for encouraging higher value production in agriculture and handicrafts. The hope is that effective use of GIs will help transfer more of the economic value of such goods, which may command a premium in high-income foreign markets, to local farmers and villages. Sustainability and biodiversity could be enhanced also to the extent that GIs promote the use of traditional production methods and development of markets for specific crops and food products.

The likelihood of such outcomes cannot be predicted with confidence because much depends on the complex economics of GIs.[12] Like other forms of intellectual property, GIs exist to address certain failures in markets for information. It is evident that consumers enjoy choosing among differentiated specialties but are willing to pay higher prices for truly higher quality. However, in markets where producers cannot certify that their goods have higher quality there is little incentive to invest in making better products.

In this context, GIs can signal the quality characteristics of what economists call "search goods" or "experience goods." Basic staple commodities, such as wheat and sugar, generally do not warrant GI protection because they can be produced with homogeneous quality in many locations. Consumers do not spend time or resources in determining the quality of such goods. However, it may be hard to determine the quality variations of differentiated goods, a task that would require significant search costs for consumers looking to find the most desirable characteristics. The experience of consuming a good permits a person to determine its quality. However, even that may not be enough to determine its true source. Thus, "credence attributes" (that is, whether a fortified wine comes from Porto or an ikat design is from Bali) often require even further protection to establish the certainty of origin.[13]

GIs permit firms to signal quality characteristics arising from regional variations and thereby considerably reduce search costs. In this way consumer markets are made more efficient and, indeed, GIs may create domestic and even global markets that would not otherwise exist. These information signals are especially important for experience goods, such as wine and cheese, where consumers appreciate quality variations from prior consumption but cannot readily distinguish among products simply by inspection.

[12] Josling (2006); Fink and Maskus (2006); Yeung and Kerr (2008).

[13] Hobbs and Kerr (2006).

Thus, laws defining and protecting GIs offer potential consumer gains by eliminating fraud and misinformation and reducing search costs. There are benefits to producers also via enhanced reputation and premium prices, permitting farmers to move away from producing undifferentiated commodity crops to filling distinctive market niches. For example, hedonic price studies have found evidence that European and Australian GIs support significant price premiums in wines, spirits and specialty meats and cheeses.[14] Some advocates also argue that there are spillover benefits from GIs, including greater community organizational skills among farmers and artisans, preservation of traditional cultures and rural development.

Set against such benefits are a daunting array of risks and costs in building and using GIs.[15] From a public administration standpoint, these costs include establishing a registration and certification system, defining and enforcing standards, defending GIs against misappropriation and providing subsidies or other support to producer groups. For example, a small group of farmers in a particular region of a poor country may not be able to marshal the significant investments needed to establish credible signals of quality and the extensive marketing costs required to interest consumers in another part of the country, let alone in foreign markets. Even if those investments could be made, the likelihood of building a sustained market demand in an overseas market in the face of significant competition and changing consumer demands is doubtful in many cases. This is a collective action problem and governments inevitably find that they must support the development and use of GIs, through both regulation and marketing subsidies.

Additional costs arise from the inherent exclusivity of the rights awarded by GIs. Defining and enforcing rules regarding production processes, geographical boundaries and conditions under which future producers may use a protected GI are likely to be contentious and subject to regulatory capture. For example, contentious litigation ensued over defining the precise boundaries of the Coonawarra designation in South Australia, since wineries lying just outside the region would not be able to benefit from it.[16] To the extent that such rules exclude alternative users who could compete under the GI without confusing consumers they are overly strong. Further, GIs may themselves become roadblocks to future innovation as producers cling to traditional methods rather than embracing newer technologies.

Policy authorities need to balance the consumer information gains and producer benefits against costs of administration, public supports, transaction costs and market power from exclusive rights. Since these effects depend on particular circumstances, it is always an empirical question as to whether GI protection is likely to work.

---

[14] Fink and Maskus (2006).

[15] Yeung and Kerr (2008).

[16] Rimmer (2009).

There are certainly cases where protection of place names in developing countries has supported market development. For example, tequila is an appellation of origin owned by the government of Mexico. The Mexican Institute of Intellectual Property (IMPI) authorizes and regulates use of the word, which is available only to certified producers in five states using Agave tequilana weber cactus grown in that region. At the top end of the quality spectrum there has been considerable product differentiation and global market growth. By one report, as of November, 2010, there were 1,232 brands of tequila available, twice the number of five years earlier, with most of that growth in artisanal varieties.[17] Another example is the successful international marketing of Ethiopian coffees from particular regions under governmental registration of foreign trademarks.[18] Producers in Argentina and Chile have developed high quality wines in a number of locations. However, none of those industries relied on rigorous EU-style geographical indications, as opposed to collective marks, trademarks and certification procedures. Moreover, at least in the case of tequila some observers claim that growth in the industry has had little positive impact on the incomes of poor farmers in the region.

Despite this mixed evidence, authorities in numerous developing countries view GIs as a positive force for economic development.[19] For example, since implementation of legislation protecting GIs in 1999, the intellectual property office of India has registered 164 domestic GIs along with eight prominent international indications, such as Napa Valley, Porto, Champagne and pisco. The vast majority of the domestic registrations are for localized handicrafts and agricultural products, suggesting that enterprises in Indian regions see value in protecting and building their reputations in this way. While few of these GIs, other than Darjeeling tea, would be recognizable outside the country, it is conceivable that sales growth in the domestic market will generate sufficient volumes to serve as a platform for exports upon registration of these GIs in foreign destinations. Thailand has also seen a significant expansion of domestic applications since passing its *sui generis* law on GIs in 2003. Some of the protected products, such as Surin Hom Mali rice, are carving out markets in Europe and elsewhere.

From this basic overview, what might be concluded about GIs and economic development? First, promising success stories exist in terms of output growth and value added, though there is little evidence available on the extent of administrative costs, marketing investments and public subsidies needed to achieve them. Second, GI protection offers some promise for generating income from traditional knowledge and handicrafts, as noted in the next section. Third, the majority of developing countries have adopted *sui generis* laws protecting geographical indications, rather than adopting the strict versions in place in the European Union. Fourth, to date relatively few GIs from poor countries have been registered in the EU. Recall, for

---

[17] Plotkin (2011)

[18] Maskus (2012).

[19] Rangnekar (2004); Maskus (2012).

example, that in the EU-Colombia-Peru FTA the two Andean partners listed just three GIs between them for protection.

In that context, a few remarks—necessarily speculative—may be made about the development potential of GIs as set out in the two agreements considered here. First, the EU-CARIFORUM EPA is far more restrictive in its expectations of policies in the Caribbean nations. Specifically, they must condition registration of GIs on both location and technical production processes, offer higher level protection for goods beyond wine and spirits and grant a form of legal priority to GIs over trademark applications. It is questionable whether such provisions will do much other than significantly raise costs of developing new GIs in these countries. In contrast, Peru and Colombia will be able to keep their more flexible registration systems in place and are not required to offer higher level protection outside the specific goods listed in the Annex. Second, as has been noted by many authors,[20] the simple registration, by itself, of domestic GIs is not likely to stimulate much business or rural development. The regime must be accompanied by complementary public policies to improve legal processes, infrastructure, governance, labor skills and other factors needed for a sound investment climate. These factors come in addition to public supports for GI development and marketing.

In this regard, it may be that the overall economic effects of these EU partnership agreements will support such policy transformations and facilitate the development role of GIs. This would be more likely to the extent the accords attract significantly more investment and technology transfer to the partner nations, a possibility that it is too early to assess. As noted earlier, some aspects of the language on technology transfer is novel and may work in this positive direction.

However, if the EU authorities wished to promote the use of GIs in its partner countries as a form of development policy, they could entertain the possibility of offering some "special and differential" treatment in this area.[21] For example, they might offer preferential access terms, including lower fees, for GIs from developing and low-income countries. They could also offer technical and financial assistance to the developing-country EPA partners to improve the administration and enforcement of GIs.

4 Genetic Resources and Traditional Knowledge

While skeptical economists might question the potential for GIs to generate much income for poor farmers, few observers doubt the commercial possibilities from international trade in goods arising from the use of genetic resources (GRs) and traditional knowledge (TK). The phrase genetic resources refers to the diverse plant materials occurring in nature from which food crops, new plant varieties, medicines

[20] Rangnekar (2004); Josling (2006).

[21] Maskus (2012).

and other biotechnological products are derived. Traditional knowledge is a broad term covering a wide range of generally informal understandings about such items as the medicinal effects of plants, artisanal designs, oral histories, cultural expressions, folklore and music. Both GRs and TK exist in a knowledge "semi-commons," often involving communal understandings but poorly defined collective ownership. Indeed, much TK is not "owned" in any proprietary sense, but is rather collectively held procedures and cultural goods passed down from prior generations.

As a matter of economics, there are major potential gains from trade if the basic ownership and sharing problems are properly worked out. Poor countries are the primary suppliers of GRs emanating from great biodiversity, yet generally lack the scientific infrastructure and commercial mechanisms to develop them. Companies and research institutions in rich countries wish to have access to genetic materials to support the production of new technologies. Regarding TK, one needs to think only of the Disney movies *Mulan* (from a Chinese folk tale) or the Weavers' hit song *The Lion Sleeps Tonight* (from a South African traditional song) to understand the economic value such knowledge contains. Traditional medicines, already a significant commercial industry in China and India, are becoming globally traded products.

Leading experts have described the potential for a "grand bargain" in materials, technologies and products that could support growth of markets based on biodiversity and genetic resources.[22] On the basis of crude statistics and methods, these authors calculate that the world markets for products developed from genetic resources already amounted to between $500 billion and $800 billion in 1999, a figure that is surely much larger today and did not consider the scope for trade in TK.

In this context, sound principles for the exploitation, use and conservation of GRs can contribute both to biodiversity and to sustainable agricultural development.[23] Benefit-sharing arrangements, in which local villagers or authorities receive payments from enterprises and scientific institutions taking resources for commercial development, can raise rural incomes and sustain incentives for in-situ conservation. Similarly, efforts to catalogue and register elements of TK can ensure that folklore, cultural expressions, music and handicraft designs find commercial markets, or, if local peoples prefer, remain outside the marketplace.

Clearly, IPRs can play an important role in building the markets and institutions to support such exchanges.[24] It is here, for example, that a legal regime of protection for GIs, in concert with trademarks, can sort out the boundaries of collective ownership for localized handicrafts and foodstuffs. Similarly, copyrights

[22] Ten Kate and Laird (1999).

[23] Dutfield (2005)

[24] Gervais (2005, 2009).

of catalogued material can help spread benefits to local peoples from the use of cultural expressions. Design patents and utility models can support small-scale innovation as traditional knowledge becomes more codified and formally enters the pool of prior art.[25]

4.1 *The EU Agreements*

The two EU partnership agreements analyzed here treat the issue of supporting GRs and TK in general terms. Article 150 in the EU-CARIFORUM EPA sets out no obligations on either side and simply recognizes the importance of all parties respecting and preserving traditional innovations and practices, supporting sustainable use of biodiverse resources and encouraging equitable benefit sharing. Both sides agree to work towards developing international *sui generis* models for protecting TK. The most affirmative declaration is that the EC and CARIFORUM states may require in their laws that an applicant for a patent using biological materials must identify the sources of the materials used. This disclosure issue is controversial internationally. It is strongly opposed within the WTO Doha Round negotiations and elsewhere by the United States, Japan and other rich countries on grounds that it raises a substantive new legal bar to patent eligibility and could force disclosure of trade secrets.[26] The EU itself seems unlikely to put such a rule into its own patent law but does not oppose it in interested countries. One reason is that the EU seeks to link approval of such disclosure to stronger protection of GIs on a global scale.

Chapter 2 of the IP section of the EU-Colombia-Peru FTA covers biodiversity and TK. Peru and Colombia are rich sources of biodiversity in GRs and have passed legislation proclaiming their sovereign rights over natural resources and setting out the need for prior informed consent and benefit sharing. Thus, the language in Chapter 2 simply affirms these sovereign responsibilities and the further importance of protecting TK. It also seeks to link such laws to the relevant provisions of the Convention on Biological Diversity (CBD), noting in particular that benefit-sharing obligations may extend to the use of IPRs arising from the use of GRs and TK. It strikes a careful balance between the technology-transfer elements of the CBD and the TRIPS Agreement. Specifically, compulsory licenses issued in this regard are subject to the disciplines of Article 31 in TRIPS. Finally, parties to the FTA “acknowledge the usefulness of requiring the disclosure of the origin or source of genetic resources,” a weaker formulation in this regard than in the EU-CARIFORUM EPA. Again, this language largely affirms what already exists in the laws governing GRs and TK in Peru and Colombia.

---

[25] Maskus (2012).

[26] Maskus (2012).

In summary, these agreements provide little in the way of affirmative support from the EU for the use and preservation of TK and GRs. They do, however, recognize the rights of trade partners to carve their own regimes in this area without committing the EU itself to any legislative reforms.

Thus, the ability of the agreements to promote sustainable development in traditional knowledge, folklore and biodiversity will depend on the implicit support for relevant intellectual property rights. In this regard, GIs may be of particular significance as noted by Dutfield[27] and Gervais.[28] It remains to be seen whether the trade agreements can muster enough expansion of technology transfer and investment to these countries in the Caribbean and South America to make IPRs a meaningful route to development. To reiterate an old point, much will depend on the surrounding institutions and economic environments established by policymakers in these countries.

5 Concluding Remarks

In this paper I have attempted to describe how the provisions covering intellectual property rights in two recent EU regional trade agreements with collections of developing countries might affect prospects for innovation and development in the latter. Such predictions cannot be made confidently because of the great complexity of the agreements, the functioning of IPRs and the potential responsiveness of people and firms in the trading partners. Indeed, to my knowledge no studies have yet been performed to analyze the impacts of any regional trade agreements on these factors. Thus, the analysis here is necessarily qualitative.

With that caveat in mind, a few tentative conclusions may be drawn from the overview of relevant provisions in the EU-CARIFORUM EPA and the EU-Colombia-Peru FTA. First, although the agreements do not commit the EU to any affirmative actions to increase technology transfer to these countries, they do contain novel provisions that may make a positive difference in this area. Specifically, commitments to encourage scientists in trading partners to participate in EU-sponsored grant programs and research networks, if they are substantively implemented, could help advance local science, technology diffusion and innovation. At the same time, the agreements do little to directly foster improvements in local innovation and investment climates, which are the key factor in expanding technology transfer.

With respect to IPRs the agreements generally recognize the importance of permitting policy flexibility in the developing-country partners. Thus, few new substantive requirements of a TRIPS-plus nature are put forward, even in medicines. One exception is the minimum periods of protection for confidential

[27] Dutfield (2005).

[28] Gervais (2009).

test data in the FTA with Colombia and Peru, but this language is consistent with requirements sought by the United States in its own agreement with those countries. In that context, the agreements are more consistent with a pro-development emphasis than are recent US-sponsored FTAs. At the same time, they set out rigorous expectations for enforcement of IPRs, especially as involves the release of financial records and use of financial disciplines in the EU-CARIFORUM EPA. Whether these countries can marshal the necessary resources to undertake significant enforcement activities remains to be seen.

As discussed, the primary sectoral interest of the EU advanced by these agreements is to achieve meaningful protection of geographical indications. Here, the EPA with the Caribbean countries may be criticized in its potential elevation of higher-level protection for products outside wines and spirits and its legal priority for GIs over registered trademarks. These provisions are likely to increase the costs of gaining protection for Caribbean GIs while raising legal uncertainty about the scope of trademark protection in the region. The FTA with Colombia and Peru permits those countries to deploy their own legal regimes covering GIs, again suggesting greater flexibility in that area. It does, however, achieve explicit recognition for a large number of EU-issued GIs.

Whether enhanced protection of GIs in these two groups of developing countries offers much scope for income growth and sustainable development in rural areas and villages is hard to predict. It is famously costly to invest in the marketing, certification and supply chains needed to ensure that high-quality products from specific locations gain a domestic or international reputation. This difficulty almost guarantees that GIs must be supported by subsidies and other public supports, raising difficult policy choices. Nonetheless, national authorities in both regions see potential for GIs to raise economic value and support international marketing for local goods and handicrafts. Geographical indications and other IPRs also can play a positive role in ensuring that local peoples share in the commercial benefits from exploitation of genetic resources, traditional knowledge and cultural expressions.

In my view, it is doubtful that the provisions on GIs *per se* in the two EU trade agreements considered here will stimulate economic growth in local regions. The simple reason is that the language largely validates legal reforms that were already in place or under consideration even in the absence of the EU accords. A far more important question is whether the economic conditions for investment and innovation will be materially enhanced by the full provisions of the trade accords. This possibility exists, for increased investment and technology transfer often accompany large-scale trade agreements. For that reason, it is conceivable that over the long term the trade agreements with the EU could facilitate important economic transformation.

References

Barton JH, Maskus KE (2006) Economic Perspectives on a Multilateral Agreement on Open Access to Basic Science and Technology. In: Evenett SJ, Hoekman BM (eds) Economic development and multilateral trade cooperation. Palgrave MacMillan, London

Branstetter L, Fisman R, Foley CF (2006) Do stronger intellectual property rights increase international technology transfer? Empirical evidence from US firm-level panel data. Q J Econ 121(1):321–349

Drexl J (2013) Intellectual property and implementation of recent bilateral trade agreements in the EU. In: Drexl J, Grosse Ruse Khan H, Nadde-Phlix S (eds) EU bilateral trade agreements and intellectual property: for better or worse? Springer, Heidelberg (this volume)

Dutfield G (2005) Legal and economic aspects of traditional knowledge. In: Maskus KE, Reichman JH (eds) International public goods and transfer of technology under a globalized intellectual property regime. Cambridge University Press, Cambridge

Fink C, Maskus KE (2006) The Debate on Geographical Indications at the WTO. In: Newfarmer R (ed) Trade, Doha and development: a window into the issues. The World Bank, Washington, pp 197–207

Gervais DJ (2005) Traditional knowledge and intellectual property: a TRIPS-compatible approach. Mich State Law Rev 2005(1):137–166

Gervais DJ (2009) Traditional knowledge: are we closer to the answers? The potential role of geographical indications. ILSA J Comp Int Law 15(2):551–567

Hobbs JE, Kerr WA (2006) Consumer information, labeling and international trade in agri-food products. Food Pol 31(1):78–89

Jaeger T (2013) IP enforcement provisions in EU Economic Partnership Agreements. In: Drexl J, Grosse Ruse Khan H, Nadde-Phlix S (eds) EU bilateral trade agreements and intellectual property: for better or worse? Springer, Heidelberg (this volume)

Josling T (2006) The war on *Terroir*: geographical indications as a Trans-Atlantic trade conflict. J Agric Econ 57(3):337–363

Maskus KE (2006) Intellectual Property Rights in the U.S.-Colombia Free Trade Agreement. In: Schott JG (ed) The free trade agreement between Colombia and the United States. Peterson Institute for International Economics, Washington

Maskus KE (2012) Private rights and public problems: the global economics of intellectual property in the 21st century. Peterson Institute for International Economics, Washington

Park WG (2008) Intellectual Property Rights and International Innovation. In: Maskus KE (ed) Intellectual property, growth and trade: frontiers of economics and globalization, vol 2. Elsevier, Amsterdam

Plotkin R (2011) Eight profitable premium tequila trends. Nc&B Forum, 8 February 2011. http://www.nightclub.com/ncb-issue/tequila-puro

Rangnekar D (2004) The socio-economics of geographical indications: a review of empirical evidence from Europe. International Centre for Trade and Sustainable Development, Issue Paper No. 8, UNCTAD-ICTSD Project on IPRs and Sustainable Development

Rimmer A (2009) The Grapes of Wrath: The Coonawarra Dispute, Geographical Indications and International Trade. In: Kenyon A, Richardson M, Ricketson S (eds) Landmarks in Australian intellectual property law. Cambridge University Press, Cambridge

Roffe P, Spennemann C (2006) The impact of FTAs on public health policies and TRIPS flexibilities. Int J Intellect Prop Manag 1(1–2):75–93

Ten Kate K, Laird SA (1999) The commercial use of biodiversity: access to genetic resources and benefit sharing. Earthscan, London

Yeung MT, Kerr WA (2008) Increasing protection of GIs at the WTO: clawbacks, greenfields and monopoly rents. Canadian Agricultural Trade Policy Research Network, working paper 2008-02

Yu PK (2011) Six secret (and now open) fears of ACTA. SMU Law Rev 64(3):975–1094

IP Enforcement Provisions in EU Economic Partnership Agreements

Thomas Jaeger

Contents

1 Scope, Objective and Methodology

Economic partnership agreements (EPAs) are not free trade agreements (FTAs) in the classic sense, but they are designed as instruments specifically to advance development objectives in the EU's trade relations with developing

This paper draws upon the findings of a longer article published in EFAR 2012, 411 (Juxtaposed to ACTA or more of the same? A look at IP enforcement under the EU's Economic Partnership Agreements).

T. Jaeger (✉)
Senior Research Fellow, Max Planck Institute for Intellectual Property and Competition Law, Marstallplatz 1, 80593 Munich, Germany
e-mail: thomas.jaeger@ip.mpg.de

J. Drexl et al. (eds.), *EU Bilateral Trade Agreements and Intellectual Property: For Better or Worse?*, MPI Studies on Intellectual Property and Competition Law 20, DOI 10.1007/978-3-642-39097-5_10,

countries.[1] As regards enforcement in particular, the EU calls these "the most elaborated provisions"[2] so far in the field of intellectual property (IP) enforcement procedures and remedies.

This contribution takes a concise look at whether the EPAs' substantive provisions deliver on that promise. The approach chosen examines the effective yield of the enforcement provisions of the EPAs in comparison to provisions that do not incorporate the EPAs' ambitious development goals. One suitable standard here is the EU's internal legislation (Enforcement Directive,[3] Border Measures Regulation (BMR),[4] E-Commerce Directive),[5] which is fully detached from a development context. Another such benchmark can be derived from general agreements concluded by the EU with markedly mercantilist aims, such as the plurilateral IP enforcement agreement known as the Anti-Counterfeiting Trade Agreement (ACTA)[6] and the EU's general FTAs.

What EPAs and FTAs have been concluded or are under negotiation thus far is laid out in detail in other papers in this volume.[7] For the present context therefore, suffice it to mention the agreements that will be examined in the following. At least for the time being,[8] an important reference point[9] for the structure and scope of future EPAs with the African-Caribbean-Pacific (ACP) group of states is marked by the agreement signed between the EU (then: EC) and the CARIFORUM states (CEPA)[10] in 2008. As the (at least thus far) most important of the EPAs, CEPA will also form the focus of the following examination. By contrast, the Association Agreement between the EU and the Central American States (CAAA) and the incomplete (and currently stalled) text of the draft EPA between the EU and the Southern African Development Community (SADC) (SAEPA) can only be drawn upon to a limited extent.

As this examination will demonstrate, CEPA's enforcement provisions are very similar or even nearly identical to those found in some parallel and subsequent

---

[1] As discussed during the workshop on Economic Partnership Agreements of the EU: A Step Ahead in Reforming International IP Law? organized by the Max Planck Institute for Intellectual Property and Competition Law (MPI) and held in Frauenchiemsee on 25 to 27 June 2011 (the MPI workshop).

[2] Information Paper July 2008.

[3] Directive 2004/48/EC.

[4] Council Regulation (EC) No 1383/2003 of 22 July 2003.

[5] Directive 2000/31/EC.

[6] Agreement text of November 2010, available at http://trade.ec.europa.eu/doclib/docs/2011/may/tradoc_147937.pdf. Accessed 19 October 2011. For a critical assessment cf. the Opinion of European Academics on ACTA, available at http://www.iri.uni-hannover.de/acta-1668.html. Accessed 19 October 2011.

[7] As discussed during the MPI workshop and as pointed out at the workshop by Pedro Roffe.

[8] DG Trade apparently seeks a change in the setup of EPAs, e.g. by excluding IP altogether.

[9] As discussed during the MPI workshop.

[10] Economic Partnership Agreement between the CARIFORUM States, of the one part, and the European Community and its Member States, of the other part.

international IP agreements of the EU. Interestingly, this similarity can be observed for EPAs (such as an early draft[11] of the EPA between the EU and the SADC group of states)[12] and for the EPA-like[13] CAAA,[14] as well as for general FTAs (such as the EU-Colombia/Peru FTA[15] and the EU-South Korea FTA).[16]

2 Overall Setup

The overall setup of the EPAs' IP enforcement is reflected in the structure of the texts. Each begins by laying out the general prerequisites of enforcement: fairness, effectiveness and proportionality.[17] This is followed by a definition of persons entitled to sue[18] and by provisions on the collection and preservation of evidence,[19]

---

[11] The July 2009 interim agreement concluded between the EU and SADC (cf. document no. CE/SADC/en, available at http://trade.ec.europa.eu/doclib/docs/2009/july/tradoc_143982.pdf; accessed 19 October 2011) is essentially limited to goods and contains no IP chapter. The interim agreement may however be followed by a wider (full) trade agreement in the future. However, also discussed during the MPI workshop was the possibility, contemplated by DG Trade, of cutting the IP chapter out of even a full EU-SADC EPA.

[12] Draft Consolidated Proposal of 5 June 2007 for an Economic Partnership Agreement between the SADC Group of States, of the one part, and the European Community and Its Member States of the other part, available at http://www.bilaterals.org/IMG/doc/280m-07_EC-SADC_EPA_draft_consolidated_June_2007-2.doc. Accessed 19 October 2011.

[13] The Central American states are, with the exception of Belize, not part of the ACP group for which the EPAs are designed. Belize is not a party to the EU's association agreement with Central America but, as a former British colony and CARICOM state, party to CEPA. Apart from this technical distinction between ACP and non-ACP states, the EU's agreement with the Central American states is similar to the EPAs in that it also pursues the aims of reinforcing political and economic stability, fostering sustainable development and deepening a process of regional integration.

[14] Agreement of 22 March 2011 establishing an association between the European Union and its member states on the one hand, and Central America on the other, available at http://trade.ec.europa.eu/doclib/press/index.cfm?id=689. Accessed 19 October 2011.

[15] Trade Agreement of 23 March 2011 between the European Union and Colombia and Peru, available at http://trade.ec.europa.eu/doclib/docs/2011/march/tradoc_147704.pdf. Accessed 19 October 2011.

[16] Free Trade Agreement between the European Union and its Member States, of the one part, and the Republic of Korea, of the other.

[17] Cf. Art. 151 CEPA (fn 10); IP Art. 13 SAEPA (fn 12); Art. 260(1) CAAA (fn 14); also Art. 234 (2) and (3) EU-Colombia/Peru FTA (fn 15); Art. 10.41 EU-South Korea FTA (fn 16).

[18] Cf. Art. 152 CEPA (fn 10); IP Art. 14 SAEPA (fn 12); Art. 261 CAAA (fn 14); also Art. 236 EU-Colombia/Peru FTA (fn 15); Art. 10.42 EU-South Korea FTA (fn 16).

[19] Cf. Arts 153 and 154 CEPA (fn 10); IP Arts 16 and 17 SAEPA (fn 12); Arts 262 et seq. CAAA (fn 14); also Arts 237 et seq. EU-Colombia/Peru FTA (fn 15); Arts 10.43 et seq. EU-South Korea FTA (fn 16).

on the extent and enforcement of a right of information of the rightholder,[20] on provisional and precautionary measures,[21] on sanctioning measures (corrective and alternative measures and injunctions),[22] on non-sanctioning measures (damages and legal costs),[23] on publicity measures regarding judicial decisions[24] and, finally, on special enforcement measures upon entry or exit of infringing goods at the border.[25] Additionally, some agreements contain flanking provisions, regarding for instance the presumption of ownership (though not in CEPA) or the elaboration of codes of conduct for IP enforcement (though not in the CAAA).[26]

There is no substantial difference in setup between the EPAs and the FTAs: The FTAs mirror this structure and contain essentially similar provisions, sometimes even with identical wording.[27] They also contain provisions on the presumption of ownership and (at least the EU-South Korea FTA) on the elaboration of codes of conduct.[28]

With this, both the EPAs and the FTAs mirror the structure of the Enforcement Directive. The Directive's order of provisions, in turn, more or less follows the sequential order in which a given issue would come up in civil proceedings, for example from the perspective of a judge or an attorney. The agreements' (as well as the Enforcement Directive's) approach to enforcement is therefore claims-based and procedure-focussed, that is, governed by the question of what claims may be pursued to what extent at what stage of the proceedings. By contrast, the enforcement part of the Agreement on Trade-Related Aspects of Intellectual Property Rights (TRIPS) is sub-divided into five sections largely along formal lines, such as provisions relating to general civil and administrative proceedings,[29] to border measures in particular[30] or to measures in criminal proceedings.[31] Unlike the

---

[20] Cf. Art. 155 CEPA (fn 10); IP Art. 18 SAEPA (fn 12); Art. 264 CAAA (fn 14); also Art. 239 EU-Colombia/Peru FTA (fn 15); Art. 10.45 EU-South Korea FTA (fn 16).

[21] Cf. Art. 156 CEPA (fn 10); IP Art. 19 SAEPA (fn 12); Art. 265 CAAA (fn 14); also Art. 240 EU-Colombia/Peru FTA (fn 15); Art. 10.46 EU-South Korea FTA (fn 16).

[22] Cf. Arts 157 to 159 CEPA (fn 10); IP Arts 20 to 22 SAEPA (fn 12); Art. 266 CAAA (fn 14); also Arts 241 et seq. EU-Colombia/Peru FTA (fn 15); Arts 10.47 et seq. EU-South Korea FTA (fn 16).

[23] Cf. Arts 160 and 161 CEPA (fn 10); IP Arts 23 and 24 SAEPA (fn 12); Arts 267 et seq. CAAA (fn 14); also Arts 244 et seq. EU-Colombia/Peru FTA (fn 15); Arts 10.50 et seq. EU-South Korea FTA (fn 16).

[24] Cf. Art. 162 CEPA (fn 10); IP Art. 24 SAEPA (fn 12); Art. 269 CAAA (fn 14); also Art. 246 EU-Colombia/Peru FTA (fn 15); Art. 10.52 EU-South Korea FTA (fn 16).

[25] Cf. Art. 163 CEPA (fn 10); IP Art. 26 SAEPA (fn 12); Art. 273 CAAA (fn 14); also Art. 249 EU-Colombia/Peru FTA (fn 15); Art. 10.67 EU-South Korea FTA (fn 16).

[26] Cf. IP Arts 15 and 27 SAEPA (fn 12); Art. 270 CAAA (fn 14); also Art. 247 EU-Colombia/Peru FTA (fn 15); Arts 10.53 and 10.68 EU-South Korea FTA (fn 16).

[27] See fn 17 to 25.

[28] See fn 26.

[29] Arts 42 et seq. TRIPS Agreement.

[30] Arts 51 et seq. TRIPS Agreement.

[31] Art. 61 TRIPS Agreement.

agreements, the order of provisions in the enforcement part of TRIPS does not follow a clear logic of claims in procedural sequence.

The EPAs' and FTAs' IP enforcement parts are designed to go beyond the TRIPS Agreement.[32] These agreements thus contain manifold TRIPS-plus provisions in the sense that a higher standard than that of TRIPS is made mandatory. The most important of these provisions will be illustrated in the remainder of this paper and compared to TRIPS, ACTA and the EU's domestic standards in particular.

3 Entitled Applicants

The TRIPS Agreement leaves its use of the term "right holders"[33] essentially open, the only specification being that federations and associations are included in its definition. By contrast, the agreements incorporate almost verbatim the respective provision of the Enforcement Directive.[34] Accordingly, these agreements not only (like TRIPS) require protection for rightholders and associations, but in addition name as eligible applicants "all other persons authorised to use such rights" under national law (e.g. licensees), "collective rights-management bodies" and "professional defence bodies", each in accordance with their laws of incorporation.[35]

In principle, this broad and detailed definition of the persons entitled to sue does not necessarily go beyond the existing provisions of national laws under the TRIPS standard: TRIPS uses an open term and is likely broad enough to accommodate all of the aforementioned groups. At the same time, TRIPS did not have to be interpreted that broadly; national provisions may therefore have well been narrower in according enforcement rights and still be in line with TRIPS. The TRIPS-plus effect of the EPAs and FTAs thus, as in the Enforcement Directive, is due to the fact that the broad interpretation of the term rightholder is, beyond the requirements of TRIPS, now made compulsory.

[32] For a definition of TRIPS-plus standards cf. Vivas-Eugui (2003), p. 4.

[33] Cf. Art. 42 TRIPS Agreement.

[34] Cf. Art. 4 Enforcement Directive.

[35] All citations Art. 152 CEPA (fn 10); identically IP Art. 14 SAEPA (fn 12); Art. 236 - EU-Colombia/Peru FTA (fn 15); Art. 10.42 EU-South Korea FTA (fn 16); similarly (rightholders, federations, associations and all licensees in accordance with national law) Art. 261(2) CAAA (fn 14).

4 Evidence

With respect to collecting and preserving evidence, the EPAs (with the exception of the CAAA) and FTAs largely adopt the standards of the Enforcement Directive. Whereas however the Enforcement Directive contains extensive and largely parallel provisions on surrender of specified evidence by the opposing party,[36] due to the fact that all relevant provisions of TRIPS must be mirrored or amended, the agreements are limited to laying down only those provisions that are TRIPS-plus.

In that respect, for IP infringements committed on a commercial scale, the agreements (with the exception of the CAAA)[37] stipulate a right for parties to demand disclosure of all appropriate (i.e. unspecified) "banking, financial or commercial documents under the control of the opposing entity, subject to the protection of confidential information".[38] This goes even further than the rules on provisional preservation of evidence contained in ACTA, which are less detailed and limited to trademark counterfeiting.[39] Similarly, as regards the preservation of evidence, the EPAs (including the CAAA) and FTAs alike depart from a laxer TRIPS standard by filling the open TRIPS requirement for "effective provisional measures"[40] with pinpointed court powers to allow for a "detailed description, with or without the taking of samples, or the physical seizure of the infringing goods, and, in appropriate cases, the materials and implements used in the production and/or distribution of these goods and the documents relating thereto."[41] This wording is again similar to, but more detailed than, that found in ACTA.[42] An optional provision provided for in the Enforcement Directive to enable states to protect the identity of witnesses used as a source of evidence[43] was not adopted by any EPA (or in ACTA).

[36] Cf. Art. 6(1) Enforcement Directive (fn 3); Art. 43(1) TRIPS Agreement.

[37] Cf. Art. 262 CAAA (fn 14).

[38] Art. 153 CEPA (fn 10); identically IP Art. 16 SAEPA (fn 12); Art. 237 EU-Colombia/Peru FTA (fn 15); Art. 10.43 EU-South Korea FTA (fn 16); similarly Art. 6(2) Enforcement Directive (fn 3).

[39] Cf. fn 42.

[40] Art. 50(1)(b) TRIPS Agreement.

[41] Art. 154 CEPA (fn 10); identically IP Art. 17 SAEPA (fn 12); Art. 263 CAAA (fn 14); Art. 238 EU-Colombia/Peru FTA (fn 15); Art. 10.44(2) EU-South Korea FTA (fn 16); Art. 7 (1) Enforcement Directive (fn 3).

[42] Cf. Art. 12(3) ACTA (fn 6): "seizure ... of goods, and of materials and implements relevant to the act of infringement, and, at least for trademark counterfeiting, documentary evidence, either originals or copies thereof".

[43] Cf. Art. 7(5) Enforcement Directive (fn 3).

5 Information Right

The EPAs (with the exception of the CAAA) and the FTAs all contain a copy of the Directive's information right for the rightholder on distribution networks for the infringing goods.[44] TRIPS contains a very weak right of information in the sense that it is only an option open to member states to lay down such a right and that it is subject to an inherent proportionality requirement.[45] The CAAA essentially mirrors that TRIPS provision,[46] thereby falling significantly behind the more ambitious enforcement level in the other EPAs and FTAs.

In the other agreements (with the exception of the CAAA), that right is significantly expanded. For one thing, the information right according to the agreements is not optional. Also, it is broader in terms of the addressees of the order for information (including not just, as in TRIPS, the infringer, but also "any other person who . . . was found in possession of the infringing goods [or] using the infringing services on a commercial scale [or] to be providing on a commercial scale services used in infringing activities"[47] or who was indicated by any of these persons) and of the scope of the right as such (not just, as in TRIPS, information on the identity of third persons and on the channels of distribution, but also any appropriate information on "names and addresses of the producers, manufacturers, distributors, suppliers and other previous holders of the goods or services, as well as the intended wholesalers and retailers [and] information on the quantities produced, manufactured, delivered, received or ordered, as well as the price obtained for the goods or services in question").[48] Finally, the already very expansive right of information applies "without prejudice to other provisions which . . . grant the rightholder rights to receive fuller information [or permit] the use in civil or criminal proceedings of the information".[49]

Apart from a general requirement for the information request of the rightholder to be proportionate to the infringement (which, as shown, is already contained in TRIPS),[50] virtually no limits for exercise of the information right are woven into

[44] Cf. Art. 155 CEPA (fn 10); IP Art. 18 SAEPA (fn 12); Art. 239 EU-Colombia/Peru FTA (fn 15); Art. 10.45 EU-South Korea FTA (fn 16); similarly Art. 8 Enforcement Directive (fn 3).

[45] Cf. Art. 47 TRIPS Agreement.

[46] Cf. Art. 264 CAAA (fn 14).

[47] Art. 155(1) CEPA (fn 10); identically IP Art. 18(1) SAEPA (fn 12); Art. 239(1) EU-Colombia/Peru FTA (fn 15); Art. 10.45(1)(a) EU-South Korea FTA (fn 16); Art. 8(1) Enforcement Directive (fn 3).

[48] Art. 155(2) CEPA (fn 10); identically IP Art. 18(2) SAEPA (fn 12); Art. 239(2) EU-Colombia/Peru FTA (fn 15); Art. 10.45(1)(b) EU-South Korea FTA (fn 16); Art. 8(2) Enforcement Directive (fn 3).

[49] Art. 155(3) CEPA (fn 10); similarly IP Art. 18(3) SAEPA (fn 12); Art. 239(3) EU-Colombia/Peru FTA (fn 15); Art. 10.45(2) EU-South Korea FTA (fn 16); Art. 8(3) Enforcement Directive (fn 3).

[50] Cf. Art. 155(1) CEPA (fn 10); IP Art. 18(1) SAEPA (fn 12); Art. 239(1) EU-Colombia/Peru FTA (fn 15); Art. 10.45(1) EU-South Korea FTA (fn 16); Art. 47 TRIPS Agreement; Art. 8 (1) Enforcement Directive (fn 3).

this provision. Like the Enforcement Directive, the agreements stipulate respect for national or international provisions governing the responsibility for misuse of the right of information, permitting a right of refusal of information in cases of self-incrimination or protecting the confidentiality of information sources or allowing personal data to remain intact, but do not by themselves incorporate such requirements.[51]

This is therefore a very sharp increase in enforcement standards in favour of rightholders as compared to TRIPS and is among the most far-reaching TRIPS-plus provisions (together, perhaps, with the obligations for disclosure of banking, financial or commercial documents[52] and for the precautionary blocking of assets[53]; the latter provision is however not contained in the EU-Colombia/Peru FTA; neither of the provisions is contained in the CAAA).

Finally, the expansion of the right of information beyond TRIPS in the EPAs (with the exception of the CAAA) and FTAs is somewhat more detailed in wording and more encompassing in scope (e.g. as regards the correlation with criminal proceedings), but for the rest very similar to what can be found in ACTA.[54] It is however more balanced than ACTA in some respects; for example, ACTA does not contain a proportionality requirement or a bar to self-incrimination. So the EPAs are not exactly like ACTA in that respect, but they are close to it.

6 Provisional Measures

Precautionary and provisional measures (other than those relating to evidence) under the EPAs (but not under the CAAA) and FTAs are significantly expanded as compared to TRIPS. Here again the respective provisions of the Enforcement Directive (and the similar provisions of ACTA) were essentially taken over.[55] Most significantly, in the case of an infringement committed on a commercial scale, the EPAs (with the exception of the CAAA)[56] and the EU-South Korea FTA (however not the EU-Colombia/Peru FTA) provide that if the applicant demonstrates circumstances likely to endanger the recovery of damages, the judicial authorities may order the precautionary seizure of the movable and immovable property of the

[51] Cf. Art. 155(3) CEPA (fn 10); IP Art. 18(3) SAEPA (fn 12); Art. 8(3) Enforcement Directive (fn 3).

[52] Cf. Art. 153 CEPA (fn 10); IP Art. 16 SAEPA (fn 12); Art. 237 EU-Colombia/Peru FTA (fn 15); Art. 10.43 EU-South Korea FTA (fn 16).

[53] Cf. Art. 156(3) CEPA (fn 10); IP Art. 19(3) SAEPA (fn 12); Art. 10.46(3) EU-South Korea FTA (fn 16).

[54] Cf. Art. 11 ACTA (fn 6).

[55] Cf. Art. 156 CEPA (fn 10); IP Art. 19 SAEPA (fn 12); Art. 240 EU-Colombia/Peru FTA (fn 15); Art. 10.46 EU-South Korea FTA (fn 16); Art. 50 TRIPS Agreement; Art. 9 Enforcement Directive (fn 3); Art. 12(3) ACTA (fn 6).

[56] Art. 265(2) CAAA (fn 14).

alleged infringer, including the blocking of his/her bank accounts and other assets. To that end, the competent authorities may order the communication of bank, financial or commercial documents, or appropriate access to the relevant information.[57]

This goes even further than the requirements under ACTA.[58] A provision for these measures to be taken inaudita altera parte contained in the Enforcement Directive[59] (and in ACTA)[60] was not adopted in CEPA or SAEPA or any of the FTAs, but only in the CAAA.[61] It is unclear whether the TRIPS requirement to order provisional and precautionary measures inaudita altera parte[62] can really fill this gap for the other agreements in relation to TRIPS-plus precautionary measures like this one, or whether, conversely, this question rests within the discretion of the parties.

A similar question arises in relation to the lack of a provision in any of the agreements with the exception of the CAAA[63] (and also contained in the Enforcement Directive, in ACTA and in TRIPS)[64] requiring the applicant to provide reasonable evidence to substantiate its claim before a precautionary measure is taken. The CAAA (like the Enforcement Directive and ACTA) also stipulates the possibility of a security payment by the applicant for such measures in order to protect the defendant.[65]

The EPAs and the FTAs also provide that injunctions must also be available against intermediaries "whose services are being used by a third party to infringe an intellectual property right".[66] Neither TRIPS nor the Enforcement Directive contain this type of obligation, but regarding EU law it is provided for by virtue of the Copyright Directive.[67] ACTA also contains this type of provision.[68] The CAAA also does not provide expressly for any such liability,[69] but it contains a provision stipulating a limitation of liability for service providers in accordance with the

---

[57] Art. 156(3) CEPA (fn 10); identically IP Art. 19(3) SAEPA (fn 12); Art. 9(2) Enforcement Directive (fn 3); similarly Art. 10.46(3) EU-South Korea FTA (fn 16).

[58] Cf. Art. 12(3) ACTA (fn 6).

[59] Cf. Art. 9(4) Enforcement Directive (fn 3).

[60] Cf. Art. 12(2) ACTA (fn 6).

[61] Cf. Art. 265(1) CAAA (fn 14).

[62] Cf. Art. 50(2) TRIPS Agreement.

[63] Cf. Art. 265(2) CAAA (fn 14).

[64] Cf. Art. 50(3) TRIPS Agreement; Art. 9(3) Enforcement Directive (fn 3); Art. 12(4) ACTA (fn 6).

[65] Cf. Art. 265(2) CAAA (fn 14); Art. 9(6) Enforcement Directive (fn 3); Art. 12(5) ACTA (fn 6).

[66] Art. 156(1) CEPA (fn 10); similarly IP Art. 19(1) SAEPA (fn 12); Art. 250 EU-Colombia/Peru FTA (fn 15); Art. 10.46(1) EU-South Korea FTA (fn 16).

[67] Cf. Art. 8(3) Directive 2001/29/EC.

[68] Cf. Art. 12(1)(a) ACTA (fn 6).

[69] Cf. Art. 265 CAAA (fn 14).

E-Commerce Directive or the national laws of the Central American parties.[70] This indicates that implicitly, third-party liability is included in the agreement. Interestingly also, the liability of service providers in the EU-Colombia/Peru FTA is woven into a set of sophisticated provisions[71] based on the model of the E-Commerce Directive[72] (differentiating between mere conduit, hosting and caching), whereas the other agreements are relatively indiscriminate vis-à-vis the activities of the intermediaries. This does however probably not imply that limitations of liability of this kind are not allowed, since this would create inconsistencies with the EU's domestic regime.

7 Corrective Measures

The provisions of the EPAs, the FTAs, the TRIPS Agreement and the Enforcement Directive run largely parallel as regards the types of measures available: desist orders, recall or definitive removal of infringing goods from the market or destruction of such goods.[73] From among the EPAs, only the CAAA grants an additional right of the plaintiff to apply for the seizure or destruction of any means of production of the infringing goods.[74] This type of provision is also contained in the FTAs, in TRIPS, the Enforcement Directive and ACTA.[75] Despite this somewhat narrower scope of CEPA and SAEPA in the field of corrective measures as compared to CAAA and the non-mercantilist agreements, the overall approach in all EPAs is also clearly TRIPS-plus, although (because of the narrower scope) they do not go quite as far as the Enforcement Directive.

The EPAs (like the FTAs) include a right to publication of infringement judgments upon the application of the rightholder,[76] something not required by TRIPS (or ACTA). While neither TRIPS nor any of the agreements (or the Enforcement Directive or ACTA) accord the infringer compensation for the

---

[70] Cf. Art. 272 CAAA (fn 14).

[71] Cf. Arts 250 et seq. EU-Colombia/Peru FTA (fn 15).

[72] Cf. Arts 12 et seq. Directive 2000/31/EC (fn 5).

[73] Cf. Arts 157, 158 and 159 CEPA (fn 10); IP Arts 20, 21 and 22 SAEPA (fn 12); Art. 241 (1) EU-Colombia/Peru FTA (fn 15); Art. 10.47(1) EU-South Korea FTA (fn 16); Arts 44 and 46 TRIPS Agreement; Arts 10, 11, 12 and 15 Enforcement Directive (fn 3); similarly (less detailed) Art. 266(1) CAAA (fn 14).

[74] Cf. Art. 266(1)(b) CAAA (fn 14).

[75] Cf. Art. 241(1) EU-Colombia/Peru FTA (fn 15); Art. 10.47(1) EU-South Korea FTA (fn 16); Art. 46, 2nd sentence TRIPS Agreement; Art 10(1), 1st sentence Enforcement Directive (fn 3); Art. 10(2) ACTA (fn 6).

[76] Cf. Art. 162 CEPA (fn 10); IP Art. 25 SAEPA (fn 12); Art. 269 CAAA (fn 14); Art. 246 - EU-Colombia/Peru FTA (fn 15); Art. 10.52 EU-South Korea FTA (fn 16); similarly Art. 15 Enforcement Directive (fn 3).

property affected,[77] all EPAs and the FTAs (like ACTA, but there optionally) in addition require the infringer to cover the expenses of any corrective measures.[78] TRIPS, by contrast, leaves the question of responsibility for enforcement expenses open, with the effect that the EPAs once more make the strictest of several possible solutions uniformly compulsory.

Likewise beyond the scope of TRIPS, all EPAs (although the CAAA only implicitly)[79] and the FTAs (as well as the Enforcement Directive and ACTA) require member states to allow for injunctions also against intermediaries "whose services are used by a third party to infringe an intellectual property right".[80] This provision, which corresponds to the responsibilities laid down for intermediaries in the field of provisional and precautionary measures,[81] aims particularly at internet access providers and file-sharing. Seeking direct injunctions against access providers may have become more important for rightholders in view of the fact that the ECJ recently limited the obligation of intermediaries (at least under the Enforcement Directive; national law may go further) to communicate personal data of internet users in order to ensure effective protection of copyright in civil proceedings for reasons of fundamental rights and data protection.[82]

Quite obviously also with a view to tackling copyright infringements on the internet and counterfeiting, the EPAs and the FTAs (like the enforcement Directive and ACTA) do away with the optional exception in TRIPS for bona fide infringements. Under TRIPS, states are free to exempt from prosecution persons not knowing or not having had reasonable grounds to know that certain goods or services infringed IP rights.[83] The corresponding provisions of all EPAs and the FTAs did away with this exemption possibility,[84] to the effect that rightholders are in principle always allowed to prosecute even such bona fide infringements. The CAAA at least has a proportionality requirement in dealing with the request for

[77] Cf. Art. 157(1) CEPA (fn 10); IP Art. 20(1) SAEPA (fn 12); Art. 266(1)(b) CAAA (fn 14); Art. 46 TRIPS Agreement; similarly Art. 10(1) Enforcement Directive (fn 3); Art. 10(1) ACTA (fn 6).

[78] Cf. Art. 157(2) CEPA (fn 10); IP Art. 20(2) SAEPA (fn 12); Art. 266(4) CAAA (fn 14); Art. 241 (2) EU-Colombia/Peru FTA (fn 15); Art. 10.47(2) EU-South Korea FTA (fn 16); similarly Art. 10 (2) Enforcement Directive (fn 3); Art. 10(3) ACTA (fn 6).

[79] Cf. fn 70 and the related main text.

[80] Art. 158 CEPA (fn 10); similarly IP Art. 21 SAEPA (fn 12); Art. 250 EU-Colombia/Peru FTA (fn 15); Art. 10.48(2) EU-South Korea FTA (fn 16); Art. 11 Enforcement Directive (fn 3); Art. 8 (1) ACTA (fn 6).

[81] See fn 66.

[82] Cf. ECJ, Judgment of 29 January 2008, Case C-275/06, *Promusicae* [2008] n.y.r., paras 61 et seq.; similarly the question in pending Case C-557/07, *LSG*, OJ 2008, C 64, 20.

[83] Cf. Art. 44(1) TRIPS Agreement.

[84] Cf. Art. 158 CEPA (fn 10); IP Art. 21 SAEPA (fn 12); Art. 266 CAAA (fn 14); Art. 242 - EU-Colombia/Peru FTA (fn 15); Art. 10.48 EU-South Korea FTA (fn 16); similarly Art. 11 Enforcement Directive (fn 3); Arts 8 and 10 ACTA (fn 6).

corrective measures,[85] which however cannot be likened in function to an exemption for bona fide infringements.

Instead of the option to let bona fide infringers go entirely free, the EPAs (with the exception of the CAAA) and the FTAs transform the bona fide exemption into an optional provision according to which states "may"[86] provide for a right of the infringer to offer to pay a pecuniary compensation instead of having other corrective measures or injunctions applied. ACTA, for comparison, does not contain this option.[87] Preconditions for the availability of this settlement possibility for bona fide infringements are that the infringer has not acted negligently and that other corrective measures would cause him harm disproportionate to the gravity of the infringement.[88] In effect therefore, the possibility for bona fide infringements incorporates a de minimis requirement in that it is probably not available where the rightholder successfully argues that strict deterrence is required and pecuniary compensation is not "reasonably satisfactory"[89] in view of the frequency or scale of infringements.

Only the CAAA contains a provision to the effect that the infringing goods may be given away as charitable donations (i.e. outside the channels of commerce) with the consent of the rightholder in individual cases or without their consent if the charitable purposes are pre-established by law.[90] A re-entry into the channels of commerce following the simple removal of the infringing feature is expressly prohibited in that provision.

ACTA contains a similarly singular (not found in any other agreement) provision in the field of injunctions, setting forth a possibility to limit remedies available against public use of the IP right.[91] However, looked at in better light, this is nothing but a restatement of government respect for the TRIPS Agreement's compulsory licensing provisions,[92] which are expressly referred to in that ACTA rule. This limited provision for public use of IP rights is therefore not a model for more public-use-friendly provisions in EPAs.

---

[85] Cf. Art. 266(3) CAAA (fn 14).

[86] Cf. Art. 159 CEPA (fn 10); identically IP Art. 22 SAEPA (fn 12); Art. 243 EU-Colombia/Peru FTA (fn 15); Art. 10.49 EU-South Korea FTA (fn 16); Art. 12 Enforcement Directive (fn 3).

[87] Cf. Art. 8 and 10 ACTA (fn 6).

[88] Cf. Art. 159 CEPA (fn 10); IP Art. 22 SAEPA (fn 12); Art. 243 EU-Colombia/Peru FTA (fn 15); Art. 10.49 EU-South Korea FTA (fn 16); similarly Art. 12 Enforcement Directive (fn 3).

[89] Cf. Art. 159 CEPA (fn 10); identically IP Art. 22 SAEPA (fn 12); Art. 243 EU-Colombia/Peru FTA (fn 15); Art. 10.49 EU-South Korea FTA (fn 16); Art. 12 Enforcement Directive (fn 3).

[90] Cf. Art. 266(2) CAAA (fn 14).

[91] Cf. Art. 8(2) ACTA (fn 6).

[92] Cf. Art. 31 and 37 TRIPS Agreement.

8 Damages

Regarding damages, TRIPS speaks of a right to receive adequate damages (without more detailed definition as to positive damages, lost profits or even moral damages) in relation to the injury, provided that the infringement was committed with a minimum degree of negligence ("reasonable grounds to know").[93] Only as an option for states, TRIPS authorizes a recovery of profits or of a lump sum for the rightholder when there is no negligence.[94] These notions are essentially repeated in (only) the CAAA, which therefore remains on the TRIPS level.[95]

The other agreements do not repeat these notions,[96] thus relying on TRIPS as regards the principles of adequate compensation and at least negligence. However, unlike TRIPS, the agreements (with the exception of the CAAA) set binding guidelines for national courts as to the calculation of damages. In doing so, the agreements in fact take the widest possible approach to the calculation of damages, which are to include lost profits as well as, where applicable, moral damages ("elements other than economic factors").[97] Here, these agreements go even beyond the standard envisaged by ACTA, which does not include moral damages.[98] As an alternative, a lump sum reflecting the amount of royalties otherwise due may be set.[99] Again, the agreements here go further than ACTA, since ACTA limits the (mandatory) availability of lump sums and pre-established damages to copyright and related rights piracy and trademark counterfeiting.[100] In addition, since a lump sum payment is evidently reasonable only where a calculation of actual damages is impossible, excessively complicated or at least overly cumbersome in view of the gravity of the infringement, the standard method for calculation of damages under the EPAs (other than the CAAA) and FTAs will likely entail the broad concept that includes lost profits and moral damages.

By filling in these notions that were left open in the TRIPS Agreement, all agreements except the CAAA establish binding standards above the level of enforcement required under a balanced interpretation of the TRIPS Agreement. In certain key aspects, they even go beyond the requirements of ACTA. However, it is

---

[93] Art. 45(1) TRIPS Agreement.

[94] Art. 45(2) TRIPS Agreement.

[95] Cf. Art. 267 CAAA (fn 14).

[96] Cf. Art. 160(1) CEPA (fn 10); IP Art. 23(1) SAEPA (fn 12); Art. 244 EU-Colombia/Peru FTA (fn 15); Art. 10.50 EU-South Korea FTA (fn 16).

[97] Art. 160(1)(a) CEPA (fn 10); identically IP Art. 23(1)(a) SAEPA (fn 12); Art. 244(1)(a) - EU-Colombia/Peru FTA (fn 15); Art. 10.50(1)(a) EU-South Korea FTA (fn 16); Art. 13(1) (a) Enforcement Directive (fn 3).

[98] Cf. Art. 9 ACTA (fn 6).

[99] Cf. Art. 160(1)(b) CEPA (fn 10); IP Art. 23(1)(b) SAEPA (fn 12); Art. 244(1)(b) EU-Colombia/ Peru FTA (fn 15); Art. 10.50(1)(b) EU-South Korea FTA (fn 16); similarly Art. 13(1) (b) Enforcement Directive (fn 3).

[100] Cf. Art. 9(3) ACTA (fn 6).

equally true that while these agreements take on the broadest possible definition of recoverable damages for IP infringements across Europe, they do not alter the level of fault required under TRIPS. That standard, by virtue of the subsidiary applicability of TRIPS, remains set at reasonable grounds for knowledge of the infringement, and more stringent national provisions allowing damages for non-negligent behaviour remain optional[101] under the agreements[102] as well.

9 Border Measures

The scope of the TRIPS provisions is expanded in the newer agreements, firstly, as regards the types of IP rights covered. Under the TRIPS Agreement, the extension of border measures to other IP rights beyond trademarks and copyright is optional.[103] By contrast, the EU's own BMR[104] and ACTA[105] both cover the full range of IP rights, including, in particular, patents, designs, geographical indications and plant variety rights.

This very broad notion is also taken up by the border measures provisions[106] of the EU-South Korea FTA.[107] CEPA and SAEPA and the EU-Colombia/Peru FTA are situated between these two, that is, they include designs and geographical indications, but not other IP rights like patents.[108] However, at least CEPA stipulates that the parties will endeavour to extend the scope of rights protected through border measures in the future.[109] The CAAA and EU-Colombia/Peru FTA, by contrast, follow the stance of TRIPS and limit border measures to trademarks and copyright.[110]

Similarly, CEPA and SAEPA and the FTAs expand upon the definition of entitled applicants. Whereas the CAAA, TRIPS and ACTA all stipulate obligations to make border measures available only in relation to rightholders,[111] the other EPAs and the FTAs (like the EU's own BMR) also include other persons authorised

[101] Cf. Art. 45(2) TRIPS Agreement.

[102] Cf. Art. 160(2) CEPA (fn 10); IP Art. 23(2) SAEPA (fn 12); Art. 244(2) EU-Colombia/Peru FTA (fn 15); Art. 10.50(2) EU-South Korea FTA (fn 16); similarly Art. 13(2) Enforcement Directive (fn 3).

[103] Cf. Art. 51 TRIPS Agreement.

[104] Cf. Art. 2(1) BMR (fn 4).

[105] Cf. Arts 5(h) and 13 ACTA (fn 6).

[106] Not, by contrast, by that FTA's section on criminal enforcement (only trademark and copyright infringements on a commercial scale); cf. Art. 10.54 EU-South Korea FTA (fn 16).

[107] Cf. Footnote 27 to Art. 10.67(1) EU-South Korea FTA (fn 16).

[108] Cf. Footnote 1 to Art. 163(1) CEPA (fn 10); Footnote 14 to IP Art. 26(1) SAEPA (fn 12); Footnote 81 to Art. 249(1) EU-Colombia/Peru FTA (fn 15).

[109] Cf. Footnote 1 to Art. 163(1) CEPA (fn 10).

[110] Cf. Art. 273 CAAA (fn 14); Art. 249(1) EU-Colombia/Peru FTA (fn 15).

[111] Cf. Art. 51 TRIPS Agreement; Art. 273(2) CAAA (fn 14); Art. 16 and 17 ACTA (fn 6).

to use the intellectual property rights, for example exporters and licensees.[112] Correspondingly, the types of acts against which border measures are to be made available is expanded in the EPAs and the EU-South Korea FTA significantly, from importation alone in the TRIPS Agreement[113] to “importation, exportation, re-exportation, entry or exit of the customs territory, placement under a suspensive procedure or placement under a customs free zone or a customs free warehouse”.[114] The CAAA, in spite of a narrower definition on the level of the applicants for border measures, likewise takes up this broad definition of the types of acts against which measures are available.[115] None of the agreements however alters the procedural standard of application for and execution of border measures.[116]

10 General Assessment

No clear pattern emerges from the foregoing analysis as regards a distinction between agreements with a purely mercantilist stance (TRIPS, ACTA, FTAs) and such that also incorporate other, non-mercantilist aims (EPAs, including the CAAA): EPAs do not homogeneously stipulate a lower level of enforcement (understood as the scope, extent and level of detail to which rightholders’ remedies are spelt out). They do also not spell out the rights of third parties (defendants) upon enforcement in any more detail than do other types of agreements. They do not contain additional rights of defence. Finally, the EPAs’ IP enforcement sections do not include more flexibility for the application of enforcement obligations. They do not incorporate any specific forms of implementation or sophistication for those non-mercantilist aims of the agreement, such as the objective of sustainable development in Art.3 of CEPA, which are typically laid out in the agreements’ general parts and in the introductions to the IP sections of those agreements. The EPAs’ enforcement sections are, in other words, neutral vis-à-vis those more general aims and provisions and do not, in particular, specifically support or facilitate their implementation within enforcement procedures in any clear way.

Compared to the EU’s domestic TRIPS-plus legislation (Enforcement Directive, BMR, E-Commerce Directive) and to the TRIPS-plus push incorporated in the final draft of ACTA, the EPAs incorporate more or less close copies of the domestic EU legislation. In this, they go beyond even the latest international framework

[112] Cf. Art. 163(2) CEPA (fn 10); IP Art. 26(2) SAEPA (fn 12); similarly Art. 249(3) - EU-Colombia/Peru FTA (fn 15); Art. 10.67(3) EU-South Korea FTA (fn 16); Art. 2(2) BMR (fn 4).

[113] Cf. Art. 51 TRIPS Agreement.

[114] Art. 163(1) CEPA (fn 10); identically IP Art. 26(1) SAEPA (fn 12); similarly Art. 10.67 (1) EU-South Korea FTA (fn 16); Art. 1(1) BMR (fn 4).

[115] Cf. Art. 273(2) CAAA (fn 14).

[116] Cf. Arts 52 et seq. TRIPS Agreement.

negotiated under ACTA. In this respect of use of the EU's domestic enforcement levels as a model, the EPAs are not significantly different from FTAs concluded by the EU. In fact, the provisions of the EPAs and FTAs often run parallel. An archetypical example here is the pairing of CEPA on the one hand and the EU-Colombia/Peru FTA on the other, where the enforcement sections are largely identical and, as such, to a great extent substantively identical to the EU's domestic legislation (especially the Enforcement Directive).

One exception to these findings however is represented by the CAAA. Although technically not an EPA,[117] the CAAA runs parallel to the classic EPAs such as CEPA and the SAEPA draft in terms of embodying non-mercantilist aims (e.g. sustainable development, public health, good governance). TRIPS-plus enforcement provisions are relatively less widespread in that agreement and it is somewhat closer at least in terms of the established enforcement level to TRIPS than to the Enforcement Directive (as the model for the levels of enforcement stipulated in the other EPAs and FTAs and, to some extent, in ACTA). It cannot be said that the CAAA warrants an overwhelmingly different assessment as compared to the other EPAs or FTAs, but several small differences exist. In relation to the overall enforcement level, for example, several instances can be pinpointed where the CAAA follows the TRIPS level instead of a higher enforcement level. Furthermore, some instances can be pinpointed where rights of defence not contained in the other EPAs (or FTAs) were taken over into the CAAA (which is in this respect modelled onto the respectively more protective model of the Enforcement Directive). The CAAA furthermore fleshes out, in the context of corrective measures, the development-driven possibility to dispose of infringing goods outside of the channels of commerce by laying down conditions for their use as charitable donations. In spite of this somewhat more balanced approach in some provisions of the CAAA, it is also more stringent with respect to some aspects of enforcement than are the other EPAs or the FTAs. Among the examples here is the introduction of additional enforcement powers for the courts (such as measures inaudita or the inclusion of production materials in correction), which were apparently deemed essential for the given enforcement context. Again, these enforcement powers can be traced back to the Enforcement Directive.

Overall, therefore, the CAAA is probably the most balanced among the agreements examined here: It is cautious in terms of the enforcement levels laid down, it seeks to heed improved rights of defence and to give effect to the general aims of the agreement through specific implementing provisions, but it also accepts certain TRIPS-plus enforcement measures where, apparently, they make sense. In turn, CEPA, which was occasionally named as the leading model agreement for a new IP enforcement approach of the EU,[118] does not—at least not in respect of IP enforcement as examined here—deserve model character for lack of a credibly implemented new and distinct approach as compared to mercantilist agreements

[117] Cf. fn 13.

[118] See fn 9; also Information Paper (fn 2).

and general IP legislation. Even so, the CAAA is far from perfect and leaves ample room for a better balancing of the interests of rightholders and third parties and for a better implementation of non-mercantilist aims: The risk of potential over-enforcement remains. A stricter correlation between enforcement and substantive law is called for here, entailing, for example, an even more detailed layout of the rights of the defence or the introduction of a complementary clause against spurious litigation.

For these reasons alone, it would be overrating the CAAA to speak of a new approach in this agreement. Nonetheless, it is at least somewhat closer to such a new approach than are the other (classic) EPAs.

References

Council Regulation (EC) No 1383/2003 of 22 July 2003 concerning customs action against goods suspected of infringing certain intellectual property rights and the measures to be taken against goods found to have infringed such rights, OJ 2003, L 196, 7

Directive 2000/31/EC of the European Parliament and of the Council of 8 June 2000 on certain legal aspects of information society services, in particular electronic commerce, in the Internal Market, OJ 2000, L 178, 1

Directive 2001/29/EC of the European Parliament and of the Council of 22 May 2001 on the harmonisation of certain aspects of copyright and related rights in the information society, OJ 2001, L 167, 10

Directive 2004/48/EC of the European Parliament and of the Council of 29 April 2004 on the enforcement of intellectual property rights, OJ 2004, L 157, 45

Economic Partnership Agreement between the CARIFORUM States, of the one part, and the European Community and its Member States, of the other part, OJ 2008, L 289, 3

Free Trade Agreement between the European Union and its Member States, of the one part, and the Republic of Korea, of the other part, OJ 2011, L 127, 6

Information Paper (July 2008) CARIFORUM-EU Economic Partnership Agreement, 16. http://trade.ec.europa.eu/doclib/docs/2008/april/tradoc_138569.pdf

Opinion of European Academics on the Anti-Counterfeiting Trade Agreement (ACTA). http://www.iri.uni-hannover.de/acta-1668.html. Accessed 19 October 2011

Vivas-Eugui (2003) Regional and bilateral agreements and a TRIPS-plus world: The Free Trade Area of the Americas (TFAA). TRIPS Issues Papers No. 1. http://www.qiap.ca/documents/FTAAUS2.pdf. Accessed 11 Nov 2011

Part IV
Implementation of IP Provisions in EU Trade Agreements

Economic Partnership Agreements and EU Trade Policy: Objectives, Competences, and Implementation

Christian Pitschas

Contents

1 Introduction

The so-called Cotonou Agreement, which governs the relationship between the EU and ACP countries at large, provides for the conclusion of "new trading arrangements" between the EU and ACP countries until 31 December 2007 at the latest.[1] These new trading arrangements, referred to as Economic Partnership Agreements (EPAs), are intended to put the trade relationship between the EU

Dr. Pitschas, LL.M., is an attorney-at-law based in Geneva who specializes in international trade/WTO law.

[1] Article 37(1) of the Cotonou Agreement.

C. Pitschas (✉)
Bernzen Sonntag Rechtsanwälte, Geneva, Switzerland
e-mail: pitschas@msbh.de

J. Drexl et al. (eds.), *EU Bilateral Trade Agreements and Intellectual Property: For Better or Worse?*, MPI Studies on Intellectual Property and Competition Law 20,
DOI 10.1007/978-3-642-39097-5_11,

and ACP countries on a new footing by complying with the rules of the World Trade Organization (WTO), progressively removing barriers to trade between the parties and enhancing cooperation in all areas relevant to trade.[2]

Given that unilateral (non-reciprocal) trade preferences to goods exported from ACP countries to the EU continued under the Cotonou Agreement, the EU and those ACP countries that are WTO members requested a waiver from the obligations of the EU (then EC) under Article I:1 of the GATT 1994—the most-favored nation (MFN) treatment obligation. The WTO Ministerial Conference granted the requested waiver but limited its duration until 31 December 2007.[3] An extension of that waiver was considered to be unfeasible due to rather fierce resistance from developing countries other than ACP countries.[4] Accordingly, the EU actively sought to conclude the EPA negotiations with the ACP regions involved before the end of 2007.[5] However, this goal could not be achieved, in particular due to the fact that the ACP regions concerned had (and still have) divergent opinions as to the desirability of concluding EPAs with the EU.

To date, only one fully fledged EPA has been concluded and is provisionally being applied: the EC-CARIFORUM EPA.[6] No other comprehensive EPA has been concluded yet but a number of interim EPAs (covering trade in goods only) with individual ACP countries have been signed and some are being provisionally applied.[7] Negotiations regarding comprehensive EPAs with the remaining ACP regions are ongoing and in various stages of progress; the negotiations with Eastern and Southern Africa (ESA) appear to have advanced the most so far.[8]

The EU has put further pressure on ACP countries by proposing to amend its Market Access Regulation (hereafter MA Regulation), which covers ACP countries

---

[2] *Id.*, Article 36(1). On WTO compatibility of EPAs see the critical appraisal of Ochieng (2007), pp. 371 et seq. See also Zimmermann (2009), pp. 3 et seq.

[3] WT/MIN(01)/15, 14 November 2001, Decision of 14 November 2001 (see para 1 of the decision).

[4] See the comments made by then EC Trade Commissioner Peter Mandelson on 5 November 2007 to the Development Committee of the European Parliament ("we are asking ACP countries to liberalise some of their trade with us over very lengthy periods. That is the price of protecting the highly preferential terms of our trading relationship from legal challenge by non-ACP developing countries who resent the privileged treatment we give to the ACP."), accessible at: http://trade.ec.europa.eu/doclib/docs/2007/november/tradoc_136678.pdf.

[5] *Id.* ("There are no alternatives that are defensible under WTO rules, or fair to other developing countries outside the ACP. I recognise that this puts pressure on the negotiations. But the pressure is external. It comes from the reasonable expectation of other developing countries that the EU and the ACP will get our house in order as we promised to do seven years ago in 2000."). See also The Economist (2008), p. 62.

[6] Economic Partnership Agreement between the CARIFORUM States, on the one part, and the European Community and its Member States, of the other part (OJ 2008 L 289, 3).

[7] See the Overview of EPA.

[8] *Id.* See also the speech delivered by EU Trade Commissioner Karel De Gucht to the EU-ACP Parliamentary Assembly on 29 May 2012, "EU-ACP: Completing a Partnership", accessible at: http://ec.europa.eu/commission_2010-2014/degucht/headlines/speeches/.

that have negotiated either comprehensive or interim EPAs.[9] This proposal would lead to the removal of a number of ACP countries from the list of countries benefitting from market access under the terms of the MA Regulation because they have either not signed or not ratified their interim EPAs.[10] If this proposal were adopted by the European Parliament (EP) and the Council, the ACP countries in question would then lose the market access preferences they currently enjoy under the MA Regulation. This loss would only be compensated in the case of those ACP countries that are least-developed countries (LDCs), as they would continue to benefit from quota-free and duty-free market access under the terms of the Everything but Arms Initiative (EBA). In contrast, ACP countries that are not LDCs would then only enjoy market access according to the trade preferences under the Generalised System of Preferences (GSP), excluding EBA treatment reserved to LDCs, or—if they are not eligible for GSP—the MFN treatment according to Article I of the GATT 1994.

Against this backdrop, this paper will address some of the issues arising in the context of EPAs. First, the paper will deal with the trade policy of the EU in general, in terms of both the policy objectives underpinning the EU trade policy and the attribution of competences to the EU in that policy area (see Sect. 2). In a second step, the paper will consider EPAs—in particular the EC-CARIFORUM EPA—and their implementation by the EU, in terms of the negotiating objectives of the EU, the commitments undertaken by the EU and their implementation within the EU (see Sect. 3). At the end, the paper will offer some conclusions (see Sect. 4).

2 EU Trade Policy

2.1 Strategic Goals of EU Trade Policy

The EU Treaties set forth the policy objectives to be pursued by the trade policy of the EU, the "common commercial policy". But these objectives are necessarily couched in broad terms and thus leave considerable discretion to EU institutions,

[9] Council Regulation (EC) No. 1528/2007 of 20 December 2007 applying the arrangements for products originating in certain states which are part of the African, Caribbean and Pacific (ACP) Group of States provided for in agreements establishing, or leading to the establishment of, Economic Partnership Agreements (OJ 2007 L 348, 1).

[10] Proposal for a Regulation of the European Parliament and of the Council amending Annex I to Council Regulation (EC) No 1528/2007 as regards the exclusion of a number of countries from the list of regions or states which have concluded negotiations, COM(2011) 598 final, 30.9.2011. This proposal was adopted by Regulation (EU) No 527/2013 of the European Parliament and of the Council of 21 May 2013, which will apply as from 1 October 2014 (OJ 2013 L 165, 59).

i.e. the European Commission, the Council and the EP, so as to determine how these objectives ought to be achieved in practice and where to set priorities.[11]

As regards EPAs, the crucial question is how these trade agreements fit in the architecture of EU trade policy, as defined by the EU Treaties and designed and executed first and foremost by the Commission.

2.1.1 Guiding Principles and Objectives of EU Trade Policy

With the entry into force of the Lisbon Treaty, EU trade policy has also formally become part and parcel of the "external action by the Union",[12] as evidenced by part five of the Treaty on the Functioning of the EU (TFEU) whose second title covers the "common commercial policy". It is not surprising therefore that EU trade policy is to "be conducted in the context of the principles and objectives of the Union's external action", according to Article 207(1), last sentence, of the TFEU.

Said principles and objectives are set forth by Article 21 of the Treaty on the EU (TEU). Article 21(3) of the TEU stresses that these principles and objectives have to be respected and pursued "in the development and implementation of the different areas of the Union's external action covered . . . by Part Five of the Treaty on the Functioning of the European Union" which includes, as noted above, the EU trade policy. Among these principles and objectives, two appear most relevant with respect to EU trade policy: (i) to foster the sustainable economic, social and environmental development of developing countries, with the primary aim of eradicating poverty[13]; and (ii) to encourage the integration of all countries into the world economy, including through the progressive abolition of restrictions on international trade.[14] These two objectives are not contradictory; rather, they may—and have to—be pursued in parallel, since the integration of developing countries into the world economy will foster their sustainable economic development.[15]

It follows that EU trade policy has to take account of considerations pertaining to the (economic) development of developing countries. However, it cannot reasonably be argued that EU trade policy ought to be primarily a tool for pursuing the (economic) development of developing countries, since Article 21 of the TEU does not establish any hierarchy among the principles and objectives set out in its second paragraph. It is left to the EU institutions to decide to what extent and by

---

[11] See Herrmann (2010), section III.

[12] On the link between the external action and trade policy of the EU see Bungenberg (2009), pp. 212 et seq.

[13] Article 21(2)(d) TEU.

[14] Article 21(2)(e) TEU.

[15] See 2010 Communication, p. 4, and the related 2010 Commission Staff Working Document, p. 58. In its 2012 communication on trade, growth, and development (p. 5), the Commission points out that "openness to trade has been a key element of successful growth and development strategies".

which means EU trade policy should foster the (economic) development of developing countries.

2.1.2 Trade Policy as a Tool for Competitiveness

The Commission has set out its vision for a "modern" trade policy of the Union in two communications. The first communication, of 2006, points out that EU trade policy must contribute to the strengthening of the EU industry's competitiveness,[16] in particular in view of the changing landscape of international trade, which is characterized by increased trade in intermediate products within global supply chains of multinational companies and the rise of new players, especially the emerging economies.[17] According to the communication, the key instrument for achieving the goal of enhanced competitiveness is far-reaching access to the markets of (particular) third countries.[18] Such market access is characterized by three features: (i) the markets of interest; (ii) the scope and depth of access to those markets; and (iii) the instruments to be used for opening up those markets.

The markets specifically targeted are those that have the highest potential in terms of their economic size and growth as well as their pervasive level of protection against EU exports.[19] Using these criteria, the communication identified as most interesting countries those associated within ASEAN, MERCOSUR and the Gulf Cooperation Council, as well as China, India, Korea, and Russia.[20]

Next, access to the specifically targeted markets should be both comprehensive and ambitious in scope, pursuant to the communication.[21] This means that access must go beyond simply reducing tariffs, since their importance is in decline (with the exception of agricultural products). Rather, effective market access requires addressing non-tariff and regulatory ("behind-the-border") measures, too, in areas such as technical barriers to trade, sanitary and phytosanitary measures, and government procurement.[22] Furthermore, the—relatively speaking—"new" trade

---

[16] 2006 Communication, p. 7.

[17] *Id.*, p. 3. The 2006 Commission Staff Working Document notes at p. 4: "Vertical integration of production – where components of a single product may be sourced in a range of countries – is replacing traditional trade in finished goods." For more information on the rise of regional and global supply chains see the Commission's Progress Report of 18 July 2012, pp. 6–8. For an analysis of the consequences for trade rules see Baldwin (2011).

[18] 2006 Communication, p. 5. The related Commission Staff Working Document states at p. 7: "We must take a robust approach to ensuring that markets are genuinely open and that international rules are applied openly and transparently." The Commission underscored this message in its 2007 Communication.

[19] 2006 Communication, p. 9.

[20] *Id.*

[21] *Id.* See generally on the issue of deep integration through international trade agreements Chauffour and Maur (2010).

[22] 2006 Communication, p. 5. See also 2006 Commission Staff Working Document, p. 8.

areas—services, foreign direct investment, competition (including subsidies), and intellectual property rights—also need to be covered so as to harness the drivers of future growth.[23]

Finally, the instruments for achieving such comprehensive and deep market access are twofold: multilateral and bilateral trade agreements. While the communication insists that the rules-based multilateral trading system—the WTO—remains crucial in terms of expanding and managing international trade,[24] the stalemate of the Doha Negotiations makes it necessary to simultaneously pursue bilateral trade agreements, especially with the abovementioned third countries.[25]

In 2010, the Commission supplemented its first communication with a second one.[26] The core message of this second communication is very similar to the first one. It stresses that trade opening results in a triple benefit for the Union: higher growth, more jobs, and lower prices.[27] As regards the abovementioned three benchmarks qualifying the Commission's market access strategy, the second communication reiterates the stance taken by the first communication. With respect to the negotiation of bilateral trade agreements with the countries specifically targeted by the Commission, the second communication emphasizes that "completing our current agenda of competitiveness-driven FTAs remains a priority".[28] It adds an important new element, however, by highlighting that cooperation with Brazil, China, India, Japan, Russia, and the US in trade matters is of a "strategic dimension for the EU".[29] As regards the substantive scope of trade policy in general, and

[23] 2006 Communication, pp. 6 et seq. See also 2006 Commission Staff Working Document, pp. 8 et seq.

[24] 2006 Communication, p. 8. In his speech to the EP's International Trade Committee on 23 November 2011 regarding the EU trade agenda for 2012, EU Trade Commissioner Karel De Gucht highlighted that "the multilateral trading system underpinned by the WTO is the only instrument to ensure that everyone plays fair in global trade now and in the future. This is why any regional or plurilateral initiatives can only complement, but never replace multilateral liberalization and rule-making."; p. 5 (accessible at: http://ec.europa.eu/commission_2010-2014/degucht/headlines/speeches/).

[25] 2006 Communication, pp. 8 et seq.

[26] 2010 Communication.

[27] *Id.*, p. 2.

[28] *Id.*, p. 10. In its 2012 Progress Report, the Commission notes on p. 3 that "the key question for the EU remains whether we will be able to conclude these agreements within a realistic timetable, at an acceptable level of ambition and with a balanced outcome of gives and takes." That report provides an overview of the state of play of the ongoing negotiations regarding trade agreements between the EU and the specifically targeted third countries, p. 9 et seq., p. 13 et seq.

[29] 2010 Communication, p. 11. The 2012 Progress Report (p. 2) adds that "two-thirds of the economic gains would come from potentially transformative agreements with the US and Japan, so reviewing the future of our relationships with these partners is crucial".

bilateral trade agreements in particular, the second communication again stresses that the "new" trade issues, such as services and investment and regulatory measures, have to be addressed in a comprehensive manner.[30]

2.1.3 Trade and Development

In view of the strong emphasis the Commission places on the negotiation of competitiveness-driven FTAs and the strategic trade relationship with certain third countries, one may wonder whether the trade relationship with developing countries in general and the ACP countries in particular has any place in the "modern" EU trade policy, as envisaged by the Commission in its aforementioned two communications. The answer to this question is "yes, but with strings attached".

To start with, the communication of 2010 addresses the issue of the trade relationship between the EU and developing countries, including the ACP countries, but in a rather limited fashion. This is in itself an indication that this specific topic is not a major concern of EU trade policy. That being said, the second communication points out, albeit in rather general terms, that developing and emerging countries are likely to account for nearly 60% of world GDP by 2030.[31] This statement suggests that developing countries should not be overlooked provided they have (future) growth potential. In line with this observation, the second communication notes that EU trade policy is employing "a carefully differentiated approach depending on the level of development of our partners".[32] In other words, the EU is not prepared to apply a "one size fits all" concept in its trade relationships with developing countries. Rather, the economic status of the developing country concerned will influence which trade measures the EU will adopt vis-à-vis that country. With respect to EPAs more specifically, the second communication describes the approach of EU trade policy as one of "fostering development by promoting regional integration, creating opportunities for trade and investment, and improving economic governance".[33] It can be deduced that for ACP countries to be eligible, in the eyes of the EU, to be party to an EPA, they must be ready to "put their house in order".[34]

---

[30] The 2010 Communication states to the point (p. 4): "What will make a bigger difference is market access for services and investment, opening public procurement, better agreements on and enforcement of protection of IPR, unrestricted supply of raw materials and energy, and, not in the least, overcoming regulatory barriers including via the promotion of international standards." See also the overview on the current state of barriers affecting EU trade set out in the 2010 Commission Staff Working Document, pp. 28 et seq.

[31] 2010 Communication, p. 4.

[32] *Id.*, p. 5.

[33] *Id.*, p. 8.

[34] The 2010 Commission Staff Working Document emphasizes (p. 58) that trade openness has to be "combined with sound domestic policies".

The link between the EU trade policy and development has been explored in more detail in a recent communication of the Commission[35] which was endorsed by the Council.[36] One of the main themes of this communication, if not the main theme, is the need, perceived by the EU, to "differentiate among developing countries to focus on those most in need".[37] This implies that development concerns as part of EU trade policy will cater to a smaller group of developing countries than in the past. According to the communication, "the EU must focus its efforts on the poorest and most vulnerable countries and make sure those efforts are tailored to their needs and constraints".[38] However, the developing countries falling into that category are expected to do their part, because the trade measures' success will depend on the willingness of the developing countries concerned "to undertake the necessary domestic reforms".[39]

As regards (the negotiation of) EPAs, the communication makes the point that "time is of the essence to finally provide certainty and predictability to operators".[40] The communication states that EPAs will include commitments on services, investment, and trade-related areas but ACP countries may liberalize partially and gradually.[41] Put differently, the EU seeks commitments from ACP countries that would provide market access to its companies in the long term, as ACP countries may soften the impact of such commitments by excluding certain sensitive sectors and providing for transition periods. The alternative to this approach is clearly spelt out in the communication: ACP countries unwilling to undertake such commitments may opt for trade preferences under the GSP "if they are eligible" but the GSP scheme would not entail the same advantages as EPAs, "particularly in terms of regional integration, enhanced investment and improved business environment".[42] Reading between the lines, it becomes apparent that the EU's patience with ACP countries is running out[43] and the proposed alternative to EPAs may not be an alternative at all if the country concerned is not eligible for the GSP scheme,

---

[35] 2012 Communication.

[36] 2012 Council Conclusions.

[37] 2012 Communication, p. 2.

[38] *Id.*, p. 9.

[39] *Id.* The communication underlines on p. 16 that domestic reforms and good governance are key to trade-led growth. The Council Conclusions, at par. 2, stress that openness to international trade has to be "accompanied by adequate domestic policies and institutional reforms".

[40] 2012 Communication, p. 13.

[41] *Id.*, p. 13.

[42] *Id.*

[43] In his speech to the EU ACP Parliamentary Assembly, EU Trade Commissioner Karel De Gucht opined that "it is not right to give the same treatment to countries that don't implement EPAs and to those that do go through deep, if ultimately beneficial, reforms.", at p. 5.

including the EBA, according to the new GSP scheme whose trade preferences will apply from 1 January 2014.[44]

2.2 Trade Policy Competence of the EU

The attribution and scope of competences in the trade policy area have developed over time with successive EU Treaties: Treaty of Rome, Treaty of Amsterdam, Treaty of Nice, and now Treaty of Lisbon. The competence of the EU in the area of trade policy has undergone a remarkable development. This development is characterized by the fact that the Member States have broadened the trade policy competence conferred on the EU, both in depth and scope, every time they have negotiated and concluded a new Treaty. Conversely, the corresponding competence of the Member States in this policy area has shrunken. Accordingly, the "enlargement" of the Union's trade policy competence is reflected in the various modifications of the respective Treaty provisions dealing with the common commercial policy of the EU, starting with Article 113 EEC, based on the original Treaty of Rome, continuing with Article 133 EC, as defined first by the Treaty of Amsterdam and subsequently modified by the Treaty of Nice, and culminating in the new Article 207 of the TFEU.

Said development is not so much a consequence of the Union's ever growing appetite for more powers (although it is undeniable that every new Treaty brought new powers for the EU, not only in the trade policy area). Rather, it is a result of the changing and equally expanding nature of international trade (law), in particular as regards (rules on) trade in services, trade and investment, and trade-related intellectually property rights. This change had to be reflected somehow in the Union's trade policy competence, given that the common commercial policy had been designed from the outset as an area of (almost) exclusive competence of the EU, in line with its nature as a customs union.

The evolving nature of international trade and the rules relating to it came to the fore with the Uruguay round of negotiations (1986–1993), which led to the establishment of the WTO. The conclusion of the Agreement Establishing the WTO, the Marrakesh Agreement, in 1993 raised the question of who had the competence of concluding that agreement: the EC alone, or only together with its Member States? The European Court of Justice gave an almost solomonic answer: the competence for concluding the Marrakesh Agreement was shared between the EC and its

[44] Regulation of the European Parliament and of the Council of 25 October 2012 applying a scheme of generalized tariff preferences, and repealing Council Regulation (EC) No 732/2008, (OJ 2012 L 303, 1); see Press release, Access to EU Markets for exporters from African, Caribbean and Pacific countries (accessible at: http://trade.ec.europa.eu/doclib/docs/2011/september/tradoc_148215.pdf).

Member States, the latter retaining some trade policy competence, in particular in the new fields covered by that agreement, namely trade in services and trade-related intellectual property rights.[45] Consequently, the Marrakesh Agreement had to be concluded as a "mixed agreement" by both the EC and its Member States. Successive changes to the Treaties were an attempt to alter the balance of power in favor of the EU and to make sure that the EU would regain its (almost) exclusive competence in the trade policy area.[46]

Against this backdrop, the following subsections address three issues in relation to the new Article 207 of the TFEU that have an impact on the implementation of international commitments undertaken by the EU on the basis of this provision, including those in the context of EPAs: (i) does the EU enjoy an exclusive competence in the area of the common commercial policy; (ii) do EU Member States retain any (residual) competence in that area; and (iii) is there a limit to the Union's exercise of its competence in that area?[47]

2.2.1 Exclusive Competence of the EU

Explicit and Implied Competences

Article 207 of the TFEU itself does not specify whether the common commercial policy falls within the exclusive competence of the EU. But Article 3(1)(e) of the TFEU explicitly provides that the Union enjoys an exclusive competence in the area of the common commercial policy.[48]

Article 3(1)(e) refers to the competence explicitly conferred by Article 207 in the area of the common commercial policy. Yet the EU also enjoys a competence implicitly conferred on it in this area ("implied powers"). In this respect, Article 3(2) of the TFEU codifies the settled case law of the Court of Justice.[49] According to this provision, the EU enjoys an exclusive competence for the conclusion of international agreements, including international trade agreements, "when its conclusion is provided for in a legislative act of the Union or is necessary to enable the Union to exercise its internal competence, or in so far as its conclusion may affect common rules or alter their scope".

---

[45] See opinion 1/94 of 15 November 1994, ECR 1994, I-5267.

[46] See Herrmann (2002), pp. 7 et seq.; Krenzler and Pitschas (2001), pp. 442 et seq.

[47] See Mylly (2013) in this volume for a discussion of EU competencies from a constitutional perspective.

[48] As explained by AG Kokott in her opinion of 26 March 2009 in case C-13/07 (*Commission v. Council*), "it is a characteristic of exclusive competence that *only the Community* is entitled to take action" (par. 57; emphasis in the original).

[49] The Court of Justice summarized its jurisprudence on this issue in opinion 1/03 (7 February 2006, ECR 2006, I-1145), pars 114 et seq.

Vertical Reach of Trade Policy Competence

In spite of its exclusiveness, the Union's trade policy competence may have its limitations, that is, it is exclusive only as far as it goes. Put differently, the concept of "exclusivity" is a relative one: it does not definitively answer the question to what extent a particular subject matter is covered by the trade policy competence; one could call this the vertical reach of the trade policy competence.[50] In particular, the vertical reach of this competence might be finite with respect to the subject matters that were added to the trade policy "portfolio" at a later stage, such as trade in services, commercial aspects of intellectual property, and, most recently, foreign direct investment.[51]

Nonetheless, two preliminary conclusions can be drawn at this stage: first, any competence (potentially) remaining with the Member States in the area of trade policy appears to be of a residual nature only given that both the explicit and implied trade policy competences are exclusive. Second, the Union's implied trade policy competence has the tendency of increasing the vertical reach of the Union's trade policy competence, since one type of this implied competence is a reflection of the Union's internal (secondary) legislation; it is a symmetrical relationship. As the body of internal legislation increases, the vertical reach of the Union's trade policy competence will increase in parallel, thereby reducing any residual competence that may yet remain with the Member States.

2.2.2 Shared Competences?

The vertical reach of the EU trade policy competence has to be ascertained by examining the subject matters that come under the common commercial policy, as defined by Article 207 of the TFEU. In the following, only the (relatively speaking) "new" subject matters will be scrutinized.

Trade in Services

According to Article 133(6) of the EC Treaty, as amended by the Treaty of Nice, the EC and the Member States shared the trade policy competence with respect to "agreements relating to trade in cultural and audiovisual services, educational

---

[50] AG Kokott used the notion of "vertical demarcation of competence" to describe the situation where "the Community is competent only in respect of certain components of a proposed act, while other components come within the competence of the Member States" (par. 113 of her opinion in case C-13/07).

[51] In her opinion in case C-13/07, AG Kokott took the view that "Article 207(1) TFEU henceforward expressly places the 'new' fields of commercial policy on the same footing as the conventional fields, and the common commercial policy as a whole is expressly assigned to the exclusive competence of the Union (Article 3(1)(e) TFEU)" (par. 63).

services, and social and human health services".[52] This provision has been abolished. In its stead, Article 207(4) of the TFEU provides that the negotiation and conclusion of agreements in the aforementioned service sectors requires a unanimous decision of the Council under certain conditions.[53] Therefore, the trade policy competence of the EU in the field of trade in services is exclusive, save for one service sector: transport services.

Article 4(2)(g) of the TFEU states that the Union and its Member States share competence in the area of transport. In accordance with this attribution of competences, Article 207(5) of the TFEU provides that international agreements in the field of transport have to be negotiated and concluded on the basis of Title VI of the TFEU, on transport.[54] Under Title VI, "transport" refers to transport by rail, road, and inland waterway, as per Article 100(1). According to the second paragraph of the latter provision, said scope can be enlarged by legislative acts jointly adopted by the European Parliament and the Council to include sea and air transport; the latter means of transport are, of course, much more important as regards international trade. The requirement to negotiate and conclude trade agreements in the field of transport services on the basis of Title VI of the TFEU applies to any trade agreement that includes rules and/or commitments on transport services, irrespective of whether transport services are the major focus of the agreement concerned. This was stressed by the ECJ in its opinion 1/08.[55] Although this opinion concerned ex-Article 133 EC, the opinion's rationale with respect to agreements in the field of transport stands, because ex-Article 133(6), third subparagraph, of the EC Treaty and Article 207(5) of the TFEU are more or less identical.[56]

---

[52] In opinion 1/08 (30 November 2009, ECR 2009, I-11129), the ECJ ruled that "the second subparagraph of Article 133(6) EC reflects a concern to prevent trade in such services being regulated by means of international agreements concluded by the Community alone under its external competence in commercial matters. Without in any way excluding a Community competence in that regard, the second subparagraph of Article 133(6) EC requires, however, that that competence which the Community in this instance shares with its Member States be exercised jointly by those States and the Community" (par. 135).

[53] On these conditions see Pitschas (2010), pp. 40 et seq.

[54] In opinion 1/08, the ECJ pointed out that "the expression 'international agreements in the field of transport' covers, *inter alia*, the field of trade concerning transport services" (par. 158).

[55] The Court of Justice stated that "the interpretation proposed by the Commission, by virtue of which only agreements exclusively or predominantly relating to trade in transport services are covered by the third subparagraph of Article 133(6) EC, would to a large extent deprive that provision of its effectiveness" (par. 163).

[56] The Court of Justice emphasized in opinion 1/08 that "the third subparagraph of Article 133(6) EC seeks to maintain, with regard to international trade in transport services, a fundamental parallelism between internal competence, whereby Community rules are unilaterally adopted, and external competence, which operates through the conclusion of international agreements, each competence remaining – as previously – anchored in the title of the Treaty specifically relating to the common transport policy" (par. 164). The opinion of AG Kokott in case C-13/07 lends support to the conclusion expressed here: "even the Treaty of Lisbon will not provide the Community with a uniform and comprehensive external trade competence for horizontal agreements because, for

Against this backdrop, it is an interesting question whether the shared competence in the field of transport could become, at some point, an exclusive competence of the EU, in line with the jurisprudence of the ECJ on implied powers.[57] If any of these instances enumerated in Article 3(2) of the TFEU were present, the EU would have the exclusive competence to conclude an international trade agreement covering the supply of transport services—but only insofar as envisaged by the legislative act, internal competence, or common rules on the basis of which the EU acquired its implied power.[58] The fact that Article 4 of the TFEU explicitly reserves a competence for the Member States in the transport area does not contradict the foregoing conclusion. One might argue that Article 3(2) of the TFEU cannot be relied on to modify the attribution of competences between the Union and its Member States, in particular in the policy areas—such as transport—that fall under the shared competence between the Union and its Member States, pursuant to Article 4 of the TFEU. However, this argument would overlook the nature of implied powers according to Article 3(2) of the TFEU. This provision is a general provision which is not confined to the policy areas enumerated in the first paragraph of Article 3 of the TFEU (this would be counterintuitive, since these areas *ipso iure* fall under the exclusive competence of the EU). Thus, Article 3(2) of the TFEU sets out the cases in which the EU will acquire an exclusive competence, irrespective of the policy area concerned. This reading is confirmed by the fact that this provision refers to a legislative act of the Union, the exercise of its internal competence, and common rules, without restricting such act, competence, or rule to any specific policy area.

Commercial Aspects of Intellectual Property

Pursuant to Article 133(5) of the EC Treaty, as modified by the Treaty of Nice, the EC enjoyed an exclusive competence for negotiating and concluding trade agreements covering the commercial aspects of intellectually property. Article 207 of the TFEU retains the exclusivity of the Union's trade policy competence in this area but introduces some changes as regards the voting procedure within the Council. As was the case under Article 133(5) of the EC Treaty, Article 207(4) of the TFEU requires the Council to act by a qualified majority. Yet, Article 133(5) of

the field of transport, Article 207(5) TFEU still requires recourse to the provisions of the common transport policy" (par. 136).

[57] For an overview of this jurisprudence see opinion 1/03 of the ECJ, supra note 49, pars 114 et seq. and Pitschas (2001), pp. 151 et seq.

[58] In opinion 1/03, the Court of Justice emphasized that "a comprehensive and detailed analysis must be carried out to determine whether the Community has the competence to conclude an international agreement and whether that competence is exclusive. In doing so, account must be taken not only of the area covered by the Community rules and by the provisions of the agreement envisaged, ... but also of the nature and content of those rules and those provisions, to ensure that the agreement is not capable of undermining the uniform and consistent application of the Community rules and the proper functioning of the system which they establish" (par. 133).

the EC Treaty contained two exceptions to this rule, whereas only one exception remains under Article 207(4), second subparagraph, of the TFEU. The Council's vote must be unanimous when trade agreements "include provisions for which unanimity is required for the adoption of internal rules". This provision seeks to ensure the principle of "parallelism" as regards the adoption of internal and external rules: where the Council is required to adopt internal rules by unanimity, the same shall apply to the adoption of trade agreements that extend to the same subject matter as the internal rules.

This immediately raises the question of whether the aforementioned exception is of any material significance as regards the commercial aspects of intellectual property, since voting within the Council by a qualified majority has become the rule under the Treaty of Lisbon. Measures for the creation of European intellectual property rights so as to provide uniform protection of intellectual property rights throughout the Union and for the setting up of centralized Union-wide authorization, coordination, and supervision arrangements do not require unanimity within the Council, pursuant to Article 118, first subparagraph, of the TFEU.[59] Therefore, the exception set out by Article 207(4), second subparagraph, of the TFEU does not apply to the negotiation and conclusion of trade agreements in the field of the commercial aspects of intellectual property.[60]

Notwithstanding the fact that the Union has an exclusive trade policy competence with respect to the commercial aspects of intellectual property, this competence only covers commercial aspects of intellectual property. The qualifier "commercial aspects" suggests that not all intellectual property rights are meant to be covered, although one may ask whether there are any intellectual property rights at all that have no commercial aspects. Leaving that issue aside, the more important question in the present context seems to be whether there is any difference between the commercial aspects of intellectual property, as referred to by Article 207 of the TFEU, and the trade-related aspects of intellectual property rights, as covered by the TRIPS Agreement.[61]

---

[59] According to the second subparagraph of Article 118 TFEU, the Council is to act unanimously when establishing "language arrangements for the European intellectual property rights". Yet this highly specific requirement has no impact on the negotiation and conclusion of trade agreements in the area of the commercial aspects of intellectual property.

[60] In her opinion in case C-13/07, AG Kokott stated in footnote 98: "When the Treaty of Lisbon enters into force the Union will acquire, under the conditions laid down in Article 83(2) TFEU, the power to establish minimum conditions for determining offences and penalties". Article 83 (2) TFEU provides that directives may establish minimum rules with regard to the definition of criminal offences and sanctions where this "proves essential to ensure the effective implementation of a Union policy in an area which has been subject to harmonisation measures". The adoption of such directives has to follow the same legislative procedure as that for adopting the harmonization measures in question. Since Article 118, first subparagraph, TFEU does not require unanimity, the adoption of a directive defining criminal sanctions and offenses so as to provide for uniform protection of intellectual property rights within the EU also does not require a unanimous vote by the Council.

[61] On the scope of the EU competence in this field see Mylly (2013) in this volume.

To begin with, it is highly likely that Article 207 of the TFEU refers to the commercial aspects of intellectual property because Article 207 is concerned with the "common commercial policy" of the EU.[62] Common commercial policy stands for the trade policy of the EU. This is evidenced by the wording of both Articles 206 and 207 of the TFEU: Article 206 refers to the "harmonious development of world trade" as well as the "progressive abolition of restrictions on international trade". Next, Article 207(1) makes it plain that the common commercial policy is based on uniform principles with regard to, *inter alia*, the conclusion of "tariff and trade agreements relating to trade in goods and services, and the commercial aspects of intellectual property". Two conclusions flow from the foregoing: first, the common commercial policy includes the conclusion of trade agreements and hence is about international trade. Second, the reference to "trade agreements relating to ... the commercial aspects of intellectual property" shows that such commercial aspects are those included in trade agreements. Put differently, there is no difference, for all practical purposes, between the commercial aspects and the trade-related aspects of intellectual property, as far as the trade policy competence of the EU is concerned.

Foreign Direct Investment

Article 133 of the EC Treaty did not encompass foreign direct investment. The Treaty of Lisbon constitutes a turning point in this respect, because it brings foreign direct investment under the Union's trade policy. Pursuant to Article 206 of the TFEU, the progressive abolition of restrictions on foreign direct investment forms a part of the tasks assigned to the Union's trade policy. Accordingly, Article 207(1) of the TFEU lists foreign direct investment as a subject matter of the Union's trade policy.

Foreign Direct Investment means the acquisition of a lasting interest in an enterprise by a foreign investor who, by virtue of this acquisition, establishes a long-term relationship with that enterprise and gains a significant degree of influence on its management.[63] By contrast, the notion of foreign direct investment does not include transactions in equity and debt securities ("portfolio investment").[64] Consequently, the Union's competence in the area of foreign direct investment does not cover portfolio investment.[65] This exclusion of portfolio investment from the realm of foreign direct investment coincides with the position taken previously by

[62] See Tietje (2009), p. 15.

[63] See the definition of direct investment (code 500) in Annex II to Regulation (EC) 184/2005 on Community statistics concerning balance of payments, international trade in services and foreign direct investment, OJ 2005 L 35/23, as last amended by Commission Regulation 707/2009, OJ 2009 L 204/3.

[64] See the definition of portfolio investment in Regulation 184/2005, *id.*

[65] Koeb and Dalleau (2010), p. 7; Krajewski (2005), p. 112; Tietje (2009), pp. 15–16.

the EC and its Member States in a WTO working group on the relationship between trade and investment.[66] It follows that any agreement that covers portfolio investment, in addition to foreign direct investment, would have to be concluded jointly by the EU and its Member States as a "mixed agreement".

What differentiates foreign direct investment from more traditional subject matters of trade policy is the fact that it is neither tied to a specific economic activity (trade in goods or trade in services) nor to a particular right that embodies an economic value (i.e. intellectual property rights). Rather, it is a short-hand reference for a certain business conduct that may occur in any economic sector unless the government has excluded a given sector from foreign investment due to overriding public interests (e.g. security concerns). This indeterminate scope of foreign direct investment is reflected in bilateral investment treaties (BITs) that have been concluded—so far—by EU Member States: these BITs subject any (type of) regulatory activity of the parties in any (covered) economic sector to their disciplines.[67] In view of the peculiar character and far-reaching scope of foreign direct investment, on the one hand, and the impact of BIT-like provisions on the exercise of regulatory power by Member States, on the other, one wonders whether there is an inherent limit to the Union's trade policy competence in the field of foreign direct investment beyond the aforementioned exclusion of portfolio investments.[68]

Apart from the foregoing issue, it has been submitted that international standards regarding the protection of foreign direct investment against (direct and indirect) expropriation fall outside the Union's trade policy competence in the area of foreign direct investment because of Article 345 of the TFEU.[69] This provision states that the Treaties are not to prejudice the rules in the Member States "governing the system of property ownership". However, the aforementioned claim seems to be based on a misunderstanding of the scope of Article 345 of the TFEU. As clarified by the Court of Justice, the guarantee offered by Article 345 is not without limits. In particular, said provision does not exempt the Member States' systems of property from the fundamental rules of the Treaty,[70] such as the free

---

[66] See references in Pitschas (2010), pp. 37, 39.

[67] Tietje (2009), p. 17. For a comprehensive overview of the various standards of protection under international investment law see Dolzer and Schreuer (2008), pp. 119 et seq.; Reinisch (2008).

[68] Tietje (2009), p. 17, argues that Article 207(6) TFEU limits the exercise of the Union's trade policy competence in this respect; see also Krajewski (2005), pp. 113-114, who contends that foreign direct investment according to Article 207 TFEU should be understood as meaning only those investment aspects which have a direct link to international trade agreements. On the limitations imposed by Article 207(6) TFEU on the exercise of the Union's trade policy competence, see Sect. 2.2.3, below.

[69] Tietje (2009), p. 15; see also Krajewski (2005), p. 114, who asserts that investment protection against expropriation is a traditional element of investment agreements (as opposed to trade agreements) and hence not covered by the Union's competence in the area of foreign direct investment.

[70] Case C-503/99, 4 June 2002, par. 44 (with further references); joined Cases T-228/99 and T-233/99, 6 March 2003, par. 192 (with further references).

movement of capital.[71] Accordingly, it is hard to see why the Union's trade policy competence in the area of foreign direct investment should be limited by Article 345,[72] also bearing in mind that standards regarding the protection of foreign direct investment against (direct and indirect) expropriation are a typical element of international investment law.[73]

Shared Competence Revisited

The foregoing analysis of the subject matters "trade in services", "commercial aspects of intellectual property", and "foreign direct investment" reveals that Member States retain very few competences in the area of the common commercial policy.

The remaining competence of Member States is most obvious as regards "trade in services", since Article 207(5) of the TFEU exempts trade agreements that extend, even if only partially, to transport services from the common commercial policy. Such agreements need to be concluded jointly by the EU and its Member States, since the competence for the common transport policy is shared between the EU and its Member States. While the "commercial aspects of intellectual property" (arguably congruent with the trade-related aspects of intellectual property) fall completely within the exclusive competence of the EU, the state of play is somewhat less clear with respect to "foreign direct investment". It is evident that "portfolio investment" is not encompassed by the Union's competence in the area of foreign direct investment; any agreement comprising portfolio investment would thus have to be ratified by the Member States, in addition to the Union's approval. Yet it is an open question whether there is an inherent limit to the Union's competence in the area of foreign direct investment beyond the exclusion of "portfolio investment".

2.2.3 Limitations on the Exercise of Trade Policy Competence

Article 207(6) of the TFEU limits the exercise of the EU's trade policy competence in two ways. The exercise of that competence must neither (i) affect the delimitation of competences between the Union and its Member States, nor (ii) lead to the harmonization of legislative or regulatory provisions of the Member States in so far as the Treaties exclude such harmonization. Given its emphasis on the exercise of the trade policy competence, this provision is highly relevant for the issue of implementing commitments that result from an exercise of the trade policy competence.

---

[71] Case C-376/98, 4 June 2002, par. 49.

[72] Hindelang (2011), p. 163.

[73] See Behrens (2007), pp. 160 et seq.

The EU exercises its trade policy competence in two directions: externally, vis-à-vis other trading partners, and internally, vis-à-vis its Member States. While the former is concerned with undertaking commitments by negotiating and concluding trade agreements (such as EPAs) with the trading partners in question, the latter is about implementing such commitments within the EU legal order. To the extent that Article 207(6) of the TFEU limits the exercise of the trade policy competence, it necessarily affects both the external and the internal aspect.

Delimitation of Competences

Article 207(6) of the TFEU states, in part, that the "exercise of the competences conferred by this Article in the field of the common commercial policy shall not affect the delimitation of competences between the Union and the Member States".

This provision focuses on the way in which the EU (potentially) uses the competence in practice and seeks to ensure that the EU refrains from using its competence in a manner that would affect, that is, alter the delimitation of competences between the Union and its Member States. In other words, when exercising its trade policy competence, the EU must not assume a competence that the Member States have not conferred on it.

Said requirement is, in essence, a restatement of the principle of conferral, established by Article 5(2) of the TEU.[74] The latter provision requires the EU "to act only within the limits of the competences conferred upon it by the Member States in the Treaties to attain the objectives set out therein." The flipside of this requirement is that "competences not conferred upon the Union in the Treaties remain with the Member States". A reading of Article 207(6) of the TFEU in light of Article 5(2) of the TFEU confirms that the former is about maintaining the "balance of powers", as it were, between the EU and its Member States: the attribution of competences between the EU and its Member States is not to be undermined by an improper (*ultra vires*) exercise of the trade policy competence (explicitly or implicitly) conferred on the EU.[75] Therefore, the EU may only enter into internationally binding obligations that have no basis in Article 207 of the TFEU if another provision of that Treaty confers a corresponding competence on the EU or if the EU enjoys an implicit competence ("implied powers") because one

[74] See Pitschas (2010), p. 42. In her opinion in case C-13/07, AG Kokott stressed that the principle of limited conferred powers "applies to both internal Community action and action of the Community under international law" (par. 45) and emphasized that "individual aspects of an agreement for which the Community has no competence internally 'infect' the agreement as a whole and make it dependent on the common accord of the Member States" (par. 121).

[75] This has been highlighted by AG Kokott in her opinion in case C-13/07: "The meaning and purpose of the first subparagraph of Article 133(6) EC Treaty [which is very similar to Article 207 (6) TFEU] is, very generally, to put the Community's internal and external powers on a parallel footing and to prevent the Community from entering into external commitments to which it would be unable to give effect internally for want of sufficient powers" (par. 142).

of the instances enumerated in Article 3(2) of the TFEU is present. If that is not the case, however, the international (trade) agreement in question has to be concluded jointly with the Member States as a "mixed agreement".[76]

If there is reason to believe that any such agreement would not respect this "balance of powers", Article 218(11) of the TFEU enables any Member State, the Parliament, the Council, or the Commission to request an opinion from the Court of Justice as to whether the agreement at stake is compatible with the Treaties, including their attribution of competences between the Union and its Member States.[77] If the Court came to the conclusion that the envisaged agreement would affect the delimitation of competences between the Union and the Member States, the agreement could not be concluded unless it were amended or concluded jointly by the EU and its Member States as "mixed agreements", or the EU Treaties were revised.

Harmonizing Measures

Article 207(6) of the TFEU states, in part, that the "exercise of the competences conferred by this Article in the field of the common commercial policy ... shall not lead to harmonization of legislative or regulatory provisions of the Member States in so far as the Treaties exclude such harmonization".

This second part of the provision is similar to its first part, addressed above, in that it focuses on the (potential) exercise of the trade policy competence by the EU. Yet the second part differs from the first in that it seeks to prevent the EU from exercising its trade policy competence in ways that would harmonize legislative or regulatory provisions of the Member States even though the Treaties exclude such harmonization.[78]

To apprehend the meaning and scope of the provision's second part, the term "harmonization" has to be interpreted. Does this term refer to harmonization in a narrow, technical sense, namely the "approximation of laws" with respect to the establishment and functioning of the internal market, as defined by Article 114 in conjunction with Article 26 of the TFEU? Or does the term refer to "harmonization" in a wide, non-technical sense, that is to say, harmonization as a

---

[76] See also Bungenberg (2009), p. 204.

[77] In opinion 1/08, the ECJ referred to its settled case law, according to which "its opinion may in particular be obtained on questions concerning the division, between the Community and the Member States, of competence to conclude a given agreement with non-member countries" (par. 109). The Commission had referred ACTA—the Anti-counterfeiting Trade Agreement—to the Court in accordance with Article 218(11) but the Union no longer pursues the ratification of this treaty, because the EP voted against it on 4 July 2012.

[78] Weiß (2011), p. 41. In opinion 1/03, the ECJ made the following statement: "If an international agreement contains provisions which presume a harmonization of legislative or regulatory measures of the Member States in an area for which the Treaty excludes such harmonization, the Community does not have the necessary competence to conclude that agreement" (par. 132).

consequence of secondary legislation enacted by the EU which has a harmonizing effect on the legislative or regulatory provisions of the Member States?

First, it must be noted that Article 207(6) of the TFEU does not speak of "approximation of laws" but of "harmonization"; this indicates that the provision's second part aims at harmonization in a wide, non-technical sense. Second, a comparison with the provision's first part corroborates this understanding, because that part refers to the delimitation of competences in all policy areas where the Treaties confer a competence on the EU; this suggests that the provision's second part refers to harmonization in a wide, non-technical sense that could occur in all policy areas where the EU is competent to adopt directives and regulations. Third, the provision's object and purpose buttress this reading: the provision is about preventing the EU from exercising its trade policy competence in an abusive manner. In particular, the provision's second part seeks to exclude a harmonization of national provisions that is not permitted by the Treaties. If the provision only applied to the "approximation of laws" in a narrow, technical sense, its object and purpose would be frustrated since it would then have no scope of application at all, given that the EU is competent to approximate the legislative, regulatory, and administrative provisions of Member States, pursuant to Article 114 of the TFEU. Therefore, the provision's second part refers to harmonization in a wide, non-technical sense.

Having established the meaning of harmonization under Article 207(6) of the TFEU, the question remains in which policy areas the Treaties exclude harmonizing measures of the EU. The most obvious candidates are the areas set out by Article 6 of the TFEU in which the EU only may "support, coordinate or supplement the actions of the Member States". This rather limited competence does not include the competence to (indirectly) harmonize the legislative or regulatory provisions of the Member States in the policy areas concerned, which are: protection and improvement of human health; industry; culture; tourism; education, vocational training, youth and sport; civil protection and administrative cooperation.

Some of these policy areas are trade-relevant, in particular as regards trade in cultural, education, health, and tourism services. With respect to these service sectors, the EU may not undertake commitments that would have a harmonizing effect on the legislative or regulatory provisions of Member States.[79] Three types of commitments have to be distinguished in this respect: commitments on market access, national treatment, and mutual recognition. It is rather unlikely that market access or national treatment commitments would have a harmonizing effect (although commitments on national treatment could eventually lead to such harmonization). In contrast, mutual recognition commitments could very well have such effect, since one way of achieving recognition is through harmonizing standards and criteria for the authorization, licensing, or certification of service suppliers. As Article 207(6) of the TFEU prohibits an exercise of the trade policy competence that would lead to harmonization of legislative and regulatory

[79] Weiβ (2011), p. 40.

provisions of the Member States in the aforementioned service sectors, an international trade agreement must not pursue mutual recognition through harmonization. Otherwise, the agreement could not be concluded by the EU alone but would have to be concluded jointly by both the EU and its Member States as a "mixed agreement".[80]

3 Implementation of Economic Partnership Agreements Within the EU

3.1 Negotiating Objectives of the EU

The Cotonou Agreement sets out objectives and principles for economic and trade cooperation between the EU and ACP countries. The "ultimate objective" of this cooperation is to enable ACP countries to play a full part in international trade.[81] To this end, the envisaged cooperation is to enhance the production, supply, and trading capacity of ACP countries and their capacity to attract investment,[82] taking account of the different needs and levels of development of the ACP countries and regions.[83] Regional integration is considered to be a "key instrument" for integrating ACP countries into the world economy.[84] These objectives and principles are to be achieved on the basis of WTO-compatible trading arrangements, the progressive removal of barriers to trade between the EU and ACP countries, and enhanced cooperation in all areas relevant to trade.[85]

In its communication on EPAs from the end of 2007, the Commission stated that "full agreements are essential to meet the ultimate objective of ACP-EU economic and trade cooperation".[86] By full agreements, the Commission means EPAs that contain provisions in "trade-related areas, trade-related rules and trade in services and include appropriate links to development co-operation".[87] The Commission emphasizes that EPAs will bring new trade opportunities for ACP countries.[88] In order to make the most of these opportunities, ACP countries are expected to create regional markets and prepare new structural reforms, trade policies, and measures

---

[80] Pitschas (2010), p. 43; Weiβ (2011), *id.*

[81] Article 34(2) of the Cotonou Agreement.

[82] *Id.*, Article 34(3).

[83] *Id.*, Article 35(3).

[84] *Id.*, Article 35(2).

[85] *Id.*, Article 36(1).

[86] 2007 Communication, p. 1.

[87] *Id.*

[88] *Id.*, p. 5.

to adjust to the changes entailed by EPAs. The Commission offers to assist and support ACP countries in this respect.[89]

In his presentation to the EP's Development Committee shortly after the publication of the aforementioned communication, then EC Trade Commissioner Peter Mandelson summarized the main elements of EPAs envisaged by the EU as follows:

> They aim to bring together: improved trade preferences for the ACP, based on a complete opening of the EU market, with progressive regional opening by the ACP to each other, and then, on a highly asymmetrical basis, to the EU; extensive EU support for this regional integration; building of rules of good economic governance; targeted development assistance to support the fiscal and other adjustments necessary to ensure this change is successful.[90]

The aforementioned communication and presentation make it crystal clear that the EU aims to conclude EPAs that go beyond the traditional approach in the trade relationship between the EU and ACP countries. In line with its overall trade-policy orientation, as set out in its communications of 2006 and 2010,[91] the EU seeks to conclude EPAs that are comprehensive in scope, covering for instance trade in services, including foreign direct investment, trade-related intellectual property rights and public procurement, in addition to trade in goods. This implies that EPAs not only include market access commitments on trade in goods and services, but also rules commitments. The goal of the EU to reach comprehensive EPAs is also evidenced by its recent communication on trade, growth, and development. In that communication, the Commission points out that making trade work for development requires much more than lowering tariffs and that modern and pro-development trade policies need to address a complex range of issues such as those mentioned above.[92]

What makes EPAs even more challenging for ACP countries is the EU's insistence that EPAs contribute to regional integration among ACP countries as a means of creating a larger market within the ACP region concerned so as to spur intra-regional trade.[93] While the economic rationale of such regional integration seems clear-cut,[94] it imposes additional burdens on the ACP countries. This is because regional integration ultimately requires ACP countries participating in an EPA to open their respective markets to each other in the same way as they have

---

[89] *Id.*

[90] Speech of 5 November 2007, supra note 4.

[91] See supra Sect. 2.1.2.

[92] 2012 Communication, p. 5. The communication also notes that a "comprehensive, regional EPA has been signed and provisionally applied with the CARIFORUM group of states in the Caribbean"; p. 7.

[93] 2012 Communication, p. 8.

[94] In his speech to the EU-ACP Parliamentary Assembly, supra note 8, EU Trade Commissioner Karel De Gucht remarked that "regional integration ... allows countries to take advantage of economies of scale. Companies that have a larger domestic market have much better chances to compete internationally. They also have the possibility to create regional level value chains".

opened their markets to the EU under the EPA in question. While ACP countries that belong to one region so far may have granted each other market access beyond their respective MFN obligations under the GATT 1994 and GATS, regional integration under an EPA is likely to take that trade opening one step further.

As was pointed out in the introduction, there is only one comprehensive EPA to date that has been provisionally applied since 2009: the EC-CARIFORUM EPA. All other EPAs are interim EPAs covering only trade in goods; negotiations between the EU and ACP countries concerned continue with the aim of either converting interim EPAs into comprehensive EPAs, along the lines of the EC-CARIFORUM EPA, or concluding interim EPAs with those (few) ACP countries that have not yet concluded interim EPAs with the EU.[95] The previously noted Commission proposals regarding the amendment of both the MA Regulation and the GSP scheme[96] are clearly intended to inject momentum into these negotiations, as the adoption of said proposals would make the market access conditions for the ACP countries that have not signed or ratified an EPA with the EU by then (far) less attractive.[97]

3.2 Implementation of International Trade Agreements by the EU

Trade agreements negotiated and concluded by the EU with third countries need to be implemented in order to have an impact on cross-border trade between the parties of the agreement in question. Without implementation, no trade agreement will be able to generate the economic benefits that such agreement is supposed to trigger. In this context, implementation means adopting in the internal legal order the legislative or administrative measures that are required to create the conditions necessary for applying the trade agreement and the commitments undertaken by the parties to that agreement in practice.[98]

Article 207(2) of the TFEU sets forth a positive obligation with respect to the implementation of the common commercial policy. Article 207(2) refers to "measures defining the framework for implementing the common commercial policy". The word "framework" suggests that Article 207(2) is concerned with measures of a general nature that provide overall direction and guidance for the

---

[95] See Overview of EPA.

[96] See supra Sects. 1 and 2.1.3.

[97] In his speech to the EU-ACP Parliamentary Assembly, supra note 8, EU Trade Commissioner Karel De Gucht commented with respect to the amendment of the MA Regulation: "the amendment allows plenty of time before the measure enters into force: sufficient time to ratify and apply existing interim EPAs as well as to conclude ongoing negotiations and put those EPAs into application".

[98] See Mylly (2013) in this volume on the implementation of international commitments undertaken by the EU.

implementation of the Union's trade policy.[99] This understanding is borne out by both the procedure on the basis of which the measures have to be adopted as well as the legal nature of these measures: they are to be adopted jointly by the European Parliament and the Council "by means of regulations in accordance with the ordinary legislative procedure". First, regulations are legal acts of the highest "order" because they have general application, are binding in their entirety, and directly applicable in all Member States.[100] Second, the ordinary legislative procedure is the "normal" procedure for the joint adoption of legal acts by the European Parliament and the Council.[101] All of this leads to the conclusion that Article 207 (2) of the TFEU seeks to ensure that the common commercial policy be implemented on the basis of a legislative framework that sets forth an overarching structure for such implementation.

The legislative framework for implementing the common commercial policy consists of all regulations that lay down the essential parameters of a given subject matter of EU trade policy. Examples of such "basic" regulations are those on trade defense instruments (e.g. the anti-dumping, anti-subsidy, and safeguards regulations), trade barriers, dual-use items, export-credit insurance, and the GSP scheme.[102] The "pool" of regulations that determine the framework for implementing EU trade policy within the meaning of Article 207(2) of the TFEU also includes the MA Regulation.[103]

It may become necessary to amend or supplement "basic" regulations constituting said legislative framework in line with developments occurring after such regulations have been adopted under the ordinary legislative procedure. The power to amend or supplement legislative acts such as the "basic" regulations by means of so-called delegated acts may be conferred on the Commission in the legislative act concerned, pursuant to Article 290(1) of the TFEU.[104] According to this provision, the Commission must confine itself to amending or supplementing "non-essential elements" of the legislative act concerned based on the "objectives,

[99] Müller-Ibold (2011), pp. 75, 85.

[100] Article 288, second subparagraph, TFEU.

[101] By requiring a "joint" adoption by the European Parliament and the Council, the ordinary legislative procedure confers on the European Parliament a "veto power" since it cannot be overruled by the Council; see Articles 289(1) and 294 TFEU; see also Krajewski (2011), pp. 55, 58.

[102] See Müller-Ibold (2011), p. 86.

[103] See Koeb and Dalleau (2010), p. 3.

[104] The conditions pertaining to the adoption of delegated acts have to be laid down explicitly in the legislative act in question, according to Article 290(2) TFEU. A "Common Understanding" sets out the practical arrangements and agreed clarifications and preferences for the inter-institutional cooperation between the Commission, the EP and the Council regarding the adoption of delegated acts.

content, scope and duration of the delegation of power ... explicitly defined in the legislative acts".[105]

As the abovementioned legislative framework for the implementation of the Union's trade policy only constitutes an overarching structure for such implementation, a subordinate second level is required to further specify how the relevant legislative acts are to be implemented. While the implementation of legislative acts adopted by the EU is, in principle, left to the Member States, Article 291(2) of the TFEU provides that legislative acts may confer implementing powers on the Commission (or in duly justified specific cases on the Council)[106] that will allow it to impose "uniform conditions for implementing legally binding Union acts" where needed.[107] Given that the common commercial policy is an area that falls almost completely within the exclusive competence of the EU,[108] uniform conditions for implementing the legislative framework in the sense of Article 207 (2) of the TFEU may be imposed by the Commission when the legislative act in question confers implementing powers on the Commission.[109]

3.3 Implementation of Commitments Undertaken by the EU in EPAs

As only one comprehensive EPA currently exists, the following observations will concentrate on this EPA, namely, the EC-CARIFORUM EPA, and its

[105] A so-called Omnibus II (2011) proposal was put forward by the Commission, covering a number of trade-related regulations, including the MA Regulation, with the aim of modifying existing decision-making procedures in these regulations (which are based on the 1999 comitology decision) so as to allow the adoption of delegated acts by the Commission, as set forth by Article 290 TFEU. According to this proposal, the MA Regulation would be amended so as to empower the Commission to adopt delegated acts as regards technical amendments to Annex II to the MA Regulation (concerning rules of origin) as well as technical amendments to the MA Regulation that may be required as a result of differences between the MA Regulation and EPAs signed with provisional application or concluded with ACP countries or regions listed in Annex I to the MA Regulation (see pp. 25–26 of the proposal).

[106] Pursuant to Article 291(3) TFEU, the rules and general principles concerning mechanisms for control by Member States of the Commission's exercise of implementing powers are to be laid down in advance. This was done by Regulation (EU) No 182/2011 of the European Parliament and of the Council of 16 February 2011, OJ 2011 L 55, 13.

[107] The Commission put forward a so-called Omnibus I (2011) proposal covering a number of trade-related regulations, including the MA Regulation, with the goal of modifying existing decision-making procedures in these regulations (which are *not* based on the 1999 comitology decision) so as to allow the conferral of implementing powers on, or the adoption of delegated acts by, the Commission. This proposal also suggests amending the MA Regulation, in particular as regards the provisions on safeguard measures and new provisions on the exercise and revocation of delegation to the Commission and objections to delegated acts adopted by the Commission (see pp. 34 et seq. of the proposal).

[108] See supra Sect. 2.2.1.

[109] See Müller-Ibold (2011), pp. 86 et seq.

implementation by the EU.[110] However, these observations would also be valid—*cum grano salis*—with respect to new comprehensive EPAs concluded by the EU and ACP countries or regions other than the Caribbean region, since the main elements of such new EPAs would in all likelihood be very similar to those of the EC-CARIFORUM EPA.

This subsection will start with an overview of commitments to be found in the EC-CARIFORUM EPA (see infra Sect. 3.3.1) and then look into the legislative measures adopted by the EU to implement these commitments in the EU legal order (see infra Sect. 3.3.2).

3.3.1 Types of Commitments

In general, three types of commitments may be differentiated in the context of a trade agreement: (i) market access commitments; (ii) rules commitments; and (iii) institutional commitments relating to the setting up of joint institutions that have the task of overseeing how the agreement in question functions in practice.[111] These categories are present, too, in the EC-CARIFORUM EPA.

Nonetheless, a distinction has to be drawn between market access and rules commitments, on the one hand, and institutional commitments, on the other. While market access and rules commitments require the adoption of legislative and administrative measures in the internal legal order of the parties to the agreement concerned with a view to effectively implementing such commitments, this is not the case with respect to institutional commitments. The latter relate to the (political) management of trade agreements, including monitoring the compliance of the parties with market access and rules commitments, as well as reviewing the implementation of the latter by the parties.[112] Consequently, institutional commitments only operate at the (governmental and, possibly, parliamentary) level of the parties and thus have no direct effect on economic operators and the

[110] On the implementation of commitments contained in EPAs see also Drexl (2013) in this volume.

[111] For a quick overview of the joint institutions created under the EC-CARIFORUM EPA (i.e. the Joint Council, Trade and Development Committee, Parliamentary Committee, Consultative Committee and Special Committee on Customs Cooperation and Trade Facilitation) and their respective tasks see The EPA Factsheet (2012), p. 7. These joint institutions are set up in accordance with Part V of the EC-CARIFORUM EPA (entitled "Institutional Provisions") and Article 36 of that Agreement (which provides for the establishment of a Special Committee on Customs Cooperation and Trade Facilitation).

[112] Article 5 of the EC-CARIFORUM EPA states, in part: "The parties undertake to monitor continuously the operation of the Agreement through their respective participative processes and institutions, as well as those set up under this Agreement, in order to ensure that . . . the Agreement is properly implemented".

markets in which they operate. It follows that institutional commitments do not require adoption of any legislative measures for purposes of implementing them in the internal legal order of the parties to the agreement.

Market Access Commitments

The EC-CARIFORUM EPA contains market access commitments in two areas: (i) trade in goods; and (ii) trade in services.

Trade in Goods

As regards trade in goods, market access commitments cover customs duties on exports of goods originating in the CARIFORUM States and imported into the EU and vice versa.[113] These export duties are to be eliminated, but the CARIFORUM States enjoy a transitional period of three years with respect to export duties set out in Annex I to the EPA.[114]

Moreover, market access commitments cover customs duties on products originating in the CARIFORUM States and imported into the EU and vice versa. The EU is not to apply such import duties, except for the products indicated in, and in conformity with the conditions of, Annex II to the EPA.[115] The CARIFORUM States are to eliminate such import duties at the latest ten years after signature of the EPA, but a process of gradually eliminating such duties has to start seven years after signature of the EPA.[116] However, CARIFORUM States may continue to apply the import duties listed in Annex III to the EPA on products originating in the EU.[117]

Furthermore, market access commitments concern government procurement of goods provided two conditions are met[118]: first, the procurement must be conducted by a procuring entity listed in Annex VI to the EPA; second, the procurement has to be above the thresholds set out in that Annex.[119] These commitments are clearly "WTO-plus" commitments for the CARIFORUM States, as none of them is a party to the WTO's plurilateral Government Procurement Agreement (GPA).[120]

---

[113] Article 14(1) of the EC-CARIFORUM EPA.

[114] *Id.*, Article 14(2).

[115] *Id.*, Article 15.

[116] *Id.*, Article 16(2)–(4).

[117] *Id.*, Article 16(1)–(2).

[118] In order to qualify as government procurement, two criteria have to be fulfilled: the procurement must be for "governmental purposes" and "not with a view to commercial resale or with a view to use in the production of goods or the supply of services for commercial sale"; Article 166 (1) of the EC-CARIFORUM EPA.

[119] Article 167(1) of the EC-CARIFORUM EPA.

[120] See the list of GPA parties and observers, accessible at: http://www.wto.org/english/tratop_e/gproc_e/memobs_e.htm.

Trade in Services

With respect to trade in services, market access commitments relate to four modes of supply: commercial presence (including economic activities by investors[121]),[122] cross-border supply (in two variations),[123] and temporary presence of natural persons for business purposes.[124] The specific commitments on market access, including any conditions and limitations, for each mode of supply are set out in Annex IV to the EPA.

In addition, market access commitments pertain to government procurement of services under the same conditions as in the case of government procurement of goods.[125] Again, these commitments represent "WTO-plus" commitments for the CARIFORUM States since they are not parties to the GPA.

Rules Commitments

The EC-CARIFORUM EPA sets forth rules commitments relating to trade in both goods and services.

As regards trade in goods, rules commitments apply, *inter alia*, to non-tariff measures,[126] customs and trade facilitation,[127] technical barriers to trade,[128] sanitary and phytosanitary measures,[129] and innovation and intellectual property.[130] The commitments on customs and trade facilitation in particular constitute "WTO-plus" commitments for both the EU and the CARIFORUM States.

With respect to trade in services (including investment), there are rules commitments of general application[131] as well as rules commitments concerning specific service sectors, such as computer services,[132] courier services,[133] telecommunications services,[134] financial services,[135] international maritime

[121] Note that measures by EPA parties relating to expropriation and investor-to-state dispute settlement such as those covered in bilateral investment treaties are not deemed to affect commercial presence, according to footnote 2 to Article 66 of the EC-CARIFORUM EPA.

[122] See Article 67 of the EC-CARIFORUM EPA.

[123] *Id.*, Article 76.

[124] *Id.*, Articles 81–83.

[125] *Id.*, Article 167(1).

[126] *Id.*, Articles 26 et seq.

[127] *Id.*, Articles 29 et seq.

[128] *Id.*, Articles 44 et seq.

[129] *Id.*, Articles 52 et seq.

[130] *Id.*, Articles 131 et seq.

[131] *Id.*, Articles 85 et seq.

[132] *Id.*, Article 88.

[133] *Id.*, Articles 89 et seq.

[134] *Id.*, Articles 94 et seq.

[135] *Id.*, Articles 103 et seq.

transport services,[136] and tourism services.[137] The rules commitments regarding the aforementioned specific service sectors partially go beyond the corresponding commitments of both the EU and CARIFORUM States in the context of the GATS.[138]

3.3.2 Implementing Measures Adopted by the EU: The MA Regulation

The EC-CARIFORUM EPA has not yet entered into force but is being applied on a provisional basis. The market access commitments entered into by the EU under this EPA are implemented on the basis of the MA Regulation, which applies to products originating in ACP countries that have negotiated but not yet signed or ratified EPAs with the EU. As the CARIFORUM States have signed (but not yet ratified) the EC-CARIFORUM EPA, the pending Commission proposal for amending the MA Regulation will not affect the CARIFORUM States.[139] Hence, their products will continue to benefit from the market access commitments set out in the EC-CARIFORUM EPA.

4 Conclusion

In light of the foregoing observations, the following conclusions may be drawn: The revised Treaty provision on the "common commercial policy" of the EU has succeeded in bringing that policy area almost entirely under the *exclusive* competence of the Union. Nonetheless, EPAs will have to be concluded *jointly* by the EU and its Member States whenever they include commitments on transport services, as in the case of the EC-CARIFORUM EPA. The same holds true for future mutual recognition agreements[140] in selected service sectors (i.e. cultural, education, health, and tourism services) if such agreements provide for the harmonization of regulatory criteria, requirements, and standards in those sectors.

Based on the assumption that the EC-CARIFORUM EPA is a "blueprint" for other full EPAs currently being negotiated, EPAs are rather comprehensive trade agreements, especially as far as rules commitments are concerned. This is in line with the Union's trade policy regarding its trade relationship with developing countries, in particular ACP countries. According to that policy, the trade

[136] *Id.*, Article 109.

[137] *Id.*, Articles 110 et seq.

[138] For a critical discussion of these rules commitments see Schloemann and Pitschas (2009).

[139] See explanatory memorandum of the proposal (supra note 10) and the press release relating thereto (supra note 44).

[140] Article 85(5) of the EC-CARIFORUM EPA envisages the conclusion of mutual recognition agreements regarding requirements, qualifications, licenses, and other regulations.

relationship with developing countries is supposed to create opportunities for trade and investment and improve economic governance in the developing countries concerned. Commitments on market access and rules inscribed in EPAs have to be seen as an instrument to achieve these goals in relation to ACP countries. While the underlying logic appears comprehensible, it is also clear that these commitments—which partially exceed corresponding WTO commitments—certainly impose a considerable burden on ACP countries in terms of implementing such commitments. The EU is providing financial support to EPA partners to help them shoulder said burden,[141] but only the future will tell whether that support will be sufficient.

References

Baldwin R (2011) 21st century regionalism: filling the gap between 21st century trade and 20th century trade rules. WTO Staff Working Paper ERSD-2011-08

Behrens P (2007) Towards the constitutionalization of international investment protection. AVR 45(2):153–179

Bungenberg M (2009) Außenbeziehungen und Außenhandelspolitik nach dem Lissaboner Vertrag. EuR Beiheft 1:195–216

Chauffour JP, Maur JC (2010) Beyond market access. The new normal of preferential trade agreements. World Bank Policy Research Working Paper 5454

Dolzer R, Schreuer C (2008) Principles of international investment law. Oxford University Press, Oxford

Drexl J (2013) Intellectual property and implementation of recent bilateral trade agreements in the EU. In: Drexl J (ed) EU bilateral trade agreements and intellectual property: for better or worse? Springer, Heidelberg (this volume). doi:10.1007/978-3-642-39097-5

EPA Factsheet (2012) How the EU is putting the EPA into practice, April 2012. Available at: http://trade.ec.europa.eu/doclib/docs/2012/april/tradoc_149286.pdf

European Commission (2006a) Communication: Global Europe: Competing in the world. A contribution to the EU's growth and jobs strategy. COM(2006) 567 final

European Commission (2006b) Commission staff working document. SEC(2006) 1230

European Commission (2007) Communication: Global Europe: a stronger partnership to deliver market access for European Exporters. COM(2007) 183 final

European Commission (2010a) Communication: trade, growth and world affairs. Trade Policy as a core component of the EU's 2020 strategy. COM(2010) 612 final

European Commission (2010b) Commission staff working document: trade as a driver of prosperity. SEC(2010) 1269

European Commission (2012a) Communication: trade, growth and development. Tailoring trade and investment policy for those countries most in need. COM(2012) 22 final

European Commission (2012b) Progress report: external sources of growth. Accessible at: http://ec.europa.eu/trade/

European Commission (2012c) Overview of EPA. State of play, updated 12 June 2012. Accessible at: http://ec.europa.eu/trade/

European Council (2011) Common understanding. 8753/11, PE 164, INST 195, 10.04.2011. Available at: http://ec.europa.eu/trade/about/policy-making/

European Council (2012) Council conclusions on EU's approach to trade, growth and development in the next decade. 3145th Foreign Affairs (Trade) Council meeting, Brussels, 16 March 2012

[141] See the Commission's EPA Factsheet, p. 6, for an overview of the financial support to be provided to the Caribbean countries in the period 2012–2015.

The Economist (5 January 2008). The sun sets on Cotonou. An end-of-year rush to replace an outdated trade agreement

Herrmann C (2002) Common commercial policy after nice: Sisyphus would have done a better job. CMLR 39:7–29

Herrmann C (2010) The Treaty of Lisbon Expands the EU's external trade and investment powers. ASIL Insight 14(28)

Hindelang S (2011) Der primärrechtliche Rahmen einer EU-Investitionsschutzpolitik: Zulässigkeit und Grenzen von Investor-Staat-Schiedsverfahren aufgrund künftiger EU-Abkommen. In: Bungenberg M, Herrmann C (eds) Die gemeinsame Handelspolitik der Europäischen Union nach Lissabon. Nomos, Baden-Baden, pp 157–184

Koeb E, Dalleau M (2010) Trade relevant provisions in the Treaty of Lisbon. Implications for economic partnership agreements. Discussion Paper No. 98. European Centre for Development Policy Management

Krajewski M (2005) External trade law and the constitution treaty: towards a federal and more democratic common commercial policy? CMLR 42:91–127

Krajewski M (2011) Die neue handelspolitische Bedeutung des Europäischen Parlaments. In: Bungenberg M, Herrmann C (eds) Die gemeinsame Handelspolitik der Europäischen Union nach Lissabon. Nomos, Baden-Baden, pp 55–74

Krenzler HG, Pitschas C (2001) Fortschritt oder Stagnation? Die gemeinsame Handelspolitik nach Nizza. EuR 36:442–461

Müller-Ibold T (2011) Die gemeinsame Handelspolitik nach Lissabon. Sekundärrechtsabhängigkeit der gemeinsamen Handelspolitik. In: Bungenberg M, Herrmann C (eds) Die gemeinsame Handelspolitik der Europäischen Union nach Lissabon. Nomos, Baden-Baden, pp 75–93

Mylly T (2013) Constitutional functions of the EU's intellectual property treaties. In: Drexl J (ed) EU bilateral trade agreements and intellectual property: for better or worse? Springer, Heidelberg (this volume). doi:10.1007/978-3-642-39097-5

Ochieng CMO (2007) The EU-ACP Economic Partnership Agreements and the "Development Question": Constraints and Opportunities Posed by Article XXIV and Special and Differential Treatment Provisions of the WTO. JIEL 10(2):363–395

Omnibus I (2011) Proposal for a Regulation of the European Parliament and of the Council amending certain regulations relating to the common commercial policy as regards the procedures for the adoption of certain measures, COM(2011) 82 final, 7.3.2011

Omnibus II (2011) Proposal for a Regulation of the European Parliament and of the Council amending certain regulations relating to the common commercial policy as regards the granting of delegated powers for the adoption of certain measures, COM(2011) 349 final, 15.6.2011

Pitschas C (2001) Die völkerrechtliche Verantwortlichkeit der Europäischen Gemeinschaft und ihrer Mitgliedstaaten. Duncker & Humblot, Berlin

Pitschas C (2010) The Treaty of Lisbon and the "New" Common Commercial Policy of the European Union. Int TLR 16(2):37-43

Reinisch A (2008) Standards of investment protection. Oxford University Press, Oxford

Schloemann H, Pitschas C (2009) Cutting the Regulatory Edge? Services Regulation Disciplines in the CARIFORUM-EU Economic Partnership Agreement. In: Qualmann R (ed) How to ensure development friendly economic partnership agreements – lessons across regions. GTZ, Eschborn, pp 101–139

Tietje (2009) Die Außenwirtschaftsverfassung der EU nach dem Vertrag von Lissabon. Beiträge zum Transantionalen Wirtschaftsrecht, Heft 83

Weiß W (2011) Handelspolitik im Europäischen Verfassungsverbund: Außenhandelskompetenz und die Lissabon-Entscheidung des Bundesverfassungsgerichts. In: Bungenberg M, Herrmann C (eds) Die gemeinsame Handelspolitik der Europäischen Union nach Lissabon. Nomos, Baden-Baden, pp 35–54

Zimmermann A (2009) Die neuen Wirtschaftspartnerschaftsabkommen der EU: WTO-Konformität versus Entwicklungsorientierung? EuZW 20(1):1–6

Constitutional Functions of the EU's Intellectual Property Treaties

Tuomas Mylly

Contents

1 Introduction

The European Union's (EU) bilateral free trade agreements (FTAs) and economic partnership agreements (EPAs) proliferate. They now typically contain a chapter dedicated to intellectual property (IP) requiring a very high standard of protection

The article has been written in the framework of the research project "How to Rule the Economy", financed by the Academy of Finland.

T. Mylly (✉)
Faculty of Law, University of Turku, Turku, Finland
e-mail: tuomyl@utu.fi

J. Drexl et al. (eds.), *EU Bilateral Trade Agreements and Intellectual Property: For Better or Worse?*, MPI Studies on Intellectual Property and Competition Law 20,
DOI 10.1007/978-3-642-39097-5_12, © Springer-Verlag Berlin Heidelberg 2014

and enforcement.[1] The enforcement provisions used by the EU have previously been less detailed and far-reaching in their demands than the comparable ones used by the US.[2] Yet now the EU uses the First Enforcement Directive[3] systematically as a benchmark when formulating such clauses.[4] It has also gone further in its demands and dropped some of the checks and balances included in the Directive. Furthermore, for example the EU's FTA with South Korea includes a sub-section containing rather far-going criminal enforcement obligations related to IP.[5] No comparable norms exist in the EU's internal laws.

The purpose of this chapter is to address the constitutional significance of the EU's FTAs and EPAs. The focus is on EU constitutional law. I argue that regulating IP with FTAs and EPAs may be politically and procedurally easier for the EU than regulating this subject matter internally. IP chapters included in trade agreements falling under the EU's exclusive Common Commercial Policy (CCP) competence could become a particularly attractive instrument with which to regulate IP. Second, I argue that the FTAs and EPAs assume constitutional functions not possible for internal legislative acts of the EU by guiding the interpretations of EU secondary law and by enabling its judicial review.

The IP chapters of the FTAs and EPAs thus form an important layer of constitutional norms. By conditioning the interpretation and legality of EU secondary law, they might even cause the development of the EU's IP law and policy to stagnate. Such international treaties inevitably constrain legislative choices and judicial creativity, which might otherwise form a threat to proprietary interests. The rise and increasing use of such international IP law measures could thus be connected to the critical discourse on new constitutionalism.[6]

I will first analyze the competence of the EU to conclude such agreements. Then I will address the multiple potential effects of such agreements in EU law. These comprise, among others, direct and interpretative effect, primacy, and the capacity of an international treaty to enable judicial review of EU secondary norms, such as decisions, regulations, and directives.

---

[1] See the EU's Strategy for Enforcement of Intellectual Property Rights in Third Countries, OJ 2005 C 129, 3.

[2] Duncan (2010), p. 109.

[3] Directive 2004/48/EC. For the earlier proposal, see COM/2003/46 final, available at http://eur-lex.europa.eu/LexUriServ/LexUriServ.do?uri=COM:2003:0046:FIN:EN:PDF.

[4] Govaere (2008), pp. 413–414.

[5] Free Trade Agreement between the European Union and its Member States, of the one part, and the Republic of Korea, of the other part, OJ 2011 L 127, 6-1343, Section C, Sub-section B. See in more detail Mylly (2012) and Jaeger (2013) about the criminal enforcement of IP in the EU.

[6] See Mylly (2014).

2 The Broadening EU Competence to Act Externally

2.1 EU External Competence in General

The increasing regulation of IP in the EU's FTAs, EPAs, and multi-party measures such as the Anti-Counterfeiting Trade Agreement[7] (ACTA) is likely to continue. The Lisbon Treaty, which entered into force in December 2009, codified parts of the pre-existing case law concerning the EU's external competence. However, it went beyond mere codification and extended the EU's external competence in several respects. The external competence of the EU is now "extremely broad", as expressed by a judge of the Court of Justice of the European Union (CJEU).[8]

The EU's external competence (exclusive or shared) now codified in Article 216 of the TFEU is formulated as broadly as the EU's internal "residual" competence based on Article 352(1) of the TFEU. The EU thus has competence, among other situations, when it is necessary to conclude an agreement or take internal action in order to achieve, within the framework of the EU's policies, one of the objectives referred to in the Treaties. Cremona has noted that the reference in Article 216 to the objectives of the Treaties might, together with the very widely drawn general external objectives expressed in Article 21 of the TEU, already enable a basis for Union action.[9]

Whereas Article 352(1) of the TFEU requires unanimity in the Council's decision-making, the comparable external competence could be exercised by qualified majority decision-making. Qualified majority decision-making now forms the main rule of external decision-making according to Articles 218(8) and 219(1) of the TFEU. Moreover, the control mechanisms based on Article 352(2), which involve the national parliaments in the supervision of the exercise of Article 352 (1), do not exist in the case of Article 216 of the TFEU and external measures. The same applies to the member-state parliaments' supervision of the principle of subsidiarity (see Article 69 TFEU). The supervision mechanism regulated in the Protocol on the application of the principles of subsidiarity and proportionality only applies to draft legislative acts.

On the other hand, the role of the European Parliament (EP) in decision-making concerning international agreements was increased through Article 218 of the TFEU.[10] The EP obtained the right to veto the conclusion of such agreements in most matters.[11] Provided the EP is also properly consulted during the negotiation stage of international agreements, the right of veto could lead to parallelism with

[7] See final text of Anti-Counterfeiting Trade Agreement, available at http://trade.ec.europa.eu/doclib/docs/2011/may/tradoc_147937.pdf.

[8] Rosas and Armati (2010), p. 209.

[9] Cremona (2011), p. 225.

[10] See e.g. Eeckhout (2011), pp. 202–205.

[11] See also Acquah (2011), pp. 434–435.

the powers of the EP in the ordinary legislative procedure. This would constitute an important development, as international agreements concluded by the EU may have direct effect and also enable judicial review of the EU's secondary legislation, as will be discussed in more detail below. The enhanced role of the EP also partially compensates for the diminished role of the member-state parliaments in the international decision-making of the EU. The role of the member-state parliaments in the EU's international decision-making is reduced by the expansion of the EU's exclusive external powers. Only mixed agreements require ratification by the member states' parliaments.

The Union's actions on the international scene are now, according to Article 21 of the TEU, connected to various principles including democracy, the rule of law, the universality and indivisibility of human rights and fundamental freedoms, respect for human dignity, and the principles of equality and solidarity. These ideals must be pursued in the development and implementation of all areas of the EU's external activity. The EP could refer to these values when exercising its power of veto in the external sphere. Its strong critique and ultimately the rejection of ACTA is one clear indication of such a potential. Yet it remains to be seen what the real impact of these values on the EU's future policy will be.

2.2 Mixed Agreements

The EU has assumed the role of the central coordinator and decision-maker with regard to many mixed agreements as well. Both the member states and the EU are involved in concluding mixed agreements with third countries or international organizations.[12] Provided a mixed agreement does not specify the division of competences between the EU and the member states, the EU member states account under EU law for the mixed agreement in its entirety due to the obligation of loyalty codified in Article 4(3) of the TEU and Article 216(2) of the TFEU. This applies even to provisions belonging to the member states' competence. Like in internal matters, in external matters the scope of application of EU law is broader than the EU competence: The member states must exercise their retained external competence consistently with EU law. They must secure the primacy of mixed agreements over national law and take all necessary measures to fulfill the obligations ensuing therein. An infringement procedure under Article 258 of the TFEU is available against a member state failing to give effect to mixed agreements, as will be discussed in more detail subsequently.

A member state may still choose the means to implement the agreement for the parts belonging to the member-state competence. It may for example decide to

[12] See about mixed agreements in more detail the contributions in Hillion and Koutrakos (2010).

grant direct effect irrespective of the EU's position concerning the same agreement.[13] However, the full responsibility of the EU for mixed agreements lacking a declaration on the division of competences renders the remaining competences of the member states strongly circumscribed by EU obligations.[14] The CJEU has assumed a broad jurisdiction to give interpretations of the provisions of mixed agreements, as typically such treaties are concluded without any allocation between the EU and the member states of their respective obligations towards the other contracting parties.[15] The rulings of the CJEU could often de facto harmonize the member states' laws even for the parts belonging to their sphere of competence.

Even if the national parliaments must ratify mixed agreements, they are in practice bound by what the Commission (often in charge of the whole negotiations) and the national government representatives have already agreed at the international level. EU member states are in practice subject to a collective management of many mixed agreements whereby the European Commission is often in charge of the negotiation and further measures needed. The states are often "little more than token contracting parties".[16] For example, the mixed nature of the WTO Agreements is hardly visible in the dispute settlement practices: The EU typically operates as a single actor, with the Commission as a litigant. Even when other WTO members address complaints to individual EU member states, the Commission has in practice taken care of the defense of the measures in question.[17] The same has applied with respect to the Cotonou Agreement with the African, Caribbean, and Pacific countries.[18]

2.3 Exclusive Union Competence and Common Commercial Policy

The exclusive competence of the EU to conclude agreements involving intellectual property rights has similarly been strengthened in the recent Treaty reforms. Being part of exclusive Union competence means not only the absence of member states in the negotiation and ratification of the agreement in question, but also that the effects of the agreement in question are determined solely by EU law and thus ultimately by the judgments of the CJEU. Hence, EU law determines the possibility for direct effect of the parts of the agreement falling under exclusive Union competence.

---

[13] Neframi (2010), pp. 334–342.

[14] See also Tietje (2008), p. 66.

[15] See e.g. Koutrakos (2010).

[16] De Witte (2008), p. 43.

[17] Neframi (2010), p. 358.

[18] De Witte (2008), p. 43.

The EU may have exclusive competence to conclude an international agreement beyond the areas exclusive by their nature, now enumerated in Article 3(1) of the TFEU.[19] Article 3(2) of the TFEU seeks to codify the pre-existing case law on exclusive competence. In addition to the areas exclusive by their nature, the competence is according to this Article 3(2) also exclusive when the conclusion of an international agreement is provided for in a legislative act of the EU or is necessary to enable the EU to exercise its internal competence, or in so far as its conclusion may affect common rules or alter their scope.

As Eeckhout points out, the difference in wording between this provision and that concerning the EU's competence in general, Article 216(1) of the TFEU (exclusive or shared), is marginal or even contradictory. For there to be exclusive competence, it is sufficient that the agreement "may" affect common rules or alter their scope, whereas for competence in general the agreement must be "likely" to do so.[20] The Lisbon Treaty also settled the controversy over the nature of the EU's competence when the conclusion of an international agreement is necessary to enable the EU to exercise its internal competence. The competence in such cases is not only implicit, but also exclusive. Although the exercise of this competence is likely irrelevant with respect to IP, due to the exclusive CCP competence discussed below, it constitutes another codification of pre-existing case law in favor of exclusive Union competence. The EU's external exclusive competence is thus considerably broader than the areas that are exclusive by their nature under Article 3(1) of the TFEU.[21]

One of the most important fields exclusive by nature is the Common Commercial Policy (CCP). The rapid development of the Community's CCP competence with regard to IP is noteworthy.[22] Less than 10 years ago, the CJEU held in its Opinion 1/94 (WTO) that only border measures relating to counterfeiting and piracy came within exclusive CCP competence.[23] According to the CJEU case law, the CCP in its conventional form as defined in Article 133(1) of the EC Treaty belonged to the exclusive competence of the Community.[24] The exclusivity of the competence under Article 133(1) EC did not necessarily extend to the competence under Article 133(5) EC created by the Treaty of Nice, which concerned trade in services and commercial aspects of IP. According to an Advocate General Opinion, the Community's external trade competence under Article 133(5) EC was neither exclusive nor parallel in nature, but a concurrent competence, which allowed the

---

[19] Article 3(1) of the TFEU lists the following as falling under the exclusive competence: the customs union; the establishing of the competition rules necessary for the functioning of the internal market; monetary policy for the member states whose currency is the euro; the conservation of marine biological resources under the common fisheries policy; and common commercial policy.

[20] Eeckhout (2011), p. 113.

[21] See also Peers (2011), p. 262 and Eeckhout (2011), p. 118.

[22] See also Acquah (2011).

[23] Opinion 1/94, (WTO) [1994] ECR I-5267, at paras 55 and 56.

[24] See for example Opinion 1/94, *supra* note 22, at paras 22 and 34 read together.

member states to act only in so far as the Community did not exercise its own power.[25]

The Lisbon Treaty included "commercial aspects of intellectual property", together with trade in services and foreign direct investment, explicitly under the exclusive CCP legal basis in Article 207(1) of the TFEU. It thus placed the new fields of commercial policy on the same footing as the conventional fields. The CCP as a whole was expressly assigned to the exclusive competence of the Union in Article 3(1)(e) of the TFEU. Thus, it is possible that all subject matter under the WTO framework now falls within the exclusive external competence of the Union.[26] This would facilitate the inclusion of IP chapters in exclusive agreements falling under the CCP competence, and thus also the regulation of IP through FTAs and similar measures. Such a position would be in line with the objective of maintaining the EU's place as a global economic actor on the international scene, where trade in services, intangible assets, and investments have now occupied the strategic position once held by trade in basic goods.

Yet the exact meaning of "commercial aspects of intellectual property" remains uncertain. It does not necessarily fully overlap with the scope of the Agreement on Trade Related Aspects of Intellectual Property Rights (TRIPS), although this was the intention of the Presidency preparing the Nice Treaty in December 2000. A specific Protocol was to connect Article 133(5) of the EC Treaty to the TRIPS Agreement. However, the Protocol was dropped from the final version of the Nice Treaty, which contained no definition of the term "commercial aspects of intellectual property".[27] There has not been much scholarly debate on the interpretation of the term. The drafting history of the term is said to suggest that it covers all trade-related aspects of IP rights within the world trading system in a dynamic fashion.[28] This, however, does not take us very far in figuring out its exact meaning.

One problem with equating "commercial aspects of intellectual property" with the scope of the TRIPS Agreement is that the EU and its member states otherwise share the competence in IP matters. The TRIPS Agreement includes substantive IP norms in areas where the EU has not yet properly legislated, such as the patent law area. The CJEU has held—before the Lisbon Treaty entered into force—that such TRIPS norms fall within a field for which the member states "remain principally competent". The CJEU has lacked the jurisdiction to interpret and define the effects of such norms.[29] Rendering the whole TRIPS Agreement under the CCP

---

[25] Opinion of Advocate General Kokott in case C-13/07, *Commission v. Council*, removed from the register on 10 June 2010, at para 85.

[26] Müller-Graff (2008), p. 192; Eeckhout (2011), p. 59. See, however, Advocate General in case C-414/11, *Daiichi Sankyo Co. Ltd and Sanofi-Aventis Deutschland GmbH v. DEMO Anonymos Viomichaniki kai Emporiki Etairia Farmakon*, Opinion presented on 31 January 2013, not yet reported. The Opinion will be discussed in more detail below.

[27] Cremona (2002), pp. 67 and 70–72.

[28] Krajewski (2005), p. 111 and Villalta Puig and Al-Haddab (2011), p. 293.

[29] See, in particular, case C-431/05, *Merck Genéricos – Produtos Farmacêuticos Ldª v. Merck & Co. Inc., Merck Sharp & Dohme Ldª*, ECR [2007] I-7001.

competence would give the CJEU jurisdiction to interpret such norms and to define their effects for the whole EU. If this is deemed possible, the EU could under the same logic introduce substantively new IP norms in its future CCP agreements—in the absence of prior EU legislation. The EU would thus effectively possess an exclusive power to harmonize IP through international treaties, though it lacks a comparable internal exclusive power.

Another problem with such an equation would be that an international treaty—a dynamic one in the case of TRIPS—would decide the contents of a core EU law concept. The CJEU will likely not let this treaty determine what constitutes commercial aspects of IP.[30] Using the *substantive contents* of the TRIPS Agreement in the interpretation of the term "commercial aspects" is not necessarily helpful. As the TRIPS Agreement harmonizes IP globally, drawing the demarcation line between commercial aspects and pure harmonization is difficult on the basis of its substantive contents. Its provisions as such are not particularly trade-related.[31] They are rendered trade-related by the Agreement being an obligatory part of the WTO pact.

The CJEU will more likely interpret the term as an autonomous concept of EU law and cherish interpretative flexibility, as also suggested by the Opinion of the Advocate General in the *Daiichi Sankyo* case.[32] Such flexibility is offered by the different wording used and the rejection of the planned Protocol connecting it to TRIPS. The deliberate choice of the term "commercial" instead of "trade-related" suggests that the CCP-related IP competence is not restricted to the application of and modifications to the TRIPS Agreement, but on the other hand does not comprise all international IP measures. The Advocate General has argued that due to conflict with shared IP competence, the term does not cover all substantive TRIPS norms, such as Article 27 of the TRIPS Agreement, which defines patentable subject matter. The CJEU could well disagree and opt for the alternative interpretation offered by the Advocate General, according to which the term now also covers the patent provision in question. It is likely that the CJEU will not define the term exhaustively. It will more probably proceed on a case-by-case basis and expand it gradually.

The exclusive CCP competence could thus cover most IP provisions included in trade agreements. In such contexts, IP provisions become part of a broader trade pact, often subject to institutional mechanisms for dispute settlement, possible trade sanctions, and so forth. Even if the CJEU were to rule in the *Daiichi Sankyo* case that patent norms of TRIPS fall under the CCP competence, it is possible that for example provisions on moral rights and detailed criminal law measures could fall

---

[30] Cf., however, Eeckhout (2011), p. 59. A third problem with equating "commercial aspects" of IP and the scope of TRIPS is that the latter does not cover all exclusive rights harmonized by the EU, such as the *sui generis* database right. New forms of IP protection may also emerge in the future.

[31] Quite the contrary, it leaves one of the most clearly trade-related aspects of intellectual property protection, the exhaustion of rights, largely untouched in its Article 6.

[32] Advocate General Opinion in case C-414/11, *supra* note 26. See also Drexl (2013).

outside the EU's CCP competence. These are excluded from TRIPS and they are not by their nature particularly commercial or trade-related aspects of IP protection either. Some aspects of the IP chapters in the EU's trade agreements might thus fall outside the EU's exclusive CCP competence under the Lisbon Treaty as well. This is typically not very problematic, as the EU's trade agreements are often broad in their scope and thus in any case may contain subject matter falling outside the EU's exclusive CCP competence. Quite often they have to be concluded as mixed agreements in any case.

The position of "pure" IP agreements, such as future WIPO conventions, is problematic from the perspective of the EU's CCP competence. Article 207(1) of the TFEU covers "commercial aspects" of IP in distinction to IP as such. The objectives of the CCP, to be found in Article 206 of the TFEU, refer to the progressive abolition of restrictions on international trade and on foreign direct investment only, to the exclusion of international IP protection. This implies that IP is within the CCP competence only to the extent that its inclusion is in conformity with the other objectives of the CCP. The drafting history of Article 207 of the TFEU supports this interpretation. "Pure" IP agreements would thus fall outside the CCP competence.

On the other hand, the limitation of the CCP competence to agreements with sufficient trade and investment elements only would mean that the EU could, on an exclusive basis and by qualified majority voting,[33] introduce identical international IP harmonization through trade and investment agreements, but not with "pure" IP agreements. Provided the CCP competence covers substantive IP harmonization in trade agreements, but does not cover "pure" IP treaties, the EU would likely favor trade agreements as an instrument harmonizing IP globally and regionally. Once such treaties proliferate, "pure" IP agreements could interfere with the exercise of the EU's CCP competence, as their material contents likely overlap with IP chapters in trade agreements. To avoid such problems, the CJEU could construct the IP-related CCP competence broadly so as to also cover specific IP measures. This would federalize IP protection on the EU's external front and undermine the shared internal competence. Moreover, how to define "pure" IP agreements in the first place? ACTA was intended to harmonize enforcement of IP. Despite its name, it was not particularly trade-related. Yet the European Commission was of the

[33] When negotiating and concluding agreements based on the CCP, the Council normally acts by a qualified majority. Yet in accordance with Article 207(4) TFEU for the negotiation and conclusion of agreements in the field of commercial aspects of IP, among others, the Council acts unanimously where such agreements include provisions for which unanimity is required for the adoption of internal rules. Article 118 TFEU enables internal measures for the creation of European IP rights and for the setting up of centralized Union-wide authorization, coordination, and supervision arrangements by recourse to qualified majority decision-making, except for language arrangements, which require unanimity. As most external trade agreements containing clauses on commercial aspects of IP do not handle language arrangements, qualified majority decision-making prevails.

opinion that, except for its criminal law provisions, ACTA fell under the EU's CCP competence.[34]

The exercise of the CCP competence cannot according to Article 207(6) of the TFEU "affect the delimitation of competences between the Union and the Member States, and cannot lead to harmonisation of legislative or regulatory provisions of the Member States in so far as the Treaties exclude such harmonisation". The latter part of the prohibition means that the exercise of the CCP competence cannot lead to harmonization in member states of subject matter listed for example in Article 6 of the TFEU, where the EU's competence is restricted to supporting, coordinating, or supplementing the actions of the member states. These areas include culture, tourism, and education. Similarly, far-going criminal law harmonization is beyond EU competence.[35]

The first part of Article 207(6) could be designed to prevent the so-called reverse ERTA effect.[36] The EU's exercise of the external CCP competence would thus not confer it an implicit internal competence to implement the agreements. The external CCP competence thus seems to cover areas where it shares the competence to legislate internally with the member states.[37] *The EU's exclusive external competence thus appears broader than its internal competence to legislate exclusively.*

The Advocate General in *Daiichi Sankyo* stated that an exclusive external competence alongside a shared internal competence would lead to a dead end.[38] However, as Krajewski argues, such an incongruence of external and internal competences is not unprecedented: For example in Germany, the federation enjoys an all-inclusive competence to conclude international agreements, but may be excluded from their implementation in favor of the states.[39] The genesis of Article 207(6) in the federalist language of the Constitutional Treaty supports this analogy. Article 207(4) of the TFEU reflects a similar premise: Subject matter falling under the external CCP competence may fall under other Treaty bases to regulate internally. Under the doctrine of implied powers, the Treaty article giving the EU an internal power to legislate would also have formed the legal basis for the conclusion of an international agreement.[40] This no longer appears to be the case with respect to the new subject matter under the CCP competence.

Article 207(4) and (6) thus seem to reflect new constitutional architecture whereby the EU could conclude international agreements regulating IP on an exclusive basis, but could not necessarily implement them internally without resorting to non-exclusive Treaty bases and the aid of the member states. The EU

[34] Commission's approach to legal basis in its Proposal for a Council Decision on the Conclusion of the Anti-Counterfeiting Trade Agreement. 28 June 2011.

[35] See Mylly (2012).

[36] See on this effect Bourgeois (1999), pp. 170–172.

[37] See also Krajewski (2005), pp. 116–118 and Villalta Puig and Al-Haddab (2011), p. 296.

[38] Advocate General Opinion in case C-414/11, *supra* note 26, at para 60.

[39] Krajewski (2005), p. 117.

[40] Eeckhout (2011), p. 61.

would have to consult the member states before the conclusion of such agreements in line with the principle of loyalty, now found in Article 4(3) of the TEU. The member states would have a comparable loyalty-based obligation to implement, especially as non-implementation would connote the liability of the EU under international law.[41] This implies that the member states do not enjoy much legislative leeway in such instances.

Hence, the EU could achieve internal harmonization of IP law through the exercise of its exclusive CCP competence by qualified majority voting in the Council. Faced with international liability, it could count on the subsequent implementation of the measure by itself or by the member states. FTAs falling under the CCP competence might thus become an increasingly appealing way for the EU to regulate IP internally.

2.4 Conclusions on EU External Competence and IP

The EU's external competence has recently expanded through Treaty amendments. The practices of the EU institutions and member states with regard to mixed agreements strengthen the trend. External law making may be easier than internal law making in terms of unanimity/qualified majority decision-making and the absence/presence of parliamentary control mechanisms, emergency brakes, and so forth. In many cases, the decision-making procedures and control mechanisms of internal law making are a heavier burden than convincing a third country to cooperate on the course of the EU's policy. This is the case especially where IP is a bargaining chip against trade concessions on the part of the EU.

Compared to internal law-making, the EU might avoid thorny questions of competence by concluding instead a mixed trade agreement for example containing a chapter criminalizing IP infringements. As mixed agreements are typically concluded without an explicit division of competences between the EU and the member states, the question of exact competence may never emerge, or it emerges as a question of internal implementation only. After the treaty is in force, it binds the EU institutions and member states under both international and European law: They must implement and apply the treaty. The EU could thus reach an end-result with a mixed agreement that it could hardly reach directly through internal measures.

The EU's exclusive CCP competence now covers "commercial aspects of intellectual property" and is broader than the EU's internal exclusive competence to legislate IP. The *Daiichi Sankyo* case, referred to above, offers the CJEU the possibility to pronounce on the scope of this competence, and as a corollary on its own powers to interpret international treaties and define their effects. Aided by a recent Treaty change and thus the presumed intention of the member states to

[41] See about loyalty in external relations Neframi (2010).

change the pre-existing situation, the CJEU likely constructs the EU competence broadly. Should this be the case, the EU could resort to its exclusive CCP competence and extensively regulate IP through trade treaties. Subsequent specific IP agreements could not in practice deviate from their provisions, as this would likely lead to an infringement of the first treaty. Most of the IP provisions in the EU's FTAs are legislative-type international norms not only applicable in contexts involving international trade relations and cross-border elements.

It is thus important that the EU secure consistency in EPAs, FTAs, and specific IP measures binding the EU and the member states.[42] The EU cannot maintain conflicting IP standards in its international treaties, as it has to comply with their provisions in its internal laws. Neither the EU nor the member states could introduce legislation departing from the standards of EPAs, FTAs, or specific IP treaties binding the EU. IP chapters in EPAs and FTAs could thus lock in the situation and tie the Union's and the member states' hands in both the internal and external spheres of law making.

3 The Constitutional Effects of FTAs and EPAs

3.1 Introduction

Not only the contents of international treaties determine their societal effects, but to a great extent also the principles regulating their effects and interpretation in the EU legal order. Direct effect of international treaties is often depicted as a managerial issue depending on the objective properties of the treaty and its applicable norm in question. However, multilateral legislative-type treaties, which also have potential effects in the private sphere, have become increasingly common. That this also applies to the IP area is evidenced for example by the TRIPS Agreement and ACTA. The IP chapters of the EU's FTAs and EPAs similarly regulate subject matter already covered by European and member-state norms, and could hence easily conflict with European and domestic laws and constitutional norms.

Due to the fragmentation of international law and the simultaneous expansion of international treaties, its norms also increasingly often conflict with each other. The principles regulating the effects of treaties are thus by no means neutral or static. They are rather an important site of judicial dynamism and political struggle. The principles in question could empower certain treaties and regimes at the expense of others. They could adapt the international treaties to the constitutional foundations of the EU's legal order, or vice versa.

Individuals may invoke directly effective norms of international agreements, and courts and public authorities are obliged to apply them. They must set aside

[42] See also Drexl (2013).

conflicting member-state laws in favor of the directly effective norms of international agreements. All member-state law and secondary EU law must also be interpreted in conformity with international treaties binding the EU. International treaties may, in addition to having interpretative and direct effect, enable judicial review of EU secondary legislation. International treaties may thus be used to quash secondary EU law, such as directives and regulations. They are thus equipped with constitutional qualities not present with internal legislative acts of the EU.

3.2 *Direct Effect and Judicial Review*

It is in theory possible that when negotiating and concluding international treaties, the EU institutions agree with the third parties concerned on what effect the provisions of the agreement will have in the internal legal order of the contracting parties. However, including such provisions in international agreements is very exceptional and would require a radical change in the negotiation practices.[43] The EU legislature may also try to exclude direct effect in the internal decision by which it accepts an international agreement. Yet the CJEU may base direct effect on the contents of the treaty itself. Thus, for example the EU's attempt to exclude direct effect before EU or member-state courts in the EU's internal decision accepting the EU–South Korea Agreement[44] is not binding on the CJEU.[45]

The EU could also try to regulate the internal applicability of international treaties through a disconnection clause.[46] However, neither most of the EU's FTAs or EPAs, nor for example ACTA contain a disconnection clause seeking to exclude their applicability in the mutual relations of the EU member states.[47] Deciding the effects of such treaties in the EU thus falls to the courts having jurisdiction in the matter.

In the EU legal order, the CJEU decides the internal effects of the agreement in the same manner as any question of interpretation relating to the application of the agreement in the EU.[48] The CJEU has adopted the role of the gatekeeper with regard to the effects of international norms in EU law. Its approach is often characterized as monist.[49] Yet the CJEU is selective with regard to measures to

---

[43] Mendez (2010a), p. 90.

[44] See e.g. Article 8 of the Council Decision of 16 September 2010 concerning the EU–South Korea free trade agreement, OJ 2010 L 127, 1.

[45] See Advocate General in Case C-149/96, *Portugal v. Council*, ECR [1999], p. I-8395, at para 20.

[46] See Cremona (2010).

[47] As the CJEU noted in Opinion 1/03, re Lugano Convention, [2006] ECR I-1145, a disconnection clause does not guarantee that the agreement does not affect Union rules but, on the contrary, provides an indication that Union rules *are* affected.

[48] See for example Case C-366/10, *Air Transport Association of America and others v. Secretary of State for Energy and Climate Change*, decided 21 December 2011, not yet reported, at para 49.

[49] Rosas (2008), p. 75.

which it grants direct effect. It has expressed that it treats directly effective international agreements binding the EU as having primacy over secondary law, but not over primary EU law.[50] This means that international agreements may be used to challenge the validity of secondary law, but they could not derogate from EU Treaty norms.

To the extent that a treaty falls within the competence of the EU, the CJEU may determine its legal effects for the member states and individuals. On the other hand, when the subject matter falls within the competence of the member states, EU law neither requires nor forbids the legal order of a member state to accord to individuals the right to rely directly on a rule included in the agreement in question, or to oblige the courts to apply that rule of their own motion.[51] When IP falls under the exclusive CCP competence, the possibility of direct effect is determined by EU law alone, in practice by the case law of the CJEU. Thus, if the entire TRIPS Agreement falls under the notion of "commercial aspects of intellectual property", EU law determines its effects even in areas where the EU has not yet legislated.[52] The same logic applies to all treaties containing IP chapters falling under the CCP competence. Their effects in the EU will thus typically be a matter to be analyzed under EU law only.

An international norm's direct effect depends on the nature and the broad logic of the international agreement as a whole and the characteristics of the particular norm in question.[53] In determining whether the nature and the broad logic of an international treaty as a whole render it capable of producing direct effect, the CJEU assesses the aim, preamble, and terms of the treaty in question. Direct effect is possible if the treaty establishes rules intended to apply directly and immediately to individuals and confers upon them rights or freedoms capable of being relied upon against states. Direct effect is thus connected to the intention of the treaty to produce individual rights or freedoms.

Lack of direct or self-executing effect in the other contracting parties does not prevent the recognition of direct effect in the EU. Similarly, a special institutional

[50] Case C-61/94 *Commission v. Germany* [1996] ECR I-3989, at para 52; case C-149/96, *supra* note 45; case C-344/04 *IATA and ELFAA*, [2006] ECR I-403, at para 35; case C-308/06, *The Queen on the application of Intertanko and Others v. Secretary of State for Transport* ECR [2008], p. I-4057, at para 42; and Case C-366/10, *supra* note 48, at para 50.

[51] See for example case C-431/05, *supra* note 29, at paras 31–35.

[52] Eeckhout (2011), pp. 285–286, presumes that direct effect of TRIPS norms on the basis of domestic law is now likely excluded under all circumstances.

[53] See e.g. Klabbers (2002) and Bronckers (2008), pp. 894–897; See for more detail for example joined cases 21–24/72, *International Fruit Company v. Produkschap voor Groenten en Fruit* [1972] ECR 1219; case 104/81, *Hauptzollamt Mainz v. C.A. Kupferberg & Cie KG a.A.* [1982] ECR I-3641; case C-213/03, *Syndicat professionnel coordination des pêcheurs de l'étang de Berre et de la région and Électricité de France (EDF)*, [2004] ECR I-7357; case C-344/04, *supra* note 50, at para 39, case C-308/06, *supra* note 50, at para 45; and case C-366/10, *supra* note 48, at paras 53 and 54.

framework for the administration and proper implementation of the agreement does not rule out direct judicial application of the agreement in the EU.[54]

In addition to the assessment concentrating on the whole treaty, its particular provisions being invoked must satisfy the general test of direct effect. The test is fulfilled when the provisions relied upon contain a clear and precise obligation that is not subject, in its implementation or effects, to the adoption of subsequent measures. The provisions in question must thus enable a judicial decision based on them, without recourse to additional implementing measures. In distinction to the analysis of the nature and the broad logic of the whole treaty, the assessment of individual provisions is context-specific and may depend on other related norms applicable in the case.

With the important exceptions of the WTO Agreements, the United Nations Convention on the Law of the Sea (UNCLOS), and the Kyoto Protocol,[55] the CJEU has recently found most international treaties before it capable of producing direct effects, provided the agreement directly governs the position of individuals.[56] According to Eeckhout, after recognizing in *Kupferberg* the potential of FTAs to produce direct effects, the CJEU has never decided against direct effect on the basis of the nature and the broad logic of free-trade, association, partnership, or even simple co-operation agreements.[57] All partnership agreements concluded by the EU thus carry the potential of direct effect.[58] The CJEU has also extended the fundamental-rights principle of effective judicial remedy to the protection of rights emanating from European Agreements.[59] Importantly, such agreements have also produced limited direct effect between private parties. Individuals could thus also invoke directly effective norms of EU external treaties for example against private sporting federations regulating working conditions collectively.[60]

The EU Court seems to treat bilateral preferential agreements more favorably in terms of their capacity for direct effect than multilateral agreements.[61] In its

[54] Case 104/81, *supra* note 53, at paras 18–20.

[55] See case C-149/96, *supra* note 45 (WTO); case C-308/06, *supra* note 50 (UNCLOS); and case C-366/10, *supra* note 48 (Kyoto Protocol).

[56] Jacobs (2008), pp. 23 and 33.

[57] Eeckhout (2011), p. 338; See for example case C-18/90, *Kziber* ECR 1991, p. I-199, at paras 15–23; case C-162/00, *Pokrzeptowicz-Meyer*, ECR 2002, p. I-1049, at paras 19–30; and case C-265/03, *Simutenkov*, ECR 2005, p. I-2579, at paras 22–29; joined Cases C-300/09 and C-301/09, *Toprak* ECR 2010, not yet reported.

[58] Similarly Tietje (2008), p. 63.

[59] See case C-327/02, *Panayotova and others v. Minister voor Vreemdelingenzaken en Integratie*, [2004] ECR I-11055 and joined cases C-23/04 to C-25/04, *Sfakianakis AEVE v. Elliniko Dimosio*, [2006] ECR I-1265.

[60] See cases C-438/00, *Kolpak* [2003] ECR I-4135 and C-265/03, *supra* note 57. In both cases a private individual was able to invoke norms of an international agreement against a sports federation.

[61] Cremona (2011), pp. 240–243; See however case C-344/04, *supra* note 50 (finding the Montreal Convention capable of producing direct effect), and case C-213/03, *supra* note 53 (finding the Barcelona Convention capable of producing direct effect). See also Mendez (2010a), pp. 94 and 98.

bilateral relations the EU may more easily than in multilateral contexts impose its own constitutional and legislative standards on others.[62] With many bilateral association, co-operation, and partnership agreements concluded by the EU, their directly effective provisions form an important layer of constitutional norms. Mendez has noted that the CJEU has recognized the treaty's capacity for direct effect more easily where member-state—and not EU—action is being challenged on the basis of international agreements binding the EU.[63]

Directly effective international treaties binding the EU have the capacity to function as a ground of invalidity for secondary EU law. The CJEU has the sole competence to declare secondary EU law invalid on this or other grounds. In addition to the EU institutions and member states, individuals may invoke international treaties capable of producing direct effect as a ground of invalidity. In *Air Transport Association of America* (*ATAA*), the CJEU explicitly connected the possibility (in that case of individuals) to use the norms of the international treaty as a ground of invalidity to direct effect.[64] The latter, in turn, is connected to the intention of the treaty to produce individual rights or freedoms. Mendez problematizes the very basis of this criterion. It is also difficult to apply in practice: Which international law instruments are intended to apply directly and immediately to individuals and how are we to discover this intention?[65]

To the extent that international IP norms now fall under the CCP and are used as part of the EPAs, FTAs, or other similar international treaties likely having the capacity to produce direct effect, they have profound constitutional implications in that *they enable judicial review of secondary EU law and guide its interpretation.* From the perspective of judicial review, such international norms function much like primary Union law: Both can be used to challenge EU secondary norms. As a consequence, it also becomes harder to modify the EU's internal IP laws once there are international norms with direct effect in place, wholly or partially reproducing the standards of existing EU IP norms. The EPAs, FTAs, and other similar international measures might thus freeze the development of internal EU IP law, at least to the extent that they contain detailed enough blueprints of existing EU IP norms.

3.3 Judicial Review in the Absence of Direct Effect?

The question of whether international treaties lacking the capacity for direct effect could also enable judicial review of secondary EU law is not fully settled. Older and the most recent case law suggests that—beyond the exceptions established in the *Fediol* and *Nakajima* cases treated below—the capacity for direct effect is needed

62 Similarly Tietje (2008), p. 63.

63 Mendez (2010a, b).

64 Case C-366/10, *supra* note 48.

65 Mendez (2010a), p. 101 and Mendez (2010b), p. 1750.

for a treaty to enable judicial review of secondary EU law in preliminary ruling procedures and direct actions alike.

However, in the *Netherlands v. European Parliament and Council* (*Biopatents*) case of the year 2001 the CJEU indicated that the claim on non-respect of an international agreement lacking direct effect could be successful.[66] It stated with respect to the Convention on Biological Diversity (CBD)[67] that it is "not strictly based on reciprocal and mutually advantageous arrangements", like the WTO Agreement. This led the CJEU to hold that even if the CBD contained provisions lacking direct effect, the CJEU could still review compliance with the obligations incumbent on the EU as a party to that agreement.

The judgment provided an escape route from the pre-existing case law denying the use of GATT/WTO Agreements for the purposes of judicial review in preliminary ruling procedures and direct actions alike. The case thus indicated that in some circumstances even international agreements lacking direct effect could be used to challenge the legality of secondary EU norms.[68] Yet the judgment left several important questions open.[69]

The CJEU did not refer to the *Biopatents* case in *ATAA* of 2011, where private parties sought to challenge a directive on the basis of the Kyoto Protocol, which according to the Court lacked the capacity for direct effect.[70] This suggests that either the *Biopatents* case is no longer valid case law or that the CJEU restricts its outcome to cases where member states or EU institutions—in distinction to individuals—challenge the validity of EU acts in direct actions. Advocate General Kokott favored the latter approach in *ATAA*. Nothing in the CJEU's judgment suggests that such a distinction exists. The Court had already rejected such a distinction with regard to GATT in *Germany v. Council* (*Bananas*).[71] As Eeckhout argues, the grounds for the review of legality should not depend on the applicable procedure or the type of party invoking the international norm in question.[72] Maintaining such a distinction would be problematic, as courts at national level would be obliged to apply secondary EU law, which would turn out to be invalid in a subsequent direct action. The question is hence not whether such a distinction should be made. It is rather whether direct effect of an international agreement makes sense as the governing criterion for judicial review in the first place. With this criterion, the language of individual rights is turned into a notion precluding judicial review.

International agreements not capable of producing direct effect may be used to challenge secondary EU law in so far as secondary EU law refers to specific

---

[66] Case C-377/98, *Netherlands v. Council and Parliament* [2001] ECR I-7079.

[67] Signed on 5 June 1992 in Rio de Janeiro.

[68] See e.g. Lenaerts and Corthaut (2006), pp. 298–299 and Mendez (2010a), p. 98.

[69] See on some of these questions Eeckhout (2011), pp. 297–298 and 322.

[70] Case C-366/10, *supra* note 48.

[71] Case C-280/93, *Germany v. Council*, [1994] ECR I-4973.

[72] Eeckhout (2011), pp. 295–296.

international-law norms or intends to implement them. This is known as the implementation effect, and was established in the cases *Nakajima* and *Fediol*.[73] However, the possibilities to review secondary EU law under this case law are limited.[74]

In *Fediol*, the conformity of a Commission decision with GATT could be reviewed by the CJEU, as what is now known as the Trade Barriers Regulation[75] implicitly referred to GATT and enabled economic operators to lodge complaints on the basis of GATT violations abroad. Judicial review of the decisions would have been meaningless without the possibility to test the conformity of the decisions with GATT provisions. A finding of inconsistency would only have led to the annulling of the Commission decision not to act on the basis of the Regulation. Thus, even a successful complaint would not have led to GATT norms producing directly applicable rights for individuals. It appears likely that the *Fediol*-based judicial review is currently restricted to the Trade Barriers Regulation.[76] For example, in *ATAA*, references to the Kyoto Protocol in directives did not enable the judicial review of these directives on the basis of the Kyoto Protocol.[77]

Similarly, the EU Courts have interpreted the *Nakajima*-based judicial review restrictively after *Italy v. Council* (*Rice*).[78] The *Nakajima* case confirmed that if the EU legislature adopts secondary law measures in order to comply with particular international obligations of the Union, the international obligations in question might be used for the purpose of judicial review of the implementing measures even when the international agreement in question lacks the potential for direct effect. In the *Chiquita* case the General Court emphasized the exceptional nature of the rule arising from *Nakajima*. It said that as an exception to the principle that individuals may not directly rely on WTO provisions before the EU judicature, that rule must be interpreted restrictively.[79] Judicial review based on *Nakajima* is possible only provided that the EU measure specifically transposes prescriptions arising from the treaty in question into Union law. Furthermore, the rule infringed must be detailed in nature. Infringement of general principles—such as national treatment, most-favored-nation treatment, and non-discriminatory application of quantitative restrictions—do not satisfy this test. A dispute settlement ruling requiring the losing party to bring a measure into compliance for example with the WTO Agreements is also of a general character. It thus appears that only new

---

[73] Case C-69/89, *Nakajima v. Council*, [1991] ECR I-2069 and case 70/87, *Fediol v. Commission*, [1989] ECR 1781.

[74] See also Drexl (2006), pp. 117–119.

[75] Council Regulation (EC) No. 3286/94 of 22 December 1994, OJ 1994 L 349, 71.

[76] Eeckhout (2011), pp. 359–360.

[77] Case C-366/10, *supra* note 48.

[78] Case C-352/96, *Italy v. Council*, ECR 1998, p. I-6937. In this case, Article XXIV:6 of GATT 1994 and para 5 of the Understanding on the Interpretation of Article XXIV of the General Agreement on Tariffs and Trade 1994 enabled the judicial review of the Regulation in question, which implemented bilateral agreements concluded under Article XXIV:6 of GATT 1994.

[79] Case T-19/01, *Chiquita v. Commission*, ECR 2005, p. II-315, at paras 117–169.

Union rules specifically transposing detailed enough treaty rules satisfy the *Nakajima* requirements enabling judicial review.[80]

Even in the absence of an international treaty's capacity to produce direct effect or implementation effect based on *Nakajima* or *Fediol*, it is possible that the treaty in question can be used in infringement proceedings initiated by the Commission against non-complying member states (under Article 258 TFEU). The Commission had earlier brought a successful infringement suit against Germany for a violation of GATT norms.[81] Similarly, it has successfully sued Ireland for its failure to comply with international treaties.[82] These actions enable the EU to operate as a unified international actor. Yet the situations may generate accusations of a double standard, as no comparable procedure exists to make the EU comply with international treaties lacking direct effect.[83] In other words, the Commission can invoke treaties lacking the capacity for direct effect against member states in infringement proceedings, but member states cannot invoke them against non-abiding Union institutions.

The foregoing demonstrates that the potential to produce direct effect is of paramount importance for the constitutional effects of the IP chapters in the FTAs and EPAs. The nature and broad logic of FTAs likely allows direct effect. The same applies to EPAs, which constitute bilateral preferential treaties. Their clear and precise IP provisions could thus also be used for the purposes of judicial review of secondary EU law. As the TRIPS Agreement lacks the capacity for direct effect and judicial review under EU law, *the IP chapters in the FTAs and EPAs change the constitutional landscape of the EU's IP law in a significant way.*

3.4 Interpretative Effect of International Agreements

The CJEU gives effect to international norms binding the EU in another manner as well: through the requirement placed on the national courts to interpret domestic norms in the light of the international norm in question. The same requirement extends to the interpretation of secondary EU norms.[84] Such an effect may in most

[80] *Ibidem.* See also case C-377/02, *Van Parys v. Belgisch Interventie- en Restitutiebureau*, ECR 2005, p. I-1465.

[81] Case C-61/94, *supra* note 50 (dairy products).

[82] Case C-13/00, *Commission v. Ireland*, [2002] ECR I-2955 (EEA Agreement and the obligation to adhere to the Berne Convention) and case C-459/03, *Commission v. Ireland* [2006] ECR I-4635 (UNCLOS).

[83] Mendez (2010a), p. 103 and Mendez (2010b), p. 1739.

[84] See case C-61/94, *supra* note 50, at para 28. In the context of the TRIPS Agreement, see cases C-53/96, *Hermes International v. FHT Marketing Choice BV* [1998] ECR I-3606; C-306/05, *Sociedad General de Autores y Editores de España (SGAE) v. Rafael Hoteles SA* [2006] ECR I-11519, at para 35; C-275/06, *Productores de Música de España (Promusicae) v. Telefónica de España SAU* [2008] ECR I-271 (at para 60) and C-431/05, *supra* note 51, at para 35.

cases bring the domestic and Union norms in compliance with the international obligations. The IP chapters of the EU's FTAs and EPAs may thus guide the interpretation of member-state law and EU secondary law. The obligation to interpret in conformity with international treaties does not depend on the direct effect of the treaty provisions in question. Where the treaty provisions lack direct effect, interpretative effect becomes the primary means with which to give effect to the treaty norms in question.

Yet the EU Courts may also be selective with interpretative effect. Drexl has pointed out that the CJEU has been less enthusiastic to extend the obligation to interpret in conformity with international norms when it is EU secondary norms and not national laws that are in question.[85] For example, in *IKEA Wholesale* the CJEU refused to interpret the EU anti-dumping regulation in conformity with WTO dispute settlement decisions and favored instead an autonomous EU-law interpretation.[86]

Moreover, in the *Microsoft* case the General Court held that the principle of consistent interpretation does not extend to primary Union law.[87] Yet in any event international treaties not capable of producing direct effect—such as the WTO Agreements—bind the EU at international level and constitute "an integral part" of Union law.[88] There is no reason to categorically exclude interpretation of EU primary norms in the light of international law.

The above examples indicate that, like with direct effect and judicial review, interpretative effect of international treaties may vary depending on the international treaty and secondary EU law in question. The EU Courts may protect specific Union interests, like the EU's anti-dumping policies. Interpretative effect may extend further when national law, in distinction to secondary EU law, is in conflict with an international norm. The EU Courts also protect the foundations of the EU's legal order by possibly excluding interpretative effect with regard to primary Union law, as in the *Microsoft* case.

3.5 Conclusions on Constitutional Effects of International Treaties

As the EU exercises its powers increasingly on the global level, the mechanisms and principles giving effect to international norms assume unprecedented constitutional relevance. Direct effect of international treaties opens the EU legal order to

---

[85] Drexl (2006), pp. 121–122.

[86] Case C-351/04, *IKEA Wholesale v. Commissioners of Customs & Excise* ECR 2007, p. I-7723. See also Eeckhout (2011), p. 356.

[87] Case T-201/04, *Microsoft Corp. v. Commission* [2007] ECR II-3601, at para 798.

[88] See also Dunoff (2009), p. 189; See cases 181/73, *R. & V. Haegeman v. Belgium* [1974] ECR I-449; 104/81, *supra* note 53; and C-431/05, *supra* note 51, at para 31.

challenge, but due to its selective nature, also protects it from international law.[89] Granting direct effect and primacy to EU norms in general has had the historical constitutional function of elevating the EU's economic constitution above potentially conflicting member-state constitutions.[90] Direct effect and primacy of international norms over secondary EU law and all member-state law enable the selected international instruments to benefit from the strong compliance force offered by the EU legal system.

By recognizing the capacity of some international treaties to produce direct effect to the exclusion of others, the CJEU inevitably forms a selected group of (types of) treaties enabling judicial review of EU secondary law and having primacy over all conflicting member-state law, including the constitutions of the member states.[91] In this way, the CJEU is building a framework of international treaties conditioning the legality of EU secondary law and the application of all member-state law. This international-law framework is becoming an increasingly essential part of EU constitutional law. The EPAs and FTAs with IP chapters form part of this constitutional framework, as they are very likely to have direct effect. IP chapters falling under the Union's external CCP competence may have direct effect determined by EU law even for the parts falling under the member states' competence to legislate internally. A member-state court could thus face an obligation to set aside a conflicting domestic norm and apply the IP chapter falling under the CCP competence instead, even when there is no other EU harmonization measure applicable to the situation.

However, as the CJEU has indicated in its much-debated *Kadi* judgment, there are substantive constitutional limits on how far international norms may interfere with the fundamental principles underlying the EU Treaties.[92] The judgment confirmed that UN resolutions could not override fundamental rights as protected in primary Union law when the CJEU exercises judicial review over secondary EU law. The constitutional order of the EU, as constructed by the CJEU, thus determines its own position with regard to international law. It also determines much of the effects of international law in the legal orders of the member states, and the possibility of member states to use international law in their own mutual relations.[93]

---

[89] Klabbers (2002), pp. 295–296 and Mendez (2010a), pp. 85–86.

[90] Scharpf (1999), p. 58 and Tuori (2010), p. 18.

[91] See also Mendez (2010a), p. 88.

[92] See joined cases C-402/05 P and C-415/05 P, *Yassin Abdullah Kadi and others v. Council* [2008] ECR I-6351.

[93] See also Cremona (2011), pp. 266–267 and Eeckhout (2011), pp. 414–415.

4 Conclusions

Even though international law obligations are still formally directed at states, international norms now often have the function of making sub-state institutions act in a particular way within their own jurisdictions. International law increasingly penetrates the surface of the sovereign state and requires governments to take specific domestic actions to meet specific aims. Its norms more often than before limit the political choices of governments and compel not only states to enact specific domestic legislation, but also the national institutions to enforce these laws and to take specific actions.[94] To the extent that such developments enable the bypassing of democratic processes, inhibit useful experimentation with alternative approaches, or empower governments and national institutions to pursue one-sided or repressive local policies, the trend is problematic.

The IP chapters of the EU's EPAs and FTAs could be seen as part of such developments. Together with multi-party measures such as ACTA, they represent what I call disciplinary globalism, which continues the previous proprietarian phase of the EU's IP law.[95] Now the EU uses international IP and trade law to take a firm grip of developing countries' IP policies in a postcolonial spirit. It also influences its own internal policies by empowering the EU legislature to drive through internal legislation that would not have been otherwise possible. In these processes, the new objectives of the EU's external activity found in Article 21 of the TEU remain mere rhetoric. It is possible to address these developments in the light of the critical discourse on new constitutionalism.[96] The EU's external IP measures form a new kind of constitutional norms for the protection of IP, having the effect of insulating proprietarian IP norms from democratic decision-making and judicial activism.

Through the notions of primacy and direct effect, the FTAs and EPAs likely assume significant constitutional functions as part of Union law: Soft norms of international law metamorphose into strict EU norms.[97] After this metamorphosis into an integral part of Union law, the sufficiently clear and precise obligations in the IP chapters of the EPAs and FTAs may replace conflicting domestic norms in application discourse, invalidate current and future EU secondary law to an extent that they are in an unavoidable conflict, and require both domestic and at least secondary EU norms to be interpreted in a manner consistent with the Europeanized international norms. Compared to the TRIPS era, which was characterized by the relative absence of directly effective IP treaties binding the EU, the constitutional architecture of disciplinary globalism, based on networks of bilateral and multi-party IP measures, is far more complex, unpredictable, and pervasive with regard to its potential multiple effects.

---

[94] Slaughter and Burke-White (2007), pp. 125–127.

[95] See Mylly (2009), pp. 262–275 on the previous phases.

[96] See Mylly (2014).

[97] On a general level see Wahl (2008), p. 18.

References

Acquah D (2011) Developments in the EU external IP and trade competence up to Lisbon: new wine in old bottles? Nordiskt Immateriellt Rättsskydd (NIR) 80(5):423–443

Bourgeois JHJ (1999) External relations powers of the European Community. Fordham Int Law J 22:149–173

Bronckers M (2008) Recent developments in the European Courts' Case Law on the WTO and beyond. J Int Econ Law 11(4):885–898

Cremona M (2002) A policy of bits and pieces? The common commercial policy after nice. In: Dashwood A, Ward A (eds) The Cambridge Yearbook of European Legal Studies. Hart, Oxford, pp 61–91

Cremona M (2010) Disconnection clauses in EU law and practice. In: Hillion H, Koutrakos P (eds) Mixed agreements revisited. The EU and its members in the world. Hart, Oxford, pp 160–186

Cremona M (2011) External relations and external competence of the European Union: the emergence of an integrated policy. In: Craig P, de Búrca G (eds) The evolution of EU law, 2nd edn. Oxford University Press, Oxford, pp 217–268

de Witte B (2008) The emergence of a European system of Public International Law: the EU and its Member States as strange subjects. In: Wouters J, Nollkaemper A, de Wet E (eds) The Europeanisation of international law. The status of international law in the EU and its Member States. T.M.C. Asser Press, The Hague, pp 39–54

Directive 2004/48/EC of the European Parliament and of the Council of 29 April 2004 on the enforcement of intellectual property rights [2004] OJ L 157, 16

Drexl J (2006) Competence of the European Community in the field of International Trade Law: limitations on Foreign Policy of the Member States and Turkey. Ankara Law Rev 3:99–127

Drexl J (2013) Intellectual property and implementation of recent bilateral trade agreements in the EU. In: Drexl J, Grosse Ruse Khan H, Nadde-Phlix S (eds) EU Bilateral Trade Agreements and Intellectual Property: for better or worse? Springer, Heidelberg (this volume)

Duncan M (2010) The Lisbon Treaty, trade agreements and the enforcement of intellectual property rights. Eur Intellect Property Rev 32(3):104–112

Dunoff JL (2009) The politics of international constitutions: the curious case of the World Trade Organization. In: Dunoff JL, Trachtman JP (eds) Ruling the world? Constitutionalism, international law, and global governance. Cambridge University Press, New York, pp 178–205

Eeckhout P (2011) EU external relations law. Oxford University Press, New York

Govaere I (2008) With eyes wide shut: the EC strategy to enforce intellectual property rights abroad. In: Dashwood A, Maresceau M (eds) Law and practice of EU external relations. Salient features of a changing landscape. Cambridge University Press, New York, pp 401–428

Hillion H, Koutrakos P (eds) (2010) Mixed agreements revisited. The EU and its members in the world. Hart, Oxford

Jacobs FG (2008) Direct effect and interpretation of international agreements in the recent case law of the European Court of Justice. In: Dashwood A, Maresceau M (eds) Law and practice of EU external relations. Salient features of a changing landscape. Cambridge University Press, New York, pp 13–33

Jaeger T (2013) IP provisions in EU economic partnership agreements. In: Drexl J, Grosse Ruse Khan H, Nadde-Phlix S (eds) EU Bilateral Trade Agreements and Intellectual Property: for better or worse? Springer, Heidelberg (this volume)

Klabbers J (2002) International law in community law: the law and politics of direct effect. Yearbook Eur Law 21:263–298

Koutrakos P (2010) Interpretation of mixed agreements. In: Hillion H, Koutrakos P (eds) Mixed agreements revisited. The EU and its members in the world. Hart, Oxford, pp 116–137

Krajewski M (2005) External trade law and the constitution treaty: towards a federal and more democratic common commercial policy? Common Market Law Rev 42:91–127

Lenaerts K, Corthaut T (2006) Of birds and hedges: the role of primacy in invoking norms of EU law. Eur Law Rev 31:287–315

Mendez M (2010a) The legal effect of community agreements: maximalist treaty enforcement and judicial avoidance techniques. Eur J Int Law 21:83–104

Mendez M (2010b) The enforcement of EU agreements: bolstering the effectiveness of treaty law? Common Market Law Rev 47:1719–1756

Müller-Graff P-C (2008) The common commercial policy enhanced by the reform Treaty of Lisbon? In: Dashwood A, Maresceau M (eds) Law and practice of EU external relations. Salient features of a changing landscape. Cambridge University Press, New York, pp 188–201

Mylly T (2009) Intellectual Property and European Economic Constitutional Law. The trouble with private informational power. IPR University Center, Helsinki

Mylly T (2012) Criminal enforcement and European Union Law. In: Geiger C (ed) Criminal enforcement of intellectual property. A handbook of contemporary research. Edward Elgar, Cheltenham

Mylly T (2014) Intellectual property and new constitutionalism. Edward Elgar, Cheltenham (forthcoming)

Neframi E (2010) The duty of loyalty: rethinking its scope through its application in the field of EU external relations. Common Market Law Rev 47:323–359

Peers S (2011) The constitutional implications of the EU Patent. Eur Constitutional Law Rev 7:229–266

Rosas A (2008) The European Court of Justice and Public International Law. In: Wouters J, Nollkaemper A, de Wet E (eds) The Europeanisation of international law. The status of international law in the EU and its Member States. T.M.C. Asser Press, The Hague, pp 71–85

Rosas A, Armati L (2010) EU Constitutional law. An introduction. Hart, Oxford

Scharpf F (1999) Governing in Europe. Effective and democratic? Oxford University Press, Oxford

Slaughter A-M, Burke-White W (2007) The future of international law is domestic (or the European way of law. In: Nijman J, Nollkaemper A (eds) New perspectives on the divide between national & international law. Oxford University Press, Oxford, pp 110–133

Tietje C (2008) The status of international law in the European Legal Order: the case of international treaties and non-binding international instruments. In: Wouters J, Nollkaemper A, de Wet E (eds) The Europeanisation of international law. The status of international law in the EU and its Member States. T.M.C. Asser Press, The Hague, pp 55–69

Tuori K (2010) The many constitutions of Europe. In: Tuori K, Sankari S (eds) The many constitutions of Europe. Ashgate, Farnham, pp 3–30

Villalta Puig G, Al-Haddab B (2011) The common commercial policy after Lisbon: an analysis of the reforms. Eur Law Rev 36:289–301

Wahl R (2008) Europeanisation beyond supremacy. In: Wouters J, Nollkaemper A, de Wet E (eds) The Europeanisation of international law. The status of international law in the EU and its Member States. T.M.C. Asser Press, The Hague, pp 17–37

Intellectual Property and Implementation of Recent Bilateral Trade Agreements in the EU

Josef Drexl

Contents

1 Introduction

The inclusion of extensive chapters on intellectual property (IP) protection in bilateral trade agreements has become an important feature of the international commercial policy of the European Union (EU). Such chapters can be found in the

J. Drexl (✉)
Max Planck Institute for Intellectual Property and Competition Law, Marstallplatz 1, Munich 80539, Germany
e-mail: Josef.drexl@ip.mpg.de

J. Drexl et al. (eds.), *EU Bilateral Trade Agreements and Intellectual Property: For Better or Worse?*, MPI Studies on Intellectual Property and Competition Law 20,
DOI 10.1007/978-3-642-39097-5_13,

EU-CARIFORUM EPA of 2008[1] and the Free Trade Agreement (FTA) with South Korea of 2010,[2] as well as the recently concluded Association Agreement with Central America[3] and the Trade Agreement with Colombia and Peru.[4] A similar chapter was made part of the negotiation mandate for the FTA with India.[5]

Another target region for the EU is the Association of Southeast Asian Nations (ASEAN). Since negotiations with the whole group of ASEAN countries turned out to be too difficult, the EU decided to enter into trade negotiations with individual ASEAN countries.[6] So far, the EU has started trade negotiations with three out of the ten: Singapore, Malaysia and Vietnam. The agreement with Singapore, which the EU seemed to have negotiated according to the model of its FTA with South Korea, will include IP provisions.[7] In 2011, IP was among the last issues on which the parties still had to reach full agreement.[8] The negotiations with Singapore were concluded on 16 December 2012.[9] The Agreement was expected to be initialed in spring 2013.[10] Negotiations with Malaysia are underway,[11] but, regarding IP, they may prove much more difficult than with Singapore.[12] According to the most

---

[1] Economic Partnership Agreement between the CARIFORUM States, of the one part, and the European Community and its Member States, of the other part. Foremost, the EPAs are intended to renew the trade preferences accorded by the EU to states of Africa, the Caribbean and the Pacific (ACP countries) under the former Cotonou Agreement of 2000: Partnership Agreement 2000/483/EC between the members of the African, Caribbean and Pacific Group of States of the one part, and the European Community and its Member States, of the other part. The Cotonou Agreement was revised in 2010 and now continues to constitute the platform for negotiating individual EPAs with regional groups of ACP countries. The EU-CARIFROUM EPA, which was the first EPA to reach the ratification stage, was initially planned as a blueprint for the following EPAs with the other regional groups of African and Pacific countries. By now, however, it seems that the EU may well abstain from including similar IP chapters in the EPAs with other ACP countries. On the current state of EPA negotiations and implementation see the website of the EU Commission: "Current state of EPA negotiations and implementation".

[2] Free Trade Agreement between the European Union and its Member States, of the one part, and the Republic of Korea, of the other part.

[3] Negotiations for this agreement were concluded in May 2010. The agreement was initialled on 22 March 2011. It still needs to be ratified by the parties.

[4] Negotiations for this agreement were concluded in March 2012.

[5] On the specific IP issues relevant in the negotiations see Centre for the Analysis of Regional Integration. The EU's intention to include substantive IP obligations in this FTA is facing fierce resistance by India. At the time of the writing of this chapter it is still unclear whether the EU will accept the Indian position according to which the FTA should not include any IP obligations that conflict with the domestic law of India.

[6] European Commission (2009).

[7] EU Centre in Singapore (2011).

[8] European Commission (2011) (information provided after a meeting of the EU Trade Commissioner in Singapore on 15 July 2011).

[9] European Commission (2012a).

[10] European Commission (2012d).

[11] ICTSD (2010).

[12] Driven by concerns about rising prices for HIV drugs, public protests arose when a leaked text for the EU-India FTA became known in Malaysia. FTA Malaysia Information (2012).

recently fixed negotiation agenda, rules on intellectual property are also planned to be included in the agreement with Vietnam.[13] Finally, another trade agreement with IP provisions is currently negotiated with Canada.[14]

With these IP provisions the EU aims "to achieve an adequate and effective level of protection and enforcement of intellectual property rights".[15] There is no doubt that they are predominantly meant to strengthen IP protection under the law of the other contracting parties in the interest of rightholders from the EU. The economic and social implications of standards of IP protection in bilateral trade agreements that go beyond the obligations contained in the Agreement of the World Trade Organization (WTO) on Trade-Related Aspects of Intellectual Property Rights (TRIPS) ("TRIPS-plus standards") in developing countries and emerging economies in particular, and the ensuing implementation challenges, have attracted considerable attention for quite some time.[16] In contrast, the implications of the IP chapters of these bilateral trade agreements for the EU's own internal legal system have largely been ignored so far. This is mostly due to the general belief that these chapters only export European standards of IP protection to other countries.

The following analysis will challenge this assumption that no implementation is needed within the EU. After a brief summary of the provisions of the EU founding treaties that are relevant for the conclusion and implementation of the agreements (Sect. 2), this paper will analyse those provisions of the EU bilateral trade agreements that may require specific action of implementation on the part of the EU. Thereby, three groups of provisions will be distinguished, namely, specific IP provisions (Sect. 3), other provisions that are not specifically IP-related (Sect. 4) and the general principles of the bilateral agreements (Sect. 5). Finally, in its concluding section, this paper will try to assess the approach of the different agreements to the obligations entered into by the EU (Sect. 6). Also, due to the lack of accessibility to the drafts of agreements currently under negotiation, the analysis will concentrate on the EU-CARIFORUM EPA and the agreements with South Korea, Central America, Columbia and Peru.

2 EU Rules on the Conclusion and Implementation of the Bilateral Agreements

In this section, the analysis will focus on the relevant provisions of the Treaty on the Functioning of the European Union (TFEU) that govern the conclusion of the abovementioned bilateral trade agreements. Thereby, it has to be recalled that the

---

[13] European Commission (2012b).

[14] Comprehensive Economic and Trade Agreement (CETA) between Canada and the European Union. On the implementation issues arising against the backdrop of the federal system of Canada see De Beer (2012).

[15] Article 10.1(b) of the EU-South Korea FTA. In Article 10.1(a), the Agreement also mentions the objective of facilitating the production and commercialisation of innovative and creative products to the Parties. It is interesting to see that the immediate goal of strengthening protection is mentioned after the indirect, more trade-related goal.

[16] Biadgleng and Maur (2011).

Economic Partnership Agreement with the CARIFORUM States[17] was concluded under the previous rules of the Nice version of the EC Treaty.

The conclusion of bilateral trade agreements falls within the competence of the EU for common commercial policy according to Articles 206 and 207 of the TFEU. Article 207(3) and (4) provides the EU with power to conclude agreements with "one or more third countries". According to Article 207(1), the EU competence for establishing a common commercial policy also covers the "commercial aspects of intellectual property".

This latter term is not explained in the Treaty; in particular, it is not quite clear how the "commercial aspects of intellectual property" are to be distinguished from other aspects of intellectual property. From a historical perspective, the inclusion of the commercial aspects of intellectual property rights serves to enlarge the external competence of the EU as compared to Opinion 1/94, in which the former ECJ (now CJEU) held that the previous provisions of the Maastricht version of the EC Treaty on common commercial policy only created exclusive competence of the EC to the extent that IP issues arise within the context of cross-border trade.[18] Accordingly, the former EC was deemed to have exclusive competence for the provisions on the WTO/TRIPS Agreement on border measures, but not for those provisions that introduced substantive standards of IP protection for the nationals of the other WTO members without specifically requiring a link with cross-border trade.[19] Although Article 207(1) of the TFEU does not use the TRIPS wording of "trade-related aspects", it seemingly has the purpose of broadening the scope of the exclusive competence of the EU to include IP-related provisions in trade agreements. This would amount to a dynamic concept of the "commercial aspects of intellectual property", according to which the EU would have discretion as to what kind of IP rules are to be included in trade agreements.[20]

---

[17] See fn. 1, above.

[18] Opinion 1/94 [1994] ECR I-5267, paras 55–71.

[19] For an analysis of the legal situation at the time of the conclusion of TRIPS, see Drexl (1996).

[20] In this sense Drexl (2010), p. 1344, para 89. The question of whether the concept of "commercial aspects of intellectual property" is identical with the "trade-related aspects" addressed in TRIPS was explicitly left open by Advocate General Kokott in her unpublished Opinion in Case C-13/07 *Commission v. Council*, para 48. The issue of the case was whether the EU can act without the Member States on the WTO Council in the framework of making a decision on the WTO accession of Vietnam. On this case see also Kokott (2010), p. 114 (maintaining that the EU has only gained exclusive competence for the commercial aspects of intellectual property under the Lisbon Treaty). The question relating to the scope of exclusive competence of the EU for the commercial aspects of intellectual property under the Lisbon Treaty has most recently been referred to the CJEU in the *Daiichi Sankyo* case (Case C-414/11). In his opinion, delivered on 31 January 2013 (not yet officially reported), Advocate General *Cruz Villalón* struggled enormously with the answer. By arguing both, namely that the Lisbon Treaty must have broadened the exclusive competence of the EU, on the one hand, and that the concept of the commercial aspects of IP must have some objective meaning that does not cover any IP provision on the sole bases that it is included in a trade agreement, on the other hand, the Advocate General tried to find some middle ground, which, however, would obviously create considerable legal uncertainty. Hence, it will be interesting to see how the CJEU will answer the referral.

In contrast, if the EU negotiates a specific IP agreement in the framework of the World Intellectual Property Organization (WIPO) in particular, such agreement should not be considered to relate to the commercial aspects of intellectual property. Nevertheless, even in regard to those latter agreements, the EU may have exclusive competence to become a party to such an agreement pursuant to Article 216(1) of the TFEU, provided that the conclusion of the agreement affects internal EU legislation.[21] To the extent that the EU legislature has neither harmonised IP rights nor introduced unitary rights, the EU can only act on the basis of joined competence and conclude the relevant agreement together with the EU Member States as a mixed agreement. This is why the Anti-Counterfeiting Trade Agreement (ACTA),[22] which would also have covered IP rights that exclusively arise from the law of the EU Member States, would have had to be concluded as a mixed agreement.[23] Despite its name this agreement neither requires a situation of cross-border trade in goods and services as a condition to be applied nor promotes higher standards of IP protection as part of a bargain for the concession of trade preferences to the other parties. Rather, ACTA is an agreement among like-minded nations that strive to set a "gold standard" for IP enforcement measures that can later be used as a blueprint for trade agreements with third states that will only agree on such standards in return for trade preferences.[24] Accordingly, ACTA cannot be considered an agreement on the commercial aspects of intellectual property in the sense of Article 207(1) of the TFEU.

The IP provisions included in the newly negotiated bilateral trade agreements of the EU do not only apply to situations in which IP-related products are traded across borders. They generally aim to enhance protection of IPRs in the territory of the other contracting parties without any direct link to cross-border trade. They therefore would largely have fallen outside of the exclusive competence of the former EC under the Maastricht Treaty as defined by the former ECJ (now CJEU) in its Opinion 1/94, but, as part of a trade agreement, these IP provisions may today well be covered by the notion of "commercial aspects of intellectual property" of the TFEU as a basis for exclusive competence.[25]

---

[21] See Drexl (2010), fn. 20, above, para 91. The last alternative of Article 216(1) TFEU enacts the so-called AETR doctrine; see Case 22/70 *Commission v Council* [1971] ECR 263, para 16 ("*AETR*").

[22] Anti-Counterfeiting Trade Agreement concluded between the European Union and its Member States, Australia, Canada, Japan, the Republic of Korea, the United Mexican States, the Kingdom of Morocco, New Zealand, the Republic of Singapore, the Swiss Federation and the United States of America.

[23] Since the European Parliament rejected ACTA in a vote on 4 July 2012 by 478 to 39 votes, with 165 abstentions, it can no longer be assumed that the EU will become a contracting party of ACTA. See European Parliament (2012). Also, since no other signatory party has ratified the agreement, it may well never enter into force. ACTA needs six ratifications to enter into force. The vote of the European Parliament also prevents the EU Member States from joining ACTA.

[24] See Grosse Ruse-Khan (2010).

[25] Case C-414/11 *Daiichi Sankyo*, on the exclusive competence of the EU for all provisions of the TRIPS agreements, which has most recently been referred to the CJEU, will have to be considered a precedent also for the assessment of EU competence to conclude IP provisions in bilateral trade agreements. On this case, see also fn. 20, above.

According to Article 216(2) of the TFEU, agreements concluded by the EU are binding on the EU institutions and the Member States. Accordingly, such international agreements are part of the legal system of the EU. However, the binding effect on EU institutions and, consequently, the EU legislature does not mean that the agreements can be relied upon by individuals before the courts within the EU and that, therefore, even if the EU legislature fails to take required internal action for the implementation of the agreement, application of the agreement would be guaranteed. Quite on the contrary, the CJEU traditionally holds that direct effect of international agreements within the EU, with the capacity of individuals to rely upon the provisions of such agreements, depends on the nature of the agreement. Concerning the WTO Agreements, the ECJ has continuously denied any direct effect.[26]

Hence, implementation is important for two reasons: First, implementation is required from the perspective of international law. If the EU fails to implement, it will violate its international obligations arising from the agreements. Second, implementation is important from an internal perspective. Without implementation there will be no guarantee that the institutions of the EU and the Member States will apply internal law in conformity with the agreements.[27]

3 Implementation Affecting IP Laws

According to Article 207(3)(2) of the TFEU, the Commission and the Council are "responsible for ensuring that the agreements negotiated are in conformity with internal Union policies and rules". While it is clear from the outset that the EU cannot conclude agreements that conflict with the provisions of the TEU and the TFEU, this rule aims at guaranteeing the conformity of agreements concluded by the EU with secondary EU law. Although Article 207(3)(2) of the TFEU relates to "negotiated" agreements, this provision does not prevent the EU from negotiating agreements that require amendment of existing EU law. Rather, the provision requires that the conformity of the agreements with internal rules has to be guaranteed at the time of the conclusion of the agreement. A good example is provided by the WIPO internet treaties—the WIPO Copyright Treaty (WCT) and the WIPO Performances and Phonograms Treaty (WPPT)—signed in 1996. The EU negotiated these agreements as mixed agreements with the Member States. However, it only joined the two agreements once the EU legislature had adopted the

---

[26] See Joined Cases C-300/98 and 392/98 *Parfums Christian Dior and Assco Gerüste* [2000] ECR I-11307, paras 41–45; Case C-89/99 *Schieving-Nijstad* [2001] 5851, paras 51–53. Note, however, that at least under the Nice version of the EC Treaty, the former ECJ maintained the power of the Member States to decide on direct effect of TRIPS to the extent that the individual case does not relate to any field in which the European Union has legislated. See C-431/05 *Merck Genéricos* [2007] ECR I-7001, para 34.

[27] Note, however, that this problem is mitigated by the CJEU's recognising an obligation of the courts in the EU Member States to interpret national law in conformity with TRIPS. See, in particular, Case C-53/96 *Hermès* [1998] ECR I-3603, para 28; Joined Cases C-300/98 and 392/98 *Parfums Christian Dior and Assco Gerüste* [2000] ECR I-11307, para 47.

Information Society Directive[28] and the Member States had concluded their implementation of this directive.[29] In addition, if the given agreement turns out to lack conformity with internal rules,[30] this will not lead to the invalidity of the agreement in terms of EU law. Rather, the EU, as a matter of international law, will have to change its internal rules or to terminate the agreement if possible.

With regard to specific IP rules, the EU—like the United States—generally aims to make its own internal rules the standard of its bilateral trade agreements. This is especially true for areas where TRIPS contains only very rudimentary rules, but where the law in the European Union takes a very specific approach, such as in the areas of geographical indications[31] and enforcement measures. Yet, on some issues, the EU refrains from exporting European standards to third countries. For instance, the EU-CARIFORUM EPA includes the protection of databases in its definition of intellectual property.[32] However, it does not contain any obligation to introduce *sui generis* protection for databases as provided for by the European Database Directive.[33] This cautious approach is incorporated in an even clearer way in the FTA with South Korea. There, the agreement only includes protection of—creative—databases as a matter of copyright law, without requiring *sui generis* protection of databases merely based on investment.[34]

3.1 The Obligation of the EU to Introduce Criminal Sanctions

Hence, it seems that the bilateral agreements do not usually contain obligations that extend protection beyond the level of substantive protection within the EU. However, a most important exception is provided by the provisions on criminal enforcement in the FTA with South Korea and the Association Agreement with Central America. To date, the EU legislature has only adopted a directive

[28] Directive 2001/29/EC.

[29] The Commission proposal of 10 November 1997 for the Information Society Directive closely followed the conclusion of the WIPO Treaties. The Directive had the objective of enabling the former EC to become a Contracting Party of the Treaties. On the interaction of the legislative process for the Directive and the ratification of the Treaties by the EC see von Lewinski and Walter (2010), paras 11.0.27–11.0.42.

[30] So far, the ECJ has constantly aimed to guarantee conformity of EU law with the WIPO copyright treaties by interpreting EU secondary law in conformity with the agreements. See, for instance, Case C-456/06 *Peek & Cloppenburg* [2008] ECR I-2731, paras 32–35 (regarding the distribution right as provided for in Article 6 of the WIPO Copyright Treaty).

[31] See, for instance, Article 145 EU-CARIFORUM EPA; Article 10.18–10.26 EU-South Korea FTA.

[32] See Article 139(3) EU-CARIFORUM EPA.

[33] Directive 96/9/EC.

[34] See Article 10.2(2)(a) EU-South Korea FTA. Similarly, Article 229(3)(a) EU-Central America Association Agreement and Article 196(5)(a) EU-Colombia and Peru Trade Agreement only include "copyright . . . in databases" on their lists of intellectual property rights.

harmonising the rules on civil enforcement,[35] while a Commission proposal for a directive on the harmonisation of criminal sanctions has so far failed to find sufficient support in the EU Parliament in particular.[36] Nevertheless, the FTA with South Korea contains a specific subsection on criminal sanctions that obliges the parties to provide for criminal procedures and sanctions at least in cases of wilful trade-mark counterfeiting and copyright and related rights piracy.[37] These provisions are mirrored by ACTA, which contains similar provisions on criminal enforcement. While it is true that criminal sanctions have already been addressed in TRIPS,[38] the FTA with South Korea and ACTA go beyond TRIPS obligations by including an obligation to introduce criminal liability of legal persons[39] and on aiding and abetting.[40]

Against this backdrop, the criminal provisions in the FTA with South Korea seem to share the objective of ACTA by being used as a blueprint for enforcement provisions that will later be transferred to bilateral agreements with states that are more reluctant to grant additional IP protection.[41]

While South Korea is a signatory of ACTA, inclusion of rules on criminal liability in the Association Agreement with Central America underlines the EU's policy to extend such obligations also to third countries, including developing countries. The provisions on criminal enforcement in the Association Agreement with Central America, however, refrain from addressing criminal liability of legal persons and do not contain any rules on aiding and abetting, but they demonstrate another feature that deserves particular attention. In its initial proposal for this agreement the EU tried to include a provision on criminal liability for wilful infringement of *any* intellectual property right. In particular, such provision would have obligated the EU to introduce criminal liability for patent infringement

[35] Directive 2004/48/EC.

[36] See Amended proposal of the Commission of 26 April 2006 for a Directive of the European Parliament and of the Council on criminal measures aimed at ensuring the enforcement of intellectual property rights, COM(2006) 168 final. For critical comments on this proposal see Hilty et al. (2006), p. 970. On the Directive see also Gibson (2012). Criminal sanctions for IP infringement are discussed in more general terms by Drexl (2012b), Griffiths (2012), and Mylly (2012).

[37] Article 10.54–10.61 EU-South Korea FTA.

[38] Article 61 TRIPS.

[39] Article 10.56 EU-South Korea FTA. This rule is highly problematic from an internal EU perspective, given that there are jurisdictions within the EU, such as Germany, that do not recognise criminal liability of legal persons as a matter of principle. An obligation regarding criminal liability of legal persons is also included in Article 23(5) ACTA. However, this provision takes a much more cautious approach by especially taking into account the consistency of such liability with the legal principles governing in the respective contracting state. The provision reads in its first sentence as follows: "Each Party shall adopt such measures as may be necessary, consistent with its legal principles, to establish the liability, which may be criminal, of legal persons for the offences specified in this Article for which the Party provides criminal procedures and penalties".

[40] Article 10.57 EU-South Korea FTA; Article 23(4) ACTA.

[41] On the criminal sanctions provisions of ACTA see Grosse Ruse-Khan (2012), pp. 183–188.

in its internal legal order, although the European Parliament had rejected such liability in the initial Commission proposal for an EU Directive on criminal liability. In the final version of the Association Agreement, the obligation to introduce criminal liability has now been limited to "wilful trade mark counterfeiting and copyright piracy on a commercial scale". However, Article 271 makes extension of criminal liability to other IPRs an option by stating as follows: "The Parties may provide for criminal procedures and penalties to be applied in other cases of infringement of intellectual property rights, in particular where they are committed wilfully and on a commercial scale."

In the light of the internal EU debate, this more cautious approach is certainly welcome. Yet, even in its final version, the Association Agreement with Central America remains problematic. It does not only provide evidence of the lack of consistency of the EU IP policy in its trade relations with other states, given that ACTA does not even consider the possibility of criminal liability beyond trademark counterfeiting and copyright piracy and that the Trade Agreement with Colombia and Peru does not contain any rule on criminal sanctions.[42] In the Association Agreement with Central America the EU should also have given more credit to the arguments against criminal liability for patent infringement that have inspired the position of the European Parliament. Patent infringement cases are technologically highly complex and often lead to lengthy disputes before courts on whether there is a case of infringement. Criminal liability for patent infringement in Central America would oblige criminal prosecutors, who may well spend most of their time on chasing drug dealers or investigating manslaughter, to assess highly complex technical questions. Allegations of wilful patent infringement can therefore easily be made by competitors with the abusive objective to distort competition to the prejudice not only of domestic manufacturers, but also, and even more so, of foreign manufacturers that try to sell their products in Central America. In the light of its own trade interest, the EU would have been much better advised to expressly exclude patent infringement from criminal liability.

In particular, the adoption of provisions on criminal enforcement as binding obligations of trade agreements will strengthen the Commission's argument in favour of getting a directive on criminal sanctions adopted by the EU legislature. Although bilateral trade agreements of the EU, such as the one with South Korea, are typically concluded as mixed agreements and, therefore, the provisions on criminal enforcement are directly binding on the Member States, the EU is also bound by these provisions and may be held liable as a matter of international law if the Member States do not have sufficient protection in place. From this analysis it has to be concluded that inclusion of binding obligations relating to criminal sanctions in bilateral trade agreements primarily serve other purposes than granting concessions to the other contracting parties under international law. Rather, there is

[42] The fact that the Agreement with Colombia and Peru does not include any provision on criminal sanctions is quite surprising since it contains other substantive TRIPS-plus obligations, such as on data exclusivity protection for pharmaceuticals, that cannot be found in the Association Agreement with Central America.

the concern that such obligations will later be used as leverage for getting internal EU legislation adopted. With regard to such provisions on criminal sanctions, the Commission and the Council have also disregarded their obligation under Article 207(3)(2) TFEU to only negotiate agreements in conformity with internal policies and rules.[43]

3.2 Protection of Genetic Resources, Traditional Knowledge and Folklore

As regards the substantive standards of protection, the bilateral trade agreements of the EU go beyond the subject-matter of European IP protection especially in the field of genetic resources, traditional knowledge and folklore. Some *sui generis* systems of protection of genetic resources, traditional knowledge and folklore can be found in a number of developing and other countries where there is a specific interest in such protection, including those that are particularly rich in biological diversity. However, no such systems of protection is currently available under the law of the EU. Yet the EU-CARIFORUM EPA, the first agreement to do so, includes a specific provision on these matters.[44] A similar provision, with basically identical wording, is found in the FTA with South Korea.[45] From a practical perspective, provisions on these topics in the Trade Agreement with Colombia and Peru are most important, since these two countries are amongst the richest in genetic resources.[46] However, these provisions only state principles of protection "subject to national legislation" and recognise the importance of taking additional measures. An even more cautious approach is adopted in the Association Agreement with Central America, where Costa Rica was one of the first countries of the world to introduce a special regime on access and benefit-sharing (ABS) regarding genetic resources.[47] This agreement only safeguards the sovereign rights of the contracting parties over the access to their genetic resources in conformity with the Convention on Biological Diversity and recognises the importance of protecting indigenous knowledge relating to genetic resources.[48]

In sum, it has to be concluded that the bilateral agreements fail to create clear obligations of the EU to protect genetic resources, traditional knowledge and folklore, although such protection is very much in the interest of the other

---

[43] It is all the more surprising that the European Parliament gave its approval to the FTA with South Korea with its rules on aiding and abetting. The Commission proposal on criminal liability was especially criticised for its lack of clarity regarding fundamental concepts of criminal law, including those on aiding and abetting.

[44] See Article 150 EU-CARIFORUM EPA.

[45] Article 10.40 EU-South Korea FTA.

[46] On the law on genetic resources and traditional knowledge in these countries see Bucher (2008).

[47] See Medaglia (2006), p. 33. With its Law on Biodiversity of 1998, Costa Rica was a pioneer in this field.

[48] Article 229(4) and (5) EU-Central America Association Agreement.

contracting parties. Yet it would not be justified to see this as evidence of a lack of balance in the IP chapters of the agreements. While it is true that the IP chapters impose a number of obligations upon the other contracting parties to improve protection mostly in the interest of EU rightholders, it is also true that there are not yet sufficiently clear internationally recognised standards of protection for genetic resources, traditional knowledge and folklore.[49] Laying the ground for future legislation and development of the field may therefore be considered the more appropriate approach.

With the more recent Nagoya Protocol to the Convention on Biological Diversity (CBD) this has changed to a certain extent.[50] After having signed the Protocol on 23 June 2011, the European Union and its Member States now have to implement this multilateral instrument.

Regarding intellectual property, the question that arises is in particular whether the national laws on access to genetic resources and benefit-sharing are in need of specific enforcement measures under patent law. Patent laws may require the person who applies for a patent, for instance on a pharmaceutical product, to disclose the origin of the underlying genetic information as an additional requirement for the patent grant. Some countries have already gone in this direction. In Germany, for instance, the Patent Act (§ 34a) stipulates that the applicant for a patent which is based on biological material "should" lay open the origin of this material. Yet German law also expressly stipulates that a violation of this duty does neither bar the grant of the patent nor constitute a ground for invalidation.[51]

Obviously, it does not suffice that access and benefit-sharing laws are only adopted in genetically rich states. Since most income will be generated in foreign markets, the need for effective sanctions gives rise to a truly international issue to which the Nagoya Protocol now reacts. The most important provision of the Nagoya Protocol is probably Article 15 which provides for obligations of all Parties to the Protocol to guarantee the respect of the access-and-benefit-sharing (ABS) rules whenever genetic resources are utilized within their jurisdictions. Article 15 reads as follows:

1. Each Party shall take appropriate, effective and proportionate legislative, administrative or policy measures to provide that genetic resources utilized within its jurisdiction have been accessed in accordance with prior informed consent and that mutually agreed terms have been established, as required by the domestic access and benefit-sharing legislation or regulatory requirements of the other Party.
2. Parties shall take appropriate, effective and proportionate measures to address situations of non-compliance with measures adopted in accordance with paragraph 1 above.
3. Parties shall, as far as possible and as appropriate, cooperate in cases of alleged violation of domestic access and benefit-sharing legislation or regulatory requirements referred to in paragraph 1 above.

---

[49] von Lewinski (2008).

[50] Nagoya Protocol (2010).

[51] In contrast, the Swiss Patent Act (§ 49a) contains a clear obligation to provide such information by using the wording "must".

As can be seen from this text, Article 15 does not require the Parties to use patent law for enforcing the ABS rules of other Parties.

The provisions on genetic resources contained in bilateral agreements, even if they were concluded prior to the Nagoya Protocol, such as of the EU-CARIFORUM EPA, have now to be read in the light of Article 15 of that Protocol. On genetic resources, the EU-CARIFORUM EPA contains two principles: first, it states that the contracting parties "agree" that the patent provisions of the EPA and the provisions of the Convention on Biological Diversity should be implemented in a mutually supportive way.[52] While this provision may already be taken as an indication in favour of having a disclosure rule in patent law, the EPA, furthermore, becomes very specific about such a rule with the following provision:

> The EC Party and the Signatory CARIFORUM States *may* require as part of the administrative requirements for a patent application concerning an invention which uses biological material as a necessary aspect of the invention, that the applicant identifies the sources of the biological material used by the applicant and described as part of the invention.[53]

A slightly different approach to the interface of genetic resources and patent law is taken by the EU Trade Agreement with Colombia and Peru. Within the rather complex provision of Article 201, paragraph 4 creates a binding obligation. However, this provision also falls short of a disclosure obligation in patent law by using wording which remains too vague. The provision reads as follows:

> In accordance with Article 15 paragraph 7 of the CBD, the Parties reaffirm their obligation to take measures with the aim of sharing in a fair and equitable way the benefits arising from the utilization of genetic resources. The Parties also recognise that mutually agreed terms may include *benefit-sharing obligations in relation to intellectual property rights* arising from the use of genetic resources and associated traditional knowledge.[54]

The second sentence of this provision may well be read as an allusion to a disclosure rule under patent law. However, this seems to make such a rule subject to further negotiations between the parties.

In sum, the EPA and the Trade Agreement with Colombia and Peru on the one hand and the Nagoya Protocol on the other hand may be considered as mutually supportive international instruments for the protection of genetic resources. Yet, even taken together, these instruments cannot be read as an obligation of the EU to implement sanctions in the framework of patent law, such as the invalidation of the patent in case of a violation of the ABS rules in the country of origin of the biological material.

In the current situation in the EU, it is also clear that no implementation of such a disclosure rule can be expected. Patents in the EU are granted by either the European Patent Office (EPO), which is an authority not of the EU but of the European Patent Organisation, or by the national patent offices. The EU had plans to adopt a Regulation on a unitary EU patent. However, these plans have meanwhile

[52] Article 150(3) EU-CARIFORUM EPA.

[53] Article 150(4) EU-CARIFORUM EPA (emphasis added).

[54] Emphasis added.

been amended, and all that can be expected now will amount to the grant of a European bundle patent under the European Patent Convention with subsequent application of a unitary effect for the territory of the participating EU Member States.[55] This would leave the rules on the patent grant under the European Patent Convention untouched. Accordingly, it does not come as a surprise that the most recent Proposal of the European Commission for a Regulation on the implementation of the Nagoya Protocol[56] abstains from establishing a nexus between the implementation of the Protocol and patent law in Europe.

In sum, it turns out that the bilateral agreements, in principle and with the important exception of criminal sanctions, do not oblige the EU to raise the level of protection existing within the EU. Nor do these agreements oblige the EU to provide for conditions and limitations which would make it more difficult to acquire rights within the EU or limit the scope of protection of such rights. With regard to genetic resources, the agreements provide for the possibility to require the disclosure of the country of origin of the biological material as a condition for the patent grant. Yet, according to the current plans concerning the implementation of the Nagoya Protocol, it cannot be expected that the EU will make use of this possibility.

4 Implementation of Obligations Outside IP Laws, Especially on Transfer of Technology and Competition Law

However, a closer analysis of the more recent trade agreements shows that third countries can be quite successful in getting rules adopted in the agreements that require the EU to become active in view of promoting the interests of these third countries outside the clear field of protecting intellectual property. This is especially so with regard to transfer of technology (Sect. 4.1). In addition, it is worthwhile to note that some of the new agreements also include general provisions on competition law, which could be used to better balance intellectual property (Sect. 4.2).

4.1 Transfer of Technology

Again, the first example of provisions with obligations regarding the promotion of transfer of technology can be found in the EU-CARIFORUM EPA. Especially Section 1 of Chapter 2 of this EPA, on "innovation", contains a number of general

---

[55] See Regulation (EU) No. 1257/2012. Whether this Regulation will ever be applied is doubtful. It is planned to be applicable as of 1 January 2014. Yet applicability depends on the entry into force of the so-called Agreement on a Unified Patent Court. This Agreement, which has been signed by 25 out of 27 Member States, needs to be ratified by at least 13 Member States, including Germany, France and the United Kingdom. Also, Spain has brought an action for annulment of the underlying regulations (Cases C-146/13 and C-147/13).

[56] European Commission (2012c).

provisions concerning the enhancement of transfer of technology. The most important provision, however, is Article 142 in Section 2, on "intellectual property", which functionally corresponds to the competition-oriented provisions of the TRIPS Agreement, namely Articles 8(2) and 40.

4.1.1 Transfer of Technology as an Objective

First, it has to be highlighted that the EPA mentions transfer of technology as an objective of the provisions of Chapter 2 along with intellectual property protection. Following Article 132(d) on IP protection, Article 132(e) postulates the "promotion of technological innovation and the transfer and dissemination of technology and know-how" as an objective of the agreement.

Putting IP protection and transfer of technology as objectives on the same level seems most important from a conceptual point of view. The approach of the EPA differs from that of Article 8(1) of the TRIPS Agreement, where the goal of promoting technology transfer is also mentioned, in two regards: first, Article 8(1) of TRIPS only recognises the power of WTO members to legislate in the interest of promoting technology transfer, whereas the EPA in itself is meant to promote technology transfer. Second, whereas Article 8(2) of TRIPS explicitly provides that domestic measures on technology transfer must not be inconsistent with other TRIPS provisions, no such priority is given to IP protection under the EPA.

Article 132(e), as a provision on the objectives, has to be taken into account for the interpretation of the subsequent provisions of the agreement, most importantly those on IP protection. In cases in which there is a conflict between IP obligations and the interest in technology transfer, equal weight will have to be given to both concerns. The question remains how the EU can guarantee that courts in the EU will interpret IP laws in the light of the goal of Article 132(e) of the EPA. It would probably be too much to claim the introduction of a specific provision in all IP laws in the EU that would require such courts to take the interest in technological innovation and technology transfer into account. Yet, as a matter of established EU law, the courts in the Member States are required to interpret internal laws in the light of international law, although the relevant international agreements may well lack direct effect in the EU.[57]

Since Article 132(e) of the EU-CARIFORUM EPA deviates from Article 8(1) of the TRIPS Agreement, the question arises of which provision prevails. In order to prevent Article 132(e) from losing all its meaning with regard to the CARIFORUM States that are also WTO members, it is to be assumed that Article 132(e) should prevail in the relations among the EPA parties.

This interpretation is not contradicted by Article 139(2). The provision reads as follows:

[57] See case-law cited at fn. 26, above.

> The EC Party and the Signatory CARIFORUM States agree that the principles set out in Article 8 of the TRIPS Agreement apply to this section. The Parties also agree that an adequate and effective enforcement of intellectual property rights should take account of the development needs of the CARIFORUM States, provide a balance of rights and obligations between right holders and users and allow the EC Party and the Signatory CARIFORUM States to protect public health and nutrition. Nothing in this Agreement shall be construed as to impair the capacity of the Parties and the Signatory CARIFORUM States to promote access to medicine.

Especially the first sentence has to be read and understood carefully. It does not mandate full application of Article 8 of the TRIPS Agreement in the framework of the EPA, but only that "the principles set out in Article 8" apply to the EPA section on intellectual property. TRIPS Article 8 safeguards the regulatory autonomy of the WTO Members with regard to certain interests. The fact that Article 139(1) EPA also deals with the regulatory autonomy of individual states is confirmed by the wording of the provision itself, which refers to the "Signatory CARIFORUM States" and not simply the "CARIFORUM States". According to Article 233(4), the agreement uses "Signatory CARIFORUM States" whenever it refers to the rights and obligations of the individual states. In addition, Article 8 of the TRIPS Agreement enumerates a whole series of interests beyond transfer of technology. By relying on the principles of Article 8 of the TRIPS Agreement, Article 139(2) fills an important gap by confirming that all of these interests are also recognised with regard to the EPA. The following sentences make clear that the EPA draws the line differently, namely more in the interest of the developing countries. In the light of the wording of the whole paragraph, it can hardly be maintained that the "consistency rule" of Article 8(1) of the TRIPS Agreement should continue to be applied between the EU and the individual signatory CARIFORUM States.

Another provision that deserves mention is Article 132(g). Therein, the EPA provides that the agreement strives to "encourage, develop and facilitate cooperative production and development activities in the creative industries between the Parties, as well as to develop lasting relationships between the Parties' creative communities". This provision, which does not relate to technology transfer in the strict sense, highlights the fact that cooperation in the field of the cultural industries, one of the biggest economic assets of the CARIFORUM States, may also help to promote sustainable development in these states.

4.1.2 General Provisions on Technology Transfer in the Section on Innovation

Section 1 of Chapter 2 of the EU-CARIFORUM EPA regulates different forms of cooperation that are meant to enhance innovation in general and transfer of technology in particular.

Article 135(1) of this EPA seems to repeat the general principle of Article 131(1) by stating that "the promotion of creativity and innovation is essential for the development of entrepreneurship and competitiveness and the achievement of the overall objectives of the Agreement".

The Parties promise to cooperate in the framework of specific development programs.[58] According to Article 135(2)(e), (f) and (g) these programs are to include the promotion of contacts and industrial cooperation between economic operators, encouraging joint investment and ventures and networks, the promotion of partnerships for research and development activities in the CARIFORUM States in order to improve their innovation systems as well as the intensification of activities to promote linkages, innovation and technology transfer between CARIFORUM and European Community partners.

According to Article 136(2), which deals in general with cooperation on science and technology, "special emphasis will be put on human potential building as a long-lasting basis of scientific and technological excellence and the creation of sustainable links between the scientific and technological communities of the Parties, at both national and regional levels".

As can be seen, none of these provisions creates any authorisation or even obligation to limit IP protection as a matter of promoting technology transfer. This is an issue which is dealt with in Section 2 on intellectual property.

4.1.3 Article 142 EU-CARIFORUM EPA on Transfer of Technology

The most important provision on transfer of technology is to be found in Article 142 of the EPA, with clear-cut obligations for the EU as well. The most important part of the provision is Article 142(2), which uses wording known from Article 40(2) of the TRIPS Agreement, on anti-competitive licensing agreements. Still, the differences make clear that Article 142(2) goes well beyond what is provided for by TRIPS with regard to licensing. The provision reads as follows:

> The EC Party and the Signatory CARIFORUM States *shall* take measures, as appropriate, to prevent or control licensing practices or conditions pertaining to intellectual property rights which may adversely affect the international transfer of technology and that constitute an abuse of intellectual property rights by right holders or an abuse of obvious information asymmetries in the negotiation of licences.[59]

The following principles may be identified for the correct understanding of this provision:

First and foremost, the provision, unlike Article 40(2) of TRIPS, does not just authorise the contracting parties to control licensing agreements, but includes an unconditional obligation to do so by using the word "shall". Since the Signatory CARIFORUM States are the recipient countries with regard to transfer of technology, this provision, above all, amounts to an obligation of the EU. Otherwise,

[58] See Articles 4 and 134 EU-CARIFORUM EPA.

[59] Emphasis added.

it would have sufficed to merely provide for an authorisation as in Article 40(2) of TRIPS.

In the context of applying competition law to licensing agreements this amounts to a legal revolution. Under Article 142(2) of the EPA, the EU is obliged to control licensing agreements between a licensor in the EU and a licensee in the signatory CARIFORUM States that only restrict the use of the intellectual property rights in these latter states. In other words, it seems that the EU now has to apply its own competition law extraterritorially. This is in clear contradiction to both the wording of Article 101(1) of the TFEU, the European prohibition on restrictive agreements, which only applies if there is a negative impact on trade between the EU Member States, and the generally accepted principle of all competition laws that these laws only protect competition in the domestic market and not in foreign markets (the so-called export cartel exemption). In the debate on the future of an international competition law it has often been argued that, in the interest of developing countries in particular, states should ban export cartels,[60] although states have never shown any tendency to go in this direction. Article 142(2) of the EU-CARIFORUM EPA seems to change this quite drastically.

In this interpretation, Article 142(2) can be seen as a major success in the negotiations of the CARIFORUM States. However, the question remains whether the EU will accept a reading of the provision in the sense of a ban on outbound restraints. Since current EU competition law does not cover such restraints, an implementing regulation would be needed on the side of the EU.

Second, Article 142(2) refers to licensing agreements that adversely affect "transfer of technology", whereas Article 40(2) of the TRIPS Agreement refers to adverse effects on "competition in the relevant market". Here, the question is whether the provision is limited to the application of competition laws only, although there is no doubt that competition law is included. In terms of its wording, Article 142(2) certainly gives more flexibility in this regard. However, it is hard to argue in the sense of a violation of the obligation of the other party by not acting against such behaviour when the argument is not one of competition law. On the one hand, the CARIFORUM States would be able to argue that the EU violated Article 142(2) if the EU did not apply its competition law relating to transfer of technology without discrimination when the effects of such agreements were only shown in the CARIFORUM States. On the other hand, one may wonder whether the CARIFORUM States may be considered to be authorised to implement regimes, such as use requirements for IP, that lie outside protecting competition but would promote transfer of technology.

Thirdly, Article 142(2) adds an additional case of intervention in the situation of unequal bargaining power based on information asymmetries between the licensor and the licensee. This is a problem of contract law and not of competition law. Still, it remains unclear why the provision in this regard is limited to information asymmetries and does not extend to unequal bargaining power in general.

[60] See, for instance, Drexl (2004), pp. 450 et seq.; Fox (2003), p. 919.

In addition, the question arises which cases should be considered those of information asymmetries. It is quite typical of licensing agreements that the licensor, based on his or her know-how, knows more than the licensee. It would go too far to consider this a sufficient ground for an information asymmetry. Rather, the supply of information is the very subject matter of all licensing transactions.

Finally, the provision relates to the concept of abuse just like Article 40(2) of the TRIPS Agreement. The concept of abuse reminds competition lawyers of the "abuse of market dominance" in the sense of Article 102 of the TFEU. However, this formula should not be understood to mean that Article 142(2) also covers unilateral conduct such as in cases of a refusal to license. It is clear from Article 40 of the TRIPS Agreement, which obviously provided the model for Article 142 (2), that the provision only applies to the control of licensing agreements. Also, Article 142(2) introduces the requirement of abuse of the right in addition ("and") to the restrictive effect of the licensing agreement on technology transfer. Hence, it is already clear from the wording that the provision applies to the control of licensing agreements only. This, however, does not mean that the EPA does not address unilateral abuse of IPRs at all. This scenario is captured by the reference in the first sentence of Article 139(2) to Article 8 of the TRIPS Agreement, which, in its second paragraph, addresses the control of the abusive use of IPRs.[61] It has to be recalled, however, that Article 8(2) of TRIPS only authorises WTO Members to apply their domestic laws to the abuse of IPRs.

In sum, it is concluded that the EPA provides for an obligation to fight anti-competitive licensing agreements extraterritorially [Article 142(2)], while it refrains from doing so with regard to unilateral conduct. At least from a conceptual point of view, this has to be seen as a clear deficiency of the EPA. However, whenever the EU acts against dominant firms in the global market whose conduct affects the CARIFORUM States, action of EU institutions to protect the European market may indirectly also protect the markets of other states.[62]

In addition, the concept of abuse in Article 142(2) does not have to be understood exclusively in a competition-law sense. It may also cover cases in the sense of the US misuse doctrine.

The other two paragraphs of Article 142 are of less legal importance. Article 142(3) provides for an obligation of the EU to facilitate and promote the use of incentives granted to institutions and enterprises in the EU for the transfer of technology to institutions and enterprises in the CARIFORM States. Article 142(1) includes a general duty to "exchange views and information" on practices and policies affecting the transfer of technology.

[61] See Heinemann (1996), pp. 241–243 (arguing that the provision does not only cover cases of "abuse of dominance" in terms of European competition law but also IP "misuse" without requiring such dominant position).

[62] This is especially true with regard to the duty imposed by the European Commission on Microsoft to provide interface information to competitors. Such a duty cannot be limited to the territory of the EU. Once the competitors receive the information they can develop competing products for the world market. See Case T-201/04 *Microsoft v Commission* [2007] ECR II-3601.

Against the background of the EU-CARIFORUM EPA and its provisions on transfer of technology, the most interesting issue concerning enforcement in the EU is whether and how the EU legislature will guarantee competition-law protection against licensing agreements that only restrict markets in the CARIFORUM States.

4.1.4 Transfer of Technology in Other Agreements

From an economic perspective, Article 142(2) of the EU-CARIFORUM EPA may remain of limited importance, since the Caribbean States, given their scarce industrial potential, will largely remain providers of agricultural products and services in the tourism business for the time being. It is therefore interesting to see how the EU deals with the promotion of technology transfer in the other agreements.

Given the level of licensing that takes place between the EU and South Korea, it is important to note that the FTA with South Korea also contains a provision that obliges both parties to act against restrictive licensing agreements that negatively affect the international transfer of technology.[63] An identical obligation is also included in the Association Agreement with Central America.[64]

In contrast to the EU-CARIFORUM EPA and the two agreements with South Korea and Central America, the Trade Agreement with Colombia and Peru, without any obvious explanation, refrains from formulating an obligation of the parties to act against restraints of competition in favour of a rule that only authorises the contracting parties to intervene under their domestic laws. Article 197(5) of this Agreement reads as follows:

> In accordance with the TRIPS Agreement, *no provision of this Title will prevent a Party* from adopting any measure necessary to prevent the abuse of intellectual property rights by right holders or the resort to practices which unreasonably restrain trade or adversely affect the international transfer of technology.[65]

In sum, the provisions on technology transfer provide a very interesting example of even the EU, at least in some bilateral agreements, accepting an international obligation regarding the application of its own competition law that goes beyond what has so far been recognised as the EU and international standard. Yet, also in this regard, the EU implements astonishingly different approaches in different bilateral agreements without any obvious justification.

---

[63] Article 10.3(2) EU-South Korea FTA.

[64] Article 231(3) EU-Central America Association Agreement.

[65] Emphasis added.

4.2 Competition Law

Competition law is a field of law that is most important for balancing protection of intellectual property from the outside. In the TRIPS Agreement, some provisions authorise WTO members to apply their competition law without creating an obligation to do so. These provisions are Article 8(2), with regard to the abuse of intellectual property, which would cover, for instance, a refusal to license as a case of abuse of market dominance, and Article 40, on restrictive licensing agreements.[66] As was pointed out above,[67] some of the new bilateral agreements go beyond this standard and create an obligation of the EU to act against practices that adversely affect international transfer of technology.

In addition, some new bilateral agreements also differ from the WTO Agreements by including a special chapter on competition policy. Yet these chapters refrain from imposing an obligation on the substantive standards of applying competition law.

Again, a good example is presented by the EU-CARIFORUM EPA. Whereas it may be argued that the contracting parties should fight anti-competitive practices flowing from the use of IPRs themselves, this, of course, remains wishful thinking to the extent that there are no working competition-law systems in place in the Caribbean States.[68] In this environment, the EPA obliges the signatory CARIFORUM States to introduce competition law within 5 years after the entry into force of the EPA and to establish competition agencies, namely, the CARICOM Competition Agency[69] and the Comisión Nacional de Defensa de la Competencia of the Dominican Republic.[70]

Intellectual property is not mentioned at all in the competition provisions of the EPA. This, however, does not mean that these provisions are not relevant to IP. On the contrary, by acknowledging that agreements substantially lessening competition and that the abuse of market power, as specific forms of anti-competitive behaviour, are to be considered incompatible with the functioning of the agreement, without mentioning IP, the EPA still makes clear that licensing agreements and the

---

[66] These provisions are generally understood as not placing limitations on the autonomy of WTO Members to act against anticompetitive conduct. See Heinemann (1996), p. 241 (arguing that WTO Members "retain their sovereignty" in the field of antitrust law); UNCTAD-ICTSD (2005), para 3.2 (p. 128).

[67] Section 4.1, above.

[68] See Article 127(1) EU-CARIFORUM EPA. In addition to the Dominican Republic, only three states, Barbados, Jamaica and Guyana, have national competition systems in place. The small island states of the Organisation of Eastern Caribbean States (OECS), as a subgroup of CARICOM, pursue the establishment of a common competition agency, the Eastern Caribbean Competition Commission (ECCC). See OECS (2008).

[69] This agency was recently established as the CARICOM Competition Commission in Suriname. See also Stewart (2012).

[70] This agency was established in 2011.

abusive use of IPRs by dominant companies are in principle also covered by the competition provisions of the agreement.

Also in this regard, the EPA goes beyond what is provided for by TRIPS by not only authorising the states to apply their laws to IP. However, the competition rules of the EPA contain no express obligation to fight anti-competitive behaviour relating to IPRs and do not provide for any guidance on how to apply competition rules in IP-related cases. In particular, the EPA with the CARIFORUM States does not contain any rule that would force the EU to strengthen its competition law regarding intellectual property.

Following the example of the EU-CARIFORUM EPA, the Association Agreement with Central America also contains a competition-law chapter.[71] The rules of this chapter are very much comparable to that of the EU-CARIFORUM EPA in that they especially oblige the Central American States to adopt a supranational competition law and to create a common competition agency, the Central American Competition Body.

A competition law chapter is also included in the FTA with South Korea. Since South Korea has a workable competition law, the provisions of this chapter, foremost, and similar to the EPA with the CARIFORUM States and the Association Agreement with Central America, oblige the parties to apply their laws effectively against restrictive agreements, abuse of market dominance and anti-competitive concentrations without, however, specifying the substantive standards.[72] The competition law chapter does not necessarily seem to implement an obligation to apply the domestic law extraterritorially. It only stipulates that competition law should be applied in such a way that restrictive business practices do not undermine the benefits flowing from trade liberalisation between the two parties.[73]

Such rules can also be found in the Trade Agreement with Colombia and Peru.[74] These provisions are to be applied, on the part of Colombia and Peru, by the competition agency they create.

5 General Principles

Of course, in the framework of implementation, the parties to an international agreement also have to take into account the general principles of the agreement. In this regard, the EU-CARIFORUM EPA is of a special interest, since, given its peculiar character, it takes into account the interest of the ACP countries in sustainable development and their social needs in particular. Accordingly, as part of its IP chapter, Article 139(2) of the EU-CARIFORUM EPA states:

[71] Articles 277–283 EU-Central America Association Agreement.

[72] Article 11.1(2) EU-South Korea FTA.

[73] Article 11.1(1) EU-South Korea FTA.

[74] See Articles 258–266 EU-Colombia and Peru Trade Agreement.

> The EC Party and the Signatory CARIFORUM States agree that the principles set out in Article 8 of the TRIPS Agreement apply to this section. The Parties also agree that an adequate and effective enforcement of intellectual property rights should take account of the development needs of the CARIFORUM States, provide a balance of rights and obligations between right holders and users and allow the EC Party and the Signatory CARIFORUM States to protect public health and nutrition. Nothing in this Agreement shall be construed as to impair the capacity of the Parties and the Signatory CARIFORUM States to promote access to medicines.

The objective of sustainable development may be considered the most important overarching principle of the EPA. In Article 3(1) of the EU-CARIFORUM EPA it is declared to be applied and integrated at every level of the economic partnership. According to Article 3(2)(a), this principle requires the parties to "take into account the human, cultural, economic, social, health, and environmental best interests of their respective population and of future generations".

The question remains of how to implement such principles. In the first place, such principles are helpful for the CARIFORUM States to justify actions that may seem to be in conflict with the black-letter law of the intellectual property provisions of the agreement. In this regard, those general principles can be used in a "defensive" way by states that have to accept higher levels of IP protection.

The more difficult question is whether these principles also raise the need for implementation within the EU. An argument against this is that especially the principle of sustainable development is a principle that regards the situation in the developing ACP countries and not the European Union. This argument rests on the territoriality principle of IP law, according to which IP rights are only protected by national law for the national territory. However, as the abovementioned discussion on disclosure rules at the interface of patent law and the protection of genetic resources demonstrates, in an increasingly globalised world, conflicts regarding sustainable development may also appear in the context of IP laws in the EU. This is especially so in the framework of a trade agreement that covers a broad range of different topics. In particular, high levels of IP protection may adversely affect the interest of poorer countries in exporting especially agricultural products to the EU.[75]

Whether, in such cases, it is indeed necessary for judges sitting on IP cases in the EU to rely on internal European rules that repeat the general principle on sustainable development in the agreement in order to achieve a better balance is nevertheless doubtful. Rather, it is argued here that judges should be aware of the particular interests of developing countries and the effect IP produces on societies worldwide when they decide intellectual property cases.[76] This seems sufficiently guaranteed

[75] This conflict more recently arose before the ECJ in Case C-428/08 *Monsanto* [2010] ECR I-6765 (on the scope of biotechnological inventions and the import of soybeans to the EU that still contained the protected DNA although the beans themselves no longer had the capacity to reproduce).

[76] A more recent example of such conflicts is provided by the cross-border seizures of products, including HIV drugs in transit in the EU on their way from India to other developing countries or emerging economies. See, on this set of cases, Drexl (2012a). See also the more recent decision of

by the duty of courts, arising from EU law, to interpret the law in conformity with the international agreements concluded by the EU.[77] Maybe even more importantly, the European legislature is well advised to pursue a better balance between the multiple interests affected by IP law internally. Such a better internal balance will reduce the likelihood that, in the international context, European law will create obstacles to sustainable development of developing countries.[78]

6 Conclusion

The analysis demonstrates that the EU largely avoids entering into obligations that would result in a need to change internal European law. The emerging exception concerning criminal sanctions pursues purposes other than granting concessions to third states. Regarding the most recent bilateral agreements, two topics that are of particular interest for the other contracting parties are worth highlighting: (1) the adoption of a disclosure requirement regarding the origin of biological material as part of the patentability requirements; and (2) the obligation to act against restraints of international transfer of technology. On the first topic, the EU avoided an international obligation by merely adopting a provision according to which the contracting parties are authorised to have such a requirement, although many of the third countries with which the EU has recently negotiated or is still in the process of negotiating bilateral agreements have a strong interest in having such a rule implemented in the EU. On the second topic, the EU has accepted an obligation to apply its competition law extraterritorially to cases in which only the markets of the other contracting parties are affected. However, in this regard as well, the EU does not seem to have sufficiently understood that there is a need for implementation in the EU legal system. Also with regard to this obligation, implementing legislation is rather unlikely to be initiated.

On both topics, the comparison of several agreements demonstrates a considerable range of different approaches. For instance, South Korea has managed to get consent from the EU for provisions similar to the agreement with the

the CJEU in Joined Cases C-446/09 and C-495/09 *Philips and Nokia* [2011] ECR I-0000 (not yet officially reported). In this case, the Court rejected the "manufacturing fiction" according to which customs authorities are authorised to seise goods in transit if these goods have infringed trademarks within the EU, provided that the goods were manufactured in the EU. The interpretation of Council Regulation (EC) No. 3295/94 of 22 December 1994 laying down measures concerning the entry into the Community and the export and re-export from the Community of goods infringing certain intellectual property rights, OJ 2004 L 341, 8, by the CJEU is in line with the principle of sustainable development as contained in the EU-CARIFORUM EPA.

[77] See fn. 26, above.

[78] Again the *Monsanto* decision of the ECJ is a good example. There, the former ECJ preferred a narrow interpretation of the scope of protection, namely, that it is limited to the functions gene sequences are expected to fulfil, with the effect that soybeans from Argentina can be more easily imported to the EU. See fn. 75, above.

CARIFORUM States, although South Korea should be much better equipped, thanks to its functional competition system, to protect its own markets against restraints of international technology transfer. In contrast, Colombia and Peru have been denied similar treatment, although such countries are certainly not better able to protect their markets against restraints of technology transfers than South Korea.

In conclusion, the policy of the EU warrants quite some criticism. The EU is imposing obligations on third states that require extensive implementation and changes with considerable impact on the life of their populations while it remains reluctant to accept amendments to the law in the EU that are in the interest of the third countries. In the rare instances where such amendments are required, the EU seems to overlook the need for implementation. Especially within the scope of the EU-CARIFORUM EPA, courts in the EU should take account of the objective of sustainable development whenever they have to deal with cases that have an economic impact on the ACP countries in the context of IP-related cases. Where, for instance, courts in the EU, in conformity with the holding in the recent *Philips and Nokia* judgment,[79] decide on the freedom of transit of generic drugs that would violate patent laws in the EU if distributed here and that are supposed to be delivered to some CARIFORUM countries, they should also spell out that such decisions are rendered in conformity with the general objectives of the EU-CARIFORUM EPA.

References

Anti-Counterfeiting Trade Agreement concluded between the European Union and its Member States, Australia, Canada, Japan, the Republic of Korea, the United Mexican States, the Kingdom of Morocco, New Zealand, the Republic of Singapore, the Swiss Federation and the United States of America. http://register.consilium.europa.eu/pdf/en/11/st12/st12196.en11.pdf. Accessed 31 Mar 2012

Biadgleng ET, Maur JC (2011) The influence of preferential trade agreements on the implementation of intellectual property rights in developing countries: a first look. Issue Paper No. 33, UNCTAD-ICTSD Project on IPRs and Sustainable Development. http://ictsd.org/downloads/2011/11/the-influence-of-preferential-trade-agreements-on-the-implementation-of-intellectual-property-rights-in-developing-countries.pdf. Accessed 7 July 2012

Bucher S (2008) Der Schutz von genetischen Ressourcen und indigenem Wissen in Lateinamerika. Nomos, Baden-Baden

Association Agreement with Central America (2011) http://trade.ec.europa.eu/doclib/press/index.cfm?id=689. Accessed 7 July 2012

Centre for the Analysis of Regional Integration at Sussex & CUTS International (2007) Qualitative analysis of a potential Free Trade Agreement between the European Union and India, Annex 3: Regulatory Issues: 94–101. http://trade.ec.europa.eu/doclib/docs/2007/july/tradoc_135348.pdf. Accessed 7 July 2012

Council of the European Union (2011) Proposal for a Regulation of the Council and the European Parliament implementing enhanced cooperation in the area of the creation of unitary patent

[79] See fn. 76, above.

protection including a Proposal for a Council Regulation implementing enhanced cooperation in the area of unitary patent protection with regard to the applicable translation arrangements. http://register.consilium.europa.eu/pdf/en/11/st11/st11328.en11.pdf. Accessed 7 July 2012

Current state of EPA negotiations and implementation. Website of the EU Commission. http://trade.ec.europa.eu/doclib/docs/2009/september/tradoc_144912.pdf. Accessed 7 July 2012

De Beer J (2012) Implementing international trade agreement in federal systems: a look at the Canada–EU CETA's intellectual property issues. Legal Issues Econ Integr 39:51–71

Directive 96/9/EC of the European Parliament and of the Council of 29 April 2004 on the legal protection of databases, OJ 1996 L 77, 20

Directive 2001/29/EC of the European Parliament and of the Council of 22 May 2001 on the harmonisation of certain aspects of copyright and related rights in the information society, OJ 2001 L 167, 10

Directive 2004/48/EC of the European Parliament and of the Council of 29 April 2004 on the enforcement of intellectual property rights, OJ 2004 L 195, 16

Drexl J (1996) The TRIPs agreement and the EC: what comes next after joint competence? In: Beier FK, Schricker S (eds) From GATT to TRIPs – the agreement on trade-related aspects of intellectual property rights. VCH, Weinheim, pp 18–58

Drexl J (2004) International competition policy after Cancún: placing a Singapore issue on the WTO development agenda. World Competition 27:419–457

Drexl J (2010) Internationales Immaterialgüterrecht. In: Rixecker R, Säcker JS (eds) Münchener Kommentar zum Bürgerlichen Gesetzbuch, vol 11. C.H. Beck, Munich, pp 1344–1491

Drexl J (2012a) EU competition law and parallel trade in pharmaceuticals: lessons to be learned for WTO/TRIPS? In: Rosén J (ed) Intellectual property at the crossroads of trade. Edward Elgar, Cheltenham, pp 3–24

Drexl J (2012b) Counterfeiting and the spare parts issue. In: Geiger C (ed) Criminal enforcement and intellectual property. Edward Elgar, Cheltenham, pp 369–385

Economic Partnership Agreement between the CARIFORUM States of the one part, and the European Community and its Member States, of the other part. OJ 2008 L 289, 3

EU Centre in Singapore (2011) The EU-Korea FTA and its implications for the future of EU-Singapore FTA, Background Brief No 4, http://www.eucentre.sg/articles/296/downloads/BackgroundBrief-The%20EU-Korea%20FTA%20and%20its%20Implications%20for%20the%20Future%20EU-Singapore%20FTA.pdf. Accessed 7 July 2012

European Parliament (2012) ACTA before the European Parliament. http://www.europarl.europa.eu/news/en/pressroom/content/20120217BKG38488/html/ACTA-before-the-European-Parliament. Accessed 7 July 2012

European Commission (2009) EU to launch FTA negotiations with individual ASEAN countries, beginning with Singapore. http://trade.ec.europa.eu/doclib/press/index.cfm?id=504&serie=307&langId=en. Accessed 7 July 2012

European Commission (2011) EU-Singapore free trade agreement negotiations progressing well. Joint statement by the EU and the Ministry of Trade and Industry of Singapore Press. http://trade.ec.europa.eu/doclib/press/index.cfm?id=729. Accessed 7 July 2012

European Commission (2012a) EU-Singapore free trade agreement negotiations progressing well. Joint statement by the EU and the Ministry of Trade and Industry of Singapore. http://trade.ec.europa.eu/doclib/press/index.cfm?id=729. Accessed 6 Dec 2012

European Commission (2012b) EU and Vietnam move closer to start trade negotiations. http://trade.ec.europa.eu/doclib/press/index.cfm?id=792. Accessed 7 July 2012

European Commission (2012c) Proposal of 4 October 2012 for a Regulation of the European Parliament and the Council on Access to Genetic Resources and the Fair and Equitable Sharing of Benefits Arising from their Utilization in the Union, COM(2012) 576 final

European Commission (2012d) EU and Singapore agree on landmark trade deal (16 December 2012). http://trade.ec.europa.eu/doclib/press/index.cfm?id=855. Accessed 15 Apr 2013

Fox EM (2003) International antitrust and the Doha Dome. Virginia J Int Law 43:911–919

Free Trade Agreement between the European Union and its Member States, of the one part, and the Republic of Korea, of the other part. OJ 2011 L 127, 6
FTA Malaysia Information (2012) Global civil society rises up over FTAs. http://www.ftamalaysia.org/article.php?aid=270. Accessed 7 July 2012
Gibson J (2012) The directive proposal on criminal sanctions. In: Geiger C (ed) Criminal enforcement of intellectual property. Edward Elgar, Cheltenham, pp 245–266
Griffith J (2012) Criminal liability for intellectual property infringement in Europe: the role of fundamental rights. In: Geiger C (ed) Criminal enforcement of intellectual property. Edward Elgar, Cheltenham, pp 191–212
Grosse Ruse-Khan H (2010) From TRIPS to ACTA: towards a New "Gold Standard" in criminal IP enforcement? Max Planck Institute for Intellectual Property and Competition Law Research Paper No. 10–06. http://papers.ssrn.com/sol3/papers.cfm?abstract_id=1592104. Accessed 31 Mar 2012
Grosse Ruse-Khan H (2012) Criminal enforcement and international IP law. In: Geiger C (ed) Criminal enforcement and intellectual property. Edward Elgar, Cheltenham, pp 171–190
Heinemann A (1996) Antitrust law of intellectual property in the TRIPs agreement of the World Trade Organization. In: Beier FK, Schricker G (eds) From GATT to TRIPs – the agreement on trade-related aspects of intellectual property. VCH, Weinheim
Hilty R et al (2006) Statement of the Max Planck Institute for Intellectual Property, Competition and Tax Law on the Proposal for a Directive of the European Parliament and of the Council on Criminal Measures aimed at ensuring the enforcement of intellectual property rights. IIC 37 (8):970–977
ICTSD (2010) EU and Malaysia Kick Off Trade Talks 7 October 2010. http://ictsd.org/i/news/bridgesweekly/86149/. Accessed 7 July 2012
Kokott J (2010) Participation in the World Trade Organization and foreign direct investment: national or European Union competences? In: Bekker PHF et al (eds) Making transnational law work in the global economy: essays in honour of Detlev Vagts. Cambridge University Press, New York, pp 108–131
Medaglia JC (2006) Costa Rica. In: Lewis-Lettington RJ, Mwanyiki S (eds) Case studies on access and benefit-sharing. International Plant Genetic Resources Institute, Rome, pp 33–74
Mylly T (2012) Criminal enforcement and European Union law. In: Geiger C (ed) Criminal enforcement of intellectual property. Edward Elgar, Cheltenham, pp 213–244
Nagoya Protocol (2010) on Access to genetic resources and the fair and equitable sharing of benefits arising from their utilization to the convention of biological diversity, of 29 October 2010, http://www.cbd.int/abs/doc/protocol/nagoya-protocol-en.pdf. Accessed 7 July 2012
Regulation (EU) No 1257/2012 of the European Parliament and of the Council of 17 December 2012 implementing enhanced cooperation in the area of the creation of unitary patent protection. OJ 2012 L 361, 1
OECS (2008) Communiqué, 47th meeting of the OECS Authority, 23th to 24th May 2008.http://www.google.de/url?sa=t&rct=j&q=eastern%20caribbean%20competition%20commission&source=web&cd=12&ved=0CFEQFjABOAo&url=http%3A%2F%2Fwww.oecs.org%2Fdoc-lib%2Fdoc_download%2F226-47th-meeting-of-theauthority&ei=_Cz4T7vuEsnOswbAtbnGBQ&usg=AFQjCNHp3bYBzJ16dlccygJP8PUmsKAFDA&cad=rja. Accessed 7 July 2012
Partnership agreement 2000/483/EC between the members of the African, Caribbean and Pacific Group of States of the one part, and the European Community and its Member States, of the other part. OJ 2000 L 317, 3
Second Revision of the Cotonou Agreement – Agreed Consolidated Text (2010). http://ec.europa.eu/development/icenter/repository/second_revision_cotonou_agreement_20100311.pdf. Accessed 7 July 2012
Stewart T (2012) Regional integration in the Caribbean: the role of competition policy. In: Drexl J et al (eds) Competition policy and regional integration in developing countries. Edward Elgar, Cheltenham, pp 161–184

Today Online (2012) EU-Singapore FTA talks to conclude by end-July. http://www.todayonline.com/Business/EDC120621-0000182/EU-Spore-FTA-talks-to-conclude-by-end-July. Accessed 7 July 2012

Trade Agreement between the European Union and its Member States and Colombia and Peru (2012) http://trade.ec.europa.eu/doclib/press/index.cfm?id=691. Accessed 7 July 2012

UNCTAD-ICTSD (2005) Resource book on TRIPS and development. Cambridge University Press, New York

Agreement on a Unified Patent Court, signed by 19 February 2013, http://www.epo.org/law-practice/unitary/patent-court.html. Accessed 15 Apr 2013

von Lewinski S (2008) Indingenous heritage and intellectual property: genetic resources, Traditional Knowledge and Folklore. Kluwer Law International, London

von Lewinski S, Walter MW (2010) European copyright law – a commentary. Oxford University Press, Oxford

Implementation Issues Arising from Intellectual Property Chapters Contained in Trade Agreements Between the EU and Developing Countries

Xavier Seuba

Contents

1 Exportation of Intellectual Property Standards

A feature that the European Union (EU), the United Sates (US) and the European Free Trade Association (EFTA) share when concluding free trade agreements (FTA)[1] is their willingness to export their respective intellectual property

[1] "FTA" will be used synonymously with economic partnership agreement (EPA), a term that will also be used.

X. Seuba (✉)
Universitat Pompeu Fabra, Barcelona, Spain

Centre d'Études Internationales de la Propriété Intellectuelle (CEIPI), Université de Strasbourg, Strasbourg, France
e-mail: xavier.seuba@upf.edu

J. Drexl et al. (eds.), *EU Bilateral Trade Agreements and Intellectual Property: For Better or Worse?*, MPI Studies on Intellectual Property and Competition Law 20,
DOI 10.1007/978-3-642-39097-5_14, © Springer-Verlag Berlin Heidelberg 2014

(IP) legal orders.[2] Their success raises numerous issues from the implementation angle that are related to both operative and systemic aspects of the reception of new international law obligations.

Comparative analysis of the IP negotiations between developed and developing countries usually allude to the "asymmetry" among partners,[3] a term that refers but it is not limited to the unequal bargaining power of each party.[4] This unbalanced context would partially explain the easy exportation of the IP legal systems of some developed countires to developed countries. Whatever the specific reasons, it seems necessary to point out a distinct dimension of that "asymmetry".

The imbalance between developed and developing partners is frequently addressed in general terms and reference is made, for instance, to the asymmetry existing between the EFTA and the Andean Community, or the EU and Mercosur. However, little attention has been paid to the internal asymmetries within each integration block, and to whether or not the existing differences should result in differentiated proposals. That is, should the EU treat Paraguay and Brazil differently when negotiating with Mercosur? Certainly Paraguay is not a "least developed country",[5] but it is also true that differences between Brazil and Paraguay can be bigger than differences existing between Brazil and the EU itself. The unwillingness to establish distinct levels of IP protection can result in inequitable texts, and may even frustrate the negotiation itself. Take for instance the case of the negotiations between the EU and the Andean Community: the lack of differentiation, together with ideological stances difficult to reconcile, were the major cause of

[2] Section 2102 of the US Bipartisan Trade Promotion Authority Act of 2002 states that "The principal negotiating objectives of the United States regarding trade-related intellectual property are ... ensuring that the provisions of any multilateral or bilateral trade agreement governing intellectual property rights that is entered into by the United States reflect a standard of protection similar to that found in United States law". The EU Strategy for the enforcement of IP rights in third countries envisages "to make the enforcement clauses in future bilateral or bi-regional agreements more operational and to clearly define what the EU regards as the highest international standards in this area and what kind of efforts it expects from its trading partners"; specifically, the "EU Directive harmonising the enforcement of IPR within the Community, as well as the new customs' Regulation on counterfeit and pirated goods may constitute an important source of inspiration and a useful benchmark" (http://trade.ec.europa.eu/doclib/docs/2005/april/tradoc_122636.pdf, p. 6).

[3] The Commission on Intellectual Property Rights stated in 2002 that "Developing countries – and in particular poor consumers of products which may be protected by IP rights – negotiate from a position of relative weakness. There is a fundamental asymmetry in relationships between developed and developing countries, based ultimately on their relative economic strength". Commission on Intellectual Property Rights (2002), p. 7.

[4] The asymmetry refers not only to the negotiation phase, but also to implementation. Section 101 of the implementation bill of the US-Central America-Dominican Republic Free Trade Agreement (US-CAFTA-DR) establishes the conditions for entry into force of the Agreement: "At such time as *the President determines that countries ... have taken measures necessary to comply* with the provisions of the Agreement that are to take effect on the date on which the Agreement enters into force with respect to those countries that provide for the Agreement to enter into force for them" (emphasis added).

[5] Article 140 of the agreement between the EU and the CARIFORUM alludes to this particular status, recalling the situation of Haiti.

the failure of the negotiations with the Andeans as a block, and the origin of the present multi-party trade agreement.[6]

The exportation of European and North-American standards is not merely a description of the resulting texts. It can also be a source of inspiration when interpreting the negotiated texts. If the "exporting" legal order is mastered, it will be possible to devise different implementation options. For instance, the EU Directive 2004/48 on civil enforcement of IP rights, which is the basis of the EU proposals regarding IP civil enforcement, originates from different European legal traditions and its language often permits several implementation options.[7] Hence, it would be interesting to draw a genealogy of the national IP systems of countries that have negotiated EPAs containing IP chapters, and identify which is the ultimate origin of its provisions. This would allow one to conclude, for instance concerning Peru, that enforcement provisions originally from Germany (such as the right of information) coexist with enforcement provisions originating in the United Kingdom and France (preservation of evidence) and also with substantive obligations originating in the US (the linkage between the patent status and the regulatory approval). This knowledge can be decisive when adopting secondary legislation, passing sentences or litigating. Sometimes the preferred option will possibly be to import from the original legal order what was missing in the proposal put forward by the IP "exporter". On other occasions, however, that knowledge may be instrumental to not repeat the errors that others may have committed. Nuanced interpretations and carefully drafted implementing legislation may improve the legal texts of origin, not to mention the trade agreement at issue.

A third reflection regarding the exportation of IP standards concerns the post-implementation of the IP system of countries that have negotiated with the US, the EU and EFTA. The resulting legal framework resembles a patchwork, since it is the outcome of a mix of obligations that collect some of the strongest though not necessarily harmonious provisions originating from OECD partners, which moreover are added to an already existing national and regional legal *acquis*. However, the patchwork is not necessarily well sewn. For instance, Andean countries' patentability standards follow the "industrial application" criterion to examine patent applications,[8] the same as the Europeans do. The agreement between Colombia and the US, though, states that a party may treat the term "capable of industrial application" as being synonymous with the term "useful",[9] something that, if literally applied, entails widening the patentable subject matter to include, among other things, inventions of exclusively experimental nature. From the

[6] Trade Agreement between the European Union and its Member States, of the one part, and Colombia and Peru, of the other part, OJ L 21.12.2012, http://eur-lex.europa.eu/LexUriServ/LexUriServ.do?uri=OJ:L:2012:354:0003:2607:EN:PDF (accessed March 2013).

[7] See, in detail, the different national traditions that influenced EU Directive 2004/48 in Heath and Petit (2008).

[8] Article 14 of Decisión 486, Régimen Común de Propiedad Industrial, 2000. Available at www.comunidadandina.org/normativa/dec/D486.htm. Accessed October 2011.

[9] See Article 16.9.1 of the Colombia-United States FTA. Available at www.ustr.gov/trade-agreements/free-trade-agreements/colombia-fta/final-text. Accessed October 2011.

systemic point of view the difficult question that arises for Colombia is how to implement both standards without denaturalizing one of them. Although this provision is drafted in terms of "may", thus allowing members to avoid the mentioned inconsistency by following the industrial application requirement, the reality is that national implementation, for many factors, has enacted both criteria in the new Colombian patentability guidelines.[10] The inherent inconsistency, moreover, raises important problems from the point of view of the Andean law.

2 Resource Implications

Studies on the economic impact of IP frequently take conflicting positions. They either introduce the social and economic gains resulting from the promotion of IP and the fight against IP infringement[11] or, conversely, point out the potential anticompetitive effects of IP and the economic burden that developing countries assume in provisions of substantive nature contained in IP chapters.[12] In the specific area of IP enforcement, most of the studies related to the economic aspects usually take the first view. There are, however, almost no studies dealing with the resource implications resulting from the introduction and implementation of new enforcement provisions.[13] In general terms, economic impact studies tend to neglect the interests of competitors and other stakeholders, such as consumers, or just assume that these are the same as those of the rightholders.

From a developing-country perspective it should be taken into account that the implementation of enforcement provisions has a cost in terms of personnel, infrastructure and institutional enhancement. These are the direct costs resulting from IP enforcement implementation, that is, the investment a country has to make in order to comply with the commitments it has made in the area of IP enforcement. These costs are relatively simple to estimate, although this is an exercise not routinely done and its magnitude has probably been overlooked.[14]

[10] Instructivo Examen de Solicitudes de Patente de Invención y Modelo de Utilidad, Memorando 12-2282-1-1, 8 February 2012, adopted by Jefe de la Oficina Asesora de Planeación de la Superintendencia de Industria y Comercio.

[11] According to the OECD positive effects can be expected in the following fields: "(*i*) general socioeconomic effects (on innovation and growth, criminal activities, environment, employment, foreign direct investment, and trade), (*ii*) effects on rights' holders (on sales volume and prices, brand value and firm reputation, royalties, firm-level investment, costs and the scope of operations), (*iii*) effects on consumers (health and safety risks and consumer utility) and (*iv*) effects on government (tax revenues, expenditures and corruption)". OECD (2007), p. 6.

[12] See for instance Li (2009), p. 75.

[13] C Fink has however reflected on the intricacies and the often forgotten aspects of IP enforcement costs and benefits. Fink (2010).

[14] When the TRIPS Agreement was adopted some international organizations developed programs to assist the implementation of the treaty. The activities financed had to do with institutional enhancement, personnel training and legislative reform, thus pertaining to the area of IP enforcement. The budget of these programs is helpful to partially approach the total quantity a country had to invest in order to implement the enforcement section of the treaty. See Finger and Schuler (1999).

A distinct resource implication of new IP undertakings is more complex to asses, both in terms of quantification as well as accurate delimitation. This distinct dimension has to do with the potential effects on welfare resulting from certain enforcement provisions, mainly arising from its impact on activities related to the supply of goods. The effects on welfare can be both positive, for instance in terms of employment protection or innovation and growth, and negative, a dimension that has do with the restriction of access to protected—or even unprotected—goods. The explanation is straightforward: "a higher level of enforcement implies a change in the institutional framework and is therefore likely to have an impact on production, investment, imports, exports and other variables. In some cases, as long as enforcement measures reinforce the position of the IP rights holder, it is likely to reduce national production, to increase imports and to reduce exports".[15]

A good example in terms of the negative impact on welfare of new IP provisions can be found in the controversy over the control of patented goods in transit that arose in 2009 between the EU and several developing countries. Whatever the most convincing legal argumentation,[16] the fact was that a very specific provision in the border enforcement legislation regarding goods protected by IP rights caused the interruption of supply of medicines to several developing countries where goods did not infringe the IP right invoked in the country of transit. The potential impact on health protection, and hence on welfare, of these provisions seems clear.

3 Internal Consistency

In addition to the resource allocation aspects of new FTA implementation, it is necessary to raise the question of the apparent inconsistency of some obligations foreseen in those agreements. In principle, all provisions contained in a treaty have been introduced with some purpose and the principles of good faith and effectiveness oblige states to implement them in a meaningful way. However, some articles contained in IP chapters of FTAs seem to establish inconsistent rules.

Examples of the inconsistency may be found in the recurrent reference to the absence of obligations with respect to the distribution of resources,[17] and the command to take into account the development situation of the country when implementing obligations pertaining to the enforcement field.[18] These references

---

[15] Seuba et al. (2010), p. 14.

[16] The July 2011 agreement between the EU and India seems to acknowledge the arguments of free trade promoters and defenders of fundamental principles of IP rights, including the territorial principle. According to this agreement, and following the European Court of Justice jurisprudence on the matter, only the existence of a real and manifest risk of diversion into the EU internal market will trigger the EU courts' jurisdiction over patented goods in transit.

[17] Article 234.4 of the treaty between Colombia, Peru and the EU states that "This Chapter does not create for the Parties ... any obligation with respect to the distribution of resources for the enforcement of intellectual property rights and for the enforcement of law in general".

[18] Article 139.2 of the CARIFORUM treaty establishes that "enforcement of intellectual property rights should take account of the development needs of the CARIFORUM States".

may be construed as a provision affirming that contracting parties are free from an obligation to devote additional resources to IP enforcement. However, if this is the correct reading, how can it be reconciled with the detailed provisions that oblige parties to create new mechanisms, build infrastructure and hire personnel to monitor IPRs? For instance, in contrast with TRIPS, which solely demands the control of importation of counterfeited or pirated goods, new provisions on border enforcement in some cases require the control of importation, exportation, re-exportation, transit, transhipment, placement under a free zone, placement under a suspensive procedure or a bonded warehouse of goods infringing an intellectual property right.[19] The activities of border authorities are thus multiplied when compared to TRIPS, which requires hiring more personnel and probably building or renting facilities in which to conduct the new tasks (inspection and storage). These are, in effect, the provisions that give place to the aforementioned investments that a signatory country to an FTA is bound to make to fulfill the treaty.

Customary principles of interpretation do not help much in finding a solution to the stated inconsistency. The principle *ut res magis valeat quam pereat*[20] could be applied when trying to reconcile provisions not only contained in distinct treaties, but also provisions within the same treaty that are in apparent contradiction. Following that principle it could be argued, for instance, that the meaningful effect of a provision that recognizes the liberty to allocate resources is, precisely, not to allocate additional resources. However, this interpretation does not seem a plausible solution from the point of view of title holders and the EU, which could argue the other way around: the meaningful effect of new enforcement undertaking necessarily implies investing additional resources.

4 Relationship with Other FTAs and TRIPS

A well-known pattern of IP chapters in new FTAs is the repetition of obligations that have already been enacted in other texts binding the same parties, such as the Agreement on Trade Related Aspects of Intellectual Property Rights (TRIPS) and other FTAs. Quite often technical debates pick up and discuss this apparently useless redundancy, a source of potential inconsistencies when words are slightly changed in different agreements, and tend to conclude that it is not clear why the repetition occurs. In fact, despite the existence of several important nuances to this operation, by virtue of the most-favored-nation treatment, advantages granted to other countries will benefit all rightholders, regardless of their nationality.

There are indeed some potential explanations, but most of them are not very convincing. It is possible, for instance, to maintain that the EU promotes the

[19] See European Union-Korea Article 10.67.1, OJ L127, 15.5.2011, p. 6.

[20] In the *Corfu Channel* case the International Court of Justice held: "It would indeed be incompatible with the generally accepted rules of interpretation to admit that a provision of this sort occurring in a Special Agreement should be devoid of purport or effect". Judgment of 9 April 1949: I.C.J. Reports, 1949, p. 24.

repetition of the same provision while not mentioning others because it tries to strike a balance in favor of the former. It is also possible to hold that the intention is merely to underpin the priority character permeating specific provisions, without intent to disregard the unmentioned articles. While deserving some merit, both explanations are highly speculative.

A more convincing explanation is that by re-enacting a provision already provided for in another treaty between the current partner and a third country, the jurisdiction of the dispute settlement of the new treaty is triggered. In effect, the jurisdiction of the dispute settlement system of each agreement is interlinked with the material breadth of the agreement. For instance, according to the agreement between Colombia, Peru and the EU, the dispute settlement title applies "with respect to any dispute concerning the interpretation and application of this Agreement".[21] Therefore, it seems plausible to defend the view that repeating provisions becomes important not in order to extend rights that already benefit rightholders, but to leave open the possibility to activate the particular dispute settlement system with respect to those rights.

5 In Search of Flexibility in the Enforcement Area[22]

In the context of the increasingly populated legal framework for the enforcement of intellectual property rights, a relevant area of research should be the policy space available in the context of the new IP enforcement obligations; that is, the performance in the enforcement area of a similar endeavor to that conducted in relation to primary norms contained in TRIPS and in other international agreements containing IP substantive norms.

One among the possible points of departure in search of flexibility in the enforcement area is to compare with the EU Enforcement Directive the enforcement provisions ensconced in the treaties promoted by the EU. In the civil enforcement area, that directive sets up the European framework to harmonize the means available for rightholders to fight the infringement of IPRs. The reasons to perform the proposed comparison are twofold. First, the EU leads the international initiatives to enhance the legal basis that permits IPRs to be enforced. Second, as mentioned above, the EU takes the Enforcement Directive as the mold to cast its partners' legal orders as far as civil enforcement is concerned.

The comparison of the Enforcement Directive with the IP chapters contained in FTAs promoted by the EU permits one to identify checks and balances that are enacted in the European legislation but that are nonexistent in the treaties promoted by the EU. Another comparison, this time among the EU treaties themselves, allows one to identify provisions that are present in some EU treaties but not in other

[21] Article 299 of the Trade Agreement between the European Union and its Member States and Colombia and Peru, in http://trade.ec.europa.eu/doclib/docs/2011/march/tradoc_147704.pdf (accessed March 2013).

[22] See in detail Seuba (2013).

treaties also promoted by the EU. In effect, while some covenants contain more flexible language and some let-out clauses, these are absent in other treaties. Both comparisons should, ideally, permit the implementation of EU FTAs by taking the best from the EU legislation and from each EU FTA, and help to achieve a more balanced IP enforcement.

Given the aforementioned similarities, it becomes apparent that the Enforcement Directive has not only been the point of departure to negotiate the enforcement provisions, but frequently the destination itself. However, in spite of the existence of important similarities, there are also remarkable differences. In the civil enforcement area, divergences are located in the provisions (or the absence thereof) that deal with the limits of rightholders' entitlements and with the rights of their competitors and of IP protected goods users. Notably, the texts promoted by the EU and frequently the resulting treaties themselves do not enshrine the majority of guarantees for competitors and for users of IPR-protected goods contained in the Enforcement Directive.

A comparison conducted between the Enforcement Directive and the EU agreements with CARIFORUM, South Korea, Central America, Peru and Colombia has permitted the identification of important differences. The impact of these differences on the balance between the rights of rightholders and the rights of their competitors and of the users of IPR-protected goods is significant. All the mentioned agreements have the same substratum, which is the Enforcement Directive. The language and most of the IP owners' rights are almost identical. They also share the same characteristic: when compared with the Enforcement Directive, most of the checks and balances provided for in the European text are absent in the trade agreements. The following paragraphs provide examples of said differences located in the articles on evidence, measures to preserve evidence and provisional measures.

With regard to evidence, EU treaties make it obligatory to empower the judicial authorities to order the opposing party to present evidence lying within his control, and affirm that the information to be produced includes banking, financial or commercial documents when the case has to do with an infringement committed on a commercial scale. The Enforcement Directive fundamentally establishes the same obligation. However, in contrast with the Directive, in the agreements concluded with CARIFORUM, South Korea, Colombia and Peru the rightholder is not obliged to specify the requested evidence, nor to present "reasonably available" evidence in order to substantiate his claims.

With regard to the measures for preserving evidence, the transposition of the resulting EU checks and balances has not occurred in the texts that the EU proposed to its trading partners. Measures for preserving evidence include, fundamentally, the description of goods and the seizure of the infringing goods—and sometimes also of the materials used to produce those goods. These *ex parte* measures are subject to the presentation of reasonably available evidence about the infringement, must be prompt and effective and may be ordered *inaudita parte*. The EU Directive has added to these requirements some additional guarantees to avoid abuse and to introduce some proportionality. However, none of the following European checks and balances are present in the abovementioned agreements: (1) notice must be given immediately after the execution of the measure; (2) the alleged infringer has the right to ask for a review of the measure; (3) in case proceedings leading to a decision are not instituted within a reasonable period of time, the revocation will be granted; (4) measures for preserving evidence may be subject to the lodging by the applicant of adequate security or an equivalent assurance; (5) the defendant may be awarded appropriate compensation.

In the EU Directive there are three main options regarding provisional and precautionary measures: the issuance of interlocutory injunctions, the seizure of allegedly infringing goods and the seizure of movable and immovable property of the alleged infringer. When the EU agreements are compared with the Enforcement Directive, some disparities become clear. For instance, as a general guarantee applicable to the three stated options, the EU Directive establishes that the claimant must show a good case (fundamentally he or she must prove that the right has been infringed or is about to be infringed). Important as it is, this condition has not been included in the agreement with Peru and Colombia, nor in the South Korean agreement. It is also noticeable that the Enforcement Directive references aimed at ensuring that provisional measures are not abused have not been included in the treaties concluded with the EU's trading partners. The first is the obligation to revoke the measures if the applicant does not institute, within a reasonable period of time, proceedings leading to a decision on the merits of the case. The second is the option to subject the measures to the lodging of adequate security or an equivalent assurance. And the third is the compensation that will follow if measures are revoked, if they lapse due to any act or omission by the applicant or if it is found that there has been no infringement or threat of infringement.

In light of the missing guarantees described above, the key question is whether their absence will nevertheless prevent the other party from implementing those or similar checks and balances. Our view on this topic is that not only is the other party not barred from implementing the missing guarantees and the overall balance, but it is actually obliged to do so. In addition to pragmatic reasons related to the efficiency and quality of the legal system, the respect of basic principles of due process and fair trial standards requires the parties to introduce those rights and guarantees that favor the alleged infringer and the consumers, which have been lost in the process of transposition of the law of IP-exporting states via the FTA.

The previously mentioned example of the measures for the preservation of evidence is useful again to show how fair-trial standards can be affected by unbalanced regimes set forth in FTAs. The European Court of Human Rights has ruled on a case dealing with Anton Piller orders, a type of civil search warrant. In *Chappel v. United Kingdom*, the Court had to assess whether the implementation of an Anton Piller order had violated the right to respect for private and family life, including home and correspondence. Reflecting on the rules that set up the Anton Piller regime, the Court held that "it is essential that this measure should be accompanied by adequate and effective safeguards against arbitrary interference and abuse".[23]

---

[23] *Chappell v. United Kingdom*, Series A No 152; Application No 10461/83 European Court of Human Rights (1990) 12 EHRR 1 30 March 1989, p. 21.

In the same case, in its report, the European Human Rights Commission assessed the legal basis for the interference at issue. In its conclusion, the Commission quoted jurisprudence of the European Court of Human Rights that fundamentally conditioned the acceptability of interference on the overall quality of the law: "The phrase 'in accordance with the law' does not merely refer back to domestic law but also relates to the quality of the law, requiring it to be compatible with the rule of law".[24]

In our view, the implementation of unbalanced measures for the preservation of evidence would entail a violation of human rights obligations related to the right to fair trial, and would facilitate violations of others' rights, such as the right to privacy.

Among other aspects of the right to a fair trial affected, the principle of equality of arms is particularly relevant. In effect, "equality of arms" means "that the same procedural rights are to be provided to all the parties unless distinctions are based on law and can be justified on objective and reasonable grounds, *not entailing actual disadvantage or other unfairness to the defendant*".[25] This requirement is hardly fulfilled in a regime on measures for the preservation of evidence in which rightholders know that no compensation in favor of the defendant will be awarded even if no infringement is found, and in which the alleged infringer will have substantially fewer chances to make his argument and to have the measure revoked.

6 Conclusion

The implementation of EU IP standards in developing countries raises many concerns. This chapter has tried to give some examples of topics pertaining to areas where said issues can be ascribed: politics (power asymmetries), economics (direct costs and welfare implications) and law (legal challenges, possible interpretations).

After sustaining that a new and more sophisticated approach should be taken with regard to the question of asymmetries, two comments were made in relation to the resource implications of agreements laying down new IP enforcement obligations. The first relates to the investment that a country that ratifies an FTA is bound to make to fulfill the treaty, mainly in terms of infrastructure and personnel. This investment only represents part of the economic impact of the agreement; the other part is its effects on welfare, both positive and negative. The second comment took the economic aspects of these agreements as an example to introduce the existence of potential inconsistencies within the treaties. The question of how to reconcile provisions that, on the one hand, affirm that countries are free to

[24] *Olsson* judgment of 24 March 1988 [Series A no. 130, p. 30, para 61 (b)].

[25] Human Rights Committee (2007), para 13 (emphasis added).

decide the allocation of resources and, on the other hand, establish very specific obligations with straightforward resource implications remains open.

The trade agreements concluded by the EU with developed and developing partners enshrine almost exclusively the Enforcement Directive institutions that are of interest for title holders. This means that some of the checks and balances present in the Enforcement Directive are neither proposed by the EU nor included in the treaties. In search of policy space in the enforcement area, the analysis of the differences between the Enforcement Directive and the EU trade agreements could be helpful to integrate into the legislation of the EU partners the public-interest-balancing provisions that the Enforcement Directive provides for. This option, which seems reasonable given the current state of affairs and the consequences of implementing the treaties with the EU simply as they read right now, nevertheless raises some fundamental questions related to the appropriateness of globalizing the EU legislation on civil enforcement.

Acknowledgments This research is funded by the Knowledge and Economy Department of the Catalan Government in the context of the COFUND Program of the EU Marie Curie Actions of the Seventh Framework Program. I thank Henning Grosse Ruse-Kahn for his comments. All errors remain mine.

References

Commission on Intellectual Property Rights (2002) Integrating intellectual property rights and development policy. London

Finger JM, Schuler P (1999) Implementation of the Uruguay round commitments: the development challenge. World Bank Development Research Group, Policy Research, Working Paper No. 2215

Fink C (2010) Enforcing intellectual property rights: an economic perspective. ICTSD, Issue Paper No. 22

Heath C, Petit L (eds) (2008) Patent enforcement worldwide. Writings in Honour of Dieter Stauder, 2nd edn. Hart, Oxford

Human Rights Committee (2007) General Comment No. 32, Right to equality before courts and tribunals and to a fair trial, CCPR/C/GC/32

Li X (2009) WCO secure: legal and economic assessments of the TRIPS-plus-plus IP enforcement. In: Li X, Correa C (eds) Intellectual property enforcement. International perspectives. Edward Elgar, Cheltenham

OECD (2007) The economic impact of counterfeiting and piracy. www.oecd.org/dataoecd/13/12/38707619.pdf. Accessed Oct 2011

Seuba X (2013) Checks and balances in the intellectual property enforcement field: reconstructing EU trade agreements. In: Geiger C (ed) Constructing European intellectual property: achievements and new perspectives. Edward Elgar, Cheltenham

Seuba X, Rovira J, Bloemen S (2010) Welfare Implications of Intellectual Property Enforcement Measures. American University Washington College of Law, PIJIP Research Paper Series, 9-1-2010. http://digitalcommons.wcl.american.edu/research/5/. Accessed Oct 2011

MIX
Papier aus verantwortungsvollen Quellen
Paper from responsible sources
FSC® C105338
FSC
www.fsc.org

If you have any concerns about our products,
you can contact us on
ProductSafety@springernature.com

In case Publisher is established outside the EU,
the EU authorized representative is:
Springer Nature Customer Service Center GmbH
Europaplatz 3, 69115 Heidelberg, Germany

Printed by Libri Plureos GmbH
in Hamburg, Germany